FOREWORD TO THE FORTY EIGHTH EDITION

This Pocketbook has come to be relied upon by many operators within the farming industry to benchmark past performance and to forecast budgets, cash flows and balance sheets. Whether for the internal use of the farm, engaging with financial institutions making decisions on farm borrowing or providing information to support a rent review, access to good information will, more than ever, be vital to steer a course through the choppy waters of the next few years. The post-Brexit landscape for agriculture will take some time to materialise. Although the UK Government has given a commitment to maintain current public spending on agriculture until the end of the Parliament, given recent events we cannot say for sure how long that will be. Neither does it guarantee that the structure of that spending will remain the same, even if the Parliament does last its intended length.

Our future trading relationships with the EU and the rest of the world, our ability to attract the labour force needed to run our farm businesses and staff our food processing and service sectors and the future regulatory framework will all have significant influence upon the profitability and resilience of the farming sector. All that is before we get into the complications of devolution and the need for a UK framework that considers, alongside policy, the trading relationships that must be established between the four component parts of the United Kingdom if, as it seems, we will be operating outside of the EU Single Market after March 2019.

On the one hand many farmers seem excited about the opportunities that might be forthcoming as we leave the EU, while on the other there are those who are anxious about the challenges and risks which lie ahead. Undoubtedly, preparation for what might arise and how each farm business should respond will be the topic of informed conversation keeping farm kitchens buzzing countrywide.

Figures in this book are projected for 2018. Thus the crops data relate to the 2018 harvest. The livestock data relate either to the 2018 calendar year (e.g. for milk production) or to 2018/19 (e.g. for winter-finished beef). The yields and prices assume a 'normal' or average season, based on trends. Looking 6-18 months ahead to 2018/19, no one can know what the actual average yield and price for that particular year will be. The figures should be adjusted as appropriate according to circumstances and price and cost differences. Assumptions are set out to enable this to be done.

John Nix ~ August 2017

FOREWORD TO THE FIRST EDITION

This booklet is intended for farmers, advisers, students and everyone else who, frequently or infrequently, find themselves hunting for data relating to farm management - whether it is for blunt pencil calculations on the back of an envelope or for feeding into a computer. The material contained is based upon the sort of information which the author finds himself frequently having to look up in his twin roles as adviser and teacher in farm management. There are several excellent handbooks already in existence, but this pocketbook endeavours to cover a wider field and thus to be substantially more comprehensive. It is intended that most of the data herein contained will have a national application, although there is inevitably some bias towards conditions in the south-eastern half of the country.

The development of farm planning techniques in recent years has outstripped the quality and quantity of data available. It is hoped that this booklet will go a little further in supplying the type of information required. It cannot, however, claim to be the ultimate in this respect. For example, there are many variations in labour requirements according to farm conditions and sizes and types of machine used and there are many more variations in sheep and beef systems than are dealt with here. More detailed data on these lines are gradually becoming available from various sources. It is hoped further to refine the material in this booklet and to keep it up to date in subsequent editions, as the information becomes available. As a help towards this end, any comments or criticisms will be gratefully received.

The author wishes to thank his many friends and colleagues who have given him so much time and help in compiling this information.

John Nix
October, 1966

First published October 1966
Forty Eighth Edition September 2017

John Nix Pocketbook

FOR FARM MANAGEMENT

For 2018

FORTY-EIGHTH EDITION

By Graham Redman

Published September 2017

Copies of this book may be obtained from:
The Pocketbook, 2 Nottingham Street
Melton Mowbray, Leicestershire LE13 1NW
Tel: 01664 564 508
Available online at www.thepocketbook.co.uk

Price £25.50 + £2.50 p&p
5 to 19 copies: £24.50
20 to 100 copies: £22.50
Over 100 copies: *call us*
Postage & Packaging free for 5 or more copies in single deliveries

ISBN 978-0-9576939-5-1

Suggested Citation:
Redman, G., 2017. *The John Nix Pocketbook for Farm Management 2018*. 48th ed. Melton Mowbray: Agro Business Consultants

CONTENTS

I. GENERAL

1. THE USE OF GROSS MARGINS

DEFINITION

The data on the crop and livestock enterprises in the Pocketbook are based on gross margins. The gross margin of an enterprise is its output less its variable costs. Enterprise output includes the market value of production retained on the farm. The variable costs must (a) be specific to the enterprise and (b) vary in proportion to the size of the enterprise, i.e. number of hectares or head of stock. The main items of variable costs are: Crops: fertiliser, seed, sprays, casual labour and contract work specific to the crop. Non-Grazing Livestock: concentrate feed, vet. and med., marketing expenses. Grazing Livestock is as for non-grazing livestock, plus forage crop variable costs.

POINTS TO NOTE

1. The gross margin is not a profit figure. The 'fixed costs' (rent, labour, machinery, general overheads) have to be covered by the total farm gross margin before arriving at a profit.

2. The gross margin of an enterprise will differ from season to season, because of yield and price differences affecting output and also because variable costs will vary, e.g. the number and type of sprays required. Different soils and other natural factors, as well as level of management, will also cause differences between farms.

3. Items of variable cost vary from farm to farm, e.g. some farmers have greater weed control costs than others; some farmers employ a contractor to combine their cereals (a variable cost), others use their own equipment (a fixed cost); some employ a contractor to deliver their sugar beet to the factory (a variable cost), others have their own lorry (a fixed cost). These differences must be borne in mind in making inter-farm comparisons.

4. Provided points 2 and 3 are borne in mind, comparison of gross margins (particularly averages over several seasons) with standards can be a useful check on technical performance.

5. The other main usefulness of gross margins lies in farm planning. This is not simply a matter of substituting high gross margin enterprises in place of low ones. The gross margin is only one feature of an enterprise, albeit an important one. It says nothing about the call the enterprise makes on the basic farm resources - labour at different times of the year, machinery, buildings, working capital requirements, etc. All these factors and more have to be taken into account in the planning process.

6. This is not to argue that these other costs should be allocated. Complete allocation of many farm expenses is only possible on an arbitrary basis, since they are shared by two or more, possibly all farm enterprises. Allocation can therefore be completely misleading when making planning decisions. The same is true even when regular labour and machinery are employed specifically on certain enterprises, if such costs are calculated on a per-hectare or per head basis. This is because when enterprises are substituted, expanded, contracted or deleted, the variable costs for each enterprise will vary in proportion to the size of that enterprise, but other costs will not, except possibly some fuel and repair costs. Most 'fixed' costs may stay the same, others will change - but not smoothly in small amounts at a time. Either the same regular labour force will cope with a revised plan or a smaller or larger number of men will be needed. The same is true of tractors, other machines and buildings. Such cost changes must be taken into account, but allocating these costs on a per-hectare or per head basis

will not aid, and may positively confuse, planning decisions. The only point of making such calculations is for efficiency comparisons, e.g. labour cost per cow.

7. Allocating fixed costs at a flat rate (e.g. per hectare) for all enterprises, deducting this from the gross margin and hence calculating a 'net profit' from each enterprise can also be misleading. It ignores the whole problem of enterprise inter-relationships, differences between enterprises in total and seasonal requirements for labour, machinery and capital, and other factors such as different quality land on the same farm.

8. Changes in the scale of an enterprise may well affect its gross margin per unit, e.g. increasing the area of winter wheat from 30% to 55% on a farm will mean more second and third crop wheats being grown and a smaller proportion of the crop being drilled under the best conditions; hence yields may fall. Even if yields remain the same, variable costs (e.g. fertiliser) may be higher.

9. Gross margins used for planning future changes should also take account of possible changes in price, and the effect of changes in production techniques.

LOW, AVERAGE AND HIGH LEVELS

The levels of production given for most crop and livestock enterprises are meant to indicate differences in natural factors, soil productivity or even managerial skill etc., given the level of variable costs. They refer, to an average for each level over several years taking trends into account. Higher variable costs do not necessarily mean greater output, but depends on other factors too such as timing of applications.

Some variable costs in the schedules are calculated according to output (P and K fertiliser is based on the average yield taken off the land and haulage and packaging are linked to output). But for the most part, variable costs demonstrate minimal change between high yielding and low yielding fields or farms. Hence the majority of costs do not vary according to yield, which is true in many sectors of farming.

The book is written with the progressive and business orientated farm manager in mind, those wanting to improve their businesses both technically and commercially. It therefore presupposes that the performance of the average Pocketbook user will exceed that of the national average farm performance, albeit only slightly. We therefore don't simply take Defra's published average yields but, in most cases, a slightly higher yield. These figures are still thoroughly achievable in most farm businesses. The 'high' yields and performances are set out for those pushing production somewhat harder.

2. COMPLETE ENTERPRISE COSTINGS

Gross margins are extremely useful for simple benchmarking and comparative tests. However, more than half of the variation in performance between farms (of all sectors) is in their overheads so won't show up on gross margin schedules. This means examining farm structure and overhead costs is crucial and understanding full costs of production is useful for business planning.

Almost everybody calculates the cost of production per litre or tonne differently thereby giving different answers to the same question. Much arbitrary allocation of 'joint costs' is required to attempt fully costed net margins, and the results are often of limited use in making farm decisions. Another problem in 'complete enterprise costing' is where to stop. For example should interest on capital be included, whether borrowed or not? If so, further problems of asset valuation and allocation are involved. Variations between farms in their financial situations are considerable as, ranging from the farmer who owns all his land without any mortgage and has no other borrowings to the one with both a rent to pay for all his land and heavy borrowings in addition.

It is natural to want to know 'unit costs' to compare, for example, with prices received. Sometimes these calculations clarify particular costs and therefore efficiency gains that could be made. For these reasons costs per litre of milk are included, although the calculation of some of the 'fixed cost' items is difficult. If a farm has only one enterprise such calculations on that farm are obviously straightforward. But, these farms are rare; even on solely dairy farms followers are usually reared or forage grown, which are separate enterprises to milk production.

If required, a cost per tonne of combinable crops can be calculated by adding the fixed costs per hectare of mainly cereals farms (according to size range, given on page 223) to the variable costs per hectare given in the enterprise gross margin data and dividing by the selected yield. Such calculations need to be interpreted with caution because the allocation of fixed costs per hectare is inevitably crude. At The Andersons Centre (the Pocketbook's owning consultancy firm), allocation of labour and machinery is made according to fuel use per hectare. This makes the resulting margins more comparable; for example grass seed with potatoes. This is not a perfect science but attributes the various costs more accurately than per hectare or per unit of yield.

The allocation of specific labour (e.g. a full-time cowman), machinery (e.g. a potato harvester) and buildings (e.g. a grain store) is relatively simple to allocate and can provide useful information both for efficiency comparisons and partial budgeting. For some enterprises on many mixed farms, there are few such specific items and the question of the other so-called fixed cost items remains if a full costing is attempted.

HISTORIC DATA

It is not the intention of The Pocketbook to include 'historical data', except for some of the material in the Agristats section. Hence total farm survey results, which are inevitably a year or two old by the time they are published, are not included, although some are used in some sections with interpretation for the forthcoming year.

3. FARM BUSINESS SURVEY DATA

Data from the Farm Business Survey is used throughout the Pocketbook being one of the most reliable sources of statistically robust farm data. It is historic data though and this book is designed for forward planning so assumptions have been made about future prices. They are explained in each case.

The Farm Business Survey (FBS) of England is a key source of farm business data in England. It is carried out on behalf of Defra by a consortium of Universities. Its site; www.farmbusinesssurvey.co.uk holds a number of sets of FBS data and publications on specialist enterprises.

The Farm Business Survey in Wales is undertaken on behalf of the Welsh Assembly Government by the University of Aberystwyth. The results are published at - https://www.aber.ac.uk/en/ibers/fbs/

In Scotland the data for the Farm Accounts Survey is collected by the Scottish Rural College. It is available in the publication 'Farm Incomes in Scotland'. See www.scotland.gov.uk/Topics/Statistics/15631/8884

The Department of Agriculture and Rural Development for Northern Ireland undertakes the Farm Business Survey in the province. Results can be found at https://www.daera-ni.gov.uk/articles/farm-business-data

4. MAIN ASSUMPTIONS

Budgeting future prices, by necessity requires making assumptions about how they are likely to move in the future from current levels (August 2017). This Edition of the Pocketbook uses the following key assumptions for 2018:

- The pound: euro exchange rate throughout the book is £1 = €1.18, equivalent to €1 = 85p.
- Fertiliser prices for nitrogen (N), phosphate (P) and potash (K) are the same throughout and are detailed in a full schedule of fertiliser valuations on page 275. To calculate the gross margins, the following are used:
  - N: 53.6 p/kg (£185/t 34.5% N) (UK Ammonium Nitrate)
  - P_2O_5: 56.5 p/kg (£260/t 46% P_2O_5) (Triple Super Phosphate)
  - K_2O: 41.7 p/kg (£250/t 60% K_2O) (Muriate of Potash)
- When calculating the gross margins' fertiliser costs, standard fertiliser recommendations from RB209 (2017) have been used, assuming an average soil type with mineral and nitrogen indexes of 2. Each gross margin accounts for the replacement of the minerals taken off the field by the harvested crop (excluding straw which is incorporated).
- In the gross margin data, seed rates vary according to soil, season, variety, drilling date etc. Home Saved Seed (HSS) cost includes grain value, cleaning, dressing, testing and BSPB levy (refer to p 282).
- Farm machinery fuel price (red diesel) is taken to be 45ppl. However, it is noted that the contract charges (page 194) are calculated on 50ppl.
- Feed wheat price (from which many other commodity prices are benchmarked), is £140/tonne. This is an ex-farm price for 2018 harvest, delivery averaged throughout the year and typical marketing dates.
- Home-saved seed (HSS) is calculated in the gross margins including grain, dressing, testing and BSPB (British Society of Plant Protection) levy (see p 283). In the seed notes, C2 refers to certified (Merchant bought) seed.
- Sprays. Refer to Agrochemical Rates on page 282. PGR refers to Plant Growth Regulators

BREXIT IN THIS POCKETBOOK

Brexit is mentioned throughout the book where relevant, particularly in Section 3 on Government Support. The decision to separate from the EU has already had a substantial impact on the value of sterling, meaning the value of many commodities has moved significantly. Input prices tend to react to currency movements in a slower manner, and so are expected to rise, a factor that has been taken into account in the costings for 2018.

Whilst politicians have promised that the total subsidy to agriculture will be provided at current level until at least 2022, we can only be sure of the Basic Payment Scheme for 2018 and 2019 (and probably 2020). After that, the allocation of support might change meaning some farmers will receive more and others less than at present.

The 2018 year might be the last complete year of full participation in the EU's Single Market. As things currently stand, the UK will formally leave the EU on the 1st April 2019, and trading arrangements might change considerably at that point. This could have profound impacts on UK farming, with some sectors being very badly affected by the changes, and others receiving considerable benefit.

II. ENTERPRISE DATA

1. CROPS

WHEAT

Feed Winter Wheat

Production level	**Low**	**Average**	**High**	
Yield: t/ha (t/ac)	7.25 (2.9)	8.60 (3.5)	10.00 (4.1)	
	£	**£**	**£**	***£/t***
Output at £140/t	1,015 (411)	1,204 (488)	1,400 (567)	*140*
Variable Costs £/ha:				
Seed......................		56 (23)		*7*
Fertiliser.................		160 (65)		*19*
Sprays....................		244 (99)		*28*
Total Variable Costs		460 (186)		*53*
Gross Margin £/ha (ac)	**555** (225)	**744** (302)	**940** (381)	***87***

Fertiliser Basis 8.6t/ha

Nutrient	Kg/t	Kg/Ha	£/Ha
N	*22*	190	£102
P	7.8	67	£38
K	5.6	48	£20

Seed:

£/t C2	£350
Kg/Ha	175
% HSS	36%
£/t HSS	£266

Sprays £/ha:

Herbicides	£98
Fungicides	£116
Insecticides	£7
PGRs	£17
Other	£5

1. *Yields*. The average yield is for all winter feed wheat, i.e. all varieties and 1st and subsequent wheats. See over for more on First and Second Wheats. The overall yield used for feed and milling wheats including spring varieties calculates as 8.5t/ha.
2. *Straw* is costed as incorporated. Average yield and price is approximately 3.5 tonnes per hectare at £60/tonne (£5 more in small bales); variable costs (string) approx. £3.50 per tonne. Unbaled straw (sold for baling): anything from £50/ha (£20/acre) to £180/ha (£73/acre), national average around £85/ha (£34/acre).
3. *Seed* is costed with a single purpose dressing. Farm-saved percentages as according to pesticide survey 2010. Up to a third of growers have an increasing requirement for additional seed treatments, in particular to supress BYDV. This can add around £138 per tonne of seed (£24.50/ha). This has not been added in the gross margins so should be taken into account.
4. This schedule does not account for severe *grass weed infestations* such as Black Grass or Sterile Brome. Costs associated with managing such problems can amount to up to £160/hectare of additional agrichemical costs. Yield losses increase as infestation rises:

Yield losses from Black Grass Infestations

Grass plants/m²	*Yield loss t/Ha*	*% yield loss*
8-12	*0.2-0.4*	*2-5%*
12-25	*0.4-0.8*	*5-15%*
100	*1-2*	*15-25%*
>300	*+3*	*37%*

References:

Roebuck, J.F. (1987). B.C.P.C. and

Blair A, Cussans J, Lutman P (1999).

Milling Winter Wheat

Production level	Low	Average	High	
Yield: t/ha (t/ac)	7.00 (2.8)	8.25 (3.3)	9.50 (3.8)	
	£	**£**	**£**	***£/t***
Output at £146/t	1,022 (414)	1,205 (488)	1,387 (562)	*146*
Variable Costs £/ha:				
Seed.......................		59 (24)		*7*
Fertiliser.................		189 (77)		*23*
Sprays....................		252 (102)		*31*
Total Variable Costs		500 (203)		*61*
Gross Margin £/ha (ac)	**522** (211)	**705** (286)	**887** (359)	***85***

Fertiliser Basis 8.25t/ha			
Nutrient	Kg/t	Kg/Ha	£/Ha
N	*30*	250	£134
P	7.8	64	£36
K	5.6	46	£19

Seed:	
£/t C2	£360
Kg/Ha	175
% HSS	25%
£/t HSS	272

Sprays £/ha:	
Herbicides	£98
Fungicides	£121
Insecticides	£7
PGRs	£17
Other	£9

5. The average *milling price* is based on a 'full specification' (NABIM Group 1) premium of £10 over feed wheat, a 'biscuit' grade (NABIM Group 2) milling specification of £6 and a 25% failure rate of achieving the specification. The average premium achieved has fallen sharply in recent years as more milling wheat is now grown and yields are higher. Full specification is defined as NABIM Group 1 wheat with a minimum Hagberg of 250, 13% protein and a bushel weight of at least 76kg/hl.
6. *Milling v. Feed.* The yield of bread and biscuit wheat (generically known as milling) was historically about 8% below feed wheat but is now less than 4% (source: *AHDB*). The price premium varies according to quality and scarcity. Not all deliveries achieve full specification. Group 2 yields are higher than Group 1. Full specification bread-making premium averaged £22/tonne from 2012 to 2017. The 2016/17 bread-wheat premium averaged £10/tonne as yield differences close. NABIM wheat group 1 varieties accounted for about 26% of 2017 wheat area.

Comparison between First and Second Feed Wheat Crops

Production level	**Average**		**High**	
Year (after break)	First	Second	First	Second
Yield: t/ha (t/ac)	8.75 (3.5)	8.05 (3.3)	10.5 (4.3)	9.66 (3.9)
	£	**£**	**£**	**£**
Output	1,225 (496)	1,127 (456)	1,470 (595)	1,352 (548)
Variable Costs £/ha:				
Seed..........................	54 (22)	98 (40)	54 (22)	98 (40)
Fertiliser.....................	158 (64)	145 (59)	189 (77)	174 (70)
Sprays........................	238 (97)	259 (105)	238 (97)	259 (105)
Variable Costs	450 (182)	502 (203)	482 (195)	531 (215)
Gross Margin £/ha (ac)	**775** (314)	**625** (253)	**988** (400)	**821** (333)

7. First v. Second (Feed) Wheat. Different types and lengths of rotational breaks affect subsequent wheat yields as well as weather, soils and varieties etc. The table above assumes a yield reduction of 8% for second wheats compared with first. Third wheats could yield 10% below second wheats; variable costs are likely to be similar. Heavy, well-structured, well-drained clay soils are best suited to second wheats.

Spring Wheat

Production level	**Low**	**Average**	**High**	
Yield: t/ha (t/ac)	5.00 (2.0)	6.00 (2.4)	7.00 (2.8)	
	£	**£**	**£**	***£/t***
Output at £146/t	730 (296)	876 (355)	1,022 (414)	*146*
Variable Costs:				
Seed......................		71 (29)		*12*
Fertiliser.................		121 (49)		*20*
Sprays....................		144 (58)		*24*
Total Variable Costs		336 (136)		*56*
Gross Margin £/ha (ac)	**394** (159)	**540** (219)	**686** (278)	***90***

Fertiliser Basis 6t/ha

Nutrient	Kg/t	Kg/Ha	£/Ha
N	*25*	150	£80
P	7.8	47	£27
K	5.6	34	£14

Seed:

£/t C2	£370
Kg/Ha	200
% HSS	15%
£/t HSS	278

Sprays £/ha:

Herbicides	£62
Fungicides	£53
Insecticides	£7
PGRs	£17
Other	£5

1. *Price:* In general, see Winter Wheat (previous pages). A higher proportion of spring wheat is sold for milling compared with winter wheat (95% here). Here we assume 25% failure rate to feed price for 2018 harvest.
2. *Straw:* See Winter Wheat but yields are considerably lower (2.5t/ha).
3. It is thought about 6% of UK wheat area is spring sown although survey data is unavailable. It is popular after root crops. The percentage is higher after a wet autumn. The area has risen in recent years because of Greening regulation obligations and to manage grass weeds and some new spring varies have long planting windows.

Red Wheat is a very hard spring wheat crop which was grown in the UK under contract until 2015 harvest. At its peak it covered several thousand hectares but is not grown in the UK any longer in any substantial way.

BARLEY

Winter Feed Barley

Production level	Low	Average	High	
Yield: t/ha (t/ac)	6.00 (2.4)	7.00 (2.8)	8.00 (3.2)	
	£	**£**	**£**	***£/t***
Output at £128/t	768 (311)	896 (363)	1,024 (415)	*128*
Variable Costs:				
Seed……………………		55 (22)		*8*
Fertiliser………………		122 (49)		*17*
Sprays…………………		186 (75)		*27*
Total Variable Costs		363 (147)		*52*
Gross Margin £/ha (ac)	**405** (164)	**533** (216)	**661** (268)	***76***

Fertiliser Basis 7t/ha

Nutrient	Kg/t	Kg/Ha	£/Ha
N	*20*	140	£75
P	7.8	55	£31
K	5.6	39	£16

Seed:

£/t C2*	£335
Kg/Ha	175
% HSS	25%
£/t HSS	260

Sprays:

Herbicides	£77
Fungicides	£79
Insecticides	£7
PGRs	£17
Other	£5

* *Not Hybrid which would be £105/ha*

1. *Prices*. Feed barley has a lower nutritional value to wheat so is normally discounted to feed wheat, by about 8% as used here (the average over 5 and 20 years is 7.5%).
2. *Straw* is costed as incorporated. Average yield is approx. 2·75 tonnes per hectare, value £65 per tonne baled ex-field, higher in the West, (£10/t more in small bales); variable cost (string) approximately £3.50 per tonne. Prices rise in years of forage shortage.

Winter Malting Barley

Production level	Low	Average	High	
Yield: t/ha (t/ac)	5.25 (2.1)	6.20 (2.5)	7.25 (2.9)	
	£	**£**	**£**	***£/t***
Output at £141.5/t	743 (301)	877 (355)	1,026 (416)	*142*
Variable Costs:				
Seed……………………		58 (23)		*9*
Fertiliser………………		95 (38)		*15*
Sprays…………………		186 (75)		*30*
Total Variable Costs		339 (137)		*55*
Gross Margin £/ha (ac)	**404** (164)	**538** (218)	**687** (278)	***87***

Fertiliser Basis 6.2t/ha

Nutrient	Kg/t	Kg/Ha	£/Ha
N	*16*	100	£54
P	7.8	48	£27
K	5.6	35	£15

Seed:

£/t C2	£350
Kg/Ha	175
% HSS	25%
£/t HSS	273

Sprays £/Ha:

Herbicides	£77
Fungicides	£79
Insecticides	£7
PGRs	£17
Other	£5

3. *Prices*. Winter Malting Barley generally has a lower malting specification to spring barley. Here, winter malting barley has a £18 per tonne premium over feed barley. This accounts for some that don't meet malting standards. For the best malting barleys the premium in the past has been £25 and in some years higher.

Spring Malting Barley

Production level	**Low**	**Average**	**High**	
Yield: t/ha (t/ac)	4.75 (1.9)	5.70 (2.3)	6.50 (2.6)	
	£	**£**	**£**	***£/t***
Output at £149.5/t	710 (288)	852 (345)	972 (394)	*150*
Variable Costs:				
Seed.......................		57 (23)		*10*
Fertiliser.................		81 (33)		*14*
Sprays....................		144 (58)		*25*
Total Variable Costs		282 (114)		*50*
Gross Margin £/ha (ac)	**428** (173)	**570** (231)	**689** (279)	***100***

Fertiliser Basis 5.7t/ha

Nutrient	Kg/t	Kg/Ha	£/Ha
N	*14*	80	£43
P	7.8	44	£25
K	5.6	32	£13

Seed:

£/t C2	£350
Kg/Ha	175
% HSS	35%
£/t HSS	286

Sprays:

Herbicides	£165
Fungicides	£47
Insecticides	£11
PGRs	£0
Other	£16

1. *Prices*. Virtually all spring barley grown is malting varieties, grown for a premium. Spring malting premiums usually exceed those for winter varieties. Here the premium over feed barley is £28 per tonne. Again, this allows for failed samples making £150 per tonne.
2. *Straw*: as per Winter Barley, but with lower yield,

Naked Barley

3. Naked barley, suitable for roasting, flaking or milling as pearl barley, is now rarely heard of. It is grown like normal barley, but yields are reckoned to be some 15% lower. It could be either autumn or spring sown.

OATS

Winter Oats

Production level	Low	Average	High	
Yield: t/ha (t/ac)	5.25 (2.1)	6.30 (2.6)	7.25 (2.9)	
	£	**£**	**£**	***£/t***
Output at £130/t (feed)	683 (277)	819 (332)	943 (382)	*130*
Variable Costs:				
Seed......................		56 (23)		*9*
Fertiliser.................		112 (45)		*18*
Sprays....................		131 (53)		*21*
Total Variable Costs		299 (121)		*47*
Gross Margin £/ha (ac)	**384** (156)	**520** (211)	**644** (261)	***83***

Fertiliser Basis 6.3t/ha			
Nutrient	Kg/t	Kg/Ha	£/Ha
N	*21*	130	£70
P	7.8	49	£28
K	5.6	35	£15

Seed:	
£/t C2	£360
Kg/Ha	175
% HSS	40%
£/t HSS	260

Sprays:	
Herbicides	£57
Fungicides	£44
Insecticides	£7
PGRs	£17
Other	£5

1. *Price:* Feed price quoted. Milling specification requires a minimum bushel weight of 50kg/Hl. Conservation grade milling oats may obtain a premium of £10-20/tonne.
2. *Straw* is costed as incorporated here. Average yield is 3.5 tonnes per hectare; value £68 per tonne according to region and season; variable costs (string) £3.50 per tonne.

Spring Oats

Production level	Low	Average	High	
Yield: t/ha (t/ac)	4.75 (1.9)	5.50 (2.2)	6.25 (2.5)	
	£	**£**	**£**	***£/t***
Output at £130/t (feed)	618 (250)	715 (290)	813 (329)	*130*
Variable Costs:				
Seed......................		60 (24)		*11*
Fertiliser.................		75 (30)		*14*
Sprays....................		91 (37)		*17*
Total Variable Costs		226 (92)		*41*
Gross Margin £/ha (ac)	**392** (159)	**489** (198)	**587** (238)	***89***

Fertiliser Basis 5.5t/ha			
Nutrient	Kg/t	Kg/Ha	£/Ha
N	*13*	70	£38
P	7.8	43	£24
K	5.6	31	£13

Seed:	
£/t C2	£370
Kg/Ha	185
% HSS	40%
£/t HSS	259

Sprays:	
Herbicides	£36
Fungicides	£34
Insecticides	£7
PGRs	£9
Other	£5

3. *Winter or Spring?* Most GB oats are winter crops although the proportion of spring oats has been rising in recent years; spring oats dominate further north with an estimated 70% winter oats in England/Wales but 20% in Scotland.

Naked Oats

Production level	Low	Average	High	
Yield: t/ha (t/ac)	4.5 (1.8)	5.50 (2.2)	6.50 (2.6)	
	£	**£**	**£**	***£/t***
Output at £190/t	855 (346)	1,045 (423)	1,235 (500)	*190*
Variable Costs £/ha:				
Seed......................		60 (24)		*11*
Fertiliser.................		104 (42)		*19*
Sprays....................		130 (53)		*24*
Total Variable Costs		294 (119)		*53*
Gross Margin £/ha (ac)	**561** (227)	**751** (304)	**941** (381)	***137***

Fertiliser Basis 5.5t/ha

Nutrient	Kg/t	Kg/Ha	£/Ha
N	*18*	100	£54
P	7.8	50	£28
K	5.6	50	£22

Seed:

£/t C2	600
Kg/Ha	100
% HSS	0%
£/t HSS	336

1. *Price:* based on contracts offering premiums 35% above the average feed wheat price. The premium can be reduced according to husk content. Contracts require a maximum moisture content of 14%, which is also recommended for long-term storage.
2. *Inputs* are lower than for wheat or barley. The agronomy is similar to that of husked oat varieties. Traditionally, high nitrogen use has not been possible due to the risk of lodging, however, new semi-dwarf varieties with stiff straw have been introduced. As well as increasing the scope for higher fertiliser applications, this means the crop is also suited to more fertile soils, and growth regulators may be avoided. Oats provide a break in the take-all cycle.
3. Naked oats have a higher protein, energy and oil content than 'traditional' oats, but the fibre content is lower – as the husk is removed during harvesting.
4. The area grown is increasing steadily. Naked oats account for over 10% of the traded tonnage of UK oats (i.e. excluding those grown for on-farm use). The traditional markets such as racehorse feed, dog food, and bird feed markets are all increasing. Over recent years the human consumption market has developed so that at least half the crop is now sold for health foods, artisan breads and breakfast cereals. In future, a further growth area is likely to be for inclusion of the crop in monogastric animal feeds. The poultry industry is looking into setting up supply chains.
5. Around a third of plantings are spring and this proportion rises after a wet autumn. The margin above is winter cropping. Past NIAB survey results have suggested that spring yields average 20%-25% less than conventional oats. The actual difference will depend on the particular season, but are likely now to be in the range 15%-20%.
6. Harvest is early (just after winter barley). New varieties are less susceptible to shedding than in the past, however care needs to be taken with both the timing of harvest, and the set-up of the combine, to ensure a clean, saleable sample.

OILSEED RAPE

Winter Oilseed Rape

Production level	Low	Average	High	
Yield: t/ha (t/ac)	3.00 (1.2)	3.50 (1.4)	4.00 (1.6)	
	£	**£**	**£**	***£/t***
Output at £310/t	930 (377)	1,085 (439)	1,240 (502)	*310*
Variable Costs:				
Seed.......................		54 (22)		*15*
Fertiliser..................		146 (59)		*42*
Sprays.....................		223 (90)		*64*
Total Variable Costs		423 (171)		*121*
Gross Margin £/ha (ac)	**507** (205)	**662** (268)	**817** (331)	***189***

Fertiliser Basis 3.5t/ha			
Nutrient	Kg/t	Kg/Ha	£/Ha
N	*54*	190	£102
P	14	49	£28
K	11	39	£16

Seed:	
£/Ha C	50
£/Ha Hy	75
£/Ha HSS	39
C:Hy:HSS	40:30:30
C = Conventional	
Hy = Hybrid	

Sprays:	
Herbicides	£108
Fungicides	£76
Insecticides	£7
PGRs	£17
Other	£14

1. *Prices*. The price assumed for the 2018 crop is £310/tonne, including oil bonuses at 44% oil content (£294 before bonus).

   The oil bonus is paid on the percentage of oil over 40 percent, at 1.5 times the sale value of the crop. For example in this case, the bonus is on 4% oil x £294 x 1.5 = £17.64. (Figures are rounded to the nearest £5.)

Spring Oilseed Rape

Production level	Low	Average	High	
Yield: t/ha (t/ac)	2.00 (0.8)	2.25 (0.9)	2.50 (1.0)	
	£	**£**	**£**	***£/t***
Output at £310/t	620 (251)	698 (282)	775 (314)	*310*
Variable Costs:				
Seed.......................		55 (22)		*25*
Fertiliser..................		71 (29)		*32*
Sprays.....................		145 (59)		*64*
Total Variable Costs		271 (110)		*120*
Gross Margin £/ha (ac)	**349** (141)	**426** (173)	**504** (204)	***190***

2. *Inputs: Seed* as per WOSR, but 50% conventional, 20% HSS. *Fertiliser:* N/P/K at 80/32/25 kg/ha. *Sprays,* Herbicides. £52, Fungicides, £55, Insecticides £7, PGRs £17 and Others £14/ha

3. *Winter Versus Spring*: As little as 8,000 hectares of spring OSR is grown in the UK which is 1.5 percent of the entire crop. As can be seen the financial reward is slim compared with other combinable crops.

LINSEED

Spring Linseed

Production level	Low	Average	High	
Yield: t/ha (t/ac)	1.50 (0.6)	1.75 (0.7)	2.00 (0.8)	
	£	£	£	*£/t*
Output at £350/t	525 (213)	613 (248)	700 (284)	*350*
Variable Costs:				
Seed.......................		90 (36)		*51*
Fertiliser.................		51 (21)		*29*
Sprays.....................		64 (26)		*37*
Total Variable Costs		205 (83)		*117*
Gross Margin £/ha (ac)	**320** (130)	**408** (165)	**495** (200)	***233***

Fertiliser Basis 1.75t/ha

Nutrient	Kg/t	Kg/Ha	£/Ha
N	*29*	50	£27
P	14	30	£17
K	11	10	£4

Seed:

£/t C2	1800
Kg/Ha	50
% HSS	0%
£/t HSS	4914

Sprays:

1. The *price* for the 2018 is OSR price plus 13%. Contract prices are normally tied to a standard 38% oil and 9% moisture. Some specialist contracts for specific varieties such as Yellow Linseed can be worth more.
2. Most *linseed is spring-sown (about 24,000 hectares)*, drilling mid-March to mid-April, no more than 1 year in 5. Too much nitrogen (over 130 kg/ha) can cause lodging, delayed maturity and excessive weed growth causing difficult harvesting, poor quality and lower yields; it should be applied early. Harvesting: spring normally end Aug-early Sept. Harvest moisture content 12-16%: Dry to 9% for storage.

Winter Linseed

Production level	Low	Average	High	
Yield: t/ha (t/ac)	2.00 (0.8)	2.25 (0.9)	2.50 (1.0)	
	£	£	£	*£/t*
Output at £350/t	700 (284)	788 (319)	875 (354)	*350*
Variable Costs:				
Seed.......................		95 (38)		*42*
Fertiliser.................		77 (31)		*34*
Sprays.....................		77 (31)		*34*
Total Variable Costs		249 (101)		*111*
Gross Margin £/ha (ac)	**451** (183)	**539** (218)	**626** (254)	***239***

3. *Output:* Price unchanged. *Inputs:* Seed rate fractionally higher, fertiliser N/P/K 90/32/25 kg/ha.
4. *Winter Linseed* area is declining, currently about 4,000 hectares grown in the UK. Yield is affected by frost heave, disease and thrips (thunder-bugs), most varieties susceptible to lodging; pigeons can be troublesome. Early sowing (early to mid-September) is best.

FIELD PEAS

Blue Peas

Production level	Low	Average	High	
Yield: t/ha (t/ac)	3.50 (1.4)	4.00 (1.6)	4.50 (1.8)	
	£	**£**	**£**	***£/t***
Output at £200/t	700 (284)	800 (324)	900 (365)	*200*
Variable Costs:				
Seed......................		84 (34)		*21*
Fertiliser.................		36 (15)		*9*
Sprays....................		150 (61)		*38*
Total Variable Costs		270 (109)		*68*
Gross Margin £/ha (ac)	**430** (174)	**530** (215)	**630** (255)	***132***

Fertiliser Basis 4t/ha

Nutrient	Kg/t	Kg/Ha	£/Ha
N	*0*	0	£0
P	8.8	35	£20
K	10	40	£17

Seed:

£/t C2	475
Kg/Ha	200
% HSS	30%
£/t HSS	297

Sprays:

Herbicides	£77
Fungicides	£53
Insecticides	£11
PGRs	£0
Other	£10

1. *Price*. All peas are grown for a premium market (not stock-feed) with only a small proportion of low-grade samples (30%) compounded for feed. Feed value is therefore not relevant as a base price.

   The overall price for *Blue Peas* is £200/tonne, taking account of human consumption values (£220/tonne) and a 30% failure rate with feed price of £160. Most peas (70% in 2017) are Blues, used for micronizing (largely for pet food) and exports.

Marrowfats

Production level	Low	Average	High	
Yield: t/ha (t/ac)	3.00 (1.2)	3.60 (1.5)	4.25 (1.7)	
	£	**£**	**£**	***£/t***
Output at £225/t	675 (273)	810 (328)	956 (387)	*225*
Variable Costs:				
Seed......................		165 (67)		*46*
Fertiliser.................		33 (13)		*9*
Sprays....................		186 (75)		*52*
Total Variable Costs		384 (156)		*107*
Gross Margin £/ha (ac)	**291** (118)	**426** (172)	**572** (232)	***118***

Fertiliser Basis 3.6t/ha

Nutrient	Kg/t	Kg/Ha	£/Ha
N	*0*	0	£0
P	8.8	32	£18
K	10	36	£15

Seed:

£/t C2	595
Kg/Ha	300
% HSS	20%
£/t HSS	374

Sprays:

Herbicides	£67
Fungicides	£92
Insecticides	£11
PGRs	£0
Other	£16

2. *Price:* Marrowfats can achieve higher prices than Blues and in recent years have achieved considerable premiums over other combinable crops but are subject to a small illiquid market. They are not priced with a premium over wheat, as the markets bear no relationship. However, for the grower, this relationship is important as all crops will, in effect, be competing for space in the arable rotation.
3. Marrowfat Peas are used for canning, packets and export trade. They are almost entirely grown on a contract thus production is restricted by demand although this is growing. They yield about 10% less than Blue Peas. The average price in this gross margin is £225/tonne being £240/tonne for 80%, £160 for the 20% that fails quality specification.

FIELD BEANS

Winter Beans

Production level	Low	Average	High	
Yield: t/ha (t/ac)	3.50 (1.4)	4.20 (1.7)	4.75 (1.9)	
	£	**£**	**£**	***£/t***
Output at £170/t	595 (241)	714 (289)	808 (327)	*170*
Variable Costs:				
Seed......................		81 (33)		*19*
Fertiliser.................		47 (19)		*11*
Sprays....................		126 (51)		*30*
Total Variable Costs		254 (103)		*61*
Gross Margin £/ha (ac)	**341** (138)	**460** (186)	**553** (224)	***109***

Fertiliser Basis 4.2t/ha

Nutrient	Kg/t	Kg/Ha	£/Ha
N	*0*	0	£0
P	11	46	£26
K	12	50	£21

Seed:

£/t C2	380
Kg/Ha	250
% HSS	60%
£/t HSS	287

Sprays:

Herbicides	£62
Fungicides	£47
Insecticides	£7
PGRs	£0
Other	£10

1. *Price*. This is based on a human consumption price of £175/tonne achieved by 60% and feed specification for the rest at £160/tonne.

   All beans are grown with a potential for sale into a human consumption market. However, insect damage, dis-colouring or other damage means some is sold for feed.

Spring Beans

Production level	Low	Average	High	
Yield: t/ha (t/ac)	3.25 (1.3)	3.90 (1.6)	4.50 (1.8)	
	£	**£**	**£**	***£/t***
Output at £175/t	569 (230)	683 (276)	788 (319)	*175*
Variable Costs:				
Seed......................		85 (34)		*22*
Fertiliser.................		44 (18)		*11*
Sprays....................		124 (50)		*32*
Total Variable Costs		253 (103)		*65*
Gross Margin £/ha (ac)	**316** (128)	**429** (174)	**534** (216)	***110***

Fertiliser Basis 3.9t/ha

Nutrient	Kg/t	Kg/Ha	£/Ha
N	*0*	0	£0
P	11	43	£24
K	12	47	£20

Seed:

£/t C2	390
Kg/Ha	250
% HSS	50%
£/t HSS	292

Sprays:

Herbicides	£62
Fungicides	£42
Insecticides	£11
PGRs	£0
Other	£10

2. *Price.* Spring beans are all grown for the human consumption market. It is only the poor quality beans (predominantly Bruchid beetle damaged) that are rejected and redirected to feed compounders. Damaged samples can be cleaned if the premium justifies it. A large proportion of the crop is exported (to North Africa). Average spring bean price is budgeted here at £175/tonne comprising 60% at £182/tonne and the rest at £160/tonne (for feed).

Winter versus Spring Beans.

The key determinant between which to crop is soil type. Winter beans are more suited to heavy soils and springs on lighter land. As the schedules illustrate, there is little real difference between the gross margins. Spring crops are retained in many rotations to help manage grass weed problems.

Peas or Beans?

For the last decade the area of peas was about 20% of the UK combinable pulse area having fallen from 50% in 1997. High quality and good yields can return high gross margins and offer wider benefits to the farming system although they can be difficult to grow and the unpredictability of pulses has put several growers off in previous years.

Beyond the Gross Margin

Page 1 explains that the gross margin is only a partial measure of crop contribution and cost to the farm business. Amongst the combinable crops this is particularly true for the legumes such as peas and beans. They fix nitrogen into the soil which is then available for uptake by subsequent crops either saving input costs of the following crop or raising its yield. The amount fixed is very difficult to predict but varies from almost nothing to over 200kg/ha in the extreme cases based on soil type, crop health, growing conditions and other factors too. A useful average figure used by the PGRO for additional nitrogen available for the following crop after a pulse crop is 50kg/ha (worth £25/ha this year). The associated input savings from the following crop, or the additional yield it achieves should therefore, for management purposes be attributed to the leguminous crop.

HERBAGE SEEDS

	Intermediate Perennial Ryegrass		Late Perennial Ryegrass	
	Average	High	Average	High
	£	£	£	£
Yield (tonnes per ha)	1.3	1.6	1.1	1.5
Price per 50 kg (£)	45		52	
Output	1,170	1,440	1,144	1,560
Variable Costs:				
Seed	50		52	
Fertiliser	198		198	
Sprays	145		145	
Cleaning / Certification	228	274	197	259
Total Variable Costs	620	667	591	653
Gross Margin per ha	**550**	**773**	**553**	**907**
Gross Margin per acre	222	313	224	367

1. *Prices* in are for certified seed for 2018 harvest. Markets for grass seed remain well-supplied after recent good harvests. High sugar varieties command a premium of £10-£20 over the values quoted. Amenity ryegrasses and fescues also command a premium for high quality sports use.
2. No allowance has been made above for *by-products*. Some crops produce 4 to 5 tonnes of threshed hay, which is of low feeding value, potentially worth £300 per hectare. Some grasses, especially spring-sown ryegrass, also provide good autumn and winter grazing.
3. *Yields* are for cleaned certified seed. The crop is risky, i.e. yields are highly variable, depending especially on the weather at, and precise timeliness of, harvesting. The margin assumes the use of growth regulators and stripper headers which reduces the risk. Most grasses give their highest yield in their first harvest year, assuming good establishment. Crops are usually replaced after two harvests.
4. *Inputs: Seed* margin assumes 10.5kg per hectare with cost split over two harvest years. Spring planted seed rates are lower. If the seed crop is undersown, the seed rate for the cover crop is reduced and nitrogen applications restricted.
5. *Chemical* costs. The margins assume an autumn-sown crop; spring costs are lower.
6. The following were the number of hectares grown for certified seed production for the main grasses and clovers in the UK for the 2016 harvest;

Italian / Westerwold Ryegrass	196	Cocksfoot	42
Early Perennial Ryegrass	118	Red Fescue	358
Inter. Perennial Ryegrass	1,846	White Clover	Nil
Late Perennial Ryegrass	2,279	Red Clover	69
Amenity Perennial Ryegrass	842	Common Vetch	148
Hybrid Ryegrass	735	Timothy	57

The ryegrasses total 6,016 ha (*14,900 acres*).
All herbage seeds total 6,690 ha (*16,500 acres*).

7. *Labour*: see page 169.

Acknowledgement: Thanks to - British Seed Houses; Herbage Seed Services; NIAB.

RYE

Production level	Low	Average	High	
Yield: t/ha (t/ac)	4.9 (2.0)	6.20 (2.5)	7.50 (3.0)	
	£	**£**	**£**	***£/t***
Output at £150/t	735 (298)	930 (377)	1,125 (456)	*150*
Variable Costs £/ha:				
Seed......................		95 (38)		*15*
Fertiliser.................		128 (52)		*21*
Sprays....................		110 (45)		*18*
Total Variable Costs		333 (135)		*54*
Gross Margin £/ha (ac)	**402** (163)	**597** (242)	**792** (321)	***96***

Fertiliser Basis 6.2t/ha			
Nutrient	Kg/t	Kg/Ha	£/Ha
N	*19*	120	£64
P	7.8	50	£28
K	5.6	80	£35

Seed:	
£/t C2	635
Kg/Ha	150
% HSS	0%
£/t HSS	235

1. The *price* of £140 per tonne for 2018 harvest is based on a £10 per tonne premium over feed wheat price at the point of sale. It assumes the milling specification is achieved. Feed grade price achieves between feed wheat and feed barley. Only a very small percentage of the crop is grown for the free market.
2. Rye is autumn-sown, drought tolerant and very hardy. It can withstand low temperatures and starts growing early in the spring. It has all-round resistance to wheat and barley diseases, e.g. eyespot, and suffers less from take-all than wheat – hence it is a possible replacement for third or fourth wheat. Its vigour keeps weeds down. Its herbicide, fungicide and fertiliser requirements are lower than for other cereals, except for growth regulators. Rye is harvested earlier than winter wheat (useful for following with oilseed rape).
3. Largely grown on light, low fertility, sandy or stony soils, not suited to other cereals. The average yield in the UK in the five years 2012 to 2016 was 4.2 tonnes per hectare, but yields were very low in both 2015 and 2016. In the previous five-year period yields averaged 6 tonnes per hectare.
4. The area grown in the UK has ranged between 6,000 and 7,000 ha for several years, but rose to over 20,000 hectares in 2015 and 2016. The latter may have been due to the three-crop rule. Rye crisp-bread is the major outlet. It is also milled into flour, used in mixed-grain bread and muesli. About two-thirds of UK requirements are imported, mainly from Canada (which produces the highest quality), Denmark, Germany and Spain. Demand for UK rye has been falling, owing to import competition in the crisp-bread market.
5. *Drawbacks*: it sprouts in a wet harvest: must therefore harvest early, at relatively high moisture. It grows very tall and lodges easily: hence high levels of nitrogen are not possible; but growth regulators help. Its heavy straw crop means slow combining (twice as long as wheat and barley), and difficult straw incorporation. Hybrid varieties, with shorter, stiffer straw, are being developed; these would improve the comparative profitability of rye on better soils.
6. Drilling: 2nd and 3rd weeks September. Harvesting: by mid-August at relatively high moisture content, then dry to 14-15% (no drying costs included in margin).

TRITICALE

Production level	Low	Average	High	
Yield: t/ha (t/ac)	4.00 (1.6)	5.00 (2.0)	7.20 (2.9)	
	£	£	£	£/t
Output at £135/t	540 (219)	675 (273)	972 (394)	*135*
Variable Costs £/ha:				
Seed......................		54 (22)		*11*
Fertiliser.................		120 (49)		*24*
Sprays....................		70 (28)		*14*
Total Variable Costs		244 (99)		*49*
Gross Margin £/ha (ac)	**296** (120)	**431** (175)	**728** (295)	***86***

Fertiliser Basis 5t/ha			
Nutrient	Kg/t	Kg/Ha	£/Ha
N	*26*	130	£70
P	7.8	50	£28
K	5.6	50	£22

Seed:	
£/t C2	400
Kg/Ha	150
% HSS	40%
£/t HSS	296

1. The price is usually £4 to £6 per tonne below feed wheat,
2. A 'man-made' cross between rye and hard wheat. It combines the hardiness of rye and the marketability of feed wheat. It is used in livestock feed, particularly pig and poultry rations, having high levels of lysine (an amino acid). After a rise to nearly 15,000ha, the cropped UK area has settled at around 10,000Ha in recent years.
3. *Yields* in the five years 2012 to 2016 averaged 4.2 tonnes/ha, a low yield resulting from being grown on light land. In these circumstances, it frequently out-yields wheat or barley, and with lower input requirements. It is less prone to damage than other cereals where rabbit grazing is a problem.
4. Less fungicide is needed because of its good disease resistance, except for ergot, but including take-all (making it a good replacement for a third or fourth wheat). It is a tall crop, which helps to suppress weeds, but it is susceptible to lodging; growth regulators are beneficial. New semi-dwarf varieties are being developed, to overcome straw strength weakness and susceptibility to rust infections.
5. The crop is best drilled early (September) on light, drought-prone soils; otherwise October is satisfactory. Harvesting is at the same time as wheat. There is more straw, which slows combining, and incorporation is difficult; this is less of a problem on poor soils as there is less straw.

Spring Triticale

Spring varieties have been introduced in the last few years. These have been grown mostly in livestock areas – the north and west of England, as well as western Scotland, Wales and N. Ireland. Being a spring crop means winter water logging is not an issue, and can be grown on a wider range of soils. In total up to 5,000 hectares of spring triticale is grown in the UK: either on its own or as part of a mixture.

It has lower yields than winter triticale. However, most is whole-cropped to produce an 'arable forage'. Often it is grown in a mixture with a protein crop. Inputs for spring triticale are lower than those for winter varieties.

BORAGE

Production level	Low	Average	High	
Yield: t/ha (t/ac)	0.1 (0.0)	0.40 (0.2)	0.7 (0.3)	
	£	**£**	**£**	***£/t***
Output at £2600/t	260 (105)	1,040 (421)	1,820 (737)	*2,600*
Variable Costs £/ha:				
Seed……………………		209 (85)		*523*
Fertiliser………………		78 (32)		*195*
Sprays…………………		40 (16)		*100*
Total Variable Costs		327 (132)		*818*
Gross Margin £/ha (ac)	**-67** -27	**713** (289)	**1,493** (605)	***1783***

Fertiliser Basis 0.4t/ha			
Nutrient	Kg/t	Kg/Ha	£/Ha
N	200	80	£43
P	87.5	35	£20
K	87.5	35	£15

Seed:	
£/Kg C2	£11.00
Kg/Ha	19
% HSS	0%
£/t HSS	£250

1. Borage is indigenous to Britain (or at least here since Roman times); it has both grown in the wild, and been cultivated for centuries. It is produced principally for use as a dietary supplement, but it may also be used in cosmetics and pharmaceuticals. The oil has a high gamma linolenic acid (GLA) content.
2. It was first grown as a field crop in the UK in the early 1980's. The usual area grown in the UK is around 5,000 hectares (12,500 acres) per year. However, due to a world-wide surplus of GLA, few, if any, contracts were offered in the years 2009 to 2011. The area has recovered since, partly due to the high quality of the UK crop compared to other sources. Contracts are expected to be available for harvest 2018.
3. The harvest crop price assumed is £2,600 per tonne for the 2018 crop. Values have recently been up to £3,000 per tonne, but the market has weakened slightly. The market tends to be volatile, it is essential for a grower to have a buy-back contract with a reputable company. The crop should not be grown speculatively.
4. The crop is spring sown (March-April) into a good seedbed. Its aggressive growth gives good weed control with a high plant density. There are no significant pests and diseases, except for powdery mildew. Low rainfall areas are preferred owing to harvesting difficulties in wet conditions. It is combined in late July/early August, after swathing and drying, which takes a minimum of two weeks. The costs of swathing are not included in the margin above. Harvesting can be difficult and seed shedding at maturity is a problem. Seed should be promptly dried to 10% for safe storage. Cleaning may be necessary.
5. Borage should only be considered by those prepared to invest sufficient time in the crop's husbandry, harvest and storage. Borage is a low yield / high risk crop – yields are from virtually nothing to 0.75 tonnes per ha (6cwt per acre); average 0.4 (3.2).

Acknowledgement: Thanks to – Frontier,; Fairking,; Premium Crops.

LUPINS

Production level	Low	Average	High	
Yield: t/ha (t/ac)	2.25 (0.9)	3.00 (1.2)	3.75 (1.5)	
	£	**£**	**£**	***£/t***
Output at £250/t	563 (228)	750 (304)	938 (380)	*250*
Variable Costs £/ha:				
Seed......................		130 (53)		*43*
Fertiliser.................		54 (22)		*18*
Sprays....................		80 (32)		*27*
Total Variable Costs		264 (107)		*88*
Gross Margin £/ha (ac)	**299** (121)	**486** (197)	**674** (273)	***162***

Fertiliser Basis 3t/ha

Nutrient	Kg/t	Kg/Ha	£/Ha
N	8.333	25	£13
P	13.33	40	£23
K	13.33	40	£18

Seed:

£/t C2	£740
Kg/Ha	175
% HSS	0%
£/t HSS	£330

1. *Price* used here is £250 per tonne (White lupins). Few lupins are traded on the open market, but the value tends to be higher than feed beans due to higher protein content (38% to 40% for white lupins) which means the price is closer to soya values.
2. A leguminous spring crop grown on light land. They are a good substitute for non-GM soya bean meal in livestock feed. Most is whole-cropped for silage but can be crimped or milled and fed directly to stock or the grain traded as a cash crop.
3. Around 2,000 hectares (5,000 acres) are grown in the UK, about 70% is white (mostly in South and East), 15-20% blue and the remainder yellow (North and Scotland due to their shorter growing season).
4. Lupins need a good cereal seedbed and pre-emergence weed control. Anthracnose is a potentially serious threat but plant health measures have so far kept it under control.
5. Appropriate variety choice is important depending on area of the country, soil pH, intended end use and growth habit required. There are three distinct species of spring lupins; white, blue and yellow. White lupins have higher protein and potentially greater yield than blues but require a longer growing season. Yellow lupins fall between blue and white on both counts.

Lupin characteristics

	White *Lupinus Albus*	**Yellow** *Lupinus Luteus*	**Blue** *Lupinus Angustifolius*
Flower Colour	white or blue	yellow	white or blue
Growth habit	semi-determinate	semi-determinate	fully or semi-determinate
pH tolerance	5 to 7.6	4.6 to 6.8	5 to 6.8
Protein	36-40%	38-42%	31-35%
Oil content	10%	5%	6%
Yield	3.0-3.5 t/ha	2.5-3.0 t/ha	3.0-3.5 t/ha

Acknowledgement: Thanks to - Soya UK.

MINORITY CROPS

Camelina Sativa

Camelina, Gold of Pleasure, or False Flax is a fast growing spring (or occasionally winter) sown crop. It is easily grown and harvested and is drought tolerant. The oil contains a range of essential fatty acids. It can be used as a food supplement or in industry as a drying oil. There is currently no commercial scale production in the UK that the authors are aware of. It is thought that current domestic usage requirements could support around 1,000 ha of the crop in the UK. Yields are in the 1.0-2.5 tonne per ha range. Price is uncertain due to the absence of a domestic market but an indicative price is likely to be around £450-£700 per tonne.

Crambe - Abyssinian Mustard

Crambe is an industrial oilseed that contains high levels of erucic acid. Converted into erucamide it is used as a slip agent in plastics and is a constituent of heat sensitive dyes. The area of crambe in the UK had grown to around 5,000 ha in the early 2000's. However, the major promoter/buyer of the crop went into receivership and little or none is being currently grown commercially.

Crambe is a cruciferous spring crop managed in a similar way to spring oilseed rape. It has a short growing season, requiring only 100-120 days to reach maturity after emergence. As with oilseed rape, timely harvesting is important. Crambe can be combined direct, desiccated and combined or swathed. The crop should be stored and marketed at a moisture content of 9% or less. Yields are in the 2.5 tonne per ha range. Contract prices offered in the past were £180 per tonne. Growing costs are likely to be around £300 per tonne.

Durum Wheat

As well as pasta, durum is used to produce semolina, couscous, biscuits, and is widely used in North African and Middle Eastern cooking. Domestic demand is relatively small; UK consumption per head is approx. 4% that of Italy and 10% that of France.

The crop started to be grown in England in the late 1970s and reached a high-point of 11,000 ha (*27,000 acres*) in 1984. The area has fluctuated since then, but had declined to well below 1,000 hectares (*2,500 acres*). At present there are no contracts being offered to produce durum in the UK. In the past, an ex-farm premium for 'Grade A' durum of £50 per tonne over feed wheat was offered.

On average the crop should yield 75%-80% of conventional feed wheat in the same situation. As with milling wheat, there is a risk of rejection if contaminated with excess foreign seeds, especially self-set cereals from previous crop; thus safer as a first cereal crop. A poor price is obtained if quality is too poor for pasta and thus has to go for feed.

Durum Wheat Gross Margin Schedule

Yield 6.2t/ha (2.5t/acre), Price £190/t ex-farm	£/ha	(£/ac)
Output	1,178	(477)
Variable Costs:		
Seed	95	(38)
Fertiliser	135	(55)
Sprays	165	(67)
Total Variable Costs	350	(142)
Gross Margin per ha (acre)................................	**828**	(335)

The crop is likely to be grown only in the driest parts of the east/south east, where it can best compete with second and third wheats. It may be either autumn or spring sown; around two-thirds is currently autumn sown and this is assumed in the table above. The crop is very sensitive to stress and frost-kill in severe winters; the spring-sown crop is more reliable, and cheaper to grow, but the yield is usually 15-20% lower. Spring crops also allow more opportunities for black grass control. The crop has a higher disease resistance than other wheats, except for eyespot and ergot.

Harvesting is a critical operation; it needs to be done as soon as the crop reaches 20% moisture content, or at most 18%: it is very prone to sprouting and the quality for semolina is reduced if harvest is delayed. Durum must be dried (slowly) to 15%. It is easier and quicker to dry than normal wheat. The straw is of poorer quality and lesser quantity than conventional wheat straw and is therefore rarely baled.

Echium

Echium is a member of the Boraginacea family like Borage. Like that crop it has high concentrations of gamma linolenic acid (GLA) but is also rich in stearidonic acid, which is used in cosmetic creams to reduce skin wrinkling and the effects of sunburn.

In past years there has been around 1,000 ha or so grown in the UK. A global glut of the active ingredient led to no contracts being offered in the years 2009 to 2017. It is believed that few if any contracts will be offered for 2018 as there is currently little to no demand for Echium oil as it is uncompetitive against marine oil alternatives. It is essential for a grower to have a buy-back contract with a reputable company, and the crop should not be grown speculatively. In the past prices have collapsed to almost nothing due to over-supply in the market.

The crop can be grown as far north as Yorkshire. It has a husbandry programme similar to that of borage but does not shed its seed as readily as borage. The seed is relatively small in size. Echium is suitable for light to medium land whereas borage performs better on a wider range of soil types.

The crop is sown in April and should come to harvest in July/August. There appear to be no significant pests of the crop. Harvesting is carried out with the use of a swather. Yields are approximately 250kg per ha (100kg per acre). Contract prices have been around £3,500 per tonne of clean seed.

Evening Primrose

This crop is an important source of gamma linolenic acid (GLA), but it is no longer grown in the UK and very little is cultivated elsewhere in Western Europe – it has been largely superseded by borage, which is easier to grow. The crop is still widely grown in China where the climate is more suitable, and labour costs are lower. Previous editions have given details of the crop and possible gross margin data.

Flax (cut flax for industrial fibre)

Flax was re-introduced into the UK during the 1990s, not as the traditional, pulled, long fibre variety used for linen textiles but as a cut, combinable crop producing shorter fibres for industrial uses – 'short-fibre flax'. As a natural, biodegradable fibre and a renewable resource it was promoted as a 'green' alternative to synthetic fibres and plastics. New markets were developed and several processing plants set up – the area of flax expanded to 20,200 ha in 1996. Following low prices and reform of the subsidy regime, the area fell to less than 2,000 ha by 2003, and the one remaining processing facility in Wales was closed. Little, if any, is currently grown.

The agronomy of flax is similar to that of linseed but it is harvested earlier. It is spring sown, suitable for most soil types although lighter soil is preferred. It is a low input crop but weed control is essential. It grows best in areas of high rainfall such as Wales and the

South-west. There are several harvesting options (described in earlier editions). Currently the preferred option is desiccation followed by combining. The straw is left to rett in the field and then baled. Retting takes 10-21 days, depending on weather conditions. The price paid for straw will reflect quality. The fibre content of a reasonable crop is 20-30%.

Hemp

The traditional use for hemp was in canvas and rope manufacture. New uses have developed over recent years in building materials and producing internal car panels for the automotive industry. The core or pith of the plant is used for horse or poultry bedding.

The area planted had been stable at around 1,000 ha in recent years. However, the UK's sole commercial processor of the crop went into administration in autumn 2013. With no buyer for the company, the processing factory has ceased operation, and no contracts will be available in the UK for the foreseeable future.

Hemp is drilled in late April/May and the fibre crop grows 3 to 3.5m (10-12 feet) tall. A minimum area of 10 ha is suggested to prevent predator damage to seedlings. A well-grown crop should have no weed or pest problems. The crop is mowed in mid to late August, and then baled when it is dry, bleached, and partially retted after 2-3 weeks. Average yields should be around 7.5 tonne per ha (*3.0t per acre*), with target yields at 9.5 tonnes per ha (*3.8t per acre*). The margin below assumes that the grower will undertake the cutting and baling operations. If contractors are used, then the variable costs will obviously be higher. The crop must be stored under cover.

The margin below is based on the past contract price of £160 per tonne delivered. Transport costs need to be taken into consideration. A figure of £15 per tonne is used in the table below.

Hemp Gross Margin Schedule

Yield 7.5t/ha (3.0t/acre), Price £160/t delivered	£/ha	(£/ac)
Output	1,200	(486)
Variable Costs:		
Seed	135	(55)
Fertiliser	143	(58)
Sprays	20	(8)
Haulage to factory (£15/tonne)	113	(46)
Total Variable Costs	410	(166)
Gross Margin per ha (acre)	**790**	(320)

Dual Hemp

Hemp may also be grown as a dual-purpose crop. In recent years, up to 10-15% of the national hemp crop was of this type. The crop is left to mature longer, and then the top can be combined for the seed before the straw is mown and retted. A yield of 1.0-1.2 tonne per ha (*0.4-0.5t per ac*) of seed is possible. The seed was worth around £500 per tonne. However, the yield of straw is lower at 5-6 tonnes per ha (*2.0-2.4t per ac*), with the price being the same as 'conventional' hemp. The seed is cold-pressed to produce high-value cooking oil, and is also used for bird feed, fishing bait and in nutritional supplements and cosmetics. Agronomy and costs are likely to be similar to a fibre crop. Because of the time needed to let the seed heads mature, an earlier-maturing variety is used. The later harvest also means that this crop is more suitable for early land in the East and South.

Grain Maize

Maize is one of the major global grains – with world output being higher than that for wheat. However, the climate of the UK has made it difficult to ripen the crop and most maize is grown for forage rather than grain. A combination of earlier varieties, the development of machinery that copes better with wet conditions, and even possibly the effects of warmer summers has improved the prospects of this crop.

There is market potential, as well over a million tonnes of grain maize are imported annually. It is used in animal rations, human foods, and in industrial processes. Marketing the UK crop is a problem at present as consignments are generally not big enough to interest the major buyers. The animal feed market is the likeliest outlet for domestic production - a specialised or local market can be developed, for example feed for pigeons or corn-fed chickens. The basis of pricing in the margin is a £10-£20 per tonne premium over feed wheat. This assumes sale into a 'niche' premium market.

There is no fundamental difference between forage and grain maize – the same varieties are simply left in the field for 3-6 weeks longer to let the cobs mature. A DEFRA survey in 2015 suggested only 5% of the total maize area was for grain.

The crop can be grown south of a line from Bristol to East Anglia, excluding the far south-west. Fields should be below 500ft in elevation and south-facing. To maximise heat units, the crop should be drilled as soon as soil temperatures are above 8°c – usually late April/May. Harvest by conventional combine with an adapted header in October/ November. In UK conditions grain maize seldom drops below 30% moisture. The crop needs to be dried to 15% for storage which can be expensive and time-consuming. On good land the crop can yield 8-10 tonnes per ha but the average is not likely to be so high.

Grain Maize Gross Margin Schedule

Yield 7.5t/ha (3.0t/acre), Price £155/t ex-farm	£/ha	(£/ac)
Output	1,163	(471)
Variable Costs:		
Seed	165	(67)
Fertiliser	90	(36)
Sprays	85	(34)
Total Variable Costs	340	(138)
Gross Margin per ha (acre)	**822**	(333)
But note high drying costs:		
£15-25/t on-farm; £20-30/t off-farm	113-225	(46-91)

The majority of grain maize is currently stored as a crimped product. This sees the crop cut at 30-35% moisture from mid-October to early November with the 'wet' grain being processed, and an additive added (usually an organic acid). The overall cost of crimping and preservative is around £12-£15 per tonne. The grain is clamped or put into large bales or bags. It provides a very digestible dairy feed of high nutrition content. Yields can be 11-13 tonnes per ha and it sells for £160-£220 per tonne ex-farm.

Acknowledgement: Thanks to - Maize Growers Association.

Millet

Millet describes a range of small-seeded grain plants covering a number of different species. The most commonly grown type in the UK is proso (also called white or common) millet. Millet has been cultivated since prehistoric times. It is a major food source in arid and semi-arid parts of the world; predominantly India, China, and parts of Africa. The crop has been grown in the UK for game cover for many years, but it has recently been commercialised to supply grain to the bird seed market.

Millet Gross Margin Schedule

Yield 3.0t/ha (1.2t/acre), Price £225/t ex-farm	£/ha	(£/ac)
Output	675	(273)
Variable Costs:		
Seed	100	(41)
Fertiliser	85	(35)
Sprays	65	(26)
Total Variable Costs	250	(101)
Gross Margin per ha (acre)................................	**425**	(172)

The UK currently imports approximately 25,000 tonnes of millet for bird and pet feed each year. Domestic plantings in 2013 were in the region of 1,000 ha, but dropped substantially from 2014 to 2017 – probably to less than 500 ha. There is the potential to raise the area to around 5,000 ha. Full import substitution is likely to be difficult as UK crop cannot compete with the very white colour of the best French white millets.

The crop can be grown on a range of soil types, but as it is drought tolerant, it is often planted on lighter land. It does not grow well in heavy or very chalky soils. The crop requires warm temperatures to ripen and is therefore best suited to the southern half of England.

The crop is late drilled, usually in May once the soil has warmed up sufficiently. It can be planted as late as June. It requires a fine seedbed. The crop grows to about a metre high and is ready to harvest after 4½ months in mid to late September. The crop is usually desiccated before harvesting with a conventional combine harvester.

Yields are in the range 2.5-4.0 tonnes per ha. The contract price for 2018 is not known at the time of writing. However, contract values have historically been around £80-£100 per tonne above the feed wheat price and a price of £225 per tonne is assumed.

Acknowledgement: Thanks to - Premium Crops.

Navy Beans

Navy beans are the basis for the familiar canned 'baked beans'. Over 100,000t of these are consumed annually in the UK – with the vast majority of these being imported from North America. A few years ago there was some interest in the crop, as varieties adapted to the soil types and climate of the UK were introduced. However, disappointing prices, variable yields, and the lack of area aid discouraged growers. It seems unlikely that the economics will encourage a resurgence of production in the foreseeable future.

The crop requires good fertile land and some care in growing. Sowing is in mid-May when there is no further frost risk. Harvesting is late August/early September. The target yield is 3.0 tonnes per ha but the average is likely to be substantially less. When budgeting, an average of around 2.0 tonnes per ha (*0.8t per acre*) could be assumed. There is very little market information available on price, but it is likely to be in the region of £250-£300 per tonne. Variable costs are likely to be in the range £300-£350 per ha.

Poppies

Commercial growing of poppies in the UK began in the early 2000's with poppy heads being processed to produce morphine for pharmaceutical purposes and the seeds being sold into the culinary market. Around 2,000 ha of the crop were grown in 2016 – all on contract to the sole UK processor. However, UK production ceased in 2017. There may be future opportunity to grow poopy seeds for the culinary market in the future, but current seed prices mean this is unlikely to be financially viable at the present time.

The crop needs free-draining alkaline soils; it is planted in the second half of March, and is harvested in early to mid-August. Under the previous contracts, the processor undertook the harvesting operation with a specialised machine. Seed was included as part of the contract, as was agronomy advice (the processor specified the pesticides to be used). The grower needed to be able to offer on-floor drying facilities. In 2016 a basic fee of £100 per ha was paid by the processor, which was then topped-up by a bonus based on the yield of the alkaloid from the crop.

Poppy Gross Margin Schedule

	£/ha	(£/ac)
Fixed Area Payment	100	(41)
Alkaloid Bonus Payment	1,200	(486)
Output	1,300	(527)
Variable Costs:		
Seed	0	(0)
Fertiliser	132	(53)
Sprays	190	(77)
Total Variable Costs	322	(130)
Gross Margin per ha (acre)................................	**978**	(396)

Soya Beans

Soya is a sub-tropical crop in origin, grown mainly in North and South America, but also to a small extent in southern Europe. The UK imports three quarters of a million tonnes each year as beans and almost a further 2 million tonnes as meal, all for animal feed, so there would appear to be a ready market for the home grown product.

Various attempts have been made to commercialise the crop in the UK. In the late 1990's new varieties were introduced and by the early 2000's the area expanded to 1,700 ha, but after several difficult years the planted area declined with less than 100 ha per year. The plant breeding process has continued and further varietal improvements in yield and earliness have been made. Problems with flea beetle in oilseed rape and soya's ability to deal with blackgrass has seen its popularity as a break crop rise again. High soya prices have made the economics more attractive at the same time. An expansion in area has been seen in the last couple of years, with the 2017 area thought to be around 1,800 ha and potential for 2018 rising as high as 6-8,000 ha.

Soya Bean Gross Margin Schedule

Yield 2.5t/ha (1.0t/acre), Price £375/t ex-farm	£/ha	(£/ac)
Output	938	(380)
Variable Costs:		
Seed	145	(59)
Fertiliser	48	(19)
Sprays	90	(36)
Total Variable Costs	283	(115)
Gross Margin per ha (acre)................................	**655**	(265)

The crop is sown in late April or early May, depending on soil temperature, into a fine moist seedbed. The crop has a requirement for high temperatures and cumulative day-degrees of heat (similar to maize). This effectively restricts the crop to the southern half of England. The crop is combine harvested in September, usually after desiccation. The crop should be cleaned and dried to 14% moisture and 2% admixture.

As a legume, soya is a good alternative break crop, largely fixing its own nitrogen. Maintenance P and K is required plus 10-20kg of N to get the crop started. Spray costs also tend to be low.

Target yield is 3.0 tonnes per ha but the average is likely to be less; an average of 2.5 tonnes per ha (*1.0t per acre*) can be assumed. The price is largely determined by the price of imported crop. The UK crop is GM free, for which a premium is paid. A further premium may be paid for Identity Preserved UK crop which goes into human consumption or for organically grown soya. For 2018 harvest the price is estimated to be £375 per tonne.

Sunflower

The UK imports the equivalent of 400,000 tonnes of sunflower seed each year, mainly as sunflower oil. None is commercially crushed in the UK. There has been continued interest in sunflower, but late harvests and low yields have restricted the development of the crop. It is unclear how much of the crop is currently been commercially grown in the UK, but it is likely to be less than 500 ha. This would produce some 1,000 tonnes of seed. Almost all UK production goes into pet-food or bird seed. Producers should satisfy themselves of the end-market before planting the crop. The birdseed market takes 20,000 tonnes of sunflower seed annually, so there is scope for import substitution. Some attempts have been made to cold-press sunflowers to produce a UK-sunflower oil, but this market is still restricted to local and small-scale production.

Extra-early maturing semi-dwarf hybrid varieties are the most suitable to conditions in the UK. The crop needs a relatively mild climate and is best grown south-east of a line from the Wash to east Dorset. Sowing is from April to early May when the soil temperature is 7-8°C. Although sunflower will grow on a broad range of soil types its capacity to do well in dry and sandy soils and areas of low rainfall is a recommendation. Pre-emergence weed control may be necessary; at the right plant density weeds should not subsequently be a problem. As it is a broad row crop, chemical or mechanical weed control is possible. Sclerotina and botrytis, in a wet season, may affect the crop; on areas of less than 6 ha bird damage can be serious. Sunflower has a low nitrogen requirement.

Harvesting is from mid-September by combine harvester. Yields of up to 2.5 tonnes per ha with oil content of 44% are possible. The crop is dried to 8-9% for safe storage, which can be expensive. The price is usually based on a premium over the price of oilseed rape (around £40-£50 per tonne), but other pricing mechanisms may be used in specialist markets. Growing costs will be in the region of £300-£350 per ha.

Others

Other crops that have been in the news in recent years as possible new crops for the future (or present crops capable of substantial development) include the following: chickpeas and lentils, ahiflower, fenugreek, meadowfoam, cuphea, peppermint, quinoa, buckwheat, honesty and herbs for their essential oils. At present there are no reliable data for these crops on average yield expectations and little on prices or variable costs, when grown on a commercial scale in this country. A number of them are either for the health food market or are sources of oil for industry as replacements for marine oils and light mineral oils. Research continues on many of them. More details may be available from the contact listed below;

Contact: NNFCC

VINING PEAS

Vining Peas

Production level	Low	Average	High	
Yield: t/ha (t/ac)	4.00 (1.6)	4.75 (1.9)	5.50 (2.2)	
	£	**£**	**£**	***£/t***
Output at £240/t	960 (389)	1,140 (462)	1,320 (535)	*240*
Variable Costs:				
Seed……………………		220 (89)		*46*
Fertiliser……………..		11 (4)		*2*
Sprays………………..		150 (61)		*32*
Total Variable Costs		381 (154)		*80*
Gross Margin £/ha (ac)	**579** (234)	**759** (307)	**939** (380)	***160***

Fertiliser Basis 4.75t/ha

Nutrient	Kg/t	Kg/Ha	£/Ha
N	*0*	0	£0
P	1.7	8	£5
K	3.2	15	£6

Seed:

Sprays:

Herbs	£77
Fungs	£53
Insect	£11
PGRs	£0
Other	£10

The table relates to vining peas grown on contract for 2018 where harvesting (approx. £80/tonne) and haulage (approx. £30/tonne) are paid for separately;

1. The *price* ranges from £200 to £370/tonne depending primarily on quality. Here we use an average of £215/tonne. The average yield is taken as 4.75 tonnes per hectare; the national average (fresh weight) for the last five years has ranged between 3.6 and 5.1 although growers are paid on frozen weight. Top quality ('150 minute') peas have to be grown within 40 miles of the factory. More distant 'long haul' peas will be in the lower price range. A pea viner costs in the region of £450,000.

   The average yield of petit pois is lower but the price averages 12 to 15% more.

2. *Fertiliser*. Many growers use no fertiliser; but RB209 suggests P&K as per the gross margin.

3. *Sprays*. Both herbicide and aphicide are commonly used with fungicides being used dependant on seasonal requirements.

4. Total UK area drilled in 2017 was 33,700 hectares. with a view to vining a 140,000-tonne crop for frozen and canned use. A small surplus might be grown that exceeds contracted requirements

Acknowledgement: Thanks to British Growers Association

POTATOES

Production level	Low	Average	High	
Yield: t/ha (t/ac)	38.5 (15.6)	45.0 (18.2)	51.5 (20.9)	
	£	**£**	**£**	***£/t***
Output at £175/t	6,738 (2,729)	7,875 (3189)	9,013 (3650)	*175*
Variable Costs:				
Seed..........................		949 (384)		*21*
Fertiliser.....................		245 (99)		*5*
Sprays........................		748 (303)		*17*
Casual labour	789 (320)	923 (374)	1056 (428)	*21*
Sundries	408 (165)	477 (193)	546 (221)	*11*
Contracting.........................		1503 (609)		*33*
Total Variable Costs	4,642 (1,880)	4,844 (1,962)	5,047 (2,044)	
Gross Margin £/ha (ac)	**2095** (849)	**3031** (1,227)	**3966** (1,606)	***67***

Fertiliser Basis 45t/ha

Nutrient	Kg/t	Kg/Ha	£/Ha
N	*3.6*	160	£86
P	1.0	45	£25
K	5.8	261	£109
MgO			£25

Casual Labour per tonne £20.50 (1) Harvest & Grading

Sundries per tonne £10.60 (2) Levies, Sacks etc.

Seed:

£/t C2	350
Kg/Ha	3,000
% HSS	40%
£/t HSS	285
Kg/Ha	2,800

Sprays:

Herbicides	£31
Fungicides	£189
Insecticides	£48
PGRs	£0
Other	£480

1. *Prices*. The price used above is £185 per tonne for ware and £30 for stock feed (assumed 7½%), which is £175 per tonne for the whole crop. Variations according to quality and market are considerable. The average price for wares between 2010 and 2016 was £166/tonne.
2. *Sprays*: herbicide, blight control, and haulm destruction. Includes Nematode (PCN) spray, which accounts for about 60% of potato land. This accounts for £440/ha.
3. *Casual Labour*. The figure in the table above is for assistance during (machine) harvesting and for grading/riddling (approx. £20.50/tonne); it is assumed that most of the labour for the latter is supplied by casuals.
4. *Contracting*: included in gross margin this year for first time. Includes destoning, ridging, planting and harvest and carting. For other contract work see page 194.
5. *AHDB-Potatoes levy*: £42.62/ha (£17.25/acre) for growers to April 2017; exempt from levy if less than 3ha grown. 2018 rates as yet unpublished.
6. *Sacks*. Approx. £8.50 per tonne, plus the cost of wire ties or stitching.
7. *Potato Land Rentals* range depending on the year, location, soil and water availability, ranging from over £650/ha (£260/acre) to as much as £1,200/ha (£500/acre), depending on terms as well as soil type such as irrigation maintenance. The late harvested potatoes depress following crop yields. As a result some have tried to increase potato rents on back of increased cereal prices.
8. *Specialised Equipment Prices*: see page 187.
9. *Potato Store Costs*: see page 231.
10. *Labour*: see p. 169.

Early Potatoes

Production level	Low	Average	High	
Yield: t/ha (t/ac)	19.5 (7.9)	23.0 (9.3)	26.5 (10.7)	
	£	**£**	**£**	***£/t***
Output at £260/t	5,070 (2,053)	5,980 (2422)	6,890 (2790)	*260*
Variable Costs:				
Seed...........................		848 (343)		*37*
Fertiliser......................		142 (58)		*6*
Sprays.........................		388 (157)		*17*
Casual labour	375 (152)	416 (169)	458 (185)	*18*
Sundries	258 (105)	305 (123)	351 (142)	*13*
Contracting.........................		1,503 (609)		*65*
Total Variable Costs	3,514 (1,423)	3,602 (1,459)	3,690 (1,494)	*157*
Gross Margin £/ha (ac)	**1556** (630)	**2378** (963)	**3200** (1,296)	***103***

Fertiliser Basis 23t/ha			
Nutrient	Kg/t	Kg/Ha	£/Ha
N	*4.4*	100	£54
P	1.0	23	£13
K	5.8	133	£55
MgO			£20

Casual per ha £145

Casual per tonne £11.80

Seed:	
£/t C2	255
Kg/Ha	3,400
% HSS	10%
£/t HSS	240
Kg/Ha	2,800

(1) Harvest & Grading

(2) Levies, Sacks etc.

Sprays:	
Herbicides	£16
Fungicides	£98
Insecticides	£25
PGRs	£0
Other	£249

1. *Prices* and *Yields*. The price assumed above is an average of £260 per tonne for a 23 tonne/ha yield. Yields increase and prices fall as the season progresses. Thus both depend on the date of lifting, e.g. late May 7t/ha, June, 15t/ha; July, 20 to 30 t/ha. Prices in late May to mid-June can be up to three times those in July; the earliest crops (early May) can exceed £1,000 per tonne, but the price could be down to £500 by mid-May and to £250 by early June. Thus the average output of £6,000 given above could be obtained from 10 tonnes at £600 per tonne, 15t at £400, 20t at £300 or 30t at £200.
2. *Sprays*: herbicide, blight control, and haulm destruction. Includes Nematode (PCN) spray, which accounts for about 60% of potato land.
3. *Casual labour for planting*: £144 per hectare, plus help with harvesting/grading at £11.80 per tonne.
4. *Contracting*: included in gross margin this year for first time. Includes destoning, ridging, planting and harvest and carting. For other contract work see page 194.
5. *AHDB-Potatoes levy*: £42.62/ha (£17.25/acre) for growers to April 2017; exempt from levy if less than 3ha grown. 2018 rates as yet unpublished.
6. *Labour*: see p. 169.

Early and Maincrop Potatoes

About 80 per cent of potatoes in the UK are maincrop (harvest in August or later), with 12 percent seed and the rest as earlies (defined as harvested before 1 August).

SUGAR BEET

Production level	Low	Average	High	
Yield: t/ha (t/ac)	66.5 (26.9)	78.0 (31.6)	89.5 (36.2)	
	£	**£**	**£**	***£/t***
Output at £27.06/t	1,799 (729)	2,111 (855)	2,422 (981)	*27*
Variable Costs:				
Seed..........................		204 (82)		*2.6*
Fertiliser....................		200 (81)		*2.6*
Sprays........................		239 (97)		*3.1*
Contract Harvest............		237 (96)		*3.0*
Transport (Contract).......	366 (148)	429 (174)	492 (199)	*5.5*
Total Variable Costs	1,245 (504)	1,308 (530)	1,372 (555)	*17*
Gross Margin £/ha (ac)	**554** (225)	**802** (325)	**1,050** (425)	***10***

Fertiliser Basis 78t/ha

Nutrient	Kg/t	Kg/Ha	£/Ha
N	*2.0*	156	£84
P	0.8	65	£37
K	1.7	131	£55
MgO			£25
Transport Charge £/t			£5.50

Seed:

£/unit	177
Unit/Ha	1.15
% HSS	0%
£/t HSS	

Sprays:

Herbicides	£165
Fungicides	£47
Insecticides	£11
PGRs	£0
Other	£16

Yield = 'Adjusted tonnes' at standard 16% sugar content

1. These figures are for the crop drilled in 2018, harvested and delivered in 2018/19.
2. *Prices*. The 'all-in' price is £27.06 per adjusted tonne. This is based on 95% sold 'in contract' at £22.50 (including former Industrial tonnage) plus sugar bonus where relevant (see below) and 5% non-contract. Non-contract beet is currently unpriced by British Sugar but priced at £15.00/tonne plus transport in this schedule.
3. Average transport of £4.75/tonne and late delivery allowances of 40p/tonne. Late delivery bonus: 26 December - 7 January: 0.8% of price; thereafter, the rate rises by 0.3% per day and at 0.4% per day from 1 March.
4. A bonus is available for growers when the average EU sugar price exceeds a trigger €475/t. This margin is converted into beet (16% sugar), sterling at the exchange rate set, and growers committing to 3-year contracts earn 25% of uplift, 1-year commitments earn 10%. For example:
   - EU sugar price of €500/t. €500-€475 = €25/t.
   - Conversion to beet (6.4t per tonne of sugar) = €3.90/t
   - Convert to sterling (at say 85p/€) = £3.32/t
   - 1-year contract earns 10%, so 33p/t, 3- year earns 25% so 83p/t
5. *Seed*; includes a standard seed dressing.
6. *Contract*. Excludes carting. For other contract work see page 194.
7. *Transport*. Contract haulage charges vary according to distance to factory. The figure assumed above is £5.50 per (unadjusted) tonne of unwashed beet including loading and cleaning (dirt and top tare assumed at 14% in total).

TOP FRUIT

The figures indicate a range within which the performance of most (established) orchards falls. The gross margin is calculated as lower yields less lower costs/higher yields less higher costs. In practice yields are not necessarily so directly linked to costs.

	Dessert Apples		*Culinary Apples*	
Production level	**Low**	**High**	**Low**	**High**
Yield: tonnes per ha	25	50	30	55
Price £/tonne	545	933	357	546
	£	£	£	£
Output	13,625	46,650	10,710	30,030
Variable Costs:				
Orchard Depreciation	635	960	510	720
Pruning/Clearing	433	865	519	952
Fertiliser/spray	870	1,455	675	1,260
Crop Sundries	165	655	215	545
Harvesting	1,685	3,365	1,665	3,055
Grading/Packing	3,550	7,100	4,260	7,810
Packaging	1,350	8,100	796	4,170
Transport	1,610	4,820	965	4,125
Commission/Levies	1,225	4,200	965	2,705
Total Variable Costs	11,523	31,520	10,570	25,342
Gross Margin per ha	**2,103**	**15,130**	**140**	**4,689**

	Cider Apples		*Pears*	
Production level	**Low**	**High**	**Low**	**High**
Yield: tonnes per ha	15	55	15	30
Price £/tonne	122	122	495	715
	£	£	£	£
Output	1,830	6,710	7,425	21,450
Variable Costs:				
Orchard Depreciation	425	640	425	720
Pruning/Clearing	300	520	459	918
Fertiliser/spray	300	800	675	1,110
Crop Sundries	30	30	165	440
Harvesting	550	2,020	1,010	2,020
Grading/Packing	30	115	2,130	4,260
Packaging	0	0	640	3,885
Transport	205	450	720	2,470
Commission/Levies	0	0	670	1,930
Total Variable Costs	1,840	4,575	6,894	17,753
Gross Margin per ha	**-10**	**2,135**	**531**	**3,697** *

Excludes Storage

1. *Price*: Average of all grades. Price is influenced by grade-out, variety, customer and pack format (which in turn may affect packing, packaging costs).

2. *Orchard Depreciation*:

Topfruit Establishment Costs	*Low*	*High*
Trees per Hectare	833	3810
£/tree & Stake	5.1	3.7
Stakes/ties/clips/guards/sundries	1.53	1.33
Other Sundries		
	£/ha	*£/ha*
Fencing (230m/ha @ £5.1)	1,173	1,173
Land Prep/ Drainage	3,060	3,060
Trees	4,248	14,097
Post & Wire	102	204
Fertiliser & Ag-Chem	184	408
Stakes/ties/clips/guards	1,274	5,067
Planting	663	1,225
Irrigation	2,040	3,570
Total Establishment	*12,745*	*28,804*
Dessert Apples Years Fruit	20	30
Culinary Apples Years Fruit	25	40
Cider Apples Years Fruit	30	45
Pears Years Fruit	30	40

This schedule provides a rough guide for typical costs required to establish a top fruit orchard.

Establishment costs vary considerably, depending on the type of top fruit and method of production.

Longevity of orchard also varies on several factors, including tree performance, new varieties, outcompeting older ones and consumer preference.

Establishment costs here, are spread over each productive year listed. Some instances might be better to calculate Return on Investment or Net Present Value calculations.

3. *Orchard Duration*: Traditional dessert apples around 20 years, with culinary and pears frequently 30 years plus. More recently planted denser apple and pear systems likely to be nearer 20 years, with full cropping reached in years 3-5 (6-9 for traditional systems). Figures above include an allowance for 5% immature trees.

4. *Crop Sundries*: Include tree ties, rabbit guards, stake replacement, tree replacement, bee hire, picking hods, bin depreciation etc.

5. *Harvesting*: Based on £67.30/t average (including supervision, Employer's NI & holiday allowance) for dessert apples and pears £55.50/t for culinary and £36.70/t for cider. In practice varies significantly with variety, yield, fruit size and quality, etc.

6. *Grading and Packing*: Based on £142 per tonne. Can vary considerably, particularly with crop quality, minimal for cider apples.

7. *Packaging*: Typical average of between £56 and £163 per tonne, although may be higher with specialist formats (e.g. overwrapped packs). Considerable variations arise from both crop quality (i.e. grade-out), customer and pack format.

8. *Transport*: allowance for farm to packer, as well as delivery to final customer.

9. *Commission/Levies*: Including both marketer's and retailer's commission, as well as levies (e.g. English Apples and Pears, AHDB). A total of 9% has been used, although charges can vary considerably. N.B. This category does not include levy payments under the Producer Organisation regime.

SOFT FRUIT

The figures – for both soil-grown and a table-top substrate crop - indicate a range within which the performance of many, but not all crops is likely to fall. The gross margins are lower yields less lower costs/higher yields less higher costs. In practice, yields are not necessarily linked to costs.

	Strawberries Raised Bed		*Strawberries Tabletop Ever-bearers*	
Production level	**Low**	**High**	**Low**	**High**
Yield: tonnes per ha	18	23	28	44
Price £/tonne	2,625	3,510	2,625	3,510
	£	**£**	**£**	**£**
Output	47,250	80,730	73,500	154,440
Variable Costs:				
Planting	3,178	4,070	12,264	20,070
Structures	5,573	8,920	7,804	11,146
Fertiliser/spray	1,033	1,725	1,552	2,592
Fieldwork	1,974	4,373	3,276	8,745
Harvesting	14,994	19,619	16,912	26,576
Grading/Packing	4,880	6,235	7,590	11,925
Packaging	6,895	8,810	10,725	16,850
Transport	3,310	4,230	5,150	8,095
Commission/Levies	4,255	7,265	6,615	13,900
Total Variable Costs	46,092	65,247	71,888	119,899
Gross Margin per ha	**1,158**	**15,483**	**1,612**	**34,541**

Strawberry Raised Bed Notes

1. *Planting* - including plants, substrate and wirework. *Plants* –35,000 per hectare with 60-day cropping in year 1 followed by 2 further years in main season production. *Plants/planting/sterilisation* written off over crop life of 3 years. Bed making not included as a variable cost.
2. *Structures* – average cost per year. Annual cost of poly-tunnels including both metalwork (w/o 10 years) and plastic (w/o 3 years). Costs also included for erection, dismantling and venting.
3. *Fertiliser, Sprays, Predators*. Relatively small component of gross margin.
4. *Fieldwork* – weeding, runner removal, leaf thinning etc.
5. *Harvesting*- including supervision, Employer's NI & holiday allowance.
6. *Grading/Packing* at £271/t. *Packaging* at £383/t, *Transport* at £184/t.
7. *Commission/Levies*: Including both marketeer's and retailer's commission, as well as levies (e.g. AHDB). A total of 9% has been used, although charges vary considerably. N.B. This does not include levy payments under the Producer Organisation regime.

Strawberries – Table-top Ever Bearer Notes:

1. *Plants* – assumes 40,000 per hectare. Plants/planting written off over crop life of one year. Cost of substrate bags w/o 3 years.
2. *Structures* – poly-tunnel cost as for June-bearers, together with annual cost of table-top system (estimated as £21,000 w/o 10 years, table-top system costs vary considerably)

3. *Fieldwork* – weeding, runner removal, leaf thinning and tucking, truss support etc.
4. *Harvesting*- including supervision, Employer's NI & holiday allowance.
5. *Grading, Packing / Packaging / Transport / Commission* - as for June bearers.

	Raspberries		***Blackcurrants***	
Production level	**Low**	**High**	**Low**	**High**
Yield: tonnes per ha	8	15	6.0	7.5
Price £/tonne	5,470	7,390	663	765
	£	**£**	**£**	**£**
Output	43,760	110,850	3,978	5,738
Variable Costs:				
Planting	1,527	1,937	747	747
Structures	5,573	8,920		
Fertiliser/spray	780	1,212	394	394
Fieldwork	3,275	5,465		
Harvesting	16,320	30,600		
Grading/Packing	3,920	7,350	135	170
Packaging	6,160	11,550	65	85
Transport	1,905	3,570	60	75
Commission/Levies	3,940	9,975	360	515
Total Variable Costs	43,400	80,579	1,761	1,986
Gross Margin per ha	**360**	**30,271**	**2,217**	**3,752**

Raspberries Notes:

1. Raspberries cover 1,500 hectares but are worth more than Blackcurrants (2,500 Ha)
2. *Plants* – 8000/ha at 44p per plant. Planting at 13.3p per plant. Land preparation and irrigation, up to £1,000/ha
3. *Structures* – as for strawberries.
4. *Wirework* – to include material and labour.
5. *Plants/planting/wirework* written off over crop life of, say 5 years (crop life typically 4 to 7 years).
6. *Harvesting* (including supervision, employer's NI & holiday allowance) – £2,040 per tonne (£2.04 per kilo).
7. *Grading/Packing* – at £490 per tonne (49 pence per kilo).
8. *Packaging* – at £770 per tonne (77 pence per kilo).
9. *Transport* – at £238 per tonne (23.8 pence per kilo).
10. *Commission/Levies*: Including both marketeer's and retailer's commission, as well as levies (e.g. AHDB). A total of 9% has been used, charges can vary considerably. N.B. This does not include levy payments under the Producer Organisation regime.

Blackcurrants

Although a soft fruit, this crop is much more of a field crop grown on arable farms with machine harvesting. Most UK blackcurrant crop is processed into cordial drink. Establishment costs approximately £7,300/ha for bushes with full production in year 2 followed by up to 10 years cropping. Contracts with processors required. Blackcurrants are grown on about 2,500 hectares in the UK, and 45 growers.

FIELD-SCALE VEGETABLES

Good quality land is required to grow field vegetable crops commercially. The overhead structure of the farm is somewhat different to that of combinable crops as is crop marketing. A market is necessary in advance of cultivation. In some cases major costs such as harvesting, packing and marketing expenses are borne by the produce company taking the crop, although the pricing structure of the product will reflect this.

Per Hectare (acre)	**Dry Bulb Onions**		**Cauliflower**		**Calabrese**	
(tons/acre)	41	(16.6)	12	(4.9)	10	(4.1)
Net Price (£/tonne)	150		386		410	
	£		£		£	
Output	6,150	(2,491)	4,550	(1,843)	4,010	(1,624)
Variable Costs:						
Seed	791	(320)	1020	(413)	881	(357)
Fertiliser	334	(135)	441	(179)	388	(157)
Sprays	660	(267)	224	(91)	257	(104)
Casual Labour			1600	(648)	1555	(630)
Packaging/consumables			279	(113)	261	
Total Variable Costs	1,785	(723)	3,564	(1,443)	3,342	(1,354)
Gross Margin	4,365	(1,768)	986	(399)	668	(271)

The unit sale of cauliflower and calabrese can differ according to retailer supplier arrangement. For example some might be sold on a pence per head basis, pounds per tray, or pound per tonne and therefore a general output calculation has been provided. Sizes of heads and percentages harvested vary enormously and therefore yield so an average yield and price calculation is also ambiguous.

Dependant on the system, field scale vegetables have a high working capital requirement relative to other cropping alternatives, and bear considerable risk (both yield of saleable product and price vary enormously according to production and also demand factors). It is therefore necessary to carefully research the potential end market in terms of its expectations and cost structure.

Cauliflower and Calabrese give an example of brassica production. The majority of fresh produce crops such as carrots, parsnips, leeks, lettuce, rhubarb, and brassicas are now grown by a few highly specialised growers with in-house marketing departments. These growers supply the multiple retailers with high volumes and work to exacting specifications. The other key market for fresh produce is the local market, usually on a smaller scale and often tied into a local food chain such as a farm shop.

HOPS

Output Data

Hops are sold to contracts and on the open market, the latter varying greatly in price. They are sold per kilogram or in 50kg lots, (historically known as Zentners). The national area of hops has fallen below 1,000 hectares, most of which is in Hereford and Worcestershire. Recent average national yields have been at the low end of this gross margin, but top producers can achieve more.

This gross margin spreads the establishment costs over 11 years and wirework structure over 40. There is no harvest in year 1 but substantial investment.

Hop Gross Margin Schedule

Production level	**Low**	**Average**	**High**
Yield: Kg per ha (Kg/Acre)	1,400 (567)	1,500 (608)	1,600 (648)
	£	**£**	**£**
Output	9,436 (3822)	10,110 (4095)	10,784
Variable Costs:			
Establishment		1060 (429)	
Growing Costs		2441 (989)	
Harvesting		3385 (1,371)	
Total Variable Costs		6886 (2,789)	
Gross Margin per ha (acre)	**2,550** (1,033)	**3,224** (1,306)	**3,898** (1,579)
Overheads		3,000 (1,215)	
Return	**-450** -(182)	**224** (91)	**898** (364)

Establishment Costs

	£/ha		**£/ha**
Ground Preparation	260	Ties & Strings	315
Plants	2,520	Fert/Spray	240
Wirework Structure	7,150	Labour	321
Planting	535	Sundries	321
Total	**11,662**	**Cost per Year**	**1,060**

1. *Growing Costs;* Fertiliser & sprays £1,025, crop sundries £206, labour £1,210/hectare
2. *Harvesting:* Including labour £1,480, drying fuel £510 per hectare
3. *Overheads:* general labour £510, power and Machinery £2,005 inc. harvesting machinery, admin & property costs £485 (rent not included). Costs per hectare.

A new hop garden (erecting the poles, wiring and planting) could cost in the order of £26,000 per hectare (£10,300 per acre), which would be expected to last 40 years. About 4,000 plants per hectare (63p each) are planted in a new hop garden, which would be expected to last 10-12 years.

Acknowledgement: Thanks to – Ali Capper, British Hops Association

VINEYARDS

The planted area under vines in England and Wales in 2017 is estimated at 2,500 hectares, three times that of 2003 (773 ha). This had fallen from a previous high of 1,065 ha in 1993 when the UK grew mainly Germanic grape varieties which then fell out of fashion. The Wine Standards Branch (WSB) of the Food Standards Agency keeps the Vineyard Register (VR) and in August 2015 it recorded 502 vineyards of 0.10 hectare or more, plus several smaller ones run as hobbies and not selling wine. However, the VR is now out-of-date and inaccurate. The average size of UK vineyards is now around 4 hectares, although there are several over 100 hectares and the 50 largest account for 75 per cent of production; more if you only consider sparkling wine. There is no EU restriction on planting vines in the UK and almost any variety may be legally planted.

Yields in 2016 were lower-than-average, with 4.07 million 75cl bottles of wine, both still and sparkling, produced. The five-year average UK yield is 1,961 litres per hectare, a low figure reflecting many young vineyards and under-performing and poorly managed vineyards in the official WSB figures. Yields in well-run, favourably sited vineyards are two to three times these levels. The last six years have included one disastrous year (2012), two difficult and very late years (2013 and 2015), one superb year (2014), and two average-to-poor years (2011 and 2016).

Most UK wines used to be white, but the proportion of red (and mainly) rosé wines has risen to around 25% of the total. Industry estimates suggest that at least 60% of the total amount produced is made into sparkling wine; a figure that will increase as many of the newer (and larger) sparkling-only vineyards start cropping. Since the very warm year of 2003, plantings of Champagne-style varieties (Chardonnay, Pinot Noir and Meunier) have increased significantly. Chardonnay and Pinot Noir are now the most widely planted varieties (about 650 ha each) and these, together with Meunier (175 ha), account for around 65% of the total vine area. Bacchus, the most widely planted still-wine variety, is becoming recognised as one from which excellent top-quality still wines can be made and is expanding, accounting for around 10% of the UK vineyard area.

The amount of UK sparkling wine for sale in any year is, smaller than the amount produced in an expanding vineyard region. This is because bottle-fermented sparkling wines take 2 to 5 years to mature after bottling and many new vineyards are still building up stocks or only just releasing their first vintages. Still-wines reach market faster. Still-wine can be for sale within 4 years of planting vines, whereas sparkling wine producers typically have 3-4 years' worth of stock to store (and finance) before they start selling wines. UK-grown wines only account for around 0.3% of the UK wine market. Many producers find that, at least initially, before they have built up a reputation for the quality of their wines, selling from the 'farm-gate' is their best route to market and helps introduce the public to their wines. However, over the last twenty years, the reputation of UK-grown sparkling wines has considerably improved and with the rising availability of these wines, more outlets, both on-trade and off-trade, are now willing to stock them. All wines sold in the UK bear the same VAT and duty irrespective of their origin and value, and the duty on sparkling wines is higher than for still-wines.

The UK market for sparkling wines is around 110 million bottles a year, of which around two-thirds is Prosecco, Cava, Asti Spumante and other less expensive wines. Champagne (for which the UK is the biggest export market) accounts for 35 million bottles a year and it is into this sector of the sparkling wine market that UK producers need to sell their wines if their enterprises are to be profitable. Although the amount of UK sparkling wine available for sale today is still quite small, given the amount of land in the UK already planted with Champagne varieties, this will rise from today's estimated 2 million bottles to around 4 million by 2018 and 6 million by 2023. What impact this increase in supply will have upon prices, currently matching those of Champagne and other top-quality sparkling wines, is unknown. Most major producers expect increased sales. Some larger producers have also started exporting their wines and this may be a route to additional sales.

A Quality Wine Scheme for England and Wales was introduced in 1991 and a Regional Wine Scheme in 1997, but in 2010 these were replaced with a new system of wine classification based upon the terms Protected Designation of Origin (PDO) and Protected Geographical Indication (PGI). PDO wines are broadly the same as Quality Wines and PGI wines the same as Regional wines. All PDO and PGI wines have to go through a testing and tasting procedure before they can use the relevant names. There are also 'Varietal Wines' which have to be 'certified' and can then can be labelled with the name of the grape variety and vintage, but not vineyard name. Wines outside of these three categories are known as 'UK Wines' and may not bear vintage or variety names, although they can state their origin. There is also a PDO for sparkling wines made from certain vine varieties which allows the term 'English Quality Sparkling Wine' to be used. The UK Vineyards Association (UKVA) has a marketing arm, English Wine Producers to promote all English wines and organise tastings and events such as the 'St. George's Day' trade tasting and English Wine Week.

The quality of wine depends on the site and, in a cool climate like the UK's, the best sites are on south-facing, well-drained land, sheltered from prevailing south-westerly winds and less than 100 metres above sea level. Coastal sites are to be avoided. The best sites are in the southern half of England or Wales with the counties of Essex, Kent, East and West Sussex, Hampshire and Surrey, the traditional fruit and hop growing counties, home to the most successful vineyards. Success should be defined not only by wine quality, but also by yield. Low to very low yields in many vineyards, whilst they might contribute to wine quality, do not help business viability. Most of the longest-established and most successful UK vineyards sell some of their wine direct to the consumer and often have tea-rooms, restaurants and even small hotels as part of the enterprise. They also offer guided tours, weddings, parties and corporate entertaining. Therefore, sites for vines should be selected with these activities in mind.

High quality vineyard management and marketing ability is essential for a successful enterprise. There is no minimum area for profitable production and a small vineyard selling wine at the farm gate and locally may be just as profitable per pound invested or per hectare as a larger one selling wine (at a considerable discount) through wholesalers and retailers. Some vineyards grow grapes under contract for other wineries who wish to spread the source of their grapes. There is a 'spot' market for grapes and prices fluctuate according to vintage.

Most UK vineyards are planted with a row width of 1.75 to 2.25 metres, an intervine distance of between 1.0 m and 1.4 m and use the Guyot cane-pruned system, either two-cane, Double Guyot or single-cane, Single Guyot. Vine density of 4,000 to 5,000 vines/hectare gives the best quality grapes and economic yield in UK conditions. Cane-pruned vines, with good establishment, should be partially cropping in their third summer and fully yielding by their fourth, although much will depend on how they establish.

Investment capital (including planting materials and labour for establishment but not the land) of £21,000 to £30,000/ha is typically required for the vineyard. A suitable tractor, mower, sprayer etc. is required to manage the vines and together these cost at least £40,000-£50,000. These prices are affected by the £-€ rate as vines, some trellising materials and vineyard equipment are imported from the Euro-zone.

There were 135 wineries in the UK in August 2015. Many are small and in modest buildings, but several are modern and as well-equipped as any in the world and cost millions to build. Many smaller vineyards take their grapes to be made into wine under contract at one of the established wineries which gives them access to state-of-the-art equipment and experienced winemakers. Temperature controlled storage space for sparkling wines is required, whether or not you have your own winery.

Depending on the quality of the site, the vine varieties grown and the style of wine produced, a well-sited, well-managed vineyard should yield on average at least 7.5

tonnes/ha (*3 tonnes/acre*) of grapes, with higher yields possible. For still wine production, around 950 x 75cl bottles will be produced from 1 tonne of grapes. For sparkling wine, production will be between 675 and 800 bottles per tonne, depending on quality, with some additional juice/wine available which will not be suitable for sparkling wine, but might be blended into still wine, depending on the vintage.

The costs below refer to a commercial enterprise on a suitable site with a broad variety range. Establishment costs would be more if the site has to be drained and provided with windbreaks and rabbit and deer fencing. Annual growing costs can also be significantly greater, depending on planting density, variety, yield and management.

	Double Guyot	
	per ha	per acre
Number of Vines	3,000 - 5,000	(1,210 - 2,020)
	£ per ha	£ per acre
Establishment Costs:	over two years	
Materials	15,000	6,070
Labour	12,500	5,059
Total Establishment Costs	**27,500**	**11,129**
Subsequent Annual Costs:		
Materials	1,500	607
Labour (growing)	6,250	2,529
Harvesting*	1,600	648
Total Variable Costs	**9,350**	**3,784**

** Harvesting costs are yield dependent. Growers without wineries also have transport costs.*

Prices: Grape prices vary according to the variety and the vintage and whether growers are under contract or not. Prices range from £1,500 to £2,500 per tonne delivered to a winery, with still varieties being less valuable and good Pinot Noir or Chardonnay for sparkling wine at the higher end.

A retail price for still wine of at least £9.50 per bottle is required to cover outgoings, capital and profit, assuming a grower uses a contract winery and sells wine at full price to the consumer with no sales costs. Larger producers, having their own wineries and selling wines via wholesalers and/or retailers and into the on-trade (hotels, bars and restaurants) have a different cost structure. Minimum prices for sparkling wine have to take account of higher costs of production, higher excise duty and finance and longer storage.

Retail price for still wine of £9.50 less 20% VAT and £2.16 ① duty = £5.76 ②

Less winery costs (materials and labour) £4.50 per bottle③ = £1.26

At 7.50 tonnes per ha and 950 bottles per tonne = £8,977/ha (£3,633/acre).

① Sparkling wine of 8.5% and up to 15% or more has a duty rate of £2.77 per 75cl bottle; still wines of the same alcoholic strength, £2.16 per 75cl bottle (2017 rates)

② If wines are sold via a wholesaler and/or retailer, gross profit margin of at least 10% (wholesaler) and 30% (retailer) on duty-paid prices must be allowed for.

③ Having still wine made under contract costs at least £4.50 a bottle. Sparkling wine will be at least £6 per bottle, plus storage costs.

Acknowledgements: Stephen Skelton MW, Viticultural Consultant: spskelton@btinternet.com and the UK Vineyards Association, Mrs Jo Cowderoy: jo@ukva.org.uk

2. GRAZING LIVESTOCK

DAIRY COWS

General Notes:

The notes below detail the general points that are pertinent to completing costings for all dairy enterprises. A number of gross margins are then presented with specific detail relating to each production system.

1. *Yield per cow:* Increases in this are usually (though not necessarily) associated with more intensive farming operations. Intensification focuses on higher gross margins per hectare, although more intensive systems will incur higher overhead costs (specifically machinery and labour requirements). Higher milk yields require different cow genetics (usually Friesian / Holstein's) and higher concentrate feeding (kg/litre), as well as other inputs.

2. *Yield*: The yield is annual herd production divided by the average number of cows and calved heifers in the herd. The average yield given for each type of production system is an estimated national figure for sizeable herds.

3. *Milk Price:* the average milk price for 2018 is budgeted at 26p per litre for a standard litre. The prices used for each gross margin are an average for the 2018 calendar year, after deducting transport costs. It incorporates adjustments for milk composition and seasonality assuming an average-size (*million litre*) herd. Payments are lower in the spring but constituents higher, making prices per litre similar for each system. Milk price variations between contracts are about 3 pence per litre (ppl), having been over 10ppl variation in 2016 when milk prices were lower.

   Smaller herds receive smaller volume bonuses and pay higher transport charges. The average price received by individual producers also depends on seasonality of production and compositional quality.

   Seasonality Price Adjustments: These vary between milk buyers. Some have payment formulae that encourage a level monthly production, with deductions and bonuses related to the individual producer's spring and autumn deliveries. Others have simple monthly adjustments per litre or on a percentage basis. The average adjustments below are for a selection of companies operating conventional adjustments are as follows in 2018/19 in pence per litre:

April	May	June	July	Aug	Sept	Oct	Nov	Dec	Jan– Mar
–4.6	–5.0	–4.5	0.8	+2.1	+3.6	+3.3	+0.7	+1.0	0.3

   Some buyers also offer a premium for a level delivery option if supplies in a calendar month are within 10% of an agreed daily volume.

   Several milk buyers have an 'A' and 'B' production payment system. This is a payment for deliveries greater than an agreed percentage of the previous year (possibly 100%) based on the open market price for milk. This means that if production from one farm increases, the payment per additional litre could be reduced.

   Compositional Quality Payments: Milk price calculations depend on the buyer and its end market. For example, cheese-makers mostly pay per percentage of butterfat and protein whereas a liquid processor pays largely base price per litre with small adjustments for butterfat. As a result, constituent values vary widely between buyers.

A *standard litre* is typically 4·10% butterfat and 3·30% protein. A typical cheese-maker might calculate milk price summarised as follows:

	% Content	*Pence per 1%*	*Price paid*
Butterfat	4.10	2.95	12.1
Protein	3.30	4.14	13.7
Total ppl			*25.8**

** Other adjustments are made to this price such as delivery volumes, collection rates, haulage hygiene and cleanliness and seasonality.*

Within Breed Quality Variation: For Holstein Friesians without going to extremes, the range can easily be: 3.5% to 4.1% butterfat and 3.1% to 3.4% protein. The difference in value between these levels combined can be up to 3.5p per 1 percent of milk solids depending on milk contract. This is being achieved by both breeding and feeding for milk quality to meet varying contractual requirements.

Proportional Split of Dairy Breeds and milk Compositions:

	Cows %	Butterfat %	Protein %
Holstein / Friesian	82	3.95	3·3
Cross Breeds	10	4.6	3.5
Jersey	3.9	5·4	3·9
Guernsey	0.5	4·7	3·6
Ayrshire	2·4	4·1	3·3
Others	1.2	3·9	3·3
All Breeds		4.0	3·3

Data from Dairy Co. & CDI

Hygiene Price Adjustments: These have been becoming more demanding in recent years and vary widely between the different milk buyers. A typical 2018/19 example is as follows:

A. *Bactoscan (bacteria measure)*

Bactoscan Reading	Price Adjustment (ppl)
0- 30,000	+0.3
30,001-50,000	0.00
50,001-70,000	-0.50
70,001-100,000	-1.00
100,001-250,001	-3.00
> 250,000	-15p

B. *Somatic Cell Count (Mastitis)*

Count	Price Adjustment (ppl)
0-200,000	+ 0.3
200,001 – 250,000	0.0
250,001-300,000	-0.5
300,001 - 400,000	-1.5
Over 400,000	-15.0

Several milk buyers have no bonus for top hygiene bands; they expect suppliers to deliver top quality milk in order to receive the standard litre price.

C. *Antibiotics.* Milk in a consignment that fails an antibiotics test is commonly charged 125 to 200 percent the value of the milk plus costs in excess of £300.

4. *Concentrate Price:* An average of £200/t has been used for dairy concentrate. This includes blends and straights which are typically lower cost than compounds by £10 to

£15 per tonne. Spring calving herds have lower protein concentrate as grazed grass has more protein than conserved feeds; conversely, autumn calvers receive higher protein concentrate. An average of £180/t has been used for spring calving herds.

All-Year-Round Calving Friesian/Holsteins (per cow per year)

	Average		High	
Yield Per Cow (litres)	*8,000*		*9,500*	
	£/Cow	*ppl*	*£/Cow*	*ppl*
Milk Output @ 26 ppl	2,080	26.0	2,470	26.0
Calf Value	117	1.5	117	1.2
Cull Value	96	1.2	108	1.1
Less, Replacement Cost @ 25% & 28% per year	-304	-3.8	-354	-3.7
Total Output	**1,989**	**24.9**	**2,341**	**24.6**
Variable Costs:				
Concentrate Costs £200/t @ 2.6t & 3.5t/cow	520	6.5	700	7.4
Purchased Bulk Feed	20	0.3	20	0.2
Vet & Med	75	0.9	78	0.8
Bedding	62	0.8	62	0.7
AI	41	0.5	43	0.5
Recording, Parlour Consumables, Sundries	76	1.0	76	0.8
Total Variable Costs	794	9.9	979	10.3
Gross Margin per cow Before Forage Costs	**1,195**	**14.9**	**1,362**	**14.3**
Forage Costs @ 2.2 Cows Per Forage Hectare	111	1.4	111	1.2
Gross Margin per Cow After Forage Costs	**1,084**	**13.6**	**1,251**	**13.2**
Gross Margin Per Forage Hectare	2,385		2,752	
Margin of Milk Over Concentrates	1,560	19.5	1,770	18.6
Sensitivity Analysis per cow				
Concentrate Price +/- £10/tonne	+- 26.0		+- 35.0	
Concentrate Price +/- £20/tonne	+- 52.0		+- 70.0	
Milk Price +/- 0.25 ppl	+- 20.0		+- 23.8	
Milk Price +/- 0.50 ppl	+- 40.0		+- 47.5	

All-year-round calving herds have higher costs of production than seasonal producers and so aim to sell their milk on a liquid premium based (supermarket supply) contract. However, these contracts are limited. Both vet and med and A.I. costs tend to increase with higher milk yield due to greater pressure on the cow and poorer fertility. As a result, herd replacement rates are also considerably higher.

See notes on page 47.

Autumn Calving Friesian/Holsteins (per cow per year)

	Average		High	
Yield Per Cow (litres)	*6,000*		*7,000*	
	£/Cow	*ppl*	*£/Cow*	*ppl*
Milk Output @ 26 ppl	1,560	26.0	1,820	26.0
Calf Value	108	1.8	108	1.5
Cull Value	81	1.4	81	1.2
Less, Replacement Cost @ 23% per year	-257	-4.3	-257	-3.7
Total Output	**1,492**	**24.9**	**1,752**	**25.0**
Variable Costs:				
Concentrate Costs £200/t @ 1.5t and 1.8t/cow	300	5.0	360	5.1
Purchased Bulk Feed	20	0.3	20	0.3
Vet & Med	50	0.8	55	0.8
Bedding	59	1.0	59	0.8
AI	30	0.5	32	0.5
Recording, Parlour Consumables, Sundries	50	0.8	50	0.7
Total Variable Costs	509	8.5	576	8.2
Gross Margin per cow Before Forage Costs	**983**	**16.4**	**1,176**	**16.8**
Forage Costs @ 2.2 Cows Per Forage Hectare	106	1.8	106	1.5
Gross Margin per Cow After Forage Costs	**877**	**14.6**	**1,070**	**15.3**
Gross Margin Per Forage Hectare	1,930		2,355	
Margin of Milk Over Concentrates	1,260	21.0	1,460	20.9
Sensitivity Analysis per cow				
Concentrate Price +/- £10/tonne	+- 15.0		+- 18.0	
Concentrate Price +/- £20/tonne	+- 30.0		+- 36.0	
Milk Price +/- 0.25 ppl	+- 15.0		+- 17.5	
Milk Price +/- 0.50 ppl	+- 30.0		+- 35.0	

Autumn calving herds (80% or more calvings between August and November) tend to have much higher overheads than spring calving herds, mainly associated with winter housing and feeding – buildings, greater silage requirements, slurry and muck handling, plus labour. Autumn calving herds benefit from a marginally higher milk price than spring or all-year-round calving herds because of seasonality, and typically sell milk to a liquid buyer. The decision between being a spring or autumn calving producer depends largely on specific circumstances, such as building facilities available, the ability of the farm to grow forage (wet or dry land) and the nearby milk buyers' requirements.

See notes on page 47.

Spring Calving Friesians (per cow per year)

	Average		High	
Yield Per Cow (litres)	*5,250*		*6,000*	
	£/Cow	*ppl*	*£/Cow*	*ppl*
Milk Output @ 25 ppl	1,313	25.0	1,500	25.0
Calf Value	108	2.1	108	1.8
Cull Value	71	1.3	71	1.2
Less, Replacement Cost @ 20% per year	-224	-4.3	-224	-3.7
Total Output	**1,267**	**24.1**	**1,455**	**24.2**
Variable Costs:				
Concentrate Costs £180/t @ 0.8t and 1.2t/cow	144	2.7	216	3.6
Purchased Bulk Feed	0	0.0	0	0.0
Vet & Med	40	0.8	45	0.8
Bedding	44	0.8	45	0.8
AI	30	0.6	34	0.6
Recording, Parlour Consumables, Sundries	50	1.0	55	0.9
Total Variable Costs	308	5.9	395	6.6
Gross Margin per cow Before Forage Costs	**959**	**18.3**	**1,060**	**17.7**
Forage Costs @ 2.4 Cows Per Forage Hectare	93	1.8	93	1.5
Gross Margin per Cow After Forage Costs	**867**	**16.5**	**967**	**16.1**
Gross Margin Per Forage Hectare	2,080		2,321	
Margin of Milk Over Concentrates	1,169	22.3	1,284	21.4
Sensitivity Analysis per cow				
Concentrate Price +/- £10/tonne	+- 8.0		+- 12.0	
Concentrate Price +/- £20/tonne	+- 16.0		+- 24.0	
Milk Price +/- 0.25 ppl	+- 13.1		+- 15.0	
Milk Price +/- 0.50 ppl	+- 26.3		+- 30.0	

Spring calving herds (80% or more calvings between February and May) typically have a lower annual average yield than other systems due to a smaller, hardier cow type but higher milk solids, typically by 10 percent ideal for a cheese/ manufacturing contract. As a result, replacement rates are lower than other systems despite the reductions from seasonality. These systems have lower overhead costs (labour, buildings and machinery) and focus on milk from grazed grass. Lower costs reflect the lower milk price received.

See notes below.

Dairy Gross Margins Notes:

1. *Value of Calves:* Average annual value per calf at 10-20 days old, allowing for 5% mortality and an average calving index of 400 days for all year round calving (AYR) and 385 days for seasonal calving herds. The average value assumed for spring and autumn calving (Seasonal) herds is comprised equally:

Calf Value (net):			
5% mortality	AYR	Seasonal	Channel Islands
Dairy bull calf (dairy x dairy)	£40	*£30*	*£20*
Dairy heifer calf (dairy x dairy)	£150	£150	£150
Cross bred bull (beef x dairy)	£180	*£170*	*£100*
Cross bred heifer (beef x dairy)	£170	*£130*	*£100*
Calving Interval (days)	*400*	*385*	*385*
Calf Mortality	*5%*	*5%*	*5%*
Average	***£117***	***£108***	***£83***

* Calves for all-year-round calving herds with higher milk yields sometimes have less beef genetics meaning dairy bull calves and beef cross animals are less valuable but higher value dairy calves.

2. *Replacement Costs:* The table below demonstrates herd replacement costs.

	AYR		Autumn	Spring	Bull
Yield per cow	*8,000*	*9,500*	*6,000*	*5,250*	
Value of new heifers (bull) (a)	1,200	1,250	1,100	1,100	1,500
Replacement Rate (b)	25%	28%	23%	20%	25%
Bull Depreciation per cow (c.)	4	4	4	4	
Herd Depreciation (a x b +c = d)	**304**	**354**	**257**	**224**	**375**
Cull Cow Value (net) (e)	400	400	360	360	800
Casualty Rate (f)	4%	4%	2%	2%	4%
Cows per Bull (g)					45
Annual Cull Value (b x e x f = h)	**96**	**108**	**81**	**71**	**192**
Calf Values (see above) (i)	**128**	**128**	**114**	**114**	
Net Replacement Cost (d-h-i)	**80**	**118**	**62**	**40**	
Cost of Bull Per cow ((a-e) x b x (1-f) / g)					**4**

Herd depreciation is the annual cost of replacing the herd i.e. the cost of a down-calving heifer divided by its life expectancy in years (or multiplied by the annual replacement rate). When the value of cull cows and calves are added (both adjusted for casualty and mortality allowance), the net replacement cost can be calculated.

3. *Concentrate Costs:*

	AYR		Autumn		Spring	
Yield per cow	*8,000*	*9,500*	*6,000*	*7,000*	*5,250*	*6,000*
Tonnes / Cow	2.60	3.50	1.50	1.80	0.80	1.20
Kg feed / Litre	0.33	0.37	0.25	0.26	0.15	0.20
Concentrate Cost (ppl)	6.50	7.37	5.00	5.14	2.74	3.60
Conc. cost p/marginal L		12.00		6.00		9.60

This table gives the costs of concentrate feed per litre of milk and crucially, the costs of concentrate per marginal (additional) litre. In other words, the cost of the extra feed required to move from the first yield to the second yield bracket in each category. The yield difference in the spring and autumn groups is small, but the yield rise for AYR herds is considerable, the cost of the last litre (to 9,500 in this instance) is always dearest, and will be more than the figure shown.

4. *Concentrate Feeding:* The table below is an example of annual concentrate use for an all-year-round calving herd.

Typical Monthly Variation in Concentrate Feeding (kg per litre, 8,000 litre herd)

Winter		Summer	
October	0.36	April	0.29
November	0.38	May	0.20
December	0.39	June	0.20
January	0.39	July	0.26
February	0.38	August	0.30
March	0.34	September	0.33
Average winter: 0.37		Average summer: 0.26	
Weighted average whole year: 0.325kg/l			

The distribution on farm varies according to factors such as seasonality of calving, milk yield, summer grazing productivity, the quality of grass, winter forages, bulk feeds, as well as turnout and housing dates. The March figure in particular will be affected by type of soil and seasonal rainfall.

Yield without concentrate and good silage can be 4,000 litres for spring calvers.

5. *Margin over Concentrates (MOC) and Concentrates per litre:* It is important to highlight in the above gross margins the differences between the margin (of milk value) over concentrates per cow; the same large variation can occur with widely differing combinations of milk yield and quantity of concentrates fed.

In the following table, for each production system, figures are given for *(a)* margin of milk value over concentrates per cow (£) and *(b)* concentrates per litre (kg).

Margin Over Concentrates (MOC) and Concentrates per Litre (C/L)

Milking System	All-Year-Round Calving				Autumn Calving		Spring Calving	
Milk Yield (litres)	8,000		9,500		6,000		5,250	
	MOC	C/L	MOC	C/L	MOC	C/L	MOC	C/L
Concentrates per cow	£	kg	£	kg	£	kg	£	kg
0.65 tonne (£117)	-	-	-	-	-	-	1196	0.12
0.75 tonne (£135)	-	-	-	-	-	-	1178	0.14
0.90 tonne (£162)	-	-	-	-	-	-	1151	0.17
1.05 tonne (£189)	-	-	-	-	1,371	0.18	1124	0.20
1.60 tonne (£320)	-	-	-	-	1,240	0.27	-	-
1.80 tonne (£360)	-	-	-	-	1,200	0.30	-	-
2.00 tonne (£400)	1,680	0.25	-	-	1,160	0.33	-	-
2.20 tonne (£440)	1,640	0.28	-	-	-	-	-	-
2.45 tonne (£490)	1,590	0.31			-	-	-	-
2.70 tonne (£540)	1,540	0.34	1930	0.28	-	-	-	-
3.00 tonne (£600)	-	-	1870	0.32	-	-	-	-
3.35 tonne (£670)	-	-	1800	0.35	-	-	-	-
3.75 tonne (£750)	-	-	1720	0.39	-	-	-	-

6. *Stocking Rate and Forage Costs:* The stocking rates used assume nearly all forage/bulk foods are obtained from the forage area, i.e. little is bought in. The stocking rates of 2.2 and 2.4 cows per forage hectare (autumn/AYR calving and spring calving respectively) assume good grassland management. Higher stocking rates are achievable, particularly in the West where natural conditions favour forage production. About 55 per cent of forage area is grazed and 45 per cent conserved for an AYR calving herd. Spring calving herds rely much less on conserved forage. Some high yielding herds are housed all-year and fed 100 percent conserved feed.

Forage costs are taken from the *Forage Variable Costs* on page 89 as follows:

	Grass	Maize	Grass	Maize	Grass	Maize
£ Cost /Ha	223	320	£/Ha		£/cow	
Spring calving	100%	0%	223	0	93	0
Autumn calving	89%	11%	198	35	90	16
All year round calving	78%	22%	174	70	79	32

An increase in stocking density can be obtained not only by intensifying grassland production, but also by buying in bulk fodder (assuming the same level of concentrate feeding). A zero-grazed farm buying in forage needs no land. In this situation, the gross margin per hectare would be extreme (and meaningless), although the cost of hauling in forage would be high.

Overheads such as labour and building depreciation are likely to increase per hectare as stocking density rises. Management challenges occur with higher stocking rates such as poaching which can be alleviated with good cow tracks. Cross Compliance and Nitrate Vulnerable Zone regulations must still be adhered to.

7. *Labour*: see page 182.
8. *Building Costs*: see page 231.

Costs of Milk Production Summary (Pence per Litre)

Production type	AYR Calving	Autumn Calving	Spring Calving
Litres per cow	*8,000*	*6,000*	*5,250*
		Pence Per Litre	
Concentrates	7.37	5.14	3.60
Forage and Bought Bulk Feed	1.38	1.80	1.55
Other Variable Costs	2.94	3.09	2.98
Total Variable Costs	**11.68**	**10.03**	**8.13**
All Labour (inc. unpaid)	4.32	5.32	5.09
Power and Machinery*	6.03	6.58	5.37
General Overheads	1.15	1.28	1.27
Total Overhead Costs	**11.50**	**13.19**	**11.73**
Less, Net Replacement Cost	1.14	1.13	0.86
Total Costs of Production	**24.32**	**24.35**	**20.72**

* *inc electricity & parlour repairs*

1. This schedule only compiles the costs of milk production. Adding milk price to it does not constitute a profit or loss as other components of the farm should be included such as BPS, youngstock enterprises, rent and finance.

2. The *Variable Costs* per litre are derived from the data (and therefore the assumptions made) under high performance in the dairy gross margin tables for each system.

3. The *Overhead Costs* assume above average financial performance. The overhead are adapted from the medium-sized 'mainly dairying' farm data in the Overhead Costs Section on page 221. Within each system, there is a marked difference between the costs achieved by the top 10% and the bottom 10% of producers (over 10ppl). The difference is mainly due to management ability. *Labour* includes the farmer and unpaid family labour but there is no management charge included. *Power and machinery* covers all machinery and equipment costs, including the use of farm vehicles, depreciation, etc. *General overheads* similarly relate to the whole farm,

including electricity and property repairs. *Rent/Rental Equivalent and Finance* assumes a modest rental charge on all land plus interest charges on a modest amount of working capital. No long-term debt is included.

4. All-year-round calving herds will have the highest overheads in absolute terms. However, well-managed high yielding herds can compete with block calving systems due to higher output. Spring calving herds may have the lowest total overheads due to a shorter housing period, less demand for winter forage and lower muck handling costs. Costs per litre might be higher though as yields are lower. Rental costs, in pence per litre terms, will be higher though due to the fixed land charge and lower output (litres) per unit area of land unless stocking rates are raised.

Once a Day and Three Times a Day Milking.

All other schedules assume twice a day milking. A growing number of farms are now milking either once a day (***OAD***) or three times a day (***TTAD***).

	OAD		**TTAD**	
Yield Per Cow (litres)	*3,400*		*10,000*	
	£/Cow	*ppl*	*£/Cow*	*ppl*
Milk Output @ 27 and 26ppl respectively	918	27.0	2,600	26.0
Calf Value	108	3.2	117	1.2
Cull Value	58	1.7	132	1.3
Less, Replacement Cost @ 15% & 35% per year	-184	-5.4	-441	-4.4
Total Output	**900**	**26.5**	**2,407**	**24.1**
Variable Costs:				
Concentrates £180/t @ 0.2t and £220 @ 4t/cow	36	1.1	720	7.2
Purchased Bulk Feed	0	0.0	43	0.4
Vet & Med	30	0.9	90	0.9
Bedding	52	1.5	52	0.5
AI	20	0.6	22	0.2
Recording, Parlour Consumables, Sundries	25	0.7	99	1.0
Total Variable Costs	163	4.8	1,026	10.3
Gross Margin per cow Before Forage Costs	**737**	**21.7**	**1,381**	**13.8**
Forage Costs @ 2.5 & 2.0 Cows / Forage Ha	93	2.7	126	1.3
Gross Margin per Cow After Forage Costs	**644**	**19.0**	**1,256**	**12.6**
Gross Margin Per Forage Hectare	1,611		2,511	
Margin of Milk Over Concentrates	882	25.9	1,880	18.8
Sensitivity Analysis per cow				
Concentrate Price +/- £20/tonne	+- 4.0		+- 80.0	
Milk Price +/- 0.25 ppl	+- 42.5		+- 25.0	

Notes on Once a Day (OAD) and Three times a day (TTAD) Milking

1. OAD milking is centred on cost stripping, as well as a lifestyle choice for the farmer. It means block calving, low yields and minimal concentrate feeding. Cows are small with low maintenance costs. The transition to OAD can take 3 seasons as cows adjust.

2. Milk solids increase in OAD, meaning milk price should be higher (hence the higher milk price) depending on milk contract. OAD milking often has a higher stocking rate to account for the reduction in milk per cow.

3. TTAD cows are larger and produce very high yields but with very high marginal costs of production. It is often associated with robotic milking. Observation and cow management is still required so costs per cow often rise, but can fall per litre. Vet and replacement costs rise considerably as well as concentrate feed. Cows are often fully housed.

4. OAD milking systems can work on farms where fields are distant from the parlour. Equally, TTAD milking systems must keep the cows close to the parlour at all times.

Acknowledgement ~ thanks to National Once a Day Farms via Pasture to Profit.

Channel Island Breeds (per cow per year)

Performance level (yield)	AYR Average	AYR High	A. Calving	S. Calving
Milk Yield per Cow (litres)	*5,450*	*6,250*	*5,000*	*4,150*
	£	**£**	**£**	**£**
Milk Value per Cow at 34 ppl	1,853	2,125	1,700	1,411
Calf Value	83	83	83	83
Cull Value	44	49	41	35
Less, Replacement Cost	-250	-280	-230	-200
Total Output	**1,730**	**1,978**	**1,594**	**1,330**
Variable Costs:				
Concentrate Costs	390	492	287	189
Purchased Bulk Feed	25	25	25	25
Vet & Med	40	44	36	32
Bedding	42	42	42	37
AI	32	34	32	30
Parlour Consumables, Sundries etc.	56	56	56	56
Total Variable Costs	**585**	**693**	**478**	**369**
Gross Margin Before Forage Costs	**1,146**	**1,285**	**1,116**	**961**
Forage Costs @ 2.5 Cows Per Forage Ha	124	124	89	89
Gross Margin After Forage Costs	**1,022**	**1,161**	**1,027**	**872**
Gross Margin Per Forage Hectare	2,555	2,902	2,567	2,179
Margin of Milk Over Concentrates	1,464	1,633	1,413	1,222

1. *Yield.* Average of Jerseys and Guernseys. See Note 1 and 2 for Holstein Friesians (page 43). Guernsey yield averages slightly higher than Jerseys and Jerseys achieve a higher butterfat and protein (see page 44).
2. *Milk Price.* This is 34p per litre (average of Jerseys and Guernseys for a level profile). This is based upon a milk solid content. Milk buyers are increasingly paying for solids, rather than a separate Channel Island contract.
3. *Concentrate Costs.* The average price taken (for 2018) is £205 per tonne (for all-year-round calving herds), £200 per tonne average for spring calving herds and £210 per tonne for autumn calving herds.

Amounts	*Milk Group*	*AYR ave.*	*AYR High*	*Spring*	*Autumn*
	kg/litre	0.315	0.384	0.217	0.280
	tonnes/cow	1.75	2.40	0.90	1.40
	pence / litre (ppl)	7.15	7.87	4.55	5.74
	pence/ marginal litre*		12.8		

** This is the additional cost of feed between yield groups, and the cost of the additional feed divided by the additional litres of production.*

4. *Net Annual Replacement Cost*: Calculated as follows (replacement rates vary by system, 20% for spring, 23% for autumn, 25% for higher yielding all-year-round calving herds):

	AYR Average	AYR High	A. Calving	S. Calving
Yield per cow	*5,450*	*6,250*	*5,000*	*4,150*
Value of new heifers (a)	1,000	1,000	1,000	1,000
Replacement Rate (b)	25%	28%	23%	20%
Bull Depreciation per cow (c.)	4	4	4	4
Herd Depreciation (a x b +c = d)	**254**	**284**	**234**	**204**
Cull Cow Value (e)	180	180	180	180
Casualty Rate (f)	2%	2%	2%	2%
Annual Cull Value (b x e x f = g)	**44**	**49**	**41**	**35**
Calf Values (h)	**83**	**83**	**83**	**83**
Net Replacement Cost (d-g-h)	**126**	**151**	**110**	**85**

*Cull cow prices for Guernseys are about £40 higher than for Jerseys.

** Allowing for calving index of 400 days and calf mortality; mixture of pure bred calves and beef crosses. Guernsey calves, especially crosses, are worth more than Jersey calves, averaging perhaps £10 more per head and substantially more for some Guernsey beef crosses.

5. *Forage Costs and Stocking Rate.* See, in general, Note 6 for Holstein Friesians (page 49). See forage section for details of improved temporary grass used here. At the average stocking rate given above for combined Channel Island breeds (2.5 cows per forage hectare) the average figure for Jerseys would be approximately 2.60 and that for Guernseys 2.40 cows per forage hectare.

DAIRY FOLLOWERS

(per Heifer reared)

Performance Level	AYR	Autumn	Spring
	£	£	£
Value of heifer (allowing for culls)	1080	990	990
Less Value of calf	158	158	158
Output	923	833	833
Variable Costs:			
Concentrate Costs	290	121	84
Bedding	88	75	61
Vet & Med	25	23	21
Other Costs	15	14	13
Total Variable Costs (excluding Forage)	418	233	179
Gross Margin per Heifer, before deducting Forage Costs	505	599	653
Forage Variable Costs	105	105	105
Gross Margin per Heifer	400	495	549
Forage Hectares (Acres) per Heifer reared	0.70 (1.7)	0.70 (1.7)	0.70 (1.7)
Gross Margin per Forage Hectare	571	707	784
Gross Margin per Forage Acre	231	286	317

B. Channel Island Breeds

Performance Level	AYR	Autumn	Spring
	£	£	£
Value of heifer (allowing for culls)	900	900	900
Less Value of calf	87	87	87
Output	813	813	813
Variable Costs:			
Concentrate Costs	216	106	74
Miscellaneous Costs	109	95	81
Total Variable Costs (excluding Forage)	324	201	154
Gross Margin per Heifer, before deducting Forage Variable Costs	488	611	658
Forage Variable Costs	94	94	94
Gross Margin per Heifer	394	517	564
Forage Hectares (Acres) per Heifer reared	0.65 (1.6)	0.65 (1.6)	0.65 (1.6)
Gross Margin per Forage Hectare	606	796	868
Gross Margin per Forage Acre	245	322	351

N.B. on average Channel Island heifers calve about three months younger than Holstein Friesian Heifers

1. *Heifer values* are based on the purchase price of calving heifers with an allowance for culls and barren animals. Most heifers are home-reared. If heifers are reared for sale, the price of whole batches is likely to be lower than the values given in the tables, by 10 or 15 per cent. On the other hand the purchaser will often take the batch a few

months before the average expected calving date, thus reducing the costs incurred by the rearer.

2. *Calf Value*; is based on the cost of a heifer dairy calf, increased to account for mortality of 5%.

3. *Concentrate cost* Other things being equal, a lower calving age requires higher levels of feeding. Feeding schedule laid out below:

		AYR	Autumn	Spring
Milk Substitute				
£1800/T	g/day	750	600	500
	days fed	63	63	63
	£/calf	£85	£68	£57
Weaning Nuts (18%)				
£275/T	kg/day	1.5	1	1.0
	days fed	84	42	35
	£/calf	£35	£12	£10
Grower Nuts (18%)				
£212/T	kg/day	2.2	2	2
	days fed	365	98	42
	£/calf	£170	£42	£18
Total Conc (£/calf)		**£290**	**£121**	**£84**
Bedding				
	t/heifer	1.3	1.1	0.9
	£/t	68	68	68

4. *Forage variable costs*. Grass for both grazing and conservation, at £142/ha, assuming all home produced. This is the variable costs for long term leys and improved permanent pasture (combined in equal parts) in the forage section on page 89, thus assuming less productive grassland is used to rear dairy heifers with the best pasture being retained for the dairy cows.

5. *A "replacement unit"* (i.e. calf + yearling + heifer) equals about 1·25 livestock units with an average calving age of 2 years 4 months. The three stocking rates used above are equivalent to approximately 0.75, 0·6 and 0·5 forage hectares (1.85, 1.48, 1.24 acres) respectively per Holstein Friesian cow (Livestock Unit). Note, this is a 2-year gross margin. It can be treated as a gross margin over a longer period of time or a margin per replacement unit, not per animal on the farm per year.

6. *Higher gross margin per hectare* figures can be achieved by intensive grazing methods, particularly if combined with alternative winter feeding systems, such as out-wintering on forage crops such as Fodder Beet or Kale.

7. *Contract Rearing*: see page 74.

8. *Labour*: see page 182.

SELF-CONTAINED DAIRY HERD: COWS AND FOLLOWERS

At average annual replacement rates (25 per cent of the milking herd), nearly one-third of a replacement unit is required for each cow in the herd, i.e. roughly one calf, yearling and heifer for every three cows (including calved heifers), allowing for mortality and culling. At average stocking rates for both, this means more than 1 hectare devoted to followers for every 3 hectares for cows. Surplus youngstock are often reared and frequently the stocking rate is less intensive, the ratio often exceeds this in practice. 1:3 is about the minimum where all replacement heifers are reared, unless their winter feeding is based largely on straw and purchased supplements, or unless there is a combination of long average herd life and early calving, i.e. all at 2 years old.

The table below shows the combined gross margin per forage hectare (acre) for the whole herd (i.e., Cows and Followers combined) for four different dairy systems assuming the same stocking rate for the dairy cows and three levels of performance, including different stocking rates, for the followers. This assumes a 3:1 land use ratio (dairy cow area: followers area) and relates to the dairying systems (gross margins) shown earlier in this section. It is important to note, however, that these are only a guide as the figures (ratio of land areas assumed) do not take account of the different herd replacement rates for each dairying system. In practise, it is likely that the amount of land required for the followers for a block spring calving herd would be less than that for a high yielding all-year-round calving herd; this is due to the fact that typically a high yielding herd would have a higher herd replacement rate and as such require more heifers and therefore land on which to rear them.

Gross Margin per Forage Hectare for Cows and Followers Combined

			G.M per Forage Hectare (acre) Dairy Cows			
		System	AYR Ave.	AYR High	Autumn	Spring
		Litres	8,000	9,500	6,000	5,250
			£	£	£	£
G.M. per			2385 (966)	2752 (1114)	1930 (782)	2080 (842)
Forage Hectare	AYR	571 (231)	1932 (782)	2207 (894)		
(acre)	Aut.	707 (286)			1624 (658)	
Followers	Spr.	784 (317)				1756 (711)

As an example, the above table indicates that for an all-year-round 8,000 litre dairy herd (AYR Average) and AYR followers, the whole farm-system gross margin per hectare (acre) figure is £1,932 (782) compared with £2,385 (966) for the dairy cows alone, a reduction of 20%.

BEEF

There are numerous systems for producing beef which are heavily influenced by factors such as feed and forage, breeds, housing, sale weights, market outlets, labour availability, enterprise scale and personal choice. Thus, the financial performance of beef enterprises is diverse. The enterprise gross margins shown on these pages represent the 'standard' systems with output prices and costs based on 2018 budgets.

Calves

The values in the table below are for 2018 and relate to dairy bulls or beef cross calves of average quality, less than three weeks old. These values have been used in the budgets for the following beef systems. There is large regional and seasonal variation in calf prices.

Calf values of various beef cattle

	Bulls	Heifers
Holstein Friesians	70	-
Hereford Cross	220	160
HF/Continental Cross	280	240

Calf Rearing

Early Weaning - Bucket Rearing (per calf)

	3 months	6 months
	£	£
Value of Calf	390	490
Less Calf Purchase	234	234
Output	**156**	**256**
Variable Costs:		
Milk Substitute	36	36
Concentrates	44	105
Hay	4	17
Vet & Med.	17	19
Bedding	7	11
Miscellaneous	4	6
Total Variable Costs	**112**	**194**
Gross Margin per Calf Reared	**44**	**62**

1. *Calf Purchase*: Equal number of male and female calves (Hereford Cross/ Continental beef cross, 1-2 weeks old). Average = £225 plus 4% mortality, mainly in first 3 weeks = £234.
2. *Milk substitute:* 20 kg @ £1,800/tonne = £36.00. Calves fed on machine or lib milk systems will use more milk powder.
3. *Calf concentrates:* to 3 months, 160 kg @ £275/tonne = £44

   Rearer Feed to 6 months, additional 290kg @ 212/tonne = £61
4. *Hay:* 50kg to 3 months, 200kg to 6 months (£64/tonne) See page 91.
5. *Miscellaneous:* Ear Tags etc.
6. *Weights*: at start = 45 to 50 kg; at 3 months = 115 kg; at 6 months = 245kg.
7. *Contract rearing charge* (both 0 to 3 months and 0 to 6 months): £14 per week. *Direct labour cost:* approximately £28 per head to 3 months, £42 per head to 6 months.
8. *Labour requirements (all beef systems):* see page 182.

Suckler Cows

Single Suckling (per Cow): Lowland

System	*Spring Calving*		*Autumn Calving*	
Performance Level	Average	High	Average	High
	£	£	£	£
Value of Calf Sold	*559*	*633*	*741*	*789*
Calf Sales / Calf Value per Cow	509	589	674	734
Less Cow and Bull Depreciation	144	144	162	162
Calf Purchases	7	7	9	9
Output	**358**	**438**	**503**	**563**
Variable Costs:				
Concentrate (Cow and Calf)	36	30	62	57
Vet & Med	30	30	32	32
Bedding	44	44	50	50
Miscellaneous	22	23	25	28
Variable Costs (ex. forage)	**132**	**127**	**170**	**167**
Gross Margin £/Cow, (ex. Forage)	225	311	333	396
Forage Variable Costs	96	78	104	86
Purchased Bulk Feeds	12	10	20	16
Gross Margin £/Cow	**118**	**222**	**209**	**294**
Cows per Ha.	1.80	2.20	1.65	2.00
Gross Margin £/Forage Ha (Acre)	**212**	**489**	**344**	**587**
	(86)	*(198)*	*(139)*	*(238)*

1. *System*: Relates to performance per cycle, i.e. for the production period. Assumed 390 days average calving interval.
2. *Performance level*: relates to variations in both outputs and inputs.

Calving Period	*Spring Calving*		*Autumn Calving*	
Performance Level	Average	High	Average	High
Calf Sale Weights (kg)	280	309	371	385
Sale Age (Days)	250	240	365	340
Sale Prices (£/kg)	£2.00	2.05	£2.00	2.05
Calves reared per 100 cows mated	91	93	91	93

3. *Cow & Bull Depreciation:*

	Spring C.	Autumn C.	Bull
Purchase Price - £	£1,500	£1,500	£4,000
Cull Price - £	£500	£500	£600
Animal Life (Years)	8	7	5
Depreciation £/cow	£125	£143	£19

4. *Calf Purchases:* £225 each, 3 per 100 cows mated (spring calving) 4 per 100 cows mated (autumn calving).

Dairy cross beef cows have better fertility performance than continental pure bred cows, but lower cull sale prices. Average 35 cows per bull.

5. *Concentrate feed:*

	Spring Calving		*Autumn Calving*	
Concentrates	Average	High	Average	High
Cow kg's	120	100	190	165
Cow - £/t	195	195	195	195
Calf kg's	60	50	120	115
Calf - £/t	212	212	212	212
Total Concentrate	£36	£30	£62	£57

6. *Straw:* where yarded in winter, straw requirements average 0.7 tonnes per cow for spring calvers and 0.8 tonnes for autumn calvers at £63/tonne.

7. *Forage Area:* includes grazing and conserved grass (silage and hay). Higher stocking rates imply better use of grassland or achieved by buying in more winter fodder, or feeding more arable by-products, including straw. Purchased bulk fodder and/or straw balancer concentrates will reduce gross margin per cow but increase gross margin per hectare. Forage cost from Long Term Ley in Forage at £172/ha on page 89.

8. *Headage Payment:* A payment is made in Scotland on three-quarter bred beef calves from Suckler Cows. This is a flat rate payment, on all eligible calves, in the region of €100 per calf on the mainland and €160 per calf on the islands. Actual rates depend on the number of calves claimed on each year. See Top-up Schemes in Chapter III.

9. *Multiple calves:* In lowland conditions rearing two or more calves per cow is an option, but needs substantially greater labour input. Output is raised by fostering a second purchased calf onto a cow soon after calving, with little impact on costs of keeping the cow. The cow breed needs to be of a quiet temperament and have enough milk to rear two calves.

Single Suckling (per Cow): Upland

System	*Spring Calving*		*Autumn Calving*	
Performance Level	Average	High	Average	High
	£	£	£	£
Value of Calf Sold	545	574	727	759
Calf Sales / Calf Value per Cow	491	528	654	698
Less Cow and Bull Depreciation	151	151	169	169
Calf Purchases	7	7	9	9
Output	**333**	**371**	**477**	**520**
Variable Costs:				
Concentrate (Cow and Calf)	38	32	63	58
Vet & Med	31	31	33	33
Bedding	49	49	55	55
Miscellaneous	22	23	25	28
Variable Costs (ex. forage)	**140**	**135**	**177**	**174**
Gross Margin £/Cow, (ex. Forage)	193	236	300	346
Forage Variable Costs	79	67	101	85
Purchased Bulk Feeds	14	12	22	18
Gross Margin £/Cow	**100**	**157**	**177**	**244**
Cows per Ha.	1.60	1.90	1.25	1.50
Gross Margin £/Forage Ha (Acre)	**160**	**298**	**221**	**366**
	(65)	*(121)*	*(89)*	*(148)*

1. *System:* Relates to performance per cycle, i.e. for the production period. Assumed 390 days average calving interval. Performance level: relates to variations in both outputs and inputs.
2. *Performance Level*

Calving Period	*Spring Calving*		*Autumn Calving*	
Performance Level	Average	High	Average	High
Calf Sale Weights (kg)	273	280	364	370
Sale Age (Days)	250	240	365	330
Sale Prices (£/kg)	£2.00	2.05	£2.00	2.05
Calves reared per 100 cows mated	90	92	90	92

3. *Cow & Bull Depreciation:*

	Spring C.	Autumn C.	Bull
Purchase Price - £	£1,500	£1,500	£4,200
Cull Price - £	£500	£500	£600
Animal Life (Years)	8	7	4
Depreciation £/cow	£125	£143	£26

4. *Calf Purchases*: £225 each, 3 per 100 cows mated (spring calving) 4 per 100 cows mated (autumn calving).

Dairy cross beef cows have better fertility performance than continental pure bred cows, but lower cull sale prices. Average 35 cows per bull.

5. *Concentrate Feed:*

	Spring Calving		*Autumn Calving*	
Concentrates	Average	High	Average	High
Cow kg's	130	110	195	170
Cow - £/t	195	195	195	195
Calf kg's	60	50	120	115
Calf - £/t	212	212	212	212
Total Concentrate	£38	£32	£63	£58

6. *Straw:* where yarded in winter, straw requirements average 0.75 tonnes per cow for spring calvers and 0.85 tonnes for autumn calvers at £65/tonne.

7. *Forage Area:* includes grazing and conserved grass (silage and hay). Higher stocking rates imply better use of grassland or higher can be achieved by buying more winter bulk fodder, or by winter feeding more arable by-products, including straw. Purchased bulk fodder and/or straw balancer concentrates will reduce gross margin per cow but increase gross margin per hectare. Forage cost from Improved Permanent Pasture in Forage page at £127/ha on page 89.

8. *Headage Payment:* A payment is made in Scotland on three-quarter bred beef calves from Suckler Cows. This is a flat rate payment, on all eligible calves, in the region of €100 per calf on the mainland and €160 per calf on the islands. Actual rates will depend on the number of calves claimed on each year. See Top-up Schemes in Chapter III.

Store Cattle

Maintenance / Keeping of Young Dairy Store Cattle **(per head)**

	Summer Keeping		*Winter Keeping*	
	Average	*High*	*Average*	*High*
	£	**£**	**£**	**£**
Store Sales	764	794	756	783
Less Purchased Store (incl. mortality)	500	495	500	495
Output	**264**	**299**	**256**	**288**
Variable Costs:				
Concentrates	5	4	53	46
Vet & Med	11	10	13	11
Bedding	0	0	50	44
Miscellaneous	17	15	21	19
Variable Costs (ex. forage)	**33**	**29**	**137**	**120**
Gross Margin £/Head, (ex. Forage)	**231**	**270**	**119**	**168**
Forage Variable Costs	30	29	66	66
Gross Margin per Head	**201**	**242**	**53**	**102**
Stock per Ha.	5.75	6.00	n/a	
Gross Margin £/Forage Ha	**1,154**	**1,449**		
Gross Margin £/Forage Acre	468	587		

1. *System*: Buying dairy cross steers and heifers at 6 months old for keeping / rearing. Animals spend 6 months in system before sale / transfer to a finishing enterprise.
2. *Sales*: at 402kg summer, 398kg winter (liveweight), both at £2.00/kg for "average" and £2.05/kg for "high".
3. *Purchases*: Both systems 245kg purchase weight @ £2.00, plus 1% mortality.
4. *Concentrates*: Winter 270kg concentrates (1.5kg/day for 180 days) @ £195 per tonne. Summer, 150g/day.
5. *Forage Costs:* Summer Keep based on 'Long Term Ley' in forage section (page 89) at £172/ha gross margin. Winter Keep: 2.9 tonnes per head grass silage consumption (2.8t/cow for "high"). Full costs of grass and ensiling are included here at contract rates making £23/tonne silage. Similarly, bought in silage will increase the forage costs over those shown. *This means that the two gross margins are not comparable as different levels of overheads are included in the calculation. Be sure what is included in the forage calculation when working out the costs.*

Finishing Cattle

Finishing of Dairy Bred Store Cattle (per head)

	Summer Finishing		*Winter Finishing*	
	Average	*High*	*Average*	*High*
	£	**£**	**£**	**£**
Finished Sales	1,105	1,117	1,118	1,130
Less Purchased Store (incl. mortality)	771	764	779	771
Output	**334**	**353**	**339**	**359**
Variable Costs:				
Concentrates	61	57	102	111
Vet & Med	13	10	20	15
Bedding	0	0	44	38
Miscellaneous	35	30	43	38
Variable Costs (ex. forage)	**109**	**97**	**209**	**202**
Gross Margin £/Head, (ex. Forage)	**225**	**256**	**130**	**157**
Stock per Ha.	3.00	3.50		
Forage Variable Costs	57	49	85	85
Gross Margin per Head	**167**	**207**	**45**	**73**
Gross Margin £/Forage Ha	**502**	**723**		
Gross Margin £/Forage Acre	203	293		

1. *System*: Finishing of dairy bred store cattle (as shown in previous margin – summer finishing cattle will have been winter stores and *vice versa*). Purchased / transferred in at 12 months old and finished over 7 months (210 days for summer finishing, 220 days winter finishing). Summer finishing takes place entirely at pasture whilst winter finishing is a housed system for the production period.
2. *Sales*: Finished sale liveweights of 598kg for summer finishing and 604kg for winter finishing. Sale price £1.97/kg in both systems.
3. *Purchases*: Purchase / transfer-in weight of 398kg (402kg for high) and 402kg (407kg high) for summer and winter finishing respectively. Cost in both cases £2.00/kg plus 1% mortality allowance.
4. *Concentrates*: Summer finishing 1.5kg/day (= 315kg); winter finishing, 3.5kg/day (=770kg) at £195 per tonne.
5. *Forage Costs*:

   Summer finishing based on 'Long Term Ley' in forage section (page 89) at £172/ha.

   Winter Finishing is housed. Uses 3.7 tonnes per head grass silage consumption. Silage production costs are full production costs (£22.87/t fresh wt. on page 89) so relevant overheads are included in this calculation. Similarly, bought in silage increases forage costs.

   This means that the two gross margins are not comparable as different levels of overheads are included in the calculation. Be sure what is included in the forage calculation when working out the costs.

Finishing of Suckler Bred Store Cattle **(per head)**

	Summer Finishing		*Winter Finishing*	
	Average	*High*	*Average*	*High*
	£	£	£	£
Finished Sales	1,130	1,198	1,063	1,104
Less Purchased Store (incl. mortality)	570	565	756	748
Output	**559**	**633**	**307**	**356**
Variable Costs:				
Concentrates	70	61	123	100
Vet & Med	13	12	21	19
Bedding	0	0	50	45
Miscellaneous	45	41	50	49
Variable Costs (ex. forage)	**128**	**113**	**244**	**213**
Gross Margin £/Head, (ex. Forage)	**431**	**520**	**63**	**142**
Stock per Ha.	3.00	3.25		
Forage Variable Costs	135	122	78	69
Gross Margin per Head	**296**	**398**	**-15**	**74**
Gross Margin £/Forage Ha	**888**	**1,295**		
Gross Margin £/Forage Acre	*360*	*524*		

1. *System*: Beef suckler progeny purchased / transferred in at 8 months old for summer finishing and 12 months old for winter finishing (summer finishing cattle will be from spring calving suckler cows, with winter finishers from autumn calving suckler cows). Summer finishers = 300 days in system, winter finishers = 180 days in system.
2. *Sales*: Summer finishing 595kg liveweight, winter finishing 560kg liveweight. Sale price of £1.90/kg in both systems.
3. *Purchase Price*: Summer and winter bought in at 280 and 371kg respectively, both at £2.00/kg and allowing 2% mortality for average and 1% for high performance.
4. *Concentrates*:

	Summer		***Winter***	
	Average	*High*	*Average*	*High*
Concentrates - kg/day	1.20	1.10	3.50	3.00
Concentrates - £/t	£195	£185	£195	£185
Total Concentrates Kg	360	330	630	540

5. *Forage Costs*:

Summer Finishing based on 'Long Term Ley' in forage section (page 89) at £172/ha.

Winter Finishing: Housed so uses 3.4 tonnes per head preserved forage. Silage production costs are full production costs (£22.87/t fresh weight on page 89) so relevant overheads are included in this calculation. Similarly, bought in silage increases forage costs.

This means that the two gross margins are not comparable as different levels of overheads are included in the calculation. Be sure what is included in the forage calculation when working out the costs.

Maize & Grass Silage Beef Finishing **(per Head Produced)**

System	*Dairy X Progeny*		*Suckler Progeny*	
Performance Level	Average	High	Average	High
	£	£	£	£
Finished Sales	1,196	1,264	1,226	1,340
Less Purchased Store (incl. mortality)	485	485	559	633
Output	**711**	**778**	**667**	**707**
Variable Costs:				
Concentrates	128	121	83	77
Vet & Med.	17	15	17	15
Misc Variable Costs	99	97	114	112
Variable Costs (ex. forage)	**244**	**233**	**214**	**205**
Gross Margin £/Head, (ex. Forage)	**467**	**545**	**453**	**502**
Forage Cost	88	79	82	74
Gross Margin per Head	**379**	**466**	**371**	**428**

1. *System*: An intensive finishing system utilising a housed forage-based system of grass silage and maize silage with heavy finished weights. Dairy cross progeny bought or transferred in at 6 months and suckler progeny at 8 months. Dairy-cross finishing period of 365 days and suckler progeny at 305 days. The gross margins are higher than in other finishing enterprises but overhead costs (fixed costs) will also be high in comparison.

	Dairy Cross		***Suckler Progeny***	
	Average	***High***	***Average***	***High***
Age at purchase	*6 months*	*6 months*	*8 months*	*8 months*
Days in System	365	365	305	305
DLWG Kg	1.10	1.20	1.20	1.30
Sale Weight - kg	647	683	646	706
Sale Price - £/kg	£1.85	£1.85	£1.90	£1.90
Purchase Weight - kg	245	245	280	309
Purchase Price - £/kg	£2.00	£2.00	£1.92	£1.92
Mortality - %	1%	1%	1%	1%
Concentrates				
Concentrates - kg/day	1.80	1.70	1.40	1.30
Concentrates - £/t	£195	£195	£195	£195

2. *Miscellaneous* Variable Costs: assumed to be proportionally higher than the store and suckler finishing enterprises shown previously. Assumed 8% premium for average performance and 5% for high performance.

3. *Forage Costs:*

Maize Cattle	***Dairy Cross***		***Suckler***	
per head	**Average**	**High**	**Average**	**High**
Tonnes Maize Silage	1.90	1.71	1.80	1.62
Total Silage Cost £/t	£24	£24	£24	£24
Tonnes Grass Silage	1.85	1.7	1.70	1.5
Total Silage Cost £/t	£23	£23	£23	£23
Total Per Cow	**£88**	**£79**	**£82**	**£74**
Total Silage T	3.75	3.38	3.50	3.15

The silage costs relate to the total operational cost of growing and harvesting the forage, but not the costs incurred in preparing/mixing rations as shown in page 89.

***Cereal Bull Beef* (per Head)**

	Continental Cross Holstein/Friesian Bulls		*Holstein Friesian Bulls*	
Performance Level	Average	High	Average	High
	£	£	£	£
Finished Sales	981	1027	831	901
Less Calf Purchase	286	284	71	71
Output	**695**	**743**	**760**	**830**
Variable Costs:				
Concentrates	429	415	429	415
Other Feed	21	19	21	19
Vet & Med	22	20	22	20
Bedding	57	57	57	57
Miscellaneous	48	48	48	48
Total Variable Costs	**576**	**559**	**576**	**559**
Gross Margin per Head	**118**	**183**	**183**	**271**

1. A traditional cereal based system for finishing cattle. Animals are housed throughout the production period and fed on a barley concentrate and straw based ration. Production period typically from 2 weeks to 14 months old. This system is highly exposed to swings in cereal commodity prices. A £10 per tonne feed price movement equates to a margin change of £22 per head.
2. *Sales:*

   Cont. cross bulls = average 530kg, high 555kg; average at £1.85/kg lwt;

   Holstein Friesian, average 475kg, high 515kg average, at £1.75/kg

   All year round production is assumed. Average slaughter age is 15 months, with killing out percentages ranging from 54% to 59%, with the better conformation continental cross bulls achieving higher percentages.
3. *Purchases:* £280 for continental cross male calves at 3 weeks of age plus mortality; £70 for dairy bulls plus mortality. Mortality, average 2%, high 1.5%.
4. *Concentrates:* £80 calf rearing (to 12 weeks inc. milk powder: see page 58) + finishing ration. Finishing ration: 17 parts barley @ £130 per tonne, 3 parts concentrate supplement at £195 per tonne; plus £17 per tonne milling and mixing cost. Total, £157 per tonne.

   Barley ration quantity; average 2,225kg, high 2,140kg (excluding calf feed to 12 weeks – see page 58).
5. *Bedding:* 0.9 tonnes at £63 per tonne

Veal

Veal consumption is low in the UK - a small fraction of the per capita consumption of France for example. Continental demand is mainly for white veal, produced in individual veal crates, a system that is illegal in the UK. There is no live calf export activity from the UK to the continent for veal production owing to animal welfare concerns and the risk of spreading Bovine Tb. There is some activity in UK 'welfare friendly' domestic veal production where calves are kept in groups in straw yards producing heavier calves with 'pink' meat known as 'Rose Veal'. This is a premium product and is considerably more expensive to produce than imported 'white veal'.

SHEEP

Spring Lambing Flocks

Lowland Spring Lambing per Ewe (selling lambs off grass)

Performance Level	Low	Average	High
Value of Lamb £/Lamb	*72*	*76*	*80*
	£/Ewe	**£/Ewe**	**£/Ewe**
Lamb Sales	93	114	135
Wool	2	2	2
Less Ewe and Ram Depreciation	20	20	20
Output	**74**	**95**	**117**
Variable Costs:			
Concentrate (Ewe and Lamb)	13	13	12
Vet & Med	8	9	10
Miscellaneous	15	15	15
Variable Costs (ex. forage)	**37**	**36**	**38**
Gross Margin £/Ewe, (ex. Forage)	**38**	**59**	**79**
Ewes with lambs per Ha.	8	10	11
Forage Variable Costs per Ewe	17	13	12
Gross Margin £/Ewe	**21**	**46**	**67**
Gross Margin £/Forage Ha (Acre)	**157**	**464**	**742**
	(64)	*(188)*	*(300)*

1. *Rearing Performance Data:*

Lambing Stats	Low	Average	High
Ewes in Lamb	92%	95%	97%
Lambing Percentage	160%	175%	190%
Lambs born per 100 ewes	147	166	184
Young Lamb Deaths	8%	6%	5%
Older Lamb Deaths	4.5%	4.0%	3.5%
Total Lamb Losses	13%	10%	9%
Lambs sold per 100 ewes put to ram	129	150	169

These performance figures are assumed for flocks of mature ewes, i.e. shearlings and older. Where ewe-lambs or mainly shearlings are included in flock performance adjustment needs to be made. The breed will have a large effect on performance data.

2. *Lamb Sales.* Prices for lambs sold for slaughter are based on the projection for the 2018 season. Average sale liveweight of 40kg, averaging £1.90/kg making £76 per average lamb

3. *Wool:* 2kg/ewe at £1.00/kg

4. *Depreciation:*

	Ewes	Ram	Per Ewe
Purchase Price - £	£150	£495	
Cull Price - £	£70	£85	
Animal Life (Years)	5.0	3.5	
Mortality	5%	5%	
Ewes per Ram		45	
Depreciation £/ewe	£17.50	£2.76	£20.26

5. *Concentrate Feeding*: Concentrate finishing of late season lambs has been common, but there has been a swing to sell as stores (for finishing on winter forage crops) rather than finish on high cost concentrates. Late season grass availability influences the store trade.

Feeding Schedule	Low	Average	High
Ewe Feed Kg	51	48	45
Ewe Feed £/t	£190	£190	£190
Ewe Feed £/Ewe	£10	£9	£9
Lamb Feed Kg/ Lamb	13	11	10
Lamb Feed £/t	£220	£220	£220
Lamb Feed £/Lamb	£2.86	£2.42	£2.20
Lamb Feed £/Ewe	£3.68	£3.62	£3.71
Total Feed Cost £/Ewe	**£13**	**£13**	**£12**

6. *Veterinary and Medicine*: includes allowance for wormer (ewes and lambs), vaccines, fly strike chemicals and foot treatments.

7. *Miscellaneous Costs*: include contract shearing @ £1.55/ewe, scanning £1.00/ewe and ewe and lamb tags £1.47/ewe (assuming slaughter batch tags are used), carcase disposal £0.74/ewe, straw £1.50/ewe, minerals and licks etc. £2.15/ewe, marketing, levy and transport £6.60/ewe.

8. *Forage Costs*: Based on Improved Permanent Pasture (£127/ha) refer to forage section, page 89. Only variable costs are included and therefore overhead costs of forage production need to be considered. Similarly, bought in grass keep and forage may increase the forage costs over those shown.

9. *Other Costs:*

   a. *Prices of Specialised Equipment*

Troughs (2.75 m)	£32 to £45
Racks (2 to 3 m)......................	£217 to £245
Foot Baths (3 m)	£100 to £180
Shearing Machines.................	£480 to £1,150
Lamb Creep Feeders	£380 to £800
Weigh Crate............................	£520 to £790
Mobile Handling System	£2,700 to £8,800

   b. *Fencing:* Approximately £6.20 per metre *for posts, sheep netting, 2 strands of barbed wired and labour inclusive. Refer to page 269.*

   c. *Labour*: see page 169.

Upland Spring Lambing per Ewe (selling lambs off grass)

Performance Level	Low	Average	High
Value of Lamb £/Lamb	*65*	*68*	*71*
	£/Ewe	**£/Ewe**	**£/Ewe**
Lamb Sales	77	97	112
Wool	2	2	2
Less Ewe and Ram Depreciation	18	18	18
Output	**61**	**80**	**96**
Variable Costs:			
Concentrate (Ewe and Lamb)	15	10	6
Vet & Med	8	9	10
Miscellaneous	15	15	15
Variable Costs (ex. forage)	**38**	**34**	**31**
Gross Margin £/Ewe, (ex. Forage)	**23**	**47**	**65**
Ewes with lambs per Ha.	4	9	10
Forage Variable Costs per Ewe	32	14	13
Gross Margin £/Ewe	**-9**	**33**	**52**
Gross Margin £/Forage Ha (Acre)	**-35**	**294**	**524**
	(-14)	*(119)*	*(212)*

1. *Rearing Performance Data:*

Lambing Stats	Low	Average	High
Ewes in Lamb	92%	95%	97%
Lambing Percentage	150%	170%	185%
Lambs born per 100 ewes	138	162	179
Young Lamb Deaths	9%	7%	7%
Older Lamb Deaths	5.0%	5.0%	5.0%
Total Lamb Losses	14%	12%	12%
Lambs sold per 100 ewes put to ram	119	142	158

These performance figures are assumed for flocks of mature ewes, i.e. shearlings and older. Where ewe lambs or mainly shearlings are included in flock performance adjustment needs to be made. The breed will obviously have a large effect on lambing percentage, liveweight gains and carcase grades.

2. *Lamb Prices.* Average market price of £1.80/kg liveweight (equivalent to £3.91/kg deadweight) has been assumed giving £68 per finished lamb at an average liveweight of 38kg. Performance variation is 5% each way caused by differences in weights, time of marketing and proportion sold finished or retained as stores.

3. *Wool:* Wool price assumed for upland flocks is £1.70 per ewe, based on a price of £1.00/kg at 1.7kg/ewe. Upland sheep wool is harsher than lowland which is softer and therefore dearer. Variations between breeds affect wool quality and ewe size affecting weight of wool produced.

4. *Depreciation*

	Ewes	Ram	Per Ewe
Purchase Price - £	£125	£490	
Cull Price - £	£55	£85	
Animal Life (Years)	5.0	3.5	
Mortality	5%	5%	
Ewes per Ram		45	
Depreciation £/ewe	£15	£3	£18

5. *Concentrate Feeding*: Concentrate finishing of late season lambs has been common, but there has been a swing to sell as stores (for finishing on winter forage crops) rather than finish on high cost concentrates. Late season grass availability influences the store trade.

Feeding Schedule	Low	Average	High
Ewe Feed Kg	59	40	24
Ewe Feed £/t	£210	£210	£210
Ewe Feed £/Ewe	£12	£8	£5
Lamb Feed Kg/ Lamb	10	6	2
Lamb Feed £/t	£230	£230	£230
Lamb Feed £/Lamb	£2.30	£1.38	£0.46
Lamb Feed £/Ewe	£2.73	£1.96	£0.73
Total Feed Cost £/Ewe	**£15**	**£10**	**£6**

6. *Veterinary and Medicine*: includes allowance for wormer (ewes and lambs), vaccines, fly strike chemicals and foot treatments.

7. *Miscellaneous Costs:* include contract shearing @ £1.58/ewe, scanning £1.00/ewe and ewe and lamb tags £1.47/ewe (assuming slaughter batch tags are used), carcase disposal £0.81/ewe, straw £1.40/ewe, minerals and licks etc. £1.65/ewe, marketing, levy and transport £6.60/ewe.

8. *Forage Costs:* Based on Improved Permanent Pasture (£127/ha) refer to forage section, page 89. Only variable costs are included and therefore overhead costs of forage production need to be considered. Similarly, bought in grass keep and forage may increase the forage costs over those shown here.

Rearing Ewe Lambs

Purchasing ewe lambs and rearing over winter & summer for breeding	
Sales:	£ Per Ewe Lamb Sold
Sale Price / Transfer Out Value	150
Wool	1
Culls for Meat, 3% at £72 per head	2
Less Purchase Price / Transfer In Value	95
Output per Ewe	**54**
Variable Costs:	
Concentrate	3
Vet and Med	6
Miscellaneous	10
Variable Costs (ex. forage)	**16**
Gross Margin £/Ewe Lamb, (ex. Forage)	**38**
Stocking Rate (Ewe lambs per forage Hectare	15.0
Forage Variable Costs (inc bought-in)	8
Gross Margin per Ewe	**29**
Gross Margin £/Forage Ha. (Ac.)	440 (178)

1. *System*: Involves rearing or purchasing ewe lambs for further breeding. Animals are purchased / transferred in late summer / autumn, grazed and outwintered, grazed on in the following summer before sale / transfer out in the autumn (i.e. 12 month system). The terminology for this system varies between regions; gimmers, thieves, shearlings and tegs all relate to the same age of female sheep.
2. *Sales*: wool, 1.4kg at £1.00/kg
3. *Purchase Price*: Assumes best quality ewe lambs are acquired at £92 per lamb than sold to market. Includes 4% mortality charge.
4. *Concentrate*: 14kg each at £200/tonne
5. *Veterinary and Medicine*: includes wormer, fly strike chemicals, vaccines and miscellaneous treatments.
6. *Miscellaneous Costs*: Shearing at £1.37/head, minerals at £1.65/head, carcase disposal at £0.32/head. Marketing and haulage costs are included at 3% sale price and £2 per lamb respectively, but not payable if for home use.
7. *Forage Costs:* Based on Improved Permanent Pasture (£1270/ha) refer to forage section, page 89. Only variable costs are included and therefore overhead costs of forage production need to be considered. Similarly, bought in grass keep and forage may increase the forage costs over those shown here.

Finishing Store Lambs

Purchasing store lambs and finishing late autumn & winter

Sales:	£ Per Lamb Finished	
Sale Price	86	
Less Purchase Price / Transfer In Value	64	
Losses	2	
Output per Lamb	**20**	
Variable Costs:		
Concentrates	3	
Vet and Med	3	
Miscellaneous	6	
Variable Costs (ex. forage)	**12**	
Gross Margin per Lamb, (Ex. Forage)	**7**	
Stocking Rate (lambs per forage Hectare	28	
Forage Variable Costs (inc bought-in)	4	
Gross Margin per Lamb	**3**	
Gross Margin £/Forage Ha. (Ac.)	92	(37)

1. *System:* lambs are batch bought in the autumn at or shortly after weaning in September or October, then drawn out and sold as they are ready in smaller groups from then through to March the following year.
2. *Sales:* Assumes 43kg liveweight @ £2.00/kg, a higher lamb price than other margins as out of season.
3. *Losses:* assumed at 4% of transfer price
4. *Concentrates:* 14kg per lamb @ £210 per tonne
5. *Veterinary and Medicine:* Allows for wormer and scab injection, clostridial vaccines and miscellaneous treatments.
6. *Miscellaneous:* Including transport, marketing, minerals, carcase disposal.
7. *Forage Costs:* Based on Low Input Permanent Pasture (£71/ha) and Stubble Turnips (£138/ha) refer to forage section, page 89. Only variable costs are included and therefore overhead costs of forage production need to be considered. Similarly, bought in grass keep and forage may increase the forage costs over those shown.
8. This is a gross margin covering only a few months of the year, but it is also worth remembering that the stubble turnips will be growing for 6 months. Fitting the enterprise into the other farm enterprises can add value to the business if carefully planned.

GRAZING AND REARING CHARGES: CATTLE AND SHEEP

Grazing charges vary greatly according to the quality of the pasture, access, fencing and infrastructure. Local supply and demand also affect the value of grazing charges. The following figures are estimated for 2017:

Summer Grazing (per head per week)

Store Cattle and in-calf heifers over 21 months, dry cows, and fattening bullocks over 18 months	£2.00 - £3.00
Heifers and Steers, 12-21 months	£2.00 - £3.00
6-12 months Cattle	£1.00 - £2.25
Cattle of mixed ages	£1.00 - £2.50
Ewes (with lambs)	£0.45 - £0.70

Winter Grazing (per head per week)

'Strong' Cattle *(including Bulk feed).*	£1.75 - £3.00
Heifers	£1.50 - £2.50
Sheep	£0.30 - £0.50

Note: the above figures assume the farmer on whose land the livestock are present does all the fencing. The livestock owner remains their keeper, else the land owner would become liable for all the livestock based cross compliance such as tagging. If the stock owner does the fencing, the figures may be much less. Prices vary on local demand.

Grass Keep

Most typically around £100-£175 per ha (£40-£70/acre), with the best £185-£275 per ha (£75-£110/acre) and lower quality keep making £62-£90 per ha (£25-£36/acre).

These figures are highly variable, especially between parts of the country and levels of local demand. Good fencing, electricity supply, mains water etc. add a premium to grass keep as does the quality of grassland and any licensor fertiliser applications. Grazing may be offered to livestock keepers at very little or no charge where the need for maintenance of grassland is the driving factor (e.g. amenity value, requirement to cross comply or meet agri-environment scheme agreements, value of cattle and sheep to 'clean-up' pasture or to provide beneficial mixed grazing). The length of grazing period offered will also influence the premium of grass keep (e.g. grazing until 30th September or until 31st December) as will permission to take a grass crop from the land (hay, haylage, silage).

The Nitrate Vulnerable Zone (NVZ) rules in England mean that demand for grass keep is high in some areas, especially where dairy enterprises are commonplace. The additional acreage helps some producers to keep within their livestock manure loading limit.

Winter Keep (Cattle per head per week)

Grazing + 9 kg hay and some straw	£9.50
Full winter housing in yards	£9.50 - £12.50
Calf bucket rearing for beef	£12.00 - £15.00

These figures would include bulk feed and straw. A typical rental for labour, buildings and maintenance diet would be £9.50 per head per week. These rates apply where feed to achieve maintenance plus some growth is supplied plus labour and buildings and bedding where applicable. A typical rental for labour, buildings and a maintenance diet would be £7.50 per head per week. In recent years the cost of bedding (usually straw) has influenced the final values of winter keeping cattle.

Heifer Rearing Charges

There have historically been two types of arrangement:

1. Farmer X sells calf to a Rearer at agreed price; the calf is then Rearer's responsibility and he pays for all expenses and bears any losses. Farmer X has first option on heifers, which he buys back two months before calving. Approximate price: £1,200 above cost of calf for Holstein Friesians. Rearer fetches calf; Farmer X supplies transport for heifer. *This system is now less common due to the increasing popularity and general transparency of option 2 below.*

2. Farmer X retains ownership of calf, but sends it to a specialist rearer. Approximate rearer charges range from £0.60 to £1.20 per head per day for winter rearing and £1.00 to £1.30 per head per day for summer rearing. Charges vary depending upon cattle, system and location. Newer agreements often include a fixed incentive payment to the Rearer if the cattle have met specification at the end of the rearing period. This is usually defined in terms of final liveweight and the level of in-calf heifers. A typical fixed fee incentive payment would be £50 per head.

   Usually the owner of the cattle is responsible for transport costs and the choice and cost of vaccine programmes. The cost of semen for artificial insemination of the heifers is also usually incurred by the owner and paid for over and above the standard rearing charge. The rearer is responsible for all standard rearing costs including for normal veterinary services and worming etc. and any animal losses over an agreed tolerance level. *Model agreements are available from industry associations and advisors.*

Contract rearing on behalf of a third party may appeal to some producers who wish to reduce borrowing exposure and / or lower capital investment in a business. A well laid out contract rearing arrangement will also provide greater cost and income clarity to both the rearer and owner and therefore reduce the risk exposure to both businesses. It also enables each business to focus and specialise to achieve optimum performance without being distracted by other enterprises. Biosecurity issues are becoming increasingly paramount where an agreement is set up. In many cases the owner of heifers will require exclusive occupancy of a rearer's farm without cattle owned by the rearer or others being present. The Bovine TB movement rules must be considered by parties entering into heifer rearing agreements including the need for pre-movement TB testing between holdings.

RED DEER

System (per 100 breeding hind)	*Breeding & Finishing*	*Breeding & Selling Stores*	*Deer Park*
Sales:	£	£	£
Stags	*14,256*	*6,750*	*8,360*
Hinds (for meat)	5,250	10,500	6,967
Hinds (for breeding)	9,450		
Less Breeding Stock Depreciation	3,200	3,200	2,325
Output	**25,756**	**14,050**	**13,002**
Variable Costs:			
Concentrate (Hinds)	1,080	312	960
Concentrate (Calves)	1,723		
Vet & Med	900	405	340
Miscellaneous	408	204	102
Variable Costs (ex. forage)	**4,111**	**921**	**1,402**
Gross Margin £/100 head	21,645	13,129	11,600
Hinds per Ha.	4.50	6.50	3.00
Forage Variable Costs	3,829	1,952	2,367
Gross Margin (Inc. Forage)	**17,816**	**11,177**	**9,233**
Gross Margin £/Ha	**802**	**727**	**277**
Gross Margin £/Acre	*325*	*294*	*112*

Assumptions	*Breeding & Finishing*		*Breeding & Selling Stores*		*Deer Park*	
Calves	***Hinds***	***Stags***	***Hinds***	***Stags***	***Hinds***	***Stags***
Deer Sale Weight - kg	50	60	£/head		50	55
Sale Price £/Kg	£5.00	£5.40	£250	£150	£3.80	£3.80
Breeding £/head	£450					
Animal Sales	42	44	42	45	37	40

Breeding Depreciation	Hinds	Stags	Hinds	Stags	Hinds	Stags
Purchase Price - £	£450	£1,500	£450	£1,500	£450	£1,500
Cull Price - £	£200	£500	£200	£500	£200	£1,000
Number Bought	8	1	8	1	8	0.75
Number Sold	7	1	7	1	7	1
£/100 head	**£2,200**	**£1,000**	**£2,200**	**£1,000**	**£2,200**	**£125**

1. *System: Lowland systems assumed. Replacements bought in.*
2. *Concentrates:* 4.5t per 100 breeding hinds for Breeding & Finishing systems and Deer Park; 1.3t per 100 breeding hinds for Breeding and Selling Store systems a cost of £240/t
3. *Forage costs*: Refer to forage section on Page 87. Breeding and Finishing system is based on Long Term Ley variable costs and includes hind plus finishing progeny; Selling Stores is based on Improved Permanent Pasture costs; Deer Park forage costs are based on Low Input Pasture.

4. *Price*: The venison price reflects projected sales for 2018 to wholesale buyers and the higher prices being paid for farmed venison by supermarkets. Higher prices will be obtained for direct sales to consumers (e.g. farm shops and farmers' markets) and caterers, but extra costs will normally be incurred.

Finishing Stag Calves

Per 100 Stags	*Average*	*High*
	£	£
Stag Sales	28,958	31,590
Less Purchased Store (incl. mortality)	15,000	15,000
Output	**13,958**	**16,590**
Variable Costs:		
Concentrates	2,210	1,920
Vet & Med	306	306
Miscellaneous	498	498
Variable Costs (ex. forage)	**3,014**	**2,724**
Gross Margin (ex. Forage)	**10,944**	**13,867**
Stock per Ha.	11	13
Forage Variable Costs	1,567	1,326
Gross Margin per 100 Head	**9,377**	**12,541**
Gross Margin £/Forage Ha	**1,032**	**1,630**
Gross Margin £/Forage Acre	*418*	*660*

	Finishing Stags	
Assumptions	*Average*	*High*
Deer Sale Weight - kg	55	60
Sale Price - £/kg	£5.40	£5.40
Animal Sales	98	98

Sources of further information: The British Deer Farms and Parks Association; Venison Advisory Service Ltd

Acknowledgement: Thanks to – Dr. John Fletcher and the Venison Advisory Service Ltd

HORSES: LIVERY

The horse industry is now reported to be the second biggest employer in the rural economy. Prior to the economic downturn it was also one of the fastest growing. Over the last 5 years the horse population has declined from its peak. Horse owners have tended to adopt spending reduction behaviours – looking for cheaper services such as DIY instead of part livery. Even so a premium segment of the market also persists, with owners of high disposable income seeking high quality services and facilities. Although there are other equine enterprises that farm businesses can operate, by far the most common is providing accommodation for horses; i.e. livery. There are many different forms of livery and the charges, therefore, vary widely also. This is apart from the effects of local supply and demand, which can lead to large price differences from one area to another. However, three fairly standard forms are offered on farms:

Grass Livery. Keep at grass, preferably with shelter, water supply and secure area to keep tack and store feed. Some grass livery will provide an exercise arena and off-road riding. Charges range from £20-£100 per week; average £45.

DIY Livery. The owner still has full care of the horse but has the facilities of a stable, grazing, and in some cases an all-weather exercise arena. The owner is responsible for mucking out, turning out, grooming, exercising and all vet./med. care and the cost of all feed and bedding. Charges range from £35-£110 per week; average £55.

Part Livery. As the above, except that the yard manager is responsible for certain tasks, such as turning out and feeding. Charges range from £50-£125.

In addition there is *Full Livery.* The yard supplies a complete service to the horse owner including tasks such as grooming and exercise. Services provided by the yard may be fitted to the needs of a horse/owner. Few farm-based liveries would offer such a high level of management unless there is equine expertise in the family. Full livery charges average £125 per week; with a range of £65-£185.

The above are only guidelines. There is a wide variation both within, and between regions.

Other Costs:

Grazing. Variable costs will average some £65 per horse per year. Average stocking rates are 0·8 ha (2 acres) for the first horse and 0·4 ha (1 acre) for each horse after if significant grazing time is allowed.

Hay. Average price £4.00 per conventional bale (approximately 20kg) (range £2.5-£6.00), depending on the season. It has to be good quality. Average consumption is one to two bales per horse per week; less in the summer depending on the grass quality/quantity and the work of the horse. Some horses now have haylage; more expensive, dust free and higher fibre and energy/protein levels; less required per head (£6.50 - £8.50/bale)

Concentrate Feed. Can range from almost nil to 3.0-4.0kg per day depending, amongst other factors, on breed, size and intensity of work. Compound feed 35 to 65p per kg.

Bedding. Averages around £12 per stabled horse per week, with some horses stabled year round and others having significant turnout in the summer, which reduces bedding cost. Typical cost £300-£400 per year. Straw might cost only half as much; however, more expensive, but preferable, alternatives (such as wood shavings, shredded paper and hemp fibre) are now increasingly being used.

Vet. and Med. Averages approximately £200 per horse per year. Some yards include worming of the horse in the livery cost.

Rates. Livery is a non-agricultural use, and therefore any buildings being used for the enterprise are liable to business rates.

The supply of livery yards appears to be stabilising. Filling a yard has become more difficult in recent years, with a good reputation paramount. The level of service and facilities expected by customers has increased – caring for owners is usually more challenging than caring for their horses! There is a trend towards greater professionalism in the running and management of livery yards. Livery contracts should be exchanged showing clearly the responsibilities of each party. Comprehensive third party insurance is also important.

To be successful, a livery enterprise needs higher quality facilities than farm livestock. To the owner the horse can be anything from a highly trained athlete to a family pet. Horses are expensive: even modest quality horses cost between £1,500 and £3,000. Good customer relations and an effective security system (including burglar and fire alarms) are crucial to success, as is good market research and effective advertising. Ensuring prompt payment of livery fees is another issue, this can be helped by payment in advance or by direct debit.

A full livery yard will require stables, a secure room to store tack, a vermin-proof hard feed store, storage for hay and bedding, a muck heap, a riding arena and parking provision with room for horse boxes. Planning permission is required for the conversion of an existing building to stabling or the erection of new, purpose-built stables. Permission is also required for construction of an all-weather arena used for training horses and exercising them in bad weather. Hay and straw should be stored away from the stables and downwind of them to minimise the fire risk. A hard standing area with a water supply and good drainage should be provided for grooming and washing down the horses.

Good ventilation in the stables is crucial as horses are prone to respiratory diseases caused by spores and dust. Provision should be made for owners to soak hay in clean water before feeding it, to reduce respiratory problems.

Fences must be sound and free of protruding nails, wire etc. Ideally fields should be fenced using post and rail, but this is expensive. Barbed wire should be avoided wherever possible or should be 'protected' with an offset electrified fence. Fields should be divided into smaller paddocks to reduce the possibility of fighting between incompatible horses and to separate mares and geldings. Paddocks may be divided using two or more strands of electrified tape or rope but wire is not advisable as it is not easily visible to the horse.

Off-road riding opportunities on the farm are a real asset. The farmer may provide riding trails, a jumping paddock, or a cross country course. An all-weather ménage for exercising horses, possibly with floodlighting, is highly desirable, and some livery yards have horse walkers too. Good facilities can be rented out to individuals or organisations such as pony clubs. It is sometimes possible to link up with nearby farms to increase the length of riding tracks available.

Construction Costs. The cost of conversion of existing buildings will depend on their quality; prefabricated hardwood and steel internal stable partitions can be purchased from upwards of £1,500 per stable, depending on size and specification. Free standing timber stables cost between £2,000 and £3,000 (plus base), depending on size and quality. As horses are fairly destructive animals (they both kick and chew) better quality stables will often prove more economic in the long run. All weather arenas (20 metres by 40 metres) cost between £20,000 and £50,000; construction is a specialist job as good drainage is essential; a badly constructed arena is worthless.

Contact: Further financial information on horse enterprises, including riding schools and equestrian centres, is available in the 'Equine Business Guide', 6th Edition, 2015, edited by Michael Haverty in conjunction with Richard Bacon (Warwickshire College) www.abcbooks.co.uk

WILD BOAR

Wild Boar is farmed in the UK on about 50 farms, with a population of 1,750 sows. Wild Boar come under the Dangerous Wild Animals Act and farms must be licensed by the Local Authority. The cost of a licence varies greatly between authorities and ranges anywhere from £150 - £700 plus veterinary inspection fees. These are annual costs following a farm inspection with renewal fees at a lower rate. Enclosures must be secure with strong fencing: at least 1.8 metres high and most authorities require 30-80cm below ground plus an additional strand of electric fence inside the main fence. The minimum cost of fencing using approved contractors is £13.50 per metre plus the hire of a digger.

Wild Boar live outdoors in groups of up to 10 sows per boar. Large arcs are suitable for a group of gestating sows, or sows running with maturing boarlets. About a hectare would be needed for 5 sows and a boar. They forage but need feeding concentrate and root crops. Gilts mature at 18 months. Farmed sows can give two litters in most years. Young sows produce 2 to 3 boarlets and mature sows 6 to 9. A well-run enterprise should average 7 boarlets per sow per year raised to maturity. Wild boar can live from 12 to 15 years, but in a commercial herd the sows are usually culled at 7 to 8 years. Wild boar take 9 to 18 months to reach a slaughter weight of 75-85 kg. This produces a 45-50 kg carcase.

Capital costs include housing and fencing at £4,200 per hectare (*£1,700 per acre*); pure-bred adult boar £500-£700; pure-bred in pig sow £350-£500. Labour requirements are low, owing to the 'hands off' nature of wild boar management. One person should manage a herd of 30-40 sows plus fatteners. There is no organised marketing system and producers develop their own outlets. There are some wholesale butchers and game dealers who will take whole carcases, but many producers organise their own processing and arrange their own retailing.

Performance Level	Low	Average	High
Finished Boarlets per Sow per Year	6	7	9
Finished Carcase Weight (over 15 months)	45	45	50
Price per kg deadweight	5.00	6.00	7.00
Sales:		£	
Meat sales per Sow per Year	1,350	1,890	3,150
Less Depreciation per Sow per Year	55	55	55
Output per Sow	**1,295**	**1,835**	**3,095**
Variable Costs:			
Concentrates sow		300	
fatteners (0.15t each at £250/t)	270	263	338
Other Feed		180	
Bedding		40	
Vet, Med and Licence		100	
Miscellaneous (inc. Water and Electricity)		30	
Total Variable Costs per Sow	**920**	**913**	**988**
Gross Margin per Sow	**375**	**922**	**2,107**
Gross Margin per Hectare (5 Sows/Ha)	**1,875**	**4,612**	**10,537**

1. *Depreciation:* Cost of sow £350, cull value £200, active herd life 5 years, plus share of boar and 5% mortality.
2. *Concentrates:* Sow includes share of boar. Sow 1.1t at £250/t. Fatteners 0.15t (0.18t for low) at £250/t.
3. *Other feed:* Includes bought-in waste vegetables, these are necessary for wild boar.

GOAT DAIRYING

Performance Level	Low	Average	High
Milk Yield (litres) per Goat	700	900	1,100
Sales:	£	£	£
Milk Value	420	540	660
Value of Kids	2.8	3.6	3.6
Less Livestock Depreciation	52	52	52
Output per doe	**370**	**491**	**611**
Variable Costs:			
Concentrates	105	153	209
Miscellaneous (inc. Vet and Med)	75	75	75
Total Variable Costs	**180**	**228**	**284**
Gross Margin per Doe, before Forage	**190**	**263**	**327**
Forage Variable Costs (Zero Grazed)	18	24	29
Gross Margin per Doe	**172**	**239**	**298**

1. *Yield:* Per 300 day lactation, kidding each year. Autumn kidders tend to yield less.
2. *Price:* 60p per litre; 55p to 65p (+) with the higher prices being in the winter months (November to February) and the lower end of the range in the summer. 12.5% solids delivered.
3. *Kid(s):* Prolificacy relates to age, breed, seasonality and feed level. Assumptions: low 140%; average and high 180%. There is very little trade in kids for meat (£2 per kid assumed).
4. *Culls and Replacements:* Replacements does at £250-300/head, bucks at £400-600/head; culls £35 to £45, average productive life 4.5 – 5 years. Bucks: 1 per 40-50 does. Does normally mate in autumn; gestation 150 days; young goats can be mated from 6 months.
5. *Concentrates:* Average 0.85kg concentrate per litre (higher for 900 litre producers), at £200 per tonne.
6. *Forage:* Average 0.5 kg DM forage per litre at £102 per tonne DM plus 20% wastage (Refer to Forage Section page 89). Goats can be grazed but are normally storage fed to avoid problems with worms, fencing, milk taints and pneumonia. Farmers able to produce maize silage will have a better forage conversion ratio.
7. *Miscellaneous:* Bedding £30, vet and med. £25 (includes treatment for out-of-season breeding, vaccination against Johnes), sundries £20.
8. *Labour:* 1 full-time person per 150 to 200 goats, dependent on technology employed.
9. *Markets:* Herd sizes in the UK range from 50 to 4,000 milking does. Average herd size is growing as established producers expand. Successful businesses have been built on producer processing and retailing, as bulk purchasers of goats' milk are few and far between. Prolificacy and technical improvements allow higher annual growth than the market and there is a cycle in milk and stock prices.

SHEEP DAIRYING

Performance Level	Low	Average	High
Milk Yield (litres per ewe per year)	150	375	450
Sales:	£	£	£
Milk Value at £1.15 /l	173	431	518
Value of Lambs	70	70	70
Wool	2	2	2
Less Livestock Depreciation (Inc. mort)	23	23	23
Output per Ewe	**222**	**480**	**567**
Variable Costs:			
Concentrates		210	
Miscellaneous (inc. Vet and Med)		25	
Total Variable Costs (excluding forage)		**235**	
Gross Margin per Ewe, (Exc. Forage)	**-13**	**245**	**332**
Stocking Rate (Ewes per Ha)	10	11	12
Forage Variable Costs	17	16	14
Gross Margin per Ewe	**-31**	**230**	**317**
Gross Margin per Hectare	**-306**	**2,527**	**3,807**

1. *Price*: 115p per litre at farm gate (range from 100p-120p per litre).
2. *Lambing %:* 175%. Assume a 300 Friesland ewe flock. Retain 60 ewe lambs for flock replacements. Sell 390 finished lambs reared from 2 days old (inc. 15% mortality) at £40. If meat-type terminal sires used then cross-bred lamb values increase to £65.
3. *Cull ewes:* Assumed 20% culled at £50 per head (average, including mortality).
4. *Concentrates:* Milking ewes: 200 days at 1.5 kg/head/day, 100 days at 0.5 kg/head/day; cost £200-£250/tonne. Ewe lamb replacements and artificially reared finished lambs at £75/head.
5. *Forage costs:* Quality silage: 1 tonne per milking ewe (or hay equivalent). Grazing: early grass in March/April; good grazing on leys or pasture; similar for dry stock and lambs. For details on *forage* refer to page 89.

   Fixed Costs per Ewe: Labour (paid) £90; Power and Machinery £33; Property Costs £17; Other £15; Total, excluding Finance and Rent, £155.

   Capital Costs of Equipment: Complete milking unit for 300 ewes (including yokes, bulk tank, dairy equipment, installation): £15,000-£30,000. A small 50 ewe unit can be put together for £10,000-£12,000. Any building works would be additional to the above costs.

Acknowledgements: thanks to – Mr. Anthony Hyde, and the British Sheep Dairying Association.

ANGORA GOATS

Angora goats produce mohair; angora rabbits produce angora; cashgora is produced by angora cross dairy goats; cashmere is produced by improved feral goats (valuable 'down' has to be separated from guard hairs; thus, with cashmere production, 'yield of down' must not be confused with 'weight of clip' as percentage down is low and can vary widely). Goat meat is sometimes called 'chevon'.

The UK Angora goat population is about 1,100 animals and produce an annual clip of about 6 tonnes. There is strong demand for angora goats from small holders and smaller farmers which is buoying stock values. The figures here are for a commercial enterprise. For semi-commercial or hobby enterprises, different criteria apply; does retained longer, mortality rates lower, doe/buck ratio different.

Performance:	Per Doe
Kids per Doe per Year	1.4
Fibre: Doe/Buck, 2 clips, 3 & 4kg/clip respectively	6.3 kg
Kids (1.4), first and second clips	4.6 kg
Wethers/Replacement Does (0.9), third clip	3.2 kg
Fibre Sales per doe:	£
Doe/Buck: 6.3kg @ £12.50/kg	79.0
Kids: 4.6kg @ £14.4/kg	66.4
Wethers/Replacements: 3.2kg @ £13.0/kg	41.0
Stock Sales:	
0.5 female kids sold for breeding @ £150 each	75.0
Wethers: 0.7 males sold for meat @ £40 each	28.0
Culls: 0.14 does @ £40 each	5.8
Skin Sales:	8.4
Less Replacements buck only	2.6
Output per Doe	**301.0**
Variable Costs:	
Concentrates	51.1
Vet and Med	12.0
Miscellaneous	20.0
Total Variable Costs per Doe	**83.1**
Gross Margin per Doe before Forage Costs	**217.9**
Forage Variable Costs	35.9
Gross Margin per Doe	**182.0**
Gross Margin per Forage hectare	873.4
Gross Margin per Forage acre	354

The 2017 mohair world price has been buoyant but is subject to fluctuations due to political uncertainty in South Africa affecting the Rand and in Britain due to Brexit. There is a world shortage of mohair and markets are volatile. The figures used in the calculations are based on prices in 2017. The producers' co-operative, British Mohair Marketing, organises a national collection and sale of mohair. Between 2010 and 2016 the entire clip was exported to South Africa where it was graded and sold by Cape Mohair auctions. However, in 2017, the clip was sold in the UK thus saving on considerable shipping costs. Some of the UK annual clip is processed for other enterprises in the UK and for hand spinning where higher prices can be achieved.

Angora goats require more management than sheep. Fencing requirements are similar but housing costs higher. Margins are sensitive to the value and number of breeding stock sold, yield and value of fibre, kidding percentage and meat values. There is a market for meat from older animals but no reliable market has yet been developed specifically for younger animals. Angoras are usually more successful as a subsidiary enterprise on a farm rather than a stand-alone operation.

1. 1.9 kids born alive per doe mated; 2% mortality to each clip. Of 0.9 surviving doe kids, the majority (0.6) are sold for breeding, the remainder (0.3) are retained for replacements. Culls (0.15) and casualties equal replacements (unless the flock size is changing). Progeny are sold after 2 clips for breeding or after 3 clips for meat. Stock may be retained for further shearing. This has become more common, as the demand for breeding stock is small, fibre quality has improved and there is little market for meat. There is increasing demand for wethers from hobbyist spinners.
2. The data for Breeding Does includes output and inputs for breeding bucks. Assumes 25 does to one buck.
3. Angora goats are usually clipped twice a year. Yield increases over first six clips, but quality decreases with age. Prices are dependent on fashion. World market is dominated by South Africa and Texas. Demand and prices are highest for the high quality kid fibre <25 microns in diameter.

   The following yields and prices have been used:-

   Clip 1 = 1.2 kg at £15.00 per kg; clip 2 = 2.1 kg at £14.00 per kg; clip 3 = 3.5 kg at £13.00 per kg. Adult doe: 3.0 kg, adult buck 4.0 kg at £12.50 per kg.

   British Mohair Marketing arranges a collection once a year, currently in September. Membership of BMM costs £30 and there is a handling/marketing levy of £1.10/kg. (Some producers process and use the fibre themselves or sell to local spinners. Commercial processing costs are significant: combing about £6.50 per kg and spinning about £40 per kg).
4. *Stock sales.* Breeding stock in commercial flocks are culled after seven years on average. Subsequent shearing stock culled after a further 4 clips. Value of all cull stock: £40 each. Depending on quality, the skin can be worth £10 before curing or up to £150 after curing. Replacement costs: does, £250; bucks, £450. Shearing stock, £20 (as transfer from breeding enterprise). Show quality stock command a premium.
5. *Skin Sales:* From cull does and males sold for meat @ £10.00
6. *Concentrates.* Quantities: Kids - 50 kg to clip 2, 15 kg to clip 3; Adults - breeding adults 90 kg per year, shearlings 40 kg per year.
7. *Veterinary* costs can be high and include vaccinations, worming & foot trimming. Membership of disease control schemes (MV/CAE) or Scrapie monitoring is extra.
8. *Miscellaneous* costs include £2.50 to £3.50 per shearing per head (it may be more) and bedding materials.
9. *Forage:* 4.8 does per hectare at £120 per hectare (grass), refer to *forage* on page 89.

Contact: *British Angora Goat Society*: www.britishangoragoats.org.uk British Mohair Marketing: www.mohairmarketing.org.uk

Acknowledgements: thanks to - Stephen Whitley, Corrymoor Angoras, Stockland,

OSTRICHES

Introduction

Ostrich has been produced in the UK for many years. Production is limited to a few small individual farms, selling most meat through farmers' markets and restaurants. There is minimal processing infrastructure in the UK. Slaughter is carried out under contract in dedicated ostrich plants and red meat slaughter plants with a ratite (flightless bird) license. Ostriches are produced primarily for meat, with their skins (for leather), fat and feathers also providing revenue potential. Skins are generally sold in minimum numbers of 200 so it can require long-term storage to build up sufficient numbers.

Adult breeding stock are normally kept in trios of one male and two females, but pairs and colonies are not unusual. A trio requires about 0.2 ha (0.5 acre) well drained land and must be able to run. A stout hedge or smooth wire fence of 1.7 metres high should surround the enclosure. Adult birds need shelter from wind and rain, and a dry floor on which to sleep. Domesticated ostrich are generally docile and easily handled. There are two systems costed here, the production of chicks from trios, and fattening the chicks.

Production

Laying Bird Trios

Performance Level	Low	Medium	High
Eggs – *per hen per year*	45	60	70
Hatching - %	65%	75%	85%
Surviving Chicks - %	50%	70%	85%
Total Chicks per hen	15	32	51
Financial Data per Trio			
Sales:			
Chicks Per Year	29	63	101
Chick Income	459	989	1,588
Output per Trio	**459**	**989**	**1,588**
Variable Costs:			
Concentrates	529	736	851
Miscellaneious	35	35	35
Bird Depreciation	86	86	86
Total Variable Costs	**650**	**857**	**972**
Gross Margin per Trio	**-190**	**132**	**616**
Stocking Rate 5 Trios per hectare			
Gross Margin per Ha	**-952**	**662**	**3,082**

Notes:

1. *Chick Income:* Chicks sold out at £15.70 per head
2. *Concentrate feed:* £230/tonne. Low production birds eat 2.4 tonnes per trio, average = 3.2 and high production birds 3.7 tonnes/trio
3. *Miscellaneous:* includes vet & med., forage etc.
4. *Bird Depreciation costs:* replacement for a trio £1,500 over 15 year's productivity less £215 cull value

Meat is the highest value, especially if marketed into the restaurant sector. This clearly requires marketing expertise. Doubling meat yields and halving the time to reach slaughter transforms the economics as is shown below. Many systems involve a high cost building and fencing layout which should be taken into consideration with the economics of the gross margins shown here.

Slaughter Birds

Performance Level	Low	Average	High
Days to Slaughter	425	300	220
Sales:	£	£	£
Meat:	300	350	400
Value of Skin/hide	54	54	54
Less Day Old Chick	16	16	16
Output per Bird	**338**	**388**	**438**
Variable Costs:			
Concentrates	181	174	101
Other Rearing Costs	110	91	60
Slaughter, Processing etc.	79	79	79
Marketing	6	6	6
Total Variable Costs	**375**	**350**	**245**
Gross Margin per Bird	**-37**	**38**	**193**
Gross Margin per year per bird	**-32**	**47**	**320**
Stocking Rate 5 birds per hectare			
Gross Margin per Ha	**-158**	**234**	**1,601**

Notes:

1. *Meat:* £10/kg, 30kg, 35kg and 40kg meat for low to high performance levels.
2. *Chicks* bought in at £15.70 each (see schedule above) but varies from £10 to £25
3. *Concentrates:* Price of feed rises as performance rises (£230, £320 and £360/t) but consumption per bird falls from 2kg/day to 1.12kg/day.
4. *Other Costs:* includes depreciation of site, vet. & med. and miscellaneous

Acknowledgement: Thanks to British Domesticated Ostrich Association BDOA

CAMELIDS

Llamas and alpacas are part of the South American Camelid family. Originally they all came from Central America. Camelids are herd animals and should not be kept in isolation but will live happily with other animals. They are usually kept as pets but do have some commercial value. Llama and Alpaca trekking is becoming an increasingly popular leisure and tourist attraction with rates of approximately £20 per Camelid-hour achievable in suitable locations.

Llamas

The llama is the largest of the Camelids, weighing up to 180kg (400lbs) and standing 1.25m (4ft) at shoulder height. Llamas are strong animals traditionally used as pack animals and kept in the UK for trekking or pets. They have a life span of 15-20 years. They produce offspring for 10-15 years.

Llamas can be kept at stocking rates of 10-12/ha (4-5/acre). They are generally hardy animals but benefit from an open fronted shelter. They eat grass and hay, with occasional supplements. They can be bought from a few hundred pounds, similar to Alpacas.

Alpacas

Alpacas are smaller with a shoulder height of 1m (3ft) and weigh around 70kg (155lb). They produce an outstanding quality fleece. Their fibres are very fine and exceptionally strong. An annual shearing produces an average fleece of 0.7 to 5kg. The saddle or prime fleece part of the shearing will, when skirted (primary clean), sell to trade processors for;

- Baby Alpaca £8 per kg coloured, £12/kg white (21 micron or below)
- Fine Alpaca £5 per kg coloured, £8 per kg white (22-26 micron)
- Coarse Alpaca £0.40 - £1.00 per kg (27+ micron)
- Retail prices are substantially higher, typically £16-35 per kg.
- Processing costs are typically around £50 - £100 per kilo to process raw fibre to Yarn which then sells for around £12 to £15 per 100g
- The value of coloured wool is rising as natural, undyed fibre is increasingly popular. High quality black or grey fibre can be as valuable as clean white fibre.

Alpacas require shearing annually with Huacaya (95% of UK alpacas) having a crimpy staple style suitable mostly for knitting yarns and Suri with longer curly locks like a Wensleydale sheep suitable for most woven cloth and some knitting.

Alpacas should be kept at 10–15 per hectare (4-6/acre). They are hardy animals well suited to the UK climate, but require shelter. They graze all year, with additional hay and a daily mineral supplement. Their feed and maintenance costs are similar to that of lowland sheep. They don't suffer from foot rot and are less likely to be fly struck as they are clean under the tail and require no tail trimming. Routine tasks include trimming of toenails every couple of months and body scoring to assess condition. In general Camelids are affected by similar parasites as sheep and are treated under the cascade system by vets – no drugs are licensed for camelids in the UK.

An alpaca can cost anything from £200 for non-breeding stock and £500 to £10,000 for female breeding stock. High quality stud males can be substantially higher but in order to improve the quality of offspring many breeders buy/sell stud services. Breeding males are therefore usually hired. Geldings/Wethers will typically cost between £200 and £700 depending on colour, quality and other factors. Price on all animals will vary according to genetics, age, fertility, fibre quality and colour. The alpaca gestation period is 11-12 months giving rise to one offspring (or Cria).

The earning potential of an Alpaca is dictated by the quality of its fleece. The UK alpaca meat market is small and is generally associated with other on-farm meat products. Typical terminal prices are £60-£75 per live animal. Animals with low quality fleeces may have a value as pets, flock guards or tourist attractions. Alpaca fleece is a luxury fibre thus only the highest quality fleeces and stock command good prices.

Breeding and Fleece Production (per alpaca)

Performance Level	Average	High
	£	£
Fleece Weight (Kg)	2.00	3.00
Fleece Sales	14	27
Progeny Sales	371	421
Less Depreciation and Purchases	239	239
Output	**146**	**209**
Variable Costs:		
Feed Supplement Costs	40	60
Vet & Med	25	25
Shearing Costs	15	20
Miscellaneious Costs	16	16
Total Variable Costs (excl. forage)	**96**	**121**
Gross Margin per Alpaca, before deducting Forage Variable Costs	50	88
Forage Variable Costs	12	8
Purchased Hay	48	48
Gross Margin per Alpaca	**-10**	**32**
Alpcas per hectare	10 (4.1)	15 (6.1)
Gross Margin per Forage Hectare (Acre)	**-97** *(-39)*	**473** *(191)*

Notes:

1. *Fleece Sales:* Average performance fleece price £7.00/ kg. High performance fleece price £9.00/ kg.
2. *Progeny Sales:* Non breeding stock sold at £250/head, breeding geldings sold at £750/head, 25% breeding stock at average performance level, 35% at high performance level.
3. *Feed Costs:* variations around 155-230g/day at 70p/kg.
4. *Bulk Feed:* 1 small hay bale per month

Acknowledgement: Thanks to British Alpaca Society

GRAZING LIVESTOCK UNITS (GLU)

Dairy cows	1.00
Beef cows (excl. calf)	0.75
Heifers in calf (rearing)	0.80
Bulls	0.65
Other cattle (excl. intensive beef):	
0-1 year old	0.34
1-2 years old	0.65
2 years old and over	0.80
Lowland ewes	0.11
Upland ewes	0.08
Hill / LFA ewes	0.06
Breeding ewe hoggets:	
½ to 1 year	0.06
Other sheep, over 1 year	0.08
Store lambs, under 1 year	0.04
Rams	0.08
Breeding sows	0.44
Gilts in pig	0.20
Maiden gilts	0.18
Boars	0.35
Other pigs	0.17
Cocks, hens, pullets in lay	0.017
Pullets, 1 week to point of lay.	0.003
Broilers	0.0017
Other table chicken	0.004
Turkeys	0.005
Ducks, geese, other poultry	0.003
Horses	0.80
Breeding nanny goats	0.16
Other goats	0.11

Source: as advised by DEFRA for the Farm Business Survey.

1. *Total livestock units on a farm* should be calculated by multiplying the above ratios by the monthly livestock numbers averaged over the whole year.
2. *The ratios are based on feed requirements*. Strictly speaking, when calculating stocking density, allowances should also be made for differences in output (e.g. milk yield per cow or liveweight gain per head), breed (e.g. Friesians v. Jerseys) and quantities of non-forage feed consumed.

FORAGE VARIABLE COSTS

Grassland	1-2 year Ley	Intensive 3-5 year Ley	Long Term Ley	Improved Permanent Pasture	Low Input Pasture
Yield t/ha *(ac)*	50 *(20)*	47 *(19)*	42 *(17)*	35 *(14)*	25 *(10)*
Years Ley	2	4	7	-	-
Kg/ha *(units/acre)*					
N	*250 (199)*	*200 (159)*	*150 (120)*	*100 (80)*	*50 (40)*
P	*35 (28)*	*33 (26)*	*29 (23)*	*25 (20)*	*18 (14)*
K	*120 (96)*	*113 (90)*	*101 (80)*	*84 (67)*	*60 (48)*
Costs £/ha *(£/ac)*					
Seed *per year*	72 (29)	36 (14)	23 (9)	16 (6)	3 (1)
Fertiliser	204 (83)	173 (70)	139 (56)	102 (42)	62 (25)
Sprays	18 (7)	14 (6)	11 (4)	8 (3)	6 (3)
Total £/ha/Yr	294 (119)	223 (90)	172 (70)	127 (51)	71 (29)
cost £/t fresh weight	5.9	4.7	4.1	3.6	2.8

Other Forages	Maize	Clover Ley	Kale	Swedes
Yield t/ha (t/acre)	40 *(16)*	40 (16)	45 (18)	70 (28)
Seed	178 (72)	29 (12)	57 (23)	175 (71)
Fertiliser	90 (36)	34 (14)	115 (47)	86 (35)
Sprays	52 (21)	18.7 (8)	52 (21)	56 (23)
Total £/ha (£/ac)	320 (130)	83 (33)	224 (91)	317 (128)
Cost £/t fresh weight	8.00	2.06	4.99	4.53

	Fodder Beet	Forage Rape	Maincrop Turnips	Stubble Turnips
Yield t/ha (t/acre)	70 (28)	35 (14)	65 (26)	35 (14)
Seed	135 (55)	30 (12)	58 (23)	19 (8)
Fertiliser	151 (61)	83 (34)	118 (48)	90 (37)
Sprays	166 (67)	27 (11)	55 (22)	29 (12)
Total £/ha (£/ac)	452 (183)	139 (56)	230 (93)	138 (56)
Cost £/t fresh weight	6.46	3.98	3.54	3.94

Forage Notes

1. *Seed costs:* vary according to the proportion of permanent pasture and length of leys.
2. *Fertiliser* is assumed to come partially from manure as well as bagged fertiliser. It is often less on permanent pasture, depending on management style which also affects stocking rates and productive levels per animal.
3. *Contract work* on maize, silage and cultivations: Refer to Page 194.
4. *Labour:* forage and conservation labour, pages 169
5. *Conservation machinery:* page 187.
6. *Standing maize* crops are typically sold for £750 to £920/ha (£300-370/acre) but can be over £1,000/ha (£400/acre), depending on the potential yield of the crop and local supply and demand which has become volatile with local demand from anaerobic digestion plants.
7. An appropriate combination of these forage gross margins is used to calculate the forage costs of all the grazing livestock margins throughout the book. In fact, for simplicity, only the grass (appropriate combination of all 5 types), maize and stubble turnips are used. Each livestock gross margin explains which forage crops are used.
8. *Plastic wrap* for baled silage = £1.75/ round bale (120cm), £4.85 to £5.40 for contract wrapping (4-6 layers).
9. *Net wrap* for bales = £0.56/round bale.

Whole Crop (feed wheat). Variable costs are as for combined crop (page 5) plus contract harvesting and clamping at £168 per ha (£68/ac.). Fresh yield averages 27.5 tonnes per ha (11 t/ac.) harvested in late June at 35% dry matter. Urea treatment (for higher dry matter) for whole-crop alkalage: £8.00/treated tonne. For urea treated grain, add £16.00 per tonne. Standing wheat auctions for about £1,050 per hectare (£425/acre). This is based on 8.5t/ha at £140 which is the opportunity cost of harvesting as grain less harvesting (£87/ha), carting (est. £20/ha) and storage costs.

TOTAL COSTS OF PRESERVED FORAGE

Cost of Preserved Forage	Clamped Grass Silage	Wrapped Grass Silage	Hay	Clamped Maize	*Grazed Grass*
Variable Costs £/ha	223	223	223	320	*223*
Operational Costs					
Mowing		56	56		
Turning		31	63		
Raking		32	32		
Harvesting & Clamping	290	290		168	
Drilling	8	8	8	45	8
Land Preparation	83	83	83	330	83
Fertilising & Spraying	49	49	49	25	49
Land based Costs £/ha	652	771	513	888	*362*
Total Costs £/fresh t	15.53	18.36	12.21	21.14	*8.62*
Fresh DM	18%	18%	18%	28%	*18%*
Preserved DM	25%	30%	85%	30%	*18%*
Sub-total £/t Preserved	21.57	30.60	57.64	22.65	*8.62*
Baling £/bale		2.6	2.6		
Wrap £/bale		5.4			
sheet £/t	1.3			1.3	
Bale Weight		600	400		
Total Costs £/t Preserved	**22.87**	**43.94**	**64.14**	**23.95**	***8.62***
Total Costs £/t dry weight	**91**	**146**	**75**	**80**	***48***

Total Forage Cost Notes:

1. *Variable Costs*: Linked to previous schedule, grass silage using 'Intensive 3-5 year' and assumes 2-cuts and a 4-year ley.
2. *Operational Costs:* Taken from contractor's charges, page 194, land preparation and drilling divided by length of rotation.
3. *All costs* are charged to the forage, despite possible late season grazing.
4. Neither *land rent or the Basic Payment Scheme* costs and incomes are included in this schedule. Depending on its use, will depend on whether you should include them in your costings. But if one is in, the other should be in most cases.

Sale Value of hay and (far less common because of its bulk) silage vary widely according to the region and season (supply/demand situation), quality and time of year:

a. *Hay* (pick-up baled) has an average ex-farm sale value of £55 to £120 per tonne, average £70. Seed hay £100 to £120 per tonne and £70-£90 per tonne for meadow hay; prices are higher in the west than the east and more after a dry summer (giving low yields of grass). Prices tend to be higher for horses as quality is higher. Big bale hay is £20 to £30/tonne cheaper.

b. *Grass silage* is typically about £37 per tonne delivered (higher when forage is very short in an area and *vice versa*), maize silage approx. £33 per tonne.

Relative Costs of Grazing, Conserved Grass, etc.

	£/t Fresh Weight	Yield DM tonnes/ha (acre)	Cost per tonne DM (£)	MJ per kg DM	Pence per MJ of ME in DM
Grazed Grass	7.22	7.6 (3.1)	£40	12.8	0.31
Grass Silage	22.14	7.6 (3.1)	£89	10.9	0.81
Big Bale Silage	30.73	7.6 (3.1)	£102	10.8	0.95
Hay	55.37	7.6 (3.1)	£65	8.8	0.74
Kale (direct drilled)	15.91	6.8 (2.7)	£106	11	0.96
Forage Turnips (d.d.)	11.11	6.8 (2.8)	£106	10.2	1.04
Brewer's Grains	40	-	£167	11.7	1.42
Concentrates	200	-	£233	12.8	1.82

1. In interpreting the above figures for use in planning feed use on farm, it is important to remember that own land, labour and capital for equipment are included here for home-produced fodder but not for purchased feed, and much more storage is required.
2. The consumption of fodder is limited by its bulk although this very much depends upon its quality/digestibility.
3. The cost of forage will vary enormously depending on growing conditions, soil fertility and type, intensity of farming practice and management ability.

3. PIGS, POULTRY, TROUT, RABBIT

PIGS

Breeding and Rearing *(to 35kg liveweight)*

Performance Level	*Average* per sow	*Average* per pig	*High* per sow	*High* per pig
	£	£	£	£
Weaners: (ave) 25.2 (1) @ £56	1412	56.0		
(high) 28.1 (2) @ £56			1575	56.0
Less Livestock Depreciation	88	3.4	109	3.8
Output	1324	52.6	1466	52.2
Variable Costs:				
Food	712	27.4	706	24.6
Miscellaneous	95	3.7	105	3.7
Total Variable Costs	807	31.0	811	28.2
Gross Margin (per year)	**517**	**21.6**	**655**	**24.0**

1. *Weaners per sow:* - average: 11.3 weaned per litter, 2.30 litters per year, 3% rearing losses = 25.2 weaners sold per sow per year. Productivity has improved markedly in the UK pig sector over the last few years.
2. *Weaners per sow:* - high: 12.2 weaned per litter, 2.35 litters per year, 2% rearing losses = 28.1 weaners sold per sow per year. For Outdoor Breeding performance figures see page 96.
3. *Price:* assumed pig cycle average. (See General Prices on page 95). Prices for 35kg weaners have varied from £15 to £65 during the past decade. Prices are currently strong due to the high finished price. There may be some weakening in the next 6-12 months.
4. *Average livestock depreciation* assumes an in-pig gilt purchase price of £200, a cull value per sow of £92 and a 55% replacement rate (i.e. approximately 4.2 litters per sow life). Sow mortality 5%. Boars (1 per 24 sows) purchased at £1,000 (40% a year replacement), sold at £85. 'High' compared with 'Average': higher gilt purchase prices, higher replacement rate and slightly fewer sows per boar assumed.
5. *Food:*

	Average Tonnes	*Average* Value £/t	*Average* Total Cost	*High* Tonnes	*High* Value £/t	*High* Total Cost
Sow	1.38	250	345	1.4	250	350
Boar	0.05	250	13	0.06	250	14
Weaner feed	1.22	290	354	1.18	290	341
Total	***2.65***	***268***	***712***	***2.63***	***268***	***706***

High performance: lower sow feed but extra piglet rearing feed for additional weaners. Piglets weaned at average 3.75 weeks, 7.5kg weight.

6. *Miscellaneous Average:* vet. and med. £35, transport £12, straw and bedding £15, miscellaneous £15, electricity and gas £11, and water £7.
7. *Direct Labour Cost* per sow: average £225, good £180; per weaner: average £8.65, good £6.25. This figure does not include labour used for 'overhead' activities – repairs etc. More pig fixed costs on page 221. *Building Costs:* see page 236.

Feeding (from 35 kg liveweight): per pig

Gross Margin	*Pork*		*Cutter*		*Bacon*	
	Average	*High*	*Average*	*High*	*Average*	*High*
	£	**£**	**£**	**£**	**£**	**£**
Sale Value	97.70	96.10	112.50	110.20	126.00	121.50
Less Weaner Cost	56.00	56.00	56.00	56.00	56.00	56.00
Mortality Charge	1.60	1.50	1.60	1.50	1.70	1.60
Output	40.10	38.60	54.90	52.70	68.30	63.90
Variable Costs:						
Feed	33.80	28.60	42.90	35.70	51.70	42.20
Miscellaneous	7.00	7.00	7.50	7.50	8.00	8.00
Total Variable Costs	**40.80**	**35.60**	**50.40**	**43.20**	**59.70**	**50.20**
Gross Margin	**-0.70**	**3.00**	**4.50**	**9.50**	**8.60**	**13.70**
Physical Data						
Liveweight (kg)	85	84	98	96	110	107
Deadweight (kg)	63	62	73.5	72	84	81
Killing Out %	74%	74%	75%	75%	76%	76%
Price per Deadweight (p)	155		153		150	
Price per Liveweight (p)	115		115		114	
Feed Conversion Rate	2.50	2.20	2.57	2.25	2.65	2.30
Feed per Pig (kg)	125	108	162	137	199	166
Average Cost of feed £/tonne	£270	£265	£265	£260	£260	£255
Food Cost per Kg l/w Gain (p)	67.5	58.3	68.1	58.5	68.9	58.7
Liveweight Gain per Day (kg)	0.78	0.78	0.8	0.8	0.82	0.82
Feeding period (days)	64	63	79	76	91	88
Mortality (%)	2.8	2.6	2.9	2.7	3.0	2.8
Direct labour costs per pig (£)	4.6	3.7	5.6	4.5	6.5	5.1
Sensitivity in Gross Margin (£)	*Pork*		*Cutter*		*Bacon*	
Price: 5p/kg dw difference	3.15	3.10	3.68	3.60	4.20	4.05
Food Cost £/t: £10 difference	1.25	1.08	1.62	1.37	1.99	1.66
FCR: 0.1 difference	1.35	1.30	1.67	1.59	1.95	1.83

1. *Weaner cost* assumes on farm transfer. If purchased (i.e., feeding only) transport and purchasing costs have to be added: these are very variable but average about £2.00 per weaner.
2. *Average of home-mixed and purchased compounds:* There can be big variations in feed costs per tonne between farms, according to whether the food is purchased as compounds or home-mixed, bought in bulk or in bags, size of unit, etc.
3. *Labour:* see page 169.
4. *Building Costs:* see page 236.

Combined Breeding, Rearing, and Feeding: per pig

This schedule is a combination of the two previous gross margins brought together as a single management system.

	Pork £		Cutter £		Bacon £	
Performance Level*	Ave.	High	Ave.	High	Ave.	High
Sale Value	97.70	96.10	112.50	110.20	126.00	121.50
Sow and Boar Deprcn	3.39	3.79	3.39	3.79	3.39	3.79
Mortality Charge	1.60	1.50	1.60	1.50	1.70	1.60
Output	**92.71**	**90.81**	**107.51**	**104.91**	**120.91**	**116.11**
Food	61.18	53.18	70.28	60.28	79.08	66.78
Miscellaneous	10.65	10.66	11.15	11.16	11.65	11.66
Total Variable Costs	**71.83**	**63.84**	**81.43**	**71.44**	**90.73**	**78.44**
Gross Margin per Pig	**20.88**	**26.97**	**26.08**	**33.47**	**30.18**	**37.67**
Gross Margin per Sow	**543**	**774**	**678**	**961**	**785**	**1081**
Labour Costs per Pig	13.25	9.97	14.25	10.77	15.15	11.37
Labour Costs per Sow	345	286	371	309	394	326

* Performance levels refer to breeding and rearing differences as on the previous 2 pages and, for feeding, differences in food conversion rate, food costs and labour cost only.

Prices - General

Pig prices are notoriously difficult to predict. Over the last five years the GB average pig price (SPP GB average DAPP beforehand) has ranged from over 170ppkg down to 115ppkg. The vast majority of UK pigs are taken to baconer weight. The level shown in the finisher margins for baconers above, of 150p, is an estimated average for late 2017 through 2018. In practice there is likely to be considerable variation around this level. The price shown is below the prevailing price at the time of writing (summer 2017). However, high prices seen both in the UK and the EU are likely to see an increase in output over this period. This may see prices fall somewhat. However, the continued weakness of Sterling should keep UK prices reasonably robust.

Further Performance Data

Source: AHDB Performance Data – 12 months to March 2017

		Performance Level	
Indoor Breeding	Average	Top Third*	Top 10%*
Replacement rate (%)	51.7	54.4	56.6
Sow and gilt mortality (%)	5.9	6.6	8.6
Litters per sow per year	2.30	2.36	2.39
Pigs weaned per litter	11.5	12.3	12.9
Pigs wened per sow per year	26.5	28.9	30.8
Weight of pigs produced (kg)	7.4	7.3	7.4
Average weaning age (days)	26.9	26.9	27.5
Sow feed per sow per year (tonnes)	1.24	1.35	1.34

* selected on basis of pigs reared per sow per year.

Pig Performance data by Level

Rearing	Average	Top Third*	Top 10%*
Weight of pigs at start (kg)...........................	7.5	7.5	7.4
Weight of pigs produced (kg).......................	37.0	35.7	37.6
Mortality (%)...	3.2	3.5	2.4
Feed conversion ratio...................................	1.71	1.52	1.39
Daily Gain (g)...	451	526	562
Feeding period (days).................................	65	53	54

Feeding/Finishing	Average	Top Third*	Top 10%*
Weight of pigs at start (kg)...........................	37.6	35.0	29.8
Weight of pigs produced (kg).......................	108.6	109.9	110.8
Carcass weight of pigs produced (kg)..........	81.6	82.9	83.0
Killing-out %	75%	75%	75%
Mortality (%)...	2.9	2.4	2.1
Feed conversion ratio...................................	2.72	2.44	2.33
Daily Gain (g)...	846	879	862
Feeding period (days).................................	85	87	96

* *selected on basis of feed cost per kg liveweight gain.*

Outdoor v Indoor Performance

Breeding	Outdoor	Indoor
Replacement rate (%)....................................	48.7	51.7
Sow and gilt mortality (%)............................	3.7	5.9
Litters per sow per year.................................	2.26	2.30
Pigs weaned per litter....................................	10.3	11.5
Pigs weaned per sow per year.......................	23.2	26.5
Weight of pigs produced (kg)........................	7.2	7.4
Average weaning age (days).........................	26.4	26.9
Sow feed per sow per year (tonnes)...............	1.55	1.24

1. *Stocking Rate for outdoor pigs* is mainly between 12 and 25 per hectare (5 and 10 per acre), 20 (8) being the most common. Good drainage is essential. A low rainfall and mild climate are also highly desirable. It is estimated that the cost of establishing a sow herd (selling weaners) would by £2,000 to £2,500 per sow place for an indoor systems and £500 to £1,000 per sow for an outdoor system.
2. *Data on the split* of indoor and outdoor herds is hard to come by. However, it is thought that about 40% of the UK breeding sow herd is now kept outdoors. A somewhat smaller proportion (probably <10%) of pigs are finished outdoors.

Further costing information can be found in 'Pig Production in England 2015-16' produced by Askham Bryan College, York on behalf of Rural Business Research.

Acknowledgement: The main data source for the margins within the Pigs section is the AHDB Pork performance data, but the pig and feed prices are the author's responsibility.

EGG PRODUCTION

Brown egg layers; 55 week laying period, 2 week changeover period. This reflects current commercial practice

	Enriched Cages				*Free Range*	
Level of Performance	Average		High		Average	
	per bird	per doz eggs	per bird	per doz eggs	per bird	per doz eggs
	£	p	£	p	£	p
Egg Returns	18.20	70.0	19.25	70.0	25.00	100.0
Less: Bird Depreciation	4.21	16.2	4.11	15.0	4.21	16.8
Output	**14.00**	**53.8**	**15.14**	**55.0**	**20.80**	**83.2**
Variable Costs:						
Food	11.50	44.2	11.25	40.9	13.25	53.0
Water	0.55	2.1	0.58	2.1	0.53	2.1
Vet & Med	0.15	0.6	0.15	0.5	0.30	1.2
Electricity	0.60	2.3	0.60	2.2	0.60	2.4
Total Variable Costs	**12.80**	**49.2**	**12.58**	**45.8**	**14.68**	**58.7**
Gross Margin	**1.20**	**4.6**	**2.55**	**9.3**	**6.12**	**24.5**

1. *Hen-housed data* are used throughout, i.e. the costs and returns are divided by the number of birds housed at the start of the laying period. Large variations in input costs and returns occur.
2. *Yields, Depreciation and Feeding* costs as detailed below:

	Average	*High*	*Free Range*
Eggs per Year	**312**	**330**	**300**
Dozens per year	26.00	27.50	25.00
Egg Price - p per doz	**70.0**	**70.0**	**100.0**
Pullet Purchase Price - £	4.10	4.10	4.10
Cull Hens Sales - £ per bird	0.10	0.15	0.10
Mortality	5.0%	4.0%	5.0%
Total Depreciation	**4.21**	**4.11**	**4.21**
Feed Use - kg	46	45	53
Feed Cost - £ per tonne	250	250	250
Total Feed Cost per Bird -	**11.50**	**11.25**	**13.25**

3. *Egg price:* If sold direct (to local shop, add 35p/doz., if sold to consumers (farm-gate) add 65p/doz. Retail margins imply a secondary enterprise.
4. *Feed* cost is dependent on breed, housing and environmental conditions, quantity purchased and type of ration.
5. *Direct Labour Costs:* average £1.50 per bird (double for free range) dependant on level of automation. See page 184.
6. *Housing Costs:* see page 236. Building at £25/place depreciate at about £1.25 per housed bird (over 20 years). Building maintenance also required.

7. *Other overhead costs:* also not included include vehicle costs, administration, bird and general insurance and clean-down between batches.
8. *Housed Stocking density:* 750cm^2/bird (13.3 birds/m^2) in enriched cage systems.
9. *Free Range Stocking density in house:* 1,111 cm^2 /bird (9 birds per m^2), stocking in multi-tier systems can be higher, if appropriate use is made of the height of the building. *Stocking density outside the house*; regulations allow 2,500 birds/ha (1,000/acre). Freedom Foods and the Lion Code allow 2,000 birds/ha (810/acre).

POULTRY MEAT & PULLETS

Notes on Table Poultry and Pullets

1. *Pullet Miscellaneous:* Excluding transport (29p), but includes full vaccination costs.
2. *Pullet Labour (43p);* deadstock depreciation (44p).
3. Broilers Building depreciation cost approximately 8p per bird sold. For capital costs of housing: see page 236.
4. Labour: 6.7p, excluding catching and cleaning out (5.3p) but includes management; see page 184.
5. Stocking density: 38kg/m^2, 263cm^2/kg
6. O.R. = Oven Ready
7. Rearing turkeys all the year round is in the hands of a few large and vertically integrated companies. Imports have outcompeted many small operators.
8. Miscellaneous Turkey costs include processing (including plucking and eviscerating) and marketing
9. Christmas Turkeys reflect smaller, seasonal enterprises using bagged feed, and otherwise redundant barns etc.

Note: With both turkey enterprises, considerable variations will occur between individual strains and because of different production systems and feeding regimes. Free range systems for example will show higher costs and returns. The figures should therefore be used only as rough guidelines.

10. There are very few indoor duck farmers left in the UK operating to this system, but they are large-scale.
11. Goose 16.5kg feed wheat at £140/t and 40kg goose concentrate at £320/t
12. Goose Farm gate output values used
13. Goose *Miscellaneous* costs include processing / marketing

POULTRY

£/Bird	Rearing Pullets	Table Poultry Broilers	*All Year Turkey*	*Christmas Turkey* *Light*	*Medium*	*Heavy*	*Large Roaster Chicken*	*Pekin Duck*	*Goose*
Sale Price £/Bird	4.00	2.05	36.26	40.26	44.24	60.00	13.92	8.40	52.00
Less Cost of Chick & Mort.	0.70	0.18	3.00	5.51	5.56	4.68	0.86	0.65	6.75
Output	**3.30**	**1.87**	**33.3**	**34.75**	**38.68**	**55.33**	**13.06**	**7.75**	**45.25**
Variable Costs:									
Feed	1.52	1.20	13.5	7.31	9.34	13.81	4.29	3.05	15.12
Miscellaneous	1.16	0.19	6.6	14.30	14.60	15.30	1.84	2.50	13.30
Total Variable Costs	**2.68**	**1.39**	**20.1**	**21.61**	**23.94**	**29.11**	**6.13**	**5.55**	**28.42**
Gross Margin	**0.62**	**0.48**	**13.2**	**13.14**	**14.74**	**26.21**	**6.93**	**2.20**	**16.83**
Sale Weight Kg		2.2	14.0	6.6	8.0	12.0	4.8	2.3	5.2
Sale price £/Kg L.Wt.		£0.93	£2.59	£6.10	£5.53	£5.00	£2.90	£3.65	£10.00
Chick Cost - p	0.68	0.17	2.75	5.15	5.15	4.25	0.78	0.59	6.37
Feed Use - kg	6.35	4.00	50	20.8	27.0	40.5	14.3	11.3	56.0
Feed Cost - £ per tonne	£240	£300	£270	£351	£346	£341	£300	£270	£270
Sale Age (Weeks unless stated)	16-17	41 days	20	18	22	22	12	7	
Total Mortality - %	3%	5%	9%	7%	8%	10%	10%	10%	6%
			Sexed Stags	Indoor Reared Slow growing sexed hens		Stags	Christmas Market		free range, dry plucked

RAINBOW TROUT (FRESHWATER)

	£ per tonne of fish
Returns: 1 tonne of fish @ £2.25 per kg	2,250
Less 4000 fingerlings @ 8.0p each	320
Output	**1,930**
Variable Costs:	
Food: 1 tonne @ £1350 per tonne	1,350
Vet and med	150
Miscellaneous	80
Total Variable Costs	**1,580**
Gross Margin	**350**

1. Fish growing to 350g from fingerlings at 4.5g.
2. Prices are estimated ex-farm to processor or wholesaler for portion sized (c.500g) freshwater rainbow trout. Higher prices of up to £4.20 per kg can be achieved by selling direct to retailers, caterers and consumers at, say farmers markets, but significant additional costs are associated with such sales.
3. Fingerlings price: varies according to quantity ordered and time of year.
4. Average feeding period, 10 months. Mortality, from fingerling to market size, 15%. Food conversion ratio 1.1:1, having a very low maintenance requirement. The price for fish food is for a pigmented high oil expanded pellet. It is a guide price, as different diets and formulations will retail at different prices and at different economies of scale depending upon volume purchased.
5. Current capital costs for construction of earth pond unit approximately £90 per cubic metre, to include buildings, holding systems and installation of water supply and services, but excluding land.
6. Labour requirement: the basic norm has in the past been 1 man per 50 tonnes of fish produced per annum on a table fish farm, but to remain competitive farmers now need to produce at least 150 tonnes per annum of table fish per man.

The figures given are illustrative and don't reflect the complexities of trout farming. Trout farming varies in the UK from Cage Farming in Scottish lochs (freshwater and marine) to 'traditional' flow through earth/pond/concrete raceway river farming. Trout farming also encompasses both the table and restocking sectors, prices given above relate to the sale of fish for the table market. As such feed costs, conversion rates etc. do vary which obviously has an effect on the costings for the enterprise. Differences in water temperature will also impact significantly on food conversion ratios, growth rates etc.

Acknowledgement: thanks to - British Trout Association

MEAT RABBITS

The UK consumption of rabbit meat is much lower than in the rest of Europe but is growing year on year. However, UK production is at an all-time low and the Smithfield Wholesalers are now having to import from countries such as France, Italy, Belgium and Spain due to the lack of UK producers. Rabbit meat is sold for human consumption and also fresh pet food; fallen stock can be sold as reptile food. There is also a growing demand for the pelts both home and abroad, if processed at the unit this aspect alone can help profit margins considerably. Demand for rabbit meat is seasonal. Sales should be concentrated between January and mid-June and from September to the end of December.

There are several varieties of rabbit suitable for meat production, the most common being American chinchillas, English and Flemish Giants. The Rex, Californians, New Zealand Whites, Silver Foxes, and Satins are also suitable for both meat and pelts. All but the Silver Foxes are highly suitable for grazing pasture. Expect to pay up to £60 for a good breeding buck and £40 each for good breeding does. Not all does are natural at raising their progeny. It is essential that the stockman should select the best natured from an early stage.

Meat rabbits require a safe environment in order to protect them from foxes, stoats, rats and other predators. A high fence (min. 1.65m) with maximum gaps of 25mm square is recommended set deeply (min. 450mm) into the ground. Three strands of electric fence set at varying distances from the fence will deter climbing predators. Adequate shelter from wind, rain and the heat of the sun is essential for a successful breeding herd. Breeding Does should be given individual accommodation particularly towards and post kindling. Barren Does can run together, progeny can also mix irrespective of sex from between 6 and 16 weeks. Rabbits can be raised indoors or out, with ventilation important for the former and good hygiene essential with the latter. The progeny are raised on a free range type system from 6 to 16 weeks.

Rabbits can be fed on fresh grass, grazed or freshly cut, plus herbs during summer months. Lactating does should receive a good dry matter supplement such as pellets, seasonal treats can be added from time to time such as fruit and vegetables. During winter months the fresh grass is substituted for hay. It is possible to make a balanced ration on the farm which saves purchasing dry feed. There is however a cost in additional labour

An outdoor rabbit unit of 200 does is a full time job, this includes 15% allowance for managerial duties, breakdowns and maintenance. Factoring for an economy of scale a 300 doe unit is considered equivalent to 1.35 man jobs. Additionally much of the work load is seasonal ranging from an estimated 57 hours per week in spring and summer, reducing to 40 hours per week over winter months (assuming a 250 to 300 Doe unit).

Meat Rabbit Gross Margin Schedule

	£ Per Doe	£ Per 200 Does
Finished Young per Doe per Year	46	9,200
Live Weight Each (at 16 weeks)	2.8	560
Price per kg to processor	2.7	540
Sales:	£	
Meat sales per Doe per Year	348	69,552
Sales of pelts	46	9,200
Less Depreciation per Doe (incl.Buck) per Year (2)	15.5	3,101
Output	**378**	**75,651**
Variable Costs:		
Feed (Doe, progeny & share of buck)	62	12,400
Bedding	3	500
Vet and Med	2	300
Miscellaneous	3	600
Total Variable Costs	**69**	**13,800**
Gross Margin	**309**	**61,851**

1. *Sales:* The prices quoted are based on the wholesale environment. Further profits can be achieved by selling retail to the public. A further income stream can be developed for pelts, £1.00 has been used above, but further profits can be achieved through self processing/marketing. Fallen stock can be sold for reptile food.

2. *Depreciation* – Doe £14.40 (incl.15% mortality), Buck £1.10 per doe (incl. 15% mortality) Average 1 buck per 10 does. Does are kept for 2 years, bucks for 6 years. Does purchased at £40 each (15% mortality), culled at £15; buck purchased at £60 (15% mortality) negligible residual value.

3. *Feed conversion*: 4:1 includes doe, progeny and 10% of buck. The feed cost assumes the availability of fresh grass/herbs on a daily basis and home grown hay in the winter.

4. Young does are bought in at between 10 and 12 weeks old, mated at 20 weeks. A ratio of one buck to 10 does is recommended. Gestation is 31 days. Average litter size is 8 to 9 of which 6 to 7 should be successfully fattened. Re mating can be immediately post-partum or up to 6 weeks afterwards. A doe can have a useful life of 10 to 12 litters over 18 months. A mortality rate of 15% can be expected. Food conversion rate is around 4:1 making rabbit compatible with poultry

Acknowledgements: Thanks to – T & S Rabbits, part of T & S Nurseries and the Abbey Vineyard Group.

4. RENEWABLE ENERGY

GENERAL

Renewable energy enterprises are commonplace across much of the UK. Returns vary as with any enterprise, but most who undertook the research carefully have been pleased with the result. As with any diversification or capital investment, a full investment appraisal is necessary for renewable energy projects, arguably particularly so now as prices paid for renewable energy have fallen. Space is fundamental to renewable energy (whether wind turbines, solar panels or anaerobic digestion), it is capital intensive and requires an entrepreneurial approach to its implementation. Agriculture, which has all these resources is therefore a natural partner for the sector.

The Renewable Energy industry is a response to incentives to cut emissions of climate changing greenhouse gases (GHGs) as a result of human activities. The main GHGs are:

- Carbon Dioxide (CO_2), which accounts for up to a quarter of the greenhouse gas effect
- Methane (CH_4) accounts for between 4% and 9% of the effect but is about 20 times more potent by volume than carbon dioxide
- Nitrous Oxide, which, whilst very low in concentration in the atmosphere, is about 300 times more potent than carbon dioxide.

In 2016, human activity in the UK accounted (provisionally) for 466 million tonnes of GHG emissions (CO_2 equivalent), 6% down from 496mt in 2015. Agriculture accounted for 49.1mt CO_2 equivalent (2015), most of which comes from the enteric fermentation of ruminating animals (methane) and the use (and manufacture) of nitrogen fertilisers (nitrous oxides).

UK GHG Emissions 2015 (measured in million tonnes of CO_2 equivalence)

	GHG Total	*Carbon Dioxide*	*Methane*	*Nitrous Oxide*	*Others*
UK	***496***	*404*	*52.2*	*23.1*	*17*
UK percentage		*81%*	*11%*	*4.7%*	*3.4%*
UK Agriculture	***49.1***	*5.2*	*27.7*	*16.3*	*0.0*
Percentage	***9.9%***	*1.3%*	*53%*	*71%*	*0%*
GWP[1]		*1*	*21*	*310*	

1. GWP is the Global Warming Potential over 100 years relative to 1 tonne CO_2
Figures from DECC.

Agriculture, being a user of natural resources (such as land) intrinsically has an unavoidable environmental footprint; it is taking resources from the earth for consumption. However, that footprint can be minimised. Crops have generally been considered sequesters of carbon and animals releasers. Different crops and technologies have differing GHG benefits and costs. Higher yields (per hectare for example), generally offer better carbon saving per unit of production, especially if it means more output per unit of input.

RENEWABLE ENERGY POLICY

Renewable energy is not currently at the top of the political agenda. Its additional cost, above that of traditional energy, both to the taxpayer and the consumer, is a major issue. The visual appearance of many of the technologies (solar farms, onshore windfarms) is becoming less of a concern as the rate of new installations slows. The direction of travel is that projects in the future will need to be viable without long term subsidy. However, support is still currently available although it has been cut.

In November 2016, the European Commission presented proposals to review the Renewable Energy Directive for post 2020 as part of a Clean Energy Package. It proposed cutting the percentage of conventional biofuels from its current mandatory 7 percent to 3.8 percent in 2030. It also set an obligation to raise the proportion of other fuels with low-emission such as electricity and advanced biofuels in transport to 6.8 percent. Energy use, the primary release of GHGs, is divided into three categories; electricity, heat and transport. The renewable generation of each is incentivised by government policy.

The Renewables Obligation (RO)

Since 2002, this has been the primary mechanism for encouraging electricity supply from large renewable sources in the UK. Since April 2017, the RO has closed to new applicants and has been replaced by Contracts For Difference (CfD). The RO will continue to operate for existing renewable electricity suppliers until their terms of agreements expire.

Contracts For Difference (CfD)

Contracts for Difference (CfDs) is a contract between a renewable electricity generator and the Low Carbon Contracts Company (LCCC), a government-owned company. The generator firm is paid the difference between the 'strike price' – a price for renewable electricity and the 'reference price'– the average wholesale price for electricity. Generators therefore supply electricity at the agreed strike price, receiving support when wholesale prices are lower than the strike price and paying back any surplus when wholesale prices are higher than the strike price.

On farm renewable electricity schemes are generally smaller and are funded through the Feed in Tariff Scheme:

Feed-in Tariffs (FIT)

Designed to facilitate the administration and subsidy receipts of small-scale electricity generators (farm-scale), Feed-in Tariffs encourage the production of renewable electricity at levels up to 5MW capacity. This is equivalent to a large offshore turbine or a very large anaerobic digestion plant. Almost all farm-scale renewable energy schemes would therefore fit within the FIT scheme. The Tariffs work as follows:

- A renewable electricity generator receives a fixed payment for each kWh electricity generated; the 'Generation Tariff'. This is set at different levels depending on technology type, installation size and start date (see below).
- The 'Export Tariff', a guaranteed market payment is available if required for its export to the wider market (currently) 5.03 p/kWh, less for existing installations.
- Generators can opt out of the Export Tariff by either selling electricity directly to an electricity consumer or making use of the electricity themselves (entirely or partially).
- The FIT payments are made by the registered Electricity Suppliers, the cost of which is redistributed among all suppliers in a pro-rata manner.

Generation Tariff rates for new installations have fallen sharply as government objectives have changed and targets met. Generation and Export Tariffs are index linked once commissioned. Tariffs are guaranteed for 20 years (25 for solar PV if installed before 1 August 2012).

As can be seen in the table, rates vary by generation type, according to Government's preferences for renewable generation and rates favour small scale rather than carbon savings. Low output schemes are arguably less carbon efficient in many cases but seen as preferable to larger scale installations.

Generation Tariffs for FITs for New Installations (non-exhaustive list)

Generation Technology	*Scale*	*Generation Tariff p/kWh*	
		1 Jan To 31 March 2018	*1 Jan To 31 March 2019*
Anaerobic Digestion	< 250kW	6.10	5.92
	250 - 500kW	5.79	5.63
	> 500kW	2.14	2.02
Hydro	< 100kW	7.77	7.71
	100kW – 2MW	6.24	6.21
	2-5MW	4.54	4.54
Photo Voltaic *	< 10kW	3.93/3.54/0.34	3.64/3.28/0.14
	10kW - 50kW	4.15/3.74/0.34	3.87/3.48/0.14
	50kW - 250kW	1.82/1.64/0.34	1.62/1.46/0.14
	250kW – 1MW	1.48	1.28
	> 1MW	0.34	0.14
	Stand Alone **	0.25	0.11
Wind	< 50kW	8.19	7.92
	50kW 100kW	4.83	4.68
	100kW - 1.5MW	3.18	3.11
	> 1.5MW	0.79	0.75
Export Tariff *of new installations*		5.03	5.03

* *If electricity supplies a building with an Energy Performance Certificate of A to D, the first, higher rate is payable. If multiple installations and most achieve A to D rating, middle band, if neither of the above, lower band.*

** *Stand Alone Systems are not attached to a building and not wired to provide electricity to an occupied building. Possibly an electric fence charger for example.*

The Renewable Heat Incentive (RHI)

Heat accounts for nearly half of energy used in the UK. The value of heat is low (possibly 1-2p/kWh thermal energy depending on local market) which rarely justifies the capital expenditure in the UK of harnessing heat or generating it from a renewable source. The RHI addresses this. The scheme is divided into domestic and non-domestic installations. RHI recipients need to meet sustainability requirements on the feedstock. This applies to all RHI payments so, for example, those using biomass boilers need to prove where their woodchip comes from.

Domestic RHI

Payments are based on estimates of heat demand and generators efficiency irrespective of installation capacity and are available for new installations. The RHI is administered by OFGEM. The Domestic RHI pays tariffs quarterly per unit of heat generated for seven years. Rates for existing recipients rise by inflation:

Levels of support for the Domestic Renewable Heat Incentive

Generation Technology	Domestic Tariff p/kWh Rates from July 2017
Air-source heat pumps	7.63
Ground source heat pumps	19.64
Biomass boilers and stoves	3.85
Solar thermal	20.06

Non-Domestic RHI

Once a RHI rate is agreed, payments are index linked but not exposed to renegotiations of the policy for the 20-year term. Payments are made quarterly based on the actual heat generated.

Levels of Support for RHI for Non Domestic Installations

Tariff name	Eligible technology	Eligible sizes	Tariff rate (p/kWh)*
Small biomass	Solid biomass; including waste	< 200 kWth	Tier 1: 2.71 Tier 2: 0.71
Medium biomass		200 - 1000 kWth	Tier 1: 4.79 Tier 2: 2.08
Large biomass		>= 1000 kWth	2.08
Large Biomass CHP			4.29
Air Source	Heat Pumps	all sizes	2.61
Deep Geothermal			5.22
Ground source	Ground and Water-source heat pumps;	Tier 1	9.09
		Tier 2	2.71
Solar thermal		< 200 kWth	10.44
Biomethane	Injection	1st 40,000 mWh	3.20
		next 40,000 mWh	1.89
		remaining mWh	1.45
Biogas	Biogas combustion	under 200 kWth	2.88
		200-600kWth	2.26
		Over 600kWth	0.86

** Tier Break is: installed capacity x 1,314 peak load hours (15% rating), i.e.: kWth x 1,314*

The Renewable Transport Fuel Obligation (RTFO) and Fuel Excise Duty

Since 2008, for every litre of biofuel that excise duty is paid on, a Renewable Transport Fuel Certificate (RTFC) is issued. Biogas 1.9 certificates are issued per kilogram supplied (1.75 RTFCs/kg biobutane or biopropane). Fuel generated from feedstocks classed as 'wastes' or 'residues' receive double certificates.

Companies supplying at least 450,000 litres of any fuel for road vehicles and (since 2013) 'non road mobile machinery' (NRMM) to the UK market annually (about 14 companies) must participate by incorporating a proportion of biofuel into their sales, buying RTFCs from another biofuel provider or paying a 'buy-out' penalty (fine) of 30p/l (index linked). As a compelling incentive, the 'buy-out fund' generated is redistributed equally to every RTFC issued by the year-end. This means that the further away the UK is from hitting the annual target, the greater the incentive to incorporate as RTFC values rise.

These subsidies make the industry viable, without them there would be no biofuel industry. The required proportion of biofuels to incorporate is 5%. The RTFO includes sustainability criteria of the Renewable Energy Directive. The criteria include minimum carbon savings requirements.

Biofuels have the same duty payable as mineral fuels for most producers. A 100% duty exemption for small scale biofuel producers of up to 2,500l biofuel per year (notionally sufficient for home use) is in place.

Fuel Excise Duty:	*Since April 2016*
Petrol, Diesel *ppl*	57.95
Bioethanol and biodiesel *ppl*	57.95
Rebated gas oil (red diesel) *ppl*	11.14
Biodiesel for non-road use *ppl*	11.14
Natural Gas (inc. biogas) *p/kg*	24.70
Liquefied Petroleum Gas *p/kg*	31.61

These figures are before VAT. Pump prices include VAT (20%)

PERENNIAL ENERGY CROPS FOR HEAT AND POWER

Biomass includes crops grown to be burnt to produce heat and/or electricity. Plant material is chipped or baled and is generally used in boilers in dedicated biomass power stations. Biomass includes short rotation coppice, Miscanthus, straw, canary reed grass and switch grass. The Basic Payment can be claimed on eligible land with these crops.

Short Rotation Coppice

Short Rotation Coppice (SRC) is a fast growing willow (occasionally poplar) that when chipped and dried is used as a fuel for heat or power generation. SRC willow needs ample moisture but grows on any cultivated land. Planting is in the spring using un-rooted cuttings at a rate of 15,000/ha. Rabbit fencing may be necessary. Crops are usually harvested on a 3-year cycle (2 or 4-year cycles depending on conditions). At this stage, the crop can be up to 7-8 metres tall. Crops should last 22 years (7 harvests). Most growers apply some fertiliser post-harvest, 60 kg/ha N is sufficient. Sewage sludge is commonly used as are animal manures.

SRC Gross Margin

Production level	**Low**	**Average**	**High**
Yield: ODT/ha (tons/acre)	7.00 (2.8)	8.00 (3.2)	9.00 (3.6)
	£	**£**	**£**
Output at £50 per ODT	350 (142)	400 (162)	450 (182)
Variable Costs:			
Establishment		80 (32)	
Fertiliser/spray		22 (9)	
Total Variable Costs	102 (41)	102 (41)	102 (41)
Gross Margin per ha (acre)	**248** (101)	**298** (121)	**348** (141)

1. *Yield:* Based on 25ODT/hectare harvested every third year.
2. *Establishment costs:* of £1750/ha (£710/ac) excluding fencing shared between 22 years.

3. *Harvest and Haulage* costs are netted from contracted price

There is one market of high volume for SRC willow – Iggesund Paperboard Mill in Cumbria - who offers long-term contracts for willow grown in the north of England and the south of Scotland. The grower pays for the establishment of the crop but receives free advice and access to low price materials (cuttings etc), meaning establishment costs are significantly lower than when growing for own use. Iggesund harvests and transports the crop meaning the price paid varies depending on the distance that the grower is from the plant. A grower in Cumbria could achieve a price of £50 per oven dry tonne (ODT).

SRC can be used for heating projects especially self-supplying private boilers. In these situations establishment costs will be higher and they will need to manage their own harvesting and woodchip drying. There are four harvesting contractors (based in Cumbria, North Yorkshire, Nottinghamshire and Warwickshire); the further the grower is from one of these contractors the higher the cost is likely to be.

Traders and self-suppliers need to consider additional costs associated with the heat market, such as Biomass Suppliers List registration and annual fees. However, greater value may be harnessed from the crop especially when RHI payments are received. Guideline areas required to provide sufficient energy are 2.7-3.5 hectares for a large farmhouse or 3.3 – 4.25 hectares for a 40,000-bird poultry shed (based on a 10.4 and 8.0 ODT/Ha). Other costs such as harvest, drying, storage etc, will be incurred.

SRC provides additional fringe benefits such as:

- Providing a means of flood mitigation (due to the dense planting and coppice nature of the crop slowing water flow)
- Reducing soil erosion
- Great potential for use as a biofilter (particularly useful if farmers have effluents they wish to dispose of cheaply and gain a yield benefit at the same time)
- Willows provide abundant sources of pollen and nectar in Jan-March providing fodder for pollinators at a time of year when there are few other sources in the countryside – this could benefit growers with insect pollinated crops such as WOSR, orchards, soft fruits, vegetables)

Miscanthus (Elephant Grass)

Miscanthus is a perennial grass crop lasting 20 years grown for energy and fibre. It is harvested annually with conventional farm machinery. Aside from biomass, Miscanthus can be used as animal bedding, paper making biopolymer or to produce bio-degradable products, such as plant pots. Miscanthus is grown throughout England. It is usually propagated from rhizomes. A mature crop suppresses weeds but weed control is very important during establishment of the crop. Wireworms can be a problem if Miscanthus is planted on former grassland without a break crop in between, but otherwise there are no significant pathogens or pests in the UK meaning agro-chemical use is minimal.

There is a single major buyer for Miscanthus, Terravesta, who offers ten-year contracts. The current price for delivered tonne (at 16% moisture) is £76 per tonne, although there are penalties if the crop is out of specification and bonuses available of £2/tonne if bales have been stored in a barn.

Miscanthus Gross Margin

Production level	Low	Average	High
Yield: oven dried tonnes/ha (tons/acre)	11 (4.5)	13 (5.3)	15 (6.1)
	£	**£**	**£**
Output at £75.96/t	835.6 (338)	987 (400)	1139.4 (461)
Variable Costs:			
Establishment		81 (33)	
Fertiliser/spray		21 (9)	
Harvest		79 (32)	
Bale	149 (60)	176 (71)	203 (82)
Cart, stack	43 (17)	51 (21)	59 (24)
Transport	176 (71)	208 (84)	240 (97)
Total Variable Costs	549 (222)	615 (249)	682 (276)
Gross Margin £/ha (ac)	**287** (100)	**372** (150)	**457** (201)

Yield accounts for average over 21 years

The crop shoots in April, and grows to 4 metres by September. The canes are harvested in February-March by which time the moisture content is below 20%. Harvest method depends on end use. For energy, the crop is cut with a mower conditioner or modified forage harvester and then baled 10 days later into Hesston bales. Contract specifications require a moisture content of 16% when sold (although they may be baled when wetter than this) and a bale weight of 525kg. For other end uses a maize harvester is used.

1. *Establishment costs:* of £1700/ha (£690/ac) including partial fencing shared between 21 years and topping at the end of the first year costing £20/ha. There are likely to be economies of scale for fencing larger areas, but is not often considered cost effective. Establishment costs for crops for own-use are likely to be significantly higher in the region of £3,000/ha including fencing.
2. *Fertiliser and agrochemicals:* Requirements are low. Whilst the harvest will remove P and K, the plant is deep rooted so accesses minerals from deeper than most crops. Sewage sludge is an ideal fertiliser. The Miscanthus gross margin has a small cost for imported slurry, biosolids or other organic manure. Some agro-chemicals will probably be required in the first 2 years.
3. *Harvest:* contracted at £79/Ha.
4. *Baling costs:* £13.50 per tonne
5. *Transport:* to Lincolnshire need to be taken into account and are likely to be in the region of £11.50-£20/tonne (included at £16/tonne in this example)

In year 2 it is possible to achieve 8 tonnes per hectare for a very good crop, but peak yields tend to be achieved from year 4 onwards. Recent precision planting machinery improvements facilitate evenly established crops, offering greater fresh weight yields on light land 9 – 12t/ha and on medium to heavy land 12 – 18 t/ha.

Small on-farm boilers have been developed to produce heat and energy which offer potential for Miscanthus growers who can benefit from the Renewable Heat Incentive (see page 105). Emissions certificates are required as well as evidence of fuel sustainability which can be registered on the Sustainable Fuel Register.

Acknowledgement ~ Thanks to Kevin Lindegaard of Crops for Energy Ltd (www.crops4energy.co.uk) and Terravesta

ANAEROBIC DIGESTION

Anaerobic Digestion (AD) is the digestion of non-woody organic material in the absence of oxygen by micro-organisms to produce biogas (a mixture of 40:60 carbon dioxide CO_2 and methane CH_4) and digestate (a soil conditioner). It works in the same way as a very large rumen. The biogas is collected and normally used in a combined heat and power (CHP) generator to produce heat and electricity for use or sale. The biogas can also be purified by removing the CO_2 and contaminant gasses (less than 1%) making biomethane and compressed for use as road fuel or in place of natural gas.

An extensive range of feedstock can be used. Livestock manure is cheap with lots of micro-organisms but has a low biogas yield and is not commercially viable as the sole feedstock. Energy crops such as maize silage offer high yields and are commonly used in AD business models. They are expensive feedstocks so add substantially to operating costs but are predictable and supply is easily managed. Non-farm waste streams from food processing companies or separated kitchen wastes offer a high return, with potential to earn revenue from gate fees. Regulatory controls and 'front-end' processing requirements are far greater when importing others' wastes though, especially if animal by-products may be included pushing up capital costs substantially. These tend to have unpredictable supply.

The rate of turnover of digestate is controlled by the rate at which feedstock enters the digester less the small (usually 3-10%) fall in volume from the production of biogas (most of the bulk is water which remains as water). Depending on feedstock and system used, digestion can take as little as a week up to 2 months in some circumstances.

Example On-Farm Feedstocks for Anaerobic Digestion

Feedstock	*Biogas Yield m³/t feedstock*	*Value of Biogas £/t feedstock**
Cattle/pig slurry	15 – 25	3.60 – 6.00
Poultry manure	30 – 100	7.25 – 24.20
Maize silage	190 – 220	46.00 – 53.00
Grass silage	150 – 200	36.00 – 48.00
Whole crop wheat	185	44.75
Maize grain	560	135
Rolled wheat grain	600	145
Crude glycerine	580 – 1,000	140 – 240
Rape meal	620	150
Fats	Up to 1,200	up to 290

** 5.79p/kWh Generation Tariff, 5.03p/kWh Export Tariff, 1p/kWh heat*

Policy

When biogas is used to generate electricity, it can be sold with Feed in Tariffs as part of the Renewables Obligation. Biomethane for road transport is technically eligible for RTFCs (see Biofuels section above) or the RHI. AD also benefits indirectly from the Landfill Directive by diverting waste from landfill to uses such as AD. AD does not facilitate NVZ implementation regulations but has been a favoured renewable energy of the Government.

Economics

The two major costs associated with AD are usually the capital set up and feedstock (if home grown or purchased feed is used). Operating and maintenance costs such as insurance, labour and utilities are usually comparatively low. A small to average size plant (2,500m³ digester and 490kW CHP generator) would cost in the region of £2.0-2.5 million to build and commission. Depending on feedstock, temperature and other settings, this size plant could digest in the region of 20,000 tonnes of feedstock per year with a 45 day retention time (spent in the digester) or 30,000t with a 30 day retention period.

Revenue from this system digesting 20,000 tonnes using the assumptions from the table above, an average gas yield per tonne of feedstock of 100m^3/tonne and an efficiency of 90% gas conversion would return income before costs and without gate fees of about £480,000 with FITs per annum.

LIQUID BIOFUELS

Liquid biofuels are road transport fuels produced from organic materials, including farm crops. *Biodiesel* is produced from oilseeds such as oilseed rape and is a replacement for diesel. *Bioethanol* is a petrol replacement, produced from starch-based crops including wheat, maize and sugar beet or cane.

Biofuels from cellulosic (woody) feedstock are referred to as 'second generation' biofuels. They enable a higher energy return per hectare and the opportunity to process household, manufacturing and agricultural organic 'wastes'. However, their production is not financially viable and requires more energy to process the cellulose than the energy released.

Supply

About 40 million tonnes of road fuel is used in the UK (diesel exceeding petrol use by about 55:45). To meet the RTFO target, about 2m tonnes of biofuel are required (5%). The RTFO does not differentiate between biofuels so one may dominate the market. Splitting the market proportionately would require roughly 1.1 million tonnes of biodiesel and 900,000 tonnes bioethanol. This would need 2.6m tonnes OSR or equivalent feedstock (at 42% extraction) covering 800,000 hectares (at 3.25t/ha) and 3m tonnes of wheat (or equivalent feedstock) covering 353,000 hectares (at 8.5t/ha).

Farmers' options on whether to grow a crop for biofuel manufacture are determined simply by price and contractual terms. Crops used in biofuel production are, in the most part, mainstream crops. There are therefore no farm-level gross margins for biofuel crops. Despite considerable investment and funding, the biofuel industry has only ever reached operating levels of about a third of capacity. It seems unlikely it will ever grow further.

SOLAR POWER

In England and Scotland most private solar installations do not require planning permission unless the building is of conservation status, is in a designated area or is a large free standing system. Installers in Wales and Northern Ireland need planning permission from their local planning authority.

Solar Photovoltaic (PV)

Solar PV panels generate electricity through the direct conversion of daylight. Panels can either be roof mounted, free-standing or integrated as a form of building material though solar slates, tiles or glass laminates.

Rates for anything above 20kW tend to be near £1,000 per kW. For example a 30kW roof mounted array with high specification panels would cost in the region of £30,000 to install, depending on connection fees, cabling, etc. a comparable 20kW system would currently cost nearer to £23,000 (£1,150/kW) to install. Smaller arrays are dearer per kW, at £1,200 to £1,400 per kW installed.

Little maintenance is required. Approximately 7-8m^2 of PV panels is required to generate 1kW of electricity. A typical panel weighs 13kg per m^2 so additional roof support may be required. Panels should last for 25 years although electricity inverters might need replacing after 5 -10 years.

Panels should be south facing at an angle of 30-40 degrees and un-shadowed. Productivity varies across the UK with levels between 1100 kWh per m^2 in the South West, to 800 kWh per m^2 in Scotland.

Solar Thermal

Solar thermal systems use the sun's energy to warm water through using either evacuated tubes or flat plate collectors fitted to a roof. A conventional boiler is then used to heat the water further. Costs are typically £3,000 to £7,000 and require little maintenance. Savings are modest; the average system provides one third of water needs, reducing heating bills by approximately £80-£160 per year.

HYDRO POWER

The UK has about 1,600MW hydro-electricity capacity. Most of the 5800GWhr (Giga Watt hours) generated each year is from large (10-100 MW) schemes. Viable sites vary from around 5kW to a few MW. Typically power output is more constant (and manageable) for hydro than wind or solar power.

Hydro, like other renewable energy projects is capital loaded, expensive to install but cheap to operate and can have a very long life. Installation costs of around £3,000 to £6,000 per kWe for small hydroelectric systems are typical, but are site dependant. Operational costs are low, generally 1-2% of capital setup. Capital cost and electrical capacity depend on the following:

- *The head (maximum vertical fall) of water:* The higher the head, the smaller the flow required to generate the same amount of electricity. Smaller flow means smaller pipe and turbine. High head is over 50 metres drop, less than 10m is low head.
- *The flow rate of water* is determined by the catchment size, amount of rainfall and the proportion of flow abstracted. The latter is determined by the environmental sensitivity of the river. Flow for small schemes is measured in litres per second.
- *Project size:* The cost of construction per kW falls as capacity rises; smallest projects take longest to repay the investment. Access affects costs. Costs for obtaining planning permission, abstraction and impoundment licenses and detailed design and specification of the equipment are similar for a 5kW scheme or a 30kW scheme.
- *Construction management:* Projects can be contracted to a single contractor to undertake design, specification, procurement and construction work, requiring little input from the landowner but is dearer. Many landowners oversee the project management which with some specialist input, costs can be greatly reduced.
- *Grid connection:* The capacity of the grid can be a major limitation, with upgrade of grid connection lines being expensive, particularly so in more rural or remote areas.
- *Development companies* take on a complete project and pay a rent to the landowner, typically 5% to 20% of income. Schemes of interest to such companies are usually at least 100 kW. There is significant competition for larger schemes.

  Typical costs of example projects:

  - 5 kW medium to low head scheme, by civil contractors with specialist hydro input. Annual generation 14 MWh. Cost around £80,000
  - 15 kW very high head. Landowner undertook project management and most civils and pipe-laying works. Annual generation 45 MWh. Cost around £52,000
  - 30 kW high head scheme. Managed by landowners using local contractors. Annual generation around 110 MWh. Cost around £77,000
  - 100 kW scheme medium head, managed by the landowner with significant time input. Annual generation around 450 MWh. Cost around £410,000
  - 300 kW scheme high head. Contractors led constructor with specialists. Annual generation around 1,200 MWh. Cost around £1,330,000

WIND TURBINES

There are 6,222 operational wind turbines spread across 1,234 wind farms throughout the UK with 10,500MW electrical generation capacity (July 2017) (renewableuk.com). Small scale turbines can have capacities of as little as 100 watts (W) up to models of 4 megawatts (MW) and 6MW for offshore turbines. Wind farms are becoming larger; the average size a decade ago was 7MW and is now 20MW, albeit with considerable offshore wind farm growth. The average onshore turbine has 1.7MW capacity with the average wind farm over 8MW.

Wind turbines in good locations produce energy equivalent to their rated capacity for around 30% of the year. For example: for a turbine rated at 40kW this calculates as 40kW x 30% x 8760 (hours in a year) = 105,120 kWh per year (105.12MWh). If this electricity is sold at 13.22p/kWh (8.19p Generation Tariff + 5.03p Export Tariff) with FITs, then a return of £13,896 per year is achieved.

Typical costs for a range of turbine capacities are in the region of the following table. Good quality constructions should have an operational life of 20 years.

Guideline Figures for Capital and Revenue of Wind Turbines

Capacity kW	*Capital Cost*	*Annual Output (kWh)*	*Revenue/yr using* FIT*
5.0	20,000	13,100	£1,720
11	70,000	28,900	£3,790
75	200,000	197,000	£19,200
250	680,000	657,000	£53,200
800	1,000,000	2,100,000	£170,000

* *Relevant FIT price as in FIT Table on page 105.*

The land surrounding a wind turbine is usually un-affected, apart from access required up to the base of the tower. A minimum average wind speed of 5 meters per second (m/s) is required; they operate at their rated capacity at 11-15m/s. Many turbines have automatic shut-down mechanisms when wind speeds exceed about 25m/s to avoid damage. Selection of the correct turbine technology and size is important.

Planning permission is required and consultation with neighbours and stakeholders for all scale turbines. Many schemes are operated by developers with land rented to them by the land owner for 20 years. In this situation, a rent will be payable to the landowner, usually at about 2-4% of income (£5,000 to £7,000 per mast per year is common plus similar construction access fees). Access to the turbines must be possible, but land between the turbines can be farmed normally. Other benefits like road improvements may also be included. An option to develop a site could be worth £1,000 to £5,000 per year.

An 11kW turbine will have a hub (mast) height of 15 to 18 metres, blade diameter of 9 metres and a 63m^3 swept area. Tip height will be up to 22.5m. A large (800kW) wind turbine has a standard hub height of 76m, a height at the maximum blade position of 102m, and a blade diameter of 53m. The area of wind captured by this size blade is 0.88ha.

5. OTHER ENTERPRISES

TURF

The turf market is predominantly supplied with seed sown turf or cultivated lawn turf. Pasture turf is still available in some areas, but its importance is small and declining. Suitable pasture for turf lifting is scarce and it can be cheaper to grow cultivated turf than treat and prepare existing pasture. Special seed mixtures and cultivation techniques produce a range of types of turfgrass that can be matched to particular sites and uses. The Turfgrass Growers Association (TGA) has quality standards. It is estimated that there are around 16,000 ha (*40,000 acres*) of turfgrass grown in the UK. Although several turfgrass companies were originally set up by farmers, the production is now in the hands of specialist turf growers but there are also farmers who use turf as part of their agricultural rotation.

Selling existing pasture turf to a turf company

This is the traditional option but it now represents very little of the turf market. Minimum 5-6 year ley/pasture generally needed for spring or autumn lifting, 8-10 year grass is better for summer cutting.

Payment varies between £750 and £1,500 per hectare (£300-£600 per acre), but mainly from £900 to £1,200 per ha (£360-£480 per acre). There is usually an initial payment plus further payments as turf is lifted. There may be a penalty clause if lifting delays prevent subsequent timely drilling. Lifting can take from two months to a year. It can be done at any time of year except when there is snow or frost on the ground. The turf company sprays against broadleaved weeds, fertilises and mows before lifting; the farmer may do these tasks, for payment. He may graze the land, for a rent, if lifting is delayed.

The effect on the land of cultivated turf production is not detrimental, the amount of topsoil removal is not much greater than other root crops; some say there are benefits (removal of accumulated pests, etc. in the top half inch of grass, roots and topsoil). Some local authorities require planning consent for turf harvesting. In some instances it has been refused on the grounds that pasture turf is not an agricultural crop. Cultivated turf, however, is deemed to be an agricultural crop. On tenanted land landlord's permission is necessary to cut pasture turf.

Farmer cutting, lifting and selling pasture turf himself

This is extremely uncommon. The turf must be treated, as in option 1. A small turf cutting machine can be hired for £65 a day. This slices off the turf which must then be cut into lengths and picked up by hand. It is slow going even in good conditions. Wastage is commonly 10-20% of the area. It is possible to hire a machine which cuts and picks up the turf but the charge will be considerably more.

Renting land to a turf company for production of cultivated turf

Turf companies rent land for turfgrass production. Typically the land is rented on a per crop basis and one or two crops grown. A turf crop usually takes 12 to 18 months from preparation to harvest but autumn sown crops may be harvested within 12 months. Rent levels depend on the quality of the land, the provision of irrigation and the profitability of competing agricultural enterprises. Currently rents are in the order of £600-£925 per hectare per crop (£240-£375 per acre) or £480-£740 per ha per year (£195-£300 per acre).

Cultivated turf production

Important features when choosing fields: good root structure, number and type of weeds, level, well-drained, stone-free land; good access. Turf has a short life once cut and stacked - a maximum 1 to 2 days in summer, 3 to 4 days in winter, depending on temperature. On their own land turf producers can grow turf continuously, taking a crop every 18 months to two years on average. On rented land (as in option 3), they take one or two crops and move on. Usually they produce a quick growing turf on rented land and cultivate more specialist and slower growing turf on their own. A high level of agronomic expertise and considerable investment in machinery are needed and labour requirements are heavy. A high degree of marketing expertise is essential. Whilst the bulk of the trade goes into general landscaping or garden centres there is an increase in the number of contracts where the quality and type of turf is specified. It is estimated that a turf farm would need to be 150-200 hectares (400-500 acres) or more in size to be viable – in order to justify the machinery and equipment necessary and to produce a succession of turf for the market. There are significant economies of scale. The cost of specialist machinery for turf production can be £350,000. A new one-man harvesting machine costs in the order of £120,000-£200,000 but significantly reduces labour costs.

Costs and Returns

Variable Costs plus Rent:	£/ha	(£/ac)
Seed	750-1,100	(300-445)
Fertiliser	350-700	(140-280)
Herbicide	90-150	(35-60)
Fungicide	100-210	(40-85)
Rent (for 15 months)	600-925	(240-375)
Total Costs	*1,890-3,085*	*(765-1,250)*

It may be necessary to irrigate and on occasions use netting to grow the grass for certain sites.

Labour: Special seed bed preparation (including subsoiling and stone burying), regular mowing (twice a week May/June), picking up clippings, harvesting (2 men on harvester plus one loading lorry) between 0.2-0.4 hectares per day (0.5-1.0 acre). The new one-man harvester can do 2 ha (5 acres) a day.

Total costs of the order of £5,000-£7,500 per ha (£2,000-£3,037 per acre), approximately 50-75p per square metre.

Value of Turf (on the field)

	per m^2	per sq. yd.	per ha*	per acre*
Pasture turf	38-43p	32-36p	£3,420-£3,850	£1,380-£1,570
Hardwearing, domestic general contract	70-95p	58-79p	£6,300-£8,550	£2,550-£3,460
Football, hockey, prestige landscape	115-145p	95-120p	£10,260-£12,825	£4,150-£5,200
High quality/specialist**	190-475p	160-405p	£17,100-£42,750	£6,910-£17,290

* assuming 90% recovery, but some producers work on 85%.

** for some contracts the price may be higher.

Delivery charges 45-55p per m^2 for a full lorry load. Higher for smaller deliveries.

Acknowledgements: Turfgrass Growers Association, www.turfgrass.co.uk. *Robert Laycock,* Littlegarth www.robertlaycock.co.uk.

GOLF

Golf development in the UK is all but dead. There are some courses where money is being spent and some developers trying to get consent for landfill and build new courses on top of the fill but new stand-alone golf courses are no longer viable and there are no areas of the UK where there is unsatisfied demand.

The golf market is aging and whilst all sorts of attempts have been made to interest youngsters, other sources of entertainment appear to hold a greater attraction. Clubs have been offering all sorts of membership deals in order just to stay alive, although those at the pinnacle of the market still seem to be doing well enough.

The only clubs which are capable of development besides those on landfill are those which have development value; some clubs which have been surrounded by built development over the years. In such circumstances developers have found new sites for clubs on agricultural land and sought permission to develop the old courses. With agricultural land prices remaining at high levels, developers can struggle to make offers tempting enough to acquire the necessary green-field land.

Agricultural land prices mean that it is now impossible to generate a profit on a stand-alone golf site. Driving range development has also virtually stopped with a declining marketplace for golf, less spend on golf equipment and less practice taking place.

The continued lack of finance from banks and institutions has meant few sales and even fewer new projects. After the Brexit vote, the uncertainty, which appears likely to last some years, will influence the availability of development finance and we are therefore unlikely to see many (if any) new courses in the near future. Some developments may occur as enabling developments – for instance supporting large housing schemes – but cannot be justified as stand-alone golf.

Whilst some Local Authorities are supporting new sports facilities, the lack of developers or development finance and government cuts give little hope for the development of new municipal golf facilities in the near future. Indeed many Local Authorities are actively seeking to dispose of golf facilities as quickly as possible. Since completed new courses are now not worth the development costs it is difficult to envision any new site being developed except in exceptional circumstances (such as to support hotel occupancy).

It is crucial to obtain professional advice at the outset for investment appraisal, feasibility study and a business plan. In the current situation, it would be wise to commission a Feasibility Study which needs only cost £10-15,000 to check that there really is a demonstrable business case on which finance can be raised.

Type of business organisation

To sell land with planning permission: The cost of development of an average new course will be significantly more than the value of the facility when it is complete. There is currently no premium over agricultural value unless the situation or planning consent offers something exceptional. The cost of obtaining permission can vary enormously depending on the sensitivity of the site but it would seldom cost less than £250,000 including design, environment impact study and Local Authority fees. The demand from Local Authorities for an ever increasing amount of supporting information and studies to accompany an application means that few developers are prepared to take the associated risks.

To let land to a developer/operator: Assuming the latter pays for constructing the course, a long lease will be required. Rental levels will depend on the expected profitability of the facility but currently, in our experience, leases remain around £30-£75,000 for an 18-hole course.

To form a joint company with a developer/operator: This obviously means the farmer shares in the success or failure. The land would be all or part of the farmer's equity. There are no known active developers in this market at present.

To develop and operate the course himself: The farmer would need good knowledge of golf and exceptional management ability besides access to substantial capital. Any such decision in today's market would be bizarre.

Returns

It will cost considerably more to build and fit out a course than it will be worth for resale. Returns on capital are therefore negative unless the course has spin off benefits such as increasing an associated hotel occupancy or room rates.

Bankable rates of return on new courses are extremely rare. Associated residential or other development could make developments profitable, but planning permission for such developments is very difficult. Such developments in the UK will be extremely rare since property around courses tends to be at the premium end of the market which has suffered greatly in the short time since the Brexit vote.

Acknowledgement: *International Design Group* www.idgplanet.com

CHRISTMAS TREES

About 7 million real Christmas trees a year are sold in the UK; this figure has reduced as the quality of artificial trees has improved. Around 70% of real trees sold are UK-produced, with the balance from imports, chiefly from Denmark. A decade ago 80% were Norway Spruce, but this is now around 15%, with Nordman Fir, which retains its needles longer, accounting for around 75%. Other firs and spruces such as Fraser Fir, Noble Fir and Blue Spruce make up the remainder. The most popular sizes are between 5 to 7 feet.

There are 400 British growers, with plantations ranging from less than one hectare to over 100 ha. It is estimated that there are in excess of 50 million trees being grown, covering up to 9,000 ha. Most sales are through garden centres, which require a uniform tree, netted and palletised, but there are many successful 'choose and cut' operations, an enterprise which works well on a farm with a farm shop. Internet sales are growing.

The enterprise is slow to make a return. Nordman Firs are typically harvested in years 7 to 9, while the quicker-growing Norway Spruce takes 5 to 7 years. This extended period from planting to marketing makes the enterprise vulnerable to changing market conditions. Typically, about 20% of the crop is harvested in the first harvesting year, 50% in the second, 30% in the third. All species need a well-drained site free from late frosts, with good access. As with any crop, the better the land, the better the crop. The margin calculation below is for an eight-year rotation.

	Nordman Fir	
	£/ha	(£/ac)
5000 5 to 7 foot trees per ha @ price of . .	£3.00 - 3.50 / ft	
Output (average)	97,500	(39,458)
Variable Costs:		
Plants	4,025	(1,629)
Planting	1,035	(419)
Fertiliser	485	(196)
Weed control	450	(182)
Plant protection	900	(364)
Pruning and shaping	5,005	(2,025)
Harvesting	4,675	(1,892)
Marketing	9,750	(3,946)
Total Variable Costs	26,325	(10,654)
Gross Margin (whole period)	71,175	(28,804)
Gross Margin per year over 8 years	**8,897**	**(3,601)**

1. *Output:* Sale number of 5,000 trees per ha is based on approx. 90% saleable from a population of 5,500 per ha (see below). Price shown is for sales to local garden centres and shops. Prices are likely to be 20-30% lower if selling to wholesalers, national garden chains or DIY stores. Prices can be 50% more for retailing direct to the public.

2. *Establishment*: Rabbit fencing (£5 per m) is necessary and possibly deer fencing (£6-£8 per m). Spacing is possible from 60cm x 60cm to 1.8m x 1.8m, but 1.2m x 1.2m gives 5,500 plants per ha allowing for 20% land loss for headlands, access, etc. Losses of up to 5% in the first year means around 250 replacements are needed in second year. Norway Spruce transplants 25p-40p each, Nordman Fir 50-90p (*70p used in margin).* Planting, by hand or machine, 15-20p/per plant (*18p used in margin*).

3. *Variable Inputs:*

   NPK or nitrogen fertiliser (depending on soil analysis) is applied in late March with a further light nitrogen application applied in September.

Weed control through residual herbicide in March at £70/ha and glyphosate at £10/ha in October/November plus spot weeding of perennial weeds until the canopy closes over.

Insect control will require aphicide at £10-£50/ha and spider mite control £5-£100/ha commencing in the year of planting and subsequently in January for Spruce and April for Firs.

In years 5 - 7 Nordman Fir will require leader control. Approximately 50% of the trees treated twice annually with cutters or growth regulators over three years at a cost of 10p/tree = £300/ha in total. Fraser Fir and Noble Fir will also require 4-6 week applications to suppress phytophthora at £30-£50/ha/application.

4. *Pruning and Shaping*: This is essential to produce the shape of tree the market demands. Nordman Fir: basal pruning in year 3 or 4 at 20p per tree plus shaping in the same year at 16p per tree and bud-rubbing every year except harvest at 5-10p per tree per year. Norway Spruce: shaping 17p per tree per year from year 3 or 4.
5. *Harvesting:* Done over 3 to 6 weeks, for dispatch Nov 20th to Dec 12th. One full-time person per 3,000 trees sold, or one person per week per 400-500 trees. Cost: Norway Spruce 70-90p per tree, Nordman Fir 75-100p. Marketing costs around 10% of output.
6. *Machinery:* Inter-row plantation tractors £15,000-£65,000; stump clearing machines £7,000-£25,000; palletiser £13,000-£14,000; mist blowers £8,000-£10,000; hydraulic netting funnel £8,000-£10,000; manual netting funnel £175; guillotine tree cutter £4,000.
7. *Labour:* Planting and pruning can be done in January/February and tagging for height and quality from August to November. Thus it fits in well with combinable cropping operations. Casual help is likely to be required for harvest and sales.
8. Further information: A newly published guide to Christmas tree growing "Christmas Trees. A Growers Guide" is available from www.ruralservice.info.

The gross margins given are high, but these will only be achieved through a high level of expertise and commitment. The long period before any return is obtained must also be stressed, together with the risk this entails.

Acknowledgement: Thanks to - British Christmas Tree Growers Association, www.bctga.co.uk. Colin Palmer, Rural Services, www.ruralservices.info

BED AND BREAKFAST

The person running bed and breakfast should enjoy meeting people, have good social skills and be prepared to work unusual hours. In a crowded market, and with rising customer expectations, the standard of the product and service is critical. Farms must provide a standard of accommodation equal to that found in hotels. This will involve some refurbishment; both before starting the enterprise, to upgrade existing B&B to rising standards and ongoing repair of wear and tear.

It is vital to know the planning, legislative and financial requirements involved in B&B. Details are available from VisitBritain in the '*The Pink Booklet' - a practical guide to legislation for accommodation providers*'. This is available online at www.accommodationknowhow.co.uk/. Advice is also provided by National Tourist Boards of England, Scotland and Wales and Regional Tourist Boards.

Marketing is important. Some establishments produce a brochure or card giving details of the B&B, its location, facilities, and quality standards rating. New routes to customers have been opened up recently by of 'peer-to-peer' renting websites such as Airbnb. To join a marketing organisation the B&B should have a Quality Assurance Standard rating. These are awarded either by the official National Tourist Board inspectorate (which in England is Quality in Tourism), or the AA. The rating is at one of five levels, expressed as stars.

As there is considerable competition it is useful for the enterprise to offer something special or different such as accommodation for visitors' horses, a welcome for pets, or access to view the working farm. Establishments that can accommodate bigger parties are gaining in popularity. The number of B&Bs offering an evening meal has declined in recent years, but providing locally grown produce can be a draw.

Prices that can be charged reflect the quality of accommodation and location but cannot be far out of line with other local B&Bs and hotels. Prices can also vary depending on length of stay and time of year. The price range for one person per night ranges from £30 to over £150 on the basis of two adults sharing a room. A higher rate per person usually applies for single occupancy. There are regional differences with higher prices generally being charged in the south and east.

The range of B&B facilities has become enormous in the last decade. Decide the marketplace that suits you by identifying your selling point. Is it low cost, luxury, access to a working farm, family comfort etc.? Prepare the B&B enterprise, target your marketing and price the rooms accordingly to meet that marketplace.

Receipts from the enterprise can be calculated as follows: If the B&B is open for 40 weeks of the year at £40 per person per night, given a 60% occupancy rate the gross return per bed place will be around £6,720. Most farmhouse B&Bs have 4-6 bed spaces, which would generate a gross return of between £27,000 to £40,000 p.a.

Costs vary considerably: As every farmhouse B&B is different and some costs are difficult to apportion between guests and family, the following provides some pointers. Variable costs are food, electricity, heating, laundry, cleaning materials and additional help. There will also be regular redecoration costs, repairs, and replacement and renewal of glassware, china, cutlery, towels and bed linen. Variable costs if no non-family labour is used average about 20% of the nightly charge. If casual labour has to be included variable costs rise to 30-35% of the nightly charge.

Fixed costs include insurance, business rates (if they apply), membership of marketing organisations, regular advertising, repayments on loans taken out for building and equipment and regular labour; they are likely to average 30-35% of charges.

Contact: Farm Stay UK, VisitBritain, Quality in Tourism,

CAMPING AND CARAVAN SITES

Camp sites and caravan parks can appear an easy way to increase farm profit with its revenue divorced from the vagaries of agricultural markets and largely unaffected or even boosted by economic downturns. To run a successful site requires capital investment and time and a suitable location. A tourist area, away from busy roads, a good view, a well-drained stone-less field (at least a half hectare), with flat areas is necessary. Water and electricity are required (some have Wi-Fi). The site needs to be licenced by the local authority (not Scotland). Exemptions apply for some camping and caravanning organisations. They also require planning permission.

Initial Capital

Infrastructure includes; toilets and hot showers with disabled access, refuse collection, electrical hook-ups for caravans, compressed gas storage and landscaping including recreational space, road and footpath improvements, land levelling (at the pitches), and screening (hedges and fences). Capital spend will vary according to existing facilities and what level of camping experience is required as suggested here for just camping.

Capital	**Low level**	**High Leve**
Planning & Licencing	1,000	1,000
Landscaping	1,500	3,000
Small toilet and shower block	10,000	25,000
Mower	2,000	2,500
Business Development	500	2,400
Other - e.g. Drainage		1,100
Total Ex-Land	**15,000**	**35,000**

Gross margin

	Low Intensity		**High Intensity**	
	Per hectare	**Per pitch**	**Per hectare**	**Per pitch**
Pitches per hectare	25		75	
Occupancy per year (1)	800	32	3,150	42
Price		15		30
Output	12,000	480	94,500	1,260
Costs				
Depreciation over 10 years	1,500	60	3,500	47
Ground maintenance (2)	980	39	3,510	47
Utilities (3)	1,000	40	2,500	33
Insurance	1,000	40	2,000	27
Staffing & Management (4)	2,600	104	10,600	141
Attributable Costs	7,080	283	22,110	295
Net Margin	4,920	197	72,390	965

(1) 32 = 75% occupancy for 6 weeks, 42 = 100% occupancy for 6 weeks.

(2) includes lawn cutting, hedge trimming, site repairs & general maintenance

(3) water, drainage, electricity, possibly Wifi

(4) receiving bookings and payment & general management

These two gross margins demonstrate differences in pitches per hectare, occupancy rates and fees paid according to location or desirability of site. The impact on output is dramatic.

LOG CABINS AND GLAMPING

A renewed interest in British short breaks and holidays has led to a popularity surge of 'alternative' accommodation as well as the more traditional cottage rentals or caravan and camping. This might be accelerated by Brexit or the subsequent fall of sterling. As with any tourism and leisure based enterprise, location is key and can determine the success or failure of the proposal. It will also determine the rental income and occupancy that can be achieved. There may also be potential for using log cabins as a substitute for 'permanent', traditional buildings for office, storage facilities etc.

Log cabins range from glorified cladded caravans on bricks to opulent, luxurious and spacious living spaces. Some have hot tubs, access to pools and sports facilities. *Full planning permission* is required for any log cabin. Professional support should be sought prior to any expenditure on equipment / groundwork.

Build Costs

Prices for cabins vary considerably, primarily linked to the size and finish (quality) of the final build and the cost of routing any mains services. The figures below are a guide to log cabin purchase and build costs, but excluding fixtures and fittings which may add £85.00 to £125.00 of additional cost per m^2. Costs in routing mains services to the cabins will depend on remoteness, topography, environmental restrictions etc. and the extent of supplies required (bottled gas and septic tanks can be used in place of mains gas and sewage):

'Fishing' Log Cabin	$30m^2$ floor space plus sleeping 'loft'	£10,000 - £42,000
'Holiday let' Log Cabin	$60m^2$ floor space with 2 bedrooms	£20,500 - £55,500

For cabins larger than the examples above, add £250.00 to £300.00 per m^2 for every m^2 over and above the sizes stated

Rental Potential

Good occupancy rates will be paramount to the viability of any investment. Annual occupancy rates will vary depending on location, seasonality of local attractions and level of discount given in the 'off' season. Rental incomes again vary considerably, but typically range from £250 to £1,100 per week, with the higher incomes being achieved where the cabins are located in more desirable locations i.e. near to areas popular for fly and course fishing, mountain biking, walking, coastal activities, tourist attractions etc. Single night stays and short breaks often command a higher income pro rata than weekly lets but more work, including administration and cleaning, as well.

Other Accommodation

Yurts, tipis and other 'high specification' camping can also be lucrative if the resources are in place and high occupancy achieved, although these may not have a long a life as the cabins. Weekly rents of £200 to £600 per week can be achieved with the right locations and glamping specification. Capital cost for a furnished yurt can be £4,000 to £10,000 depending on size and specification. Ground and site maintenance as well as yurt preparation and booking administration should also be accounted for.

COARSE FISHING

In excess of 1.5 million people regularly coarse fish in the UK and numbers are rising. It is a freshwater method of line fishing usually from the banks of a watercourse. Coarse fish species include Rudd, Roach, Bream, Barbel, Tench, Chub, Perch, Pike, Carp, exclude sea species and 'game' fish like salmon and trout (usually caught by 'fly fishing'). Coarse fish are returned to the water after catching and weighing. Facilities can be rivers, streams, canals, lakes, ponds and even drains. The close season for coarse fishing is 15th March to 15th June although most canals and still waters are exempt from the close season. Anyone fishing must have a rod licence (available from the Environment Agency). Take advice before starting a fishing enterprise.

Fishing permit prices vary depending on the location, quality of the fishing, species etc. They will be higher if the water is actively managed to attract more or certain fish species. Maintenance and landscaping of the water banks will add a premium to a facility as will secure car parking and easy access to fishing pegs (platforms). Typically permits cost:

- Half-Day Ticket (per rod) £4.00 to £7.00
- Full-Day Ticket (per rod) £5.00 to £13.00
- Season Ticket (per rod) £50.00 to £180

Typical Net Margin for Coarse Fishing Lake, Labour excluded

1 Hectare (2.4 acre) Lake	**per peg**	**per Lake**
	£	**£**
Fishing Permits	1,080	10,800
Fish Sales	80	800
Output	1,160	11,600
Costs		
Setup Capital	128	1,275
Peg Maintenance	11	110
Fish Restocking	21	210
Feed Feed	150	1,500
Plants and Ground Maint.	40	400
Total Variable Costs	350	3,495
Gross Margin per ha (acre)	731	7,305

The figures above are a guide based on 30 half-day tickets per peg per year (£5 each), 30 full-days (£8 each), and 6 season tickets (at £115). There are 10 pegs on this lake. It takes time and commitment to build up a good reputation. Pegs should be spaced at no less than 25m apart (dictating income potential). A 2 acre carp lake would cost around £5,000 to initially stock with annual feeding costs of £1,500. Plants and other costs would total around £3,000 initially and will then need maintaining.

The larger the fish the higher the price that can be charged therefore the smaller fish can be routinely removed and sold. The total income from a two acre well-managed lake should be £10-15,000. Further diversifying into accommodation (log cabins) on a two acre lake stocked with 30lb carp could demand up to £1,000 per week for 4 anglers. Labour could become significant to manage the permits, stock and landscape. Generating this return might take some building up of regular fishers, managing the layout and facilities and so on and requires an existing suitable lake.

GAME SHOOTING

Game shooting is rising in popularity. It is the shooting of game species which include both feathered and fur animals. The most common birds shot in the UK include pheasant, partridge, duck, woodcock, snipe and grouse. Most feathered game are reared in captivity and then released but wild populations can be enhanced by different management techniques. There are strict and differing shooting seasons for different species, both game and pests.

'Driven' game shooting is the most popular method of game shooting in the UK whereby game birds are 'flighted' towards a standing line of guns. The quality and type of driven shoot varies according to landscape and management as well as the number of birds present. These variances also have a major impact on the cost of partaking in a shoot.

	per bird	**per Gun**	**per Shoot Day**	**per Season**
		22 birds	8 guns	8 shoots
	£	**£**	**£**	**£**
Charge for Gun	35.00	770	6,160	49,280
Other charges				1,500
Output	35	770	6,160	50,780
Costs				
Bird Placing	12.00	264	2,112	16,896
Bird Feed	2.30	51	405	3,238
Hospitality		75	600	4,800
Beaters & Pickers		80	600	4,800
Ground Maint. Costs			*625*	5,000
Capital depreciation			*500*	4,000
Gamekeeper			*1,000*	8,000
Attributable Costs	14.30	470	5,842	46,734
Net Margin	2.87	63	506	4,046

1. *Bird Placings:* at £4/head. Many more are placed than shot; this example is 3-fold.
2. *Beaters and Pickers:* 15 beaters per shoot and pickers
3. *Capital Depreciation:* Bird pens, feeders, water, etc.
4. *Gamekeeper:* Part time wage included here. May include imputed costs.

Gamekeeper costs vary depending on the scale of the shoot. In small-scale shoots, owners may themselves be the gamekeepers, but the opportunity cost of the owner's time should still be taken into account when computing margins. Also not included above is the cost of the land used for rearing and for game cover which may have an opportunity cost even if the land is already owned, although there may be other benefits obtained from this too, such as income earned from environmental schemes.

As a rough guide, a 200-bird day driven shoot will cost in the range of £800 per gun (participant), at £32 per bird. A driven shoot normally has 7 to 9 guns with up to 8 'drives' in a day. The expensive nature of most driven game shoots is required by the amount of work and cost involved in running a shoot (buying birds, feeding, structural equipment costs, game plot establishment, game keeper and beater's costs, shoot day hospitality etc.) and so margins may be small given the investment required.

Further information: British Association for Shooting and Conservation

OTHER DIVERSIFICATION

Well calculated diversification is to be encouraged. Non-agricultural enterprises managed in conjunction with the farming operation can offer several benefits to the business. These include:

- Spreading risks of returns; if the economics of agricultural production declines, revenue from non-commodity based enterprises may boost business income.
- Resource efficiency; most farm systems have quieter and busier periods for staff and management which may be switched into other roles for examples.
- Increased profit.

Any new enterprise will have its own risks associated with it. These must be clearly and objectively calculated (this will be a requirement if borrowed money is necessary). Each resource employed will have its own opportunity cost (what could it be earning if it was not being used for this new venture?). Cash (return on capital) is the obvious one, what could it earn elsewhere? Labour is less straight forward. For example, a B&B might require minimal new capital under some circumstances, but tie somebody to the house at key times of the day, restricting other employment opportunities.

Before a major investment or change in business structure to incorporate new diversifications, business plans and market research to assess the income potential are needed. Most new enterprises require new skills (such as different production systems, new marketing and sales techniques). These may take time and dedication to acquire. Developing new ideas and expanding a novel business venture can be exciting and time consuming; maintaining sufficient management time on the existing farm business is a common problem.

Nevertheless, many ventures exist where entrepreneurial skills have achieved notable success. Conversion of surplus farm buildings, for offices, workshops, retail and storage, has been the primary farm diversification activity up to date. Well over half of all farms have some kind of diversification, but if letting farm buildings is stripped out, the percentage of diversified farms falls to between a quarter and a third. Arable farms tend to be more diversified than livestock and farms in the South East are more diversified than elsewhere in the UK. Diversified enterprises might have a different VAT and taxation treatment. Check in advance with your accountant.

Some 'diversification' enterprises have been included above. There are many others, such as;

Novel crops/livestock
- Herbs
- Carp and crayfish
- Quails
- Snails & worms
- Maggots

Barn conversions
- Business lets
- Dwelling let

Sporting
- Fisheries
- Stalking
- Clay pigeon shooting

Horses
- Riding school
- Trekking

Drinks
- Brewing
- Distilling

Tourism
- Holiday cottages

Vertical integration
- Yoghurt / ice cream
- Farm shop
- Meat sales

Adventure Games
- Motor sports
- Go-karting

Many of these have been taken to new levels in recent years. For example the farm shop has moved on substantially from where it was 10 years ago and is now a vibrant and growing industry for high-end shoppers in market towns and motorway service stations. Camping has given rise to Glamping, again focussing at the more affluent end of the market keen on luxury and service, one that is covered in the book now. Brexit and its economic impacts could lead to other local opportunities.

6. FORESTRY

ESTABLISHMENT COSTS (BEFORE GRANT)

Unit Cost of Operations

Year/s	Operation	Cost (£)
1.	Trees for planting[1]	
	(i) Bare rooted:	
	Conifers	220-350 per 1,000
	Broadleaves	250-450 per 1,000
	(ii) Cell grown:	
	Conifers	270-355 per 1,000
	Broadleaves	330-450 per 1,000
1.	Tree Protection	
	(i) Fencing (materials and erection)	
	Rabbit	4.40-6.30 per metre
	Stock	4.35-5.40 per metre
	Deer	6.80-8.90 per metre
	Deer and Rabbit	8.40-11.00 per metre
	Split post and rail	5.70-8.90 per metre
	(ii) Tree guards/shelters	
	Spiral and canes (750mm)	40-45 per 100
	Plastic tubes (1,200mm)	140-190 per 100
	Stakes	75-100 per 100
1.	Spot spraying	80-100 per 1,000 trees
1.	Hand planting	
	Conifers	370-630 per 1,000 trees
	Broadleaves[2]	370-630 per 1,000 trees
	Machine planting (loams and sand based on 2,250 plants per ha)	235-475 per ha
2-3.	Replacing dead trees[3]	
	Operation	115-210 per ha
	Plant supply	95-160 per ha
1-4.	Weeding per operation	
	Herbicide[4]	75-135 per ha weeded
2.	Inter-row mowing	75-210 per ha

Costs specific to location		Upland	Lowland
1. Ground Preparation:	ploughing	140-220 per ha	70- 105 per ha
	mounding	290-405 per ha	290-405 per ha
1. Drainage		90-115 per ha	—
1. Fertilising		132-297 per ha	—

1. Price dependent on size and species.
2. Includes cost of erecting guards/shelters.
3. Replacing dead trees (beating up) may be necessary, once in the second year and again in the third year. Costs depend on number of trees.
4. Up to two weeding operations may be necessary in each of the first four years in extreme situations. Costs are inclusive of materials.

Access roads may need to be constructed and can typically cost between £13,500 and £33,000 per kilometre run (£21,700 to £53,000 per mile) depending on availability of road stone and the number of culverts and bridges required.

Total Establishment Costs up to Year 3

1. *Conifer—Lowland Sites:* On a fairly typical lowland site, requiring little or no clearing or draining, the approximate cost before grant of establishing a conifer plantation would be in the range of £3,500-£6,000 per hectare. Up to eight separate weeding operations may be required.
2. *Conifer—Upland Sites:* Establishing a similar conifer plantation on an upland site could cost £3,000 to £5,500 per hectare. Normally some form of site preparation and drainage is required but only one weeding operation may be necessary. Overall costs tend to be £500 per hectare less than on lowland sites.
3. *Hardwoods:* Costs of establishing hardwood plantations are highly dependent on the fencing and/or tree protection required. If tubes are needed, the overall costs will be influenced by the number of trees per hectare. Costs could be in the range of £4,000-£8,000 per hectare. Site conditions normally mean that hardwoods being grown for timber production are restricted to lowland sites.
4. *Farm Woodlands:* Establishment costs for farm woodlands may be lower than those indicated for hardwoods in (3) above if lower planting densities are used; costs of about £6,800 per ha for woods under 3 ha and £5,500 per ha for woods of 3 to 10 ha would be typical. However, it should be noted planting at lower densities may increase maintenance cost and will lead to production of lower-quality material.
5. *Size Factor:* Savings in fencing and other economies of scale may reduce average costs per ha by 10 to 20% where large plantations are being established.
6. *Method of Establishment:* A range of organisations and individuals undertake forestry contracting work and competitive tendering can help to control costs.

The costs of establishment given above, and those for maintenance given below, are estimates for England. Costs in Scotland tend to be lower.

Re-Stocking Costs

Once trees on a site have been felled, the Forestry Commission usually requires the site to be restocked as a condition of awarding a felling licence. This can be done by replanting or through natural regeneration, leaving a proportion of the trees standing and using seed from these trees to re-stock. Site preparation is usually required for natural regeneration through scarification and ongoing maintenance will be required to encourage a viable crop. Re-stocking a clear felled area would incur similar costs to those above.

MAINTENANCE COSTS

Once trees have been established they normally require some maintenance and management work each year. For trees being grown primarily for timber production on a large scale, operations required may include ride and fence maintenance, pest control, fire protection, management fee and insurance premiums. Costs are normally £60-£90 per ha per annum depending on the size of the plantation and the complexity of management. In upland areas, fertiliser is occasionally applied once or more times in the first 20 years of the tree's life, depending on the quality of the site. The estimated cost of this is £110-£275 per ha, depending on elements applied. For trees being grown for sporting and amenity purposes, annual maintenance costs are likely to be less and may range up to about £30 per ha.

Brashing is no longer practised on large-scale conifer plantations as a result of mechanical harvesting techniques.

PRODUCTION

Production is usually measured in terms of cubic metres (m^3) of marketable timber per hectare and will vary according to the quality of the site, species planted and thinning policy. Sites in lowland Britain planted to conifers typically produce an average of 12 to 18 m^3 of timber per ha per year over the rotation as a whole and would accordingly be assessed as falling in yield classes 12 to 18. Under traditional management systems, thinning begins 18 to 25 years after planting and is repeated at intervals of approximately 5-7 years until a conifer wood is clear-felled at between 40 and 60 years, or a broadleaf wood at 80-120 years. Approximately 40-45% of total production will be from thinnings. Broadleaves typically produce an average of between 4 and 8 m^3 of timber per hectare per year and fall in yield classes 4 to 8.

Prior to a thinning sale, the trees normally have to be marked and measured at an estimated cost of 75p - £1 per m^3. For a clear-felling sale the cost can range from £300 to £400 per ha, or about £1.50 per m^3 where a full tariff applies. These costs associated with mensuration and marking can vary significantly and will correlate to the value of the crop to be harvested.

Felling permission is required when more than 5m^3 is to be removed in any one calendar quarter. This requires an application to the Forestry Commission for a Felling Licence which will vary in complexity depending on the size and variety of the woodland. A felling licence must be obtained from the Forestry Commission before any felling takes place, unless a Woodland Management Plan has already been approved by them. Grants are available for preparing a Woodland Management Plan under Countryside Stewardship in England. Similar provisions operate in other parts of the UK.

TIMBER PRICES

Prices for standing timber are extremely variable, depending on species, tree size and quality; ease of extraction from site; geographical location (nearness to end user); quantity being sold; world market prices and effectiveness of marketing method used. The use of wood for energy generation continues to provide a market for poorer quality hardwood, conifer logs and forest residues.

Conifers/Softwood

Coniferous Standing Sales Price for Great Britain from the Forestry Enterprise Estate

Year to:	Average Price (per m^3 overbark)	
	Nominal terms	Real terms (2016 prices)
31st March 2010	9.61	10.60
31st March 2011	13.70	14.84
31st March 2012	14.10	15.06
31st March 2013	13.29	13.90
31st March 2014	15.62	16.07
31st March 2015	18.48	18.74
31st March 2016	16.79	16.91
31st March 2017	19.05	18.84

Source: Forestry Commission: Timber Price Indices. May 2017.

Hardwoods

The hardwood trade is very complex. Merchants normally assess and value all but the smallest trees on a stem by stem basis. Actual prices fetched can show considerable variation depending on species, size, form, quality and marketing expertise of the seller. Felling usually takes place in the winter months.

Some indicative prices for hardwoods are given below but it is important to note that actual prices fetched can vary quite widely. Wood quality is particularly important in determining prices and is particularly relevant when considering selling into the UK's developing export markets. Ash for internal joinery and poplar for plywood are in demand but size specification and seasonality of felling are crucial.

Product	Price per Unit
Poplar for the domestic market (standing)	£0-£5 per tonne
Quality poplar for the export market (standing)	£10-£25 per tonne
Ash logs (roadside)	£3-£7 per hoppus foot[1]
Oak logs – milling timber (roadside)	£3-£8 per hoppus foot[1]
Firewood (standing)	£18-£22 per tonne
Softwood sawlogs (standing)	£25-£50 per tonne
Cricket bat willow (standing)	£200-£250 per tree
Ash Hurley stick butts (standing)	£180-£200 per m^3

1. A hoppus foot is an imperial measurement that is still used in the hardwood trade (but not for softwood). It estimates what volume of a round log would be usable timber after processing (allowing for wastage). Because of the wastage factor a hoppus foot is larger than a cubic foot. $1m^3 = 27.736074$ hoppus feet.

TIMBER MARKETING

In-house marketing by the owner or agent can be cost effective but only if they have detailed, up-to-date knowledge of timber buyers in the market place. The alternative is marketing through a forestry manager or management company.

Sales can take place of either standing timber or felled timber at roadside. Standing sales place felling and extraction costs onto the purchaser who will usually pay for the timber on an outturn basis, whether by weight (tonne) or volume (m^3). These types of sales suit thinning and lower quality material. Roadside sales require the owner to pay for trees to be felled and extracted to a collection point where they can be accurately measured and inspected by potential purchasers. These types of sales are generally suitable for higher value timber.

Nationwide electronic sales of timber by auction and tender are now available for all types and quantities of timber.

MARKET VALUE OF ESTABLISHED PLANTATIONS AND WOODS

The value of woods depends on many factors such as location, access, species, age and soil type. The table below gives an indication of the range of current (2016) market values of commercial woodlands of different ages, based on recent sales. From years 20 to 25 onwards, prices of commercial woods will also be increasingly influenced by the quantity of merchantable timber they contain. Depending on the time of clear-felling, the timber may be worth between £900 and £6,000 per hectare (£360 to £2,500 per acre).

Relatively small woods or those with high amenity or Ancient Woodland status often command a premium over prices for commercial woodlands as can those that are freehold with minerals or sporting rights; this is particularly true in southern England. Conversely, conservation designation can restrict value due to a perception of preventing economic forest management; however this need not be the case. Recent sales of predominately broadleaved, amenity woodlands range from £10,000/ha to £20,000/ha with exceptional woodlands exceeding this by over 20%. The value of woods containing mature hardwoods will depend on the quality and value of the timber they contain and the quality of access.

Market Value of Commercial Conifer Woodlands

Age of Commercial Woods and Plantations	Price Range for crop and land £/ha	£/acre
0-10 years	5,000-5,500	(2,020-2,220)
11-20 years	7,800-8,400	(3,150-3,400)
21-30 years	8,100-8,600	(3,280-3,480)
31-40 years	8,200-8,700	(3,310-3,520)
40+ years	6,200-7,500	(2,510-3,060)

WOODLAND GRANTS

Each part of the UK has its own woodland grant scheme funded via the Rural Development Programme (RDP) and administered by the Forestry Commission. Details of all the schemes are on the Forestry Commission's website (www.forestry.gov.uk) or www.gov.uk.

Countryside Stewardship - England

The main priority of Countryside Stewardship (CS) is to protect and enhance the natural environment, in particular the diversity of wildlife (biodiversity). Water quality is another important priority as are flood management, the historic environment, landscape, genetic conservation and educational access.

The scheme is jointly run by Natural England (NE), Forestry Commission England (FC) and the Rural Payments Agency on behalf of Defra. Applications are competitively scored and must demonstrate that they meet the specific scheme priorities/statement of priorities.

To enter into any of the Countryside Stewardship schemes, applicants need to have all the following in place:

- Single Business Identifier (SBI)/Business Name;
- Land registered on the Rural Land Register (RLR);
- Registered on the Rural Payments Service and hold a Customer Reference Number.

CS provides both capital grants and funding for ongoing management. Capital grants are available for;

- Woodland Creation;
- Tree Health measures;
- The creation of a Woodland Management Plan.

A Management Plan must be in place for any woodland that is to be entered into an ongoing Higher Tier management agreement for Woodland Improvement.

1. *Woodland Creation:* The 2017 application window closed at the end of May 2017 but is expected to open again in early 2018 for Woodland Creation schemes.

- Woodland creation £1.28/tree with spiral guard + various supplements for enhanced protection measures – maximum £6,800 per hectare;
- Maintenance £200 per hectare per year for 10 years.

2. *Woodland Tree Health:* Grants are available for restoration and improvement but only available for trees infected by ash dieback (widely referred to as *Chalara* dieback of ash, but now scientifically described as *Hymenoscyphus fraxineus*) or *Phytopthora ramorum.* Official confirmation of infection by Forestry Commission Plant Health is required to be eligible for this grant.

3. *Woodland Management Plans:* Capital grants are available for the production of Woodland Management Plans on a rolling basis (no application window). They can secure 10 years' felling permission by the creation of a Plan of Operations.

- Minimum grant is £1,000 for three hectares and over of woodland;
- First 100 hectares is paid at £20 per hectare; £10 per hectare thereafter with no further limit.

4. *Woodland Improvement Grant (WD2(£100/ha per year):* This is a competitive multi-year scheme (five years) offering annual payments to undertake practices that will benefit the environment including; thinning, ride management and deer/squirrel control. It falls under the 'higher tier' of CS. Infrastructure grants and Capital grants to support the management objectives are also available under this scheme.

   Some example capital items that can be applied for under the WIG are as follows:

Option	Funding
Rhododendron Control	£2,800-£4,400 per Ha
Deer High Seats	£300 per unit
Deer fencing	£7.20 per metre

CARBON FUNDING

The Forestry Commission will not fund applications for new woodland creation that include carbon co-funding if there is any link between the proposals and use of the term 'offsetting'. It will, however, allow co-funding provided certain criteria are met and appropriate language is used. This has been formalised with the Forestry Commission's Woodland Carbon Code under which new plantations can be registered to verify their CO_2 sequestration and allow it to be marketed as a potentially valuable asset to be sold or reported in the short or longer term. Carbon is currently being valued at around £7-15 per tonne however, at the end of 2015, the Department of Energy and Climate Change predicted that values would continue growing, particularly from 2020 onwards. A typical broadleaved planting on a no-thin option may sequester over 500 tonnes of carbon per hectare over 60 years (http://www.forestry.gov.uk/carboncode).

WOODLAND TAXATION

Income from commercial woodlands is not subject to income tax and tax relief cannot be claimed for the cost of establishing new woodlands. In general, grants are tax free but annual Farm Woodland Payments are regarded as compensation for agricultural income forgone and are liable to income tax. The sale of timber does not attract capital gains tax, although the disposal of the underlying land may give rise to an assessment.

Woodlands which are managed commercially or which are ancillary to a farming business may be eligible for business property relief or agricultural property relief respectively, for inheritance tax purposes, if owned for more than two years.

Acknowledgement: The above estimates are based on information supplied by Justin Mumford of Lockhart Garratt Ltd.

7. ORGANIC FARMING

The Organic Sector:

The land area fully converted to organic status fell for the 6th consecutive time in the UK in 2016. When the land in conversion is included, it has been falling each year since 2008. Pigs, poultry and cattle numbers increased in 2016, but sheep numbers decreased. The total number of registered organic producers and processors rose 5% to 6,363, of whom 3,559 are producers.

In 2016, 2.9% of UK agricultural land (excluding common grazing) was registered as organic and is summarised as follows:

Area in '000 Hectares	*Fully Organic*	*In conversion*	*Total*	*% of Agric. Area*	*% of UK Organic Area*	*Number of Organic Producers*
England	282	15	297	3.3	58	2,434
Wales	74	8	82	4.9	16	618
Scotland	119	2	121	2.2	24	355
N. Ireland	8	0	8	0.8	2	145
Area in hectares						
2016	***482,700***	***25,200***	***507,900***	***2.9***		
2015	*500,800*	*20,600*	*521,400*	*3.0*		
2014	*529,000*	*19,700*	*548,600*	*3.2*		
2013	*550,999*	*24,350*	*575,349*	*3.3*		
2012	*573,406*	*32,223*	*605,629*	*3.6*		
2011	*619,073*	*36,914*	*655,987*	*3.8*		
2010	*667,551*	*50,794*	*718,345*	*4.0*		
2009	*619,268*	*119,441*	*738,709*	*3.7*		
2008	*594,413*	*149,103*	*743,516*	*3.6*		

The long term decline in UK organic farming has been led by a comparable fall of organic consumption having fallen by 32% since 2008 despite sales of all 'ethical produce' having risen annually since 2007 (*Food Statistics Pocketbook 2016*). The premium for organic goods is dearer than most other 'conscience-based' brands. However, a small upturn of land in conversion in 2015 and 2016 might lead the increase in organic farming.

Organic Prices

The table below gives an indication of prices comparing organic with conventional. Note it is not possible to simply change the prices or even gross margins in a farm system, the overhead structure would also change, probably considerably.

Farm Gate Prices

	Organic	*Conventional*	*Difference*	
Feed Wheat	*£260*	*£140*	*£120*	*85%*
*Milling Wheat**	*£290*	*£146*	*£144*	*99%*
Feed Barley	*£240*	*£128*	*£112*	*88%*
Milling Oats	*£270*	*£130*	*£140*	*108%*
Beans	*£300*	*£170*	*£130*	*76%*
Finished Beef (R4L Steer)	*£4.80/kg dw*	*£3.52*	*£1.28/kg*	*36%*

Stores (lowland Suckler)	*£2.30/kg*	*£1.90*	*40p/kg*	*21%*
Finished Lamb	*£4.65/kg dw*	*£4.22*	*43p/kg*	*10%*
Finished Pig	*2.45*	*1.45*	*£1.00*	*69%*
Milk	*36p/l*	*26p/l*	*10ppl*	*38%*
Free Range Eggs (med.)	*£1.65/doz*	*£1.00*	*£0.70/doz*	*65%*

* *Organic milling wheat specification tends to be 12.0% protein as opposed to 13.0% for conventional*

More resources are needed in organic farming so the goods are more expensive than conventional farming systems; for example yields per hectare or per unit of labour tend to be lower meaning more land and labour is needed per unit of product. Higher sale prices (or greater subsidisation) are therefore necessary to make organic farming as financially viable.

Two thirds of UK organic land is extensive permanent pasture and rough grazing, land which has less farming per hectare (and fewer non-organic inputs per hectare making conversion easier). The largest increase in organic land in 2016 is in woodland. Below are the land use statistics of producers of organic and in-conversion crop areas and livestock numbers for the applicable years:

Organic Land Use according to Crop Type (UK)

'000 ha	**2012**	**2013**	**2014**	**2015**	**2016**	***year on year % change***
Cereals	47.8	43.7	42.2	39.6	38.4	-3.2
Other arable crops	8.3	7.5	7.3	6.9	7.3	4.7
Fruit & Nut	2.1	2.1	2.1	1.9	1.9	-0.4
Vegetables & Pots	12.2	11.3	9.4	10.4	10.2	-1.2
Herbs & Ornam's	5.8	6.8	0.3	6.2	5.8	-7.5
Temporary pasture	106	98.9	93.7	92.2	92.1	-0.2
Permanent pasture	406	387	370	347	335	-3.5
Woodland	7.4	7.6	15.3	6.9	7.4	6.1
Unused Land	10.2	10.4	8.7	10.0	9.9	-0.7
Total area ha	***605***	***575***	***549***	***521***	***508***	**-2.6**

Organic Livestock Numbers (UK)

'000 head	**2012**	**2013**	**2014**	**2015**	**2016**	***year on year % change***
Cattle	290	283	304	292	296	1.7
Sheep	1,152	999	959	845	841	-0.5
Pigs	35	30	28	30	32	5.0
Poultry	2,458	2,488	2,399	2,560	2,821	10.2
Other Livestock	4.1	4.0	5.7	4.3	3.4	-22.1

Economics of Organic Farming

It has been no easier to make profits out of commodity farming in the organic sector than in the conventional systems in most areas of farming in the last year. Sales of organic farm goods have retained a premium over conventional commodities but they have increased as the base price has also risen. Mostly, only those adding value to the output, making a product from the farm commodity are making better margins, thereby the added-value enterprise is capturing the value rather than the farming *per se*.

When market volume declines, it changes at varying rates, meaning the demand for some products will be out of balance with others. Indeed, with livestock (several cuts of varying cost), it is sometimes a challenge to capture the organic premium for the entire beast and some fifth and fore-quarter (lower value) meats do not find organic homes. Indeed, by definition, the organic market being added-value trade means this is not uncommon.

Organic livestock farming is usually easier in the summer when forage is easily available, but costs of keeping stock rise in winter and this is exaggerated in the organic sector with high cost feeds.

Aid for Organic Farmers:

In England, support for organic farmers has previously been through the Organic Entry Level Stewardship (OELS) (see Section III). Existing OELS schemes will continue to their completion, but no new ones are being issued. Organic farming now receives support under the Countryside Stewardship Scheme, which grants an agreement to all those organic farmers who apply (i.e. it is not competitive). This provides support for the two-year conversion period of £50-£450/ha/year depending on land use. Rates then drop to a 'maintenance' level thereafter at £8-£300/ha. There are also specific organic related 'options'. Organic farming in Wales is supported under Glastir Organic whilst in Scotland support is provided under the Agri-environment Climate Scheme.

Further Information:

No gross margin data for organic enterprises are included in this section because a specialist publication is available on the subject: the '2017 Organic Farm Management Handbook', (11th Edition) by Nic Lampkin, Mark Measures and Susanne Padel, Organic Research Centre, Elm Farm, Newbury. Tel: 01488 658 298.

8. SUMMARY OF GROSS MARGINS

This page summarises the key figures of the gross margins over the previous pages. There are well in excess of 100 gross margins in the Pocketbook and additional data for other enterprises too. They cannot all be directly compared on a like for like basis, as different resources are required in order to produce each one and some offer whole farm benefits beyond the gross margin. Some, for example require different resources such as higher quality land, more overheads in terms of machinery, labour, buildings or working capital than others. Management requirement varies from one enterprise to another. Others are subject to having a supply contract with the processor.

Summary of Arable Crop Gross Margins

Crop	Price £/t	Yield t/ha	Output £/ha	Variable Costs £/ha	Gross Margin £/ha	Gross Margin £/t
Winter feed wheat	£140	8.60	£1,204	£460	£744	£87
Winter milling wheat	£146	8.25	£1,205	£500	£704	£85
Spring milling wheat	£146	6.00	£876	£336	£540	£90
First feed wheat	£140	8.75	£1,225	£450	£775	£89
Second feed wheat	£140	8.05	£1,127	£502	£625	£78
Winter feed barley	£128	7.00	£896	£363	£533	£76
Winter malting barley	£142	6.20	£877	£339	£538	£87
Spring malting barley	£150	5.70	£852	£282	£570	£100
Winter oats	£130	6.30	£819	£299	£520	£83
Spring oats	£130	5.50	£715	£226	£489	£89
Naked oats	£190	5.50	£1,045	£294	£751	£137
Winter rape	£310	3.50	£1,085	£423	£662	£189
Spring rape	£310	2.25	£698	£271	£426	£190
Spring linseed	£350	1.75	£613	£205	£408	£233
Winter linseed	£350	2.25	£788	£249	£539	£239
Winter beans	£170	4.20	£714	£254	£460	£109
Spring beans	£175	3.90	£683	£253	£429	£110
Blue peas	£200	4.00	£800	£270	£530	£132
Marofats	£225	3.60	£810	£384	£426	£118
Herbage seed ryegrass	£900	1.30	£1,170	£620	£550	£423
Late perennial	£1,040	1.10	£1,144	£591	£553	£502
Rye	£150	6.20	£930	£333	£597	£96
Triticale	£135	5.00	£675	£244	£431	£86
Borage	£2,600	0.40	£1,040	£327	£713	£1,783

Summary of Arable Crop Gross Margins (Continued)

Crop	Price £/t	Yield t/ha	Output £/ha	Variable Costs £/ha	Gross Margin £/ha	Gross Margin £/t
Lupins	£250	3.00	£750	£264	£486	£162
Durum wheat	£190	6.20	£1,178	£350	£828	£134
Crambe	£180	2.50	£450	£300	£150	£60
Hemp	£160	7.50	£1,200	£410	£790	£105
Grain maize	£155	7.50	£1,163	£340	£822	£110
Millet	£225	3.00	£675	£250	£425	£142
Poppies	£650	2.00	£1,300	£322	£978	£489
Soya	£375	2.50	£938	£283	£655	£262
Vining peas	£240	4.75	£1,140	£381	£759	£160
Maincrop potatoes	£175	45.0	£7,875	£4,844	£3,031	£67
Early potatoes	£260	23.0	£5,980	£3,602	£2,378	£103
Sugarbeet	£27	78.0	£2,111	£1,308	£802	£10
Dessert apples	£739	37.5	27,713	21,521	£6,191	£165
Culinary apples	£452	42.5	19,189	17,956	£1,233	£29
Cider apples	£122	35.0	£4,270	£3,208	£1,063	£30
Pears	£605	22.5	13,613	12,324	£1,289	£57
Raised bed strawb.s	£3,068	20.5	62,884	55,670	£7,214	£352
Everbearer strawb.s	£3,068	36.0	110,430	95,894	14,537	£404
Raspberries	£6,430	11.5	73,945	61,989	11,956	£1,040
Blackcurrants	£714	6.75	£4,820	£1,874	£2,946	£436
Dry bulb onions	£150	41.0	£6,150	£1,785	£4,365	£106
Cauliflower	£386	12.0	£4,632	£3,564	£1,068	£89
Calabrese	£410	10.0	£4,100	£3,342	£758	£76
Hops (£/kg)	£6.74	1.50	10,110	£6,886	£3,224	£2,149
SRC /year	£50	8.0	£400	£102	£298	£37
Miscanthus	£76	13.0	£987	£615	£372	£29
Christmas trees	£3.25/ft		£12,188	£3,291	£8,897	

Summary of Livestock Gross Margins

Livestock		Output	Variable Costs	Gross Margin /Head	Gross margin £/Ha
Dairy					
All-Year-Round calving Holstein	per Cow	£1,989	£905	£1,084	£2,385
Autumn calving Fries./Hol.	per Cow	£1,492	£615	£877	£1,930
Spring calving Friesians	per Cow	£1,267	£401	£867	£2,080
Channel Island	per Cow	£1,594	£567	£1,027	£2,567
Friesian followers	per Head	£833	£338	£495	£707
Channel followers	per Head	£813	£295	£517	£796
Beef Cattle					
Bucket reared calf 3 month	per Calf	£156	£112	£44	
Bucket reared calf 6 month	per Calf	£256	£194	£62	
Spring calving lowland sucklers	per Cow	£358	£240	£118	£212
Autumn calving lowland suckler	per Cow	£503	£294	£209	£344
Spring calving upland suckler	per Cow	£333	£233	£100	£160
Autumn calving upland sucklers	per Cow	£477	£300	£177	£221
Store cattle keeping summer	per Head	£264	£63	£201	£1,154
Store cattle keeping winter	per Head	£256	£203	£53	
Summer store finishers	per Head	£334	£167	£167	£502
Winter store finishers	per Head	£339	£294	£45	
Summer finished sucklers	per Head	£559	£263	£296	£888
Winter finished sucklers	per Head	£307	£322	-£15	
Maize finishing (dairy)	per Head	£711	£332	£379	
Maize finishing (suckler)	per Head	£667	£296	£371	
Cereal bull beef (continental)	per Head	£695	£576	£118	
Cereal bull beef (dairy)	per Head	£760	£576	£183	
Sheep					
Lowland spring lamb	per Ewe	£95	£49	£46	£464
Upland spring lamb	per Ewe	£80	£48	£33	£294
Rearing ewe lambs	per Head	£54	£25	£29	£440
Finishing store lambs	per Head	£20	£16	£3	£92

Summary of Livestock Gross Margins (Continued)

Livestock		Output	Variable Costs	Gross Margin /Head	Gross margin £/Ha
Pigs					
Weaners	per Sow	£1,324	£807	£517	
Pork	per Pig	£40	£41	-£0.70	
Cutter	per Pig	£55	£50	£4.50	
Bacon	per Pig	£68	£60	£8.60	
Combined pork	per Pig	£93	£72	£20.88	
Combined cutter	per Pig	£108	£81	£26.08	
Combined bacon	per Pig	£121	£91	£30.18	
Poultry					
Enriched caged eggs	per Bird	£14.00	£12.80	£1.20	
Free range eggs	per Bird	£20.80	£14.68	£6.12	
Pullets	/Bird Reared	£3.30	£2.68	£0.62	
Broilers	£/Bird	£1.87	£1.39	£0.48	
All year turkey	£/Bird	£33.26	£20.10	£13.16	
Christmas turkey	£/Bird	£38.68	£23.94	£14.74	
Large roaster chickens	£/Bird	£13.06	£6.13	£6.93	
Ducks	£/Bird	£7.75	£5.55	£2.20	
Geese	£/Bird	£45.25	£28.42	£16.83	
Other Livestock					
Breeding & finishing deer	/100 Hinds	£25,756	£7,940	£17,816	£802
Breeding and selling stores	/100 Hinds	£14,050	£2,873	£11,177	£727
Deer park	/100 Hinds	£13,002	£3,769	£9,233	£277
Finishing stag calves	/100 Stags	£13,958	£4,580	£9,377	£1,032
Wild boar	per Sow	£1,835	£913	£922	£4,612
Dairy goats	per Doe	£491	£252	£239	
Dairy sheep	per Ewe	£480	£251	£230	£2,527
Angora goats	per Doe	£301	£119	£182	£873
Ostriches ~ laying trios	per Trio	£989	£857	£132	£662
Ostriches ~ fatteners	per bird	£388	£350	£38	£234
Alpacas	Per head	£146	£156	-£10	-£97
Rabbits	/200 Does	£75,651	£13,800	£61,851	
Trout	/tonne Fish	£1,930	£1,580	£350	

III. GOVERNMENT SUPPORT

1. INTRODUCTION

Agricultural support to farmers and the rural economy is largely provided through the European Union's Common Agricultural Policy (CAP), and delivered in the UK by the devolved Governments of England, Wales, Scotland and Northern Ireland. The World Trade Organisation (WTO) provides a global tier in the hierarchy of agricultural (trade) policy.

The CAP has two main budgets (or Pillars). Pillar 1 includes the Basic Payment Scheme (BPS), which provides direct aid to farm businesses and also market support for agricultural produce – the latter once being the mainstay of CAP support, but now much reduced in importance. Pillar 2 is support through Rural Development and provides direct support to farmers and also to rural communities. In 2016, Pillar 1 accounted for approximately 76 per cent of support paid to English Farmers and 24 per cent for Pillar 2. Market support (which is not paid direct to farmers) is not included.

In individual situations businesses should always check with the latest legislation and their devolved administrations' publications.

2. SUPPORT POST BREXIT

The UK is timetabled to leave the EU at the end of March 2019. Until it formally leaves, it remains subject to EU policies, including the CAP and all the support measures and legislation included in this chapter. The UK's decision to leave the EU will mean on departure, it will no longer receive support through the Common Agricultural Policy (CAP). There will be a British Agricultural Policy and as agriculture is a devolved policy, we may see different parts of the UK diverging on farm support. The Government has pledged to keep spending on farm support at current levels until the end of the next Parliament, whilst this is supposed to be 2022, there seems a strong possibility that there will be another election before then. It must be noted though, there is no mention of inflation and also it only refers to the budget and not the way in which support is delivered. It cannot be assumed that a BPS-like system will be in place until 2022. It is likely that a new system will be phased in from 2020.

3. THE BASIC PAYMENT SCHEME

The Basic Payment Scheme was introduced from 1st January 2015 and is scheduled to last to December 2019 and possibly beyond then if agreement on the next round has not been completed as happened last time. Many decisions on implementation were left to member states. Agriculture, being a devolved policy meant in the UK, England, Scotland, Wales and Northern Ireland each made their own decisions as detailed in following pages.

ENTITLEMENTS AND REDISTRIBUTION

The Basic Payment Scheme (BPS) replaced the Single Payment Scheme (SPS) from January 1st 2015. They are similar (see page 148 for details); entitlements have to be matched against eligible land which then generates a yearly payment as long as certain land management rules are followed (cross-compliance). But unlike the SPS, the BPS forms the 'foundations' of the new support arrangements, with a system of top-up payments that are available from the Pillar 1 budget. These are discussed in detail below. Regardless of how many top-ups are used in each member state, the total funds for Pillar 1 (the National Ceiling) in any region remains unchanged, they simply allocate the funds differently:

- ***Entitlement Roll-over.*** England and other countries already operating the regional payment system were able to roll-over existing entitlements into the new system. There was therefore no re-grant of entitlements in England – SPS entitlements held by farmers at the end of 2014 were converted into BPS ones for 2015. However, excess entitlements held in 2015 (more entitlements than eligible hectares), were confiscated.

- ***Entitlement Grant.*** Countries operating the historic system (including Wales and Scotland) issued new BPS entitlements on the basis of land occupied in 2015. Entitlements were only granted to those that received a payment (of any size) under the SPS in 2013. There are mechanisms for cases where this did not happen: A 'national reserve', comprising up to 3% of funds, deals with hardship claims. Farmers growing certain crops in 2013 (fruit, vegetables, potatoes, ornamentals and vineyards) were eligible to establish entitlements even if they did not claim the SPS in 2013. There were rules to deal with 'mergers and scissions' of holdings between 2013 and 2015 and there was also the Private Contract Clause. This applied where all or part of a holding was sold or leased between 2013 and 15th May 2015.

- ***Internal Convergence.*** This is the term for the move to a flat rate regional payment in countries which operated the historic system (e.g. Wales and Scotland).

  Scotland and Wales are phasing in the flat rate system fully by 2019. This is happening in equal steps of 20% per year i.e. in 2018 a farmer's entitlement value will be made up of 20% of the historic value and 80% of the flat regional payment (see below). This will mean farmer's entitlement values change each year until 2019. England went through this process between 2005 and 2012. There will be winners (extensive producers) and losers (intensive producers). Examples of estimated payment rates are given at the end of this section.

- ***Regions.*** The flat rate regional payment is equal throughout the region the land is in. Member states are able to divide their countries into sub-regions so the regional payment rates reflect the intensity of farming possible on each hectare. This can make the transition from historic to flat rate less pronounced as the less productive land can be given a lower rate and the better, more productive land, a higher flat rate payment.

  In ***England*** under SPS, there were three regions; Lowland, Severely Disadvantaged Areas (SDA) and Moorland. These were retained for the BPS. Entitlements are not tradable across these regions, but in order to 'move money up the hills', from 2015 the Lowland rate reduced slightly and the SDA rate increased to match the Lowland value. The Moorland rate also increased from 2014 levels.

  Scotland created three regions. Better land (arable and grassland) is one payment region (approximately 1.8m ha) – Region 1. Rough grazing has been split to avoid over compensation for the least productive land. This has been done using the Less Favoured Area Support Scheme (LFASS) classification (see Rural Development Section). Rough grazing in the non-LFA and in LFASS grazing categories B, C and D, are in one payment region (approx. 1m ha) – Region 2. The least productive rough grazing land in LFASS grazing category A forms the third region covering approximately 2m ha. In this region coupled support for beef and sheep enterprises is available - see Top-Up Schemes later.

  Wales initially decided to create three regions. But following a legal challenge a decision was made to introduce a flat rate payment system across all of Wales by 2019 in five equal steps. A *Redistributive Payment* (see below) applies to the first 54 hectares (133 acres) of any claim, rising to the estimated rate of €129 per hectare in 2019.

GREENING

Greening is the biggest change for farmers under the BPS. It requires farmers to provide environmental benefits in return for their direct payments. It is seen as a way of making farm support more acceptable to tax payers and voters. Greening payments account for 30% of the BPS. Therefore it will change as a result of the 'internal convergence' mechanism set out above.

Under the Rules of 'Equivalence' if a member state can demonstrate to the EU Commission that existing or proposed schemes (national environmental certification schemes) provide equivalent environmental benefit to greening, then this can replace the basic greening requirement. None of the UK administrations used this measure, all adopting the three basic EU measures of crop diversification, permanent pasture retention, and Ecological Focus Areas (EFAs). Claimants are exempt from greening on organic land although the greening payment is still made.

- ***Land Definitions***. Under greening there are three types of land, all three categories added together are known as the claimant's eligible area;

  - Permanent Pasture – land that has been in grass for five years or longer. The sixth time it is entered as grass on the subsidy claim form it becomes permanent pasture. It doesn't matter if it has been reseeded, it is the length of time the land has been out of the arable rotation. A catch crop (e.g. stubble turnips) could break the sequence but it would have to be demonstrated.

  - Permanent Crops – land in crops that are in place for five years or more without replanting and that yield repeated harvests e.g. vines, orchards, short rotation coppice, Miscanthus, nurseries.

  - Arable Land – any eligible land that is not permanent pasture or permanent crops, including fallow land and temporary grass.

- ***Crop Diversification***. Where a claimant's arable land area (as defined above) is between 10-30 hectares a minimum of two crops are required. Three crops will be needed when the arable land area is above 30 hectares. No crop should cover more than 75% of the farm area. Where three crops are required, the two main crops together should not exceed 95% of the area. The crop diversification requirement does not apply where;
  - more than 75% of the arable land is used for temporary grass or left fallow (as long as the remaining arable land area is below 30 hectares)
  - more than 75% of the entire holding is permanent or temporary grass (again, subject to a 30 hectare limit on the remaining arable land area).

  A crop is defined by its *genus* and *species*. Wheat, barley, oats, oilseed rape, linseed, potatoes, sugar beet etc. are all classed as separate crops. Spring and winter crops are also treated as separate crops. Fallow is a 'crop type', as is temporary grass. There are some oddities though so refer to scheme guidance.

- ***Permanent Pasture***. Permanent pasture area has to be maintained, enforceable at member state (not farm) level. The overall percentage of permanent grassland in each country compared to the total agricultural area must not fall by more than 5%.

  Ecological Focus Areas (EFAs). Claimants must put 5% of their eligible *arable* land into EFAs. The EU Commission has confirmed it will remain at 5% for 2018 and 2019. Countries can choose from a list of possible features to offer to farmers as eligible EFAs. This includes landscape features (hedges and trees), buffer strips, fallow land, protein-fixing crops, agro-forestry and short-rotation coppice. A matrix system converts linear features (e.g. hedges) into EFA area equivalents and gives some features extra value. E.g. in England a 1m stretch of hedge can be worth $10m^2$ of EFA. Some claimants are exempt; EFAs are not required on farms where more than 75% of the land is grassland (temporary or permanent) as long as the remaining arable area is less than 30 hectares. Farms with less than 15 hectares of arable land are also exempt from the EFA requirement. Farmers need to re-calculate their EFA requirement annually and different EFAs can be used each year. The table below shows the features available in each devolved region.

The EFA requirement, apart from woodland (& coppice) options, must be sited on or within 5m of arable land i.e. hedges between permanent pasture fields are not eligible but a hedge separated from arable land by a track < 5m wide is eligible.

Other Points Regarding Greening

- ***Double funding and Agri-environment schemes.*** This is where farmers could potentially be paid twice for the same action. This is not allowed under EU rules. Some Agri-Environment Scheme options are similar to EFA options and so are seen as double funding, in which case a reduction is made on some Agri-Environment Payments.

- ***Penalties.*** Penalties for not complying with greening are based on the shortfall in requirement and range from 0 to 15% for each of the Crop Diversification and EFA rules separately on arable land only i.e. up to a maximum of 30% (100% of the greening payment). From 2017 further administrative penalties for non-compliance were introduced increasing the penalty to 120% of the greening payment. In 2018 this rises to 125%.

EFA Options in England, Scotland and Wales

Feature	Notes	EFA area m² (1m length or 1m² =)		
		England	Scotland	Wales
Fallow land	The 'default' EFA option. No production is allowed during the fallow period. Each devolved region has its own fallow period.	1.0	1.0	1.0
Hedges	Refer to scheme literature for management rules.	Both sides 10 One side 5	n/a	Both sides 10 One side 5
Traditional Stone Walls	Min. height 1m, Max. width 4m. No cement allowed.	n/a	n/a	1.0
Buffer strips	Must be next to a watercourse or parallel with and on a slope leading to a watercourse (Eng.) The same buffer strip can be used for Greening and Cross Compliance rules.	9.0	1.5	n/a
Field Margins	Can include hedges and ditches. Min. width 1m, max. 20m.	n/a	1.5	n/a
Catch crops & green cover	England and Scotland only but different management rules	0.3	0.3	n/a
Nitrogen fixing crops	Includes beans, peas, lupins, clover (plus soya, sainfoin and lucerne in Eng. & Wales plus alfalpha, chickpea, vetch and trefoil in Scot.). Scotland requires at least two of these crops to be grown, distinctively, not as a mixture. *	0.7	0.7	0.7
Short Rotation Coppice	Includes Alder, Silver Birch, European Ash, Sweet Chestnut, Willow, Poplar, Hazel, Lime and Sycamore.	n/a	n/a	1.0
Forested Areas	Areas used to claim the SPS in 2008 and are now afforested under the WGS, FWPS, Better Woodlands for Wales, Improved Land Premium or Glastir.	n/a	n/a	1.0

***Note**: This table only summarises the features in each country. Each has detailed management rules which differ depending on which country it is in. Claimants should consult scheme literature for further guidance. * Check rules of allowable input use carefully.*

TOP-UP SCHEMES

The Basic Payment Scheme and Greening form the 'foundation' of the direct support arrangements, but a system of top-up payments is available from the Pillar 1 budget.

- ***Young Farmers Scheme***. A mandatory scheme for all member states, funded by a minimum of 2% of the BPS budget. It provides a 25% top-up to the value of entitlements for 5 years to those under 40 years old. In Wales and Scotland, the top-up is equivalent to 25% of the final (2019) payment rate. There is a limit on how many hectares qualify – the average farm size in the region, but with a minimum and maximum area of 25 and 90 hectares. In England and Scotland it is 90 hectares. In Wales it is 25. At 90 hectares the extra payment is worth around £3,500 per year. Rules apply regarding having at least 50% of business accountability and dates since that began.

- ***Coupled Support***. There are no coupled payments in England or Wales. Scotland has coupled support for beef and sheep enterprises. Cattle with 75% beef genetics receive an annual payment, dependant on the number of animals claimed each year but is approximately €100 per calf. Additionally there is a coupled top-up for beef producers on the islands in the region of €160 per calf. There is coupled support for sheep producers who farm in Scotland's rough grazing areas (80% of BPS area in region 3 and less than 200ha in region 1). Payment rates vary annually depending on the number of animals claimed but is around €100 per eligible yearling ewe.

- ***Redistributive payment***. This provides a 'top-up' on the first few entitlements held by each claimant. It is optional for member states and is limited to the initial 30 hectares, or the average national farm size if larger (54 hectares in the UK). Only Wales has taken up this measure – see Regions earlier.

- ***Small Farmers Scheme.*** This is optional for member states. Participants would face less stringent cross-compliance regime and not be subject to greening in return for a fixed annual payment. No UK administrations took this up.

- ***Hill Support.*** It is possible for member states to pay additional support to hill areas from the Pillar 1 (BPS) budget. This is limited to 5% of total funds and is in the form of a top-up to entitlement values. None of the GB regions are making use of this.

ELIGIBILITY AND RESTRICTIONS ON AID

- ***Active Farmer***. To be eligible for the BPS, a claimant must be an 'active farmer', defined in two parts: A simple 'negative list' of entities not eligible by default for the Basic Payment; operators of airports, water companies, railways, sports grounds and real estate services. Member states can add to this list with the permission of the EU Commission (GB devolved regions have not). If claimants are one of the above, they may still be eligible for the BPS if one of the following apply:

    - If the claimant received less than €5,000 direct payment the previous year
    - In England if the claimant has more than 36 hectares of eligible land (or 21 in Wales) they are automatically an 'active farmer'. Scotland does not have an area readmission route.

Or by the income routes:

- If the amount of direct payments is at least 5% of the receipts obtained from non-agricultural activities in the most recent fiscal year, or

- If receipts from farming is at least 40% (33% in Scotland) of total business receipts, or If agricultural activity is a principle business objective i.e. is in the founding documents (Scotland Only)

Secondly, if more than 50% of a claimant's land is in 'areas naturally kept in a state suitable for grazing or cultivation' and they do not comply with the minimum activity rule (see below) the claimant is deemed not to be an 'active farmer'.

- ***Minimum Agricultural Activity***. Minimum activity levels are set on 'areas naturally kept in a state suitable for grazing or cultivation'. ***England*** has no land in this classification. In ***Wales*** saltmarsh and coastal dunes have been identified as such. If such land covers more than half of the farm, to be an active farmer, claimants must have either a minimum stocking density of 0.01 to 0.05 European Livestock Units per hectare or maintain stock proof fencing and provide water, or control injurious invasive plants. In ***Scotland*** Payment Regions two and three (see earlier) are designated. If over half of the holding is located in these regions to be classed as an active farmer a minimum activity must take place. There must either be an average stocking level of 0.05 Livestock Units per hectare for 183 days in each scheme year or an Annual Environmental Assessment must be carried out.
- ***Minimum Claim size***. The EU's minimum claim size is 1 hectare or €100. The minimum BPS claim size in each of the GB regions is higher at;
  - England – 5 hectares
  - Scotland – 3 hectares
  - Wales – 5 hectares
- ***Degressivity.*** This was new for BPS, mandatory for all member states. It is a minimum 5% reduction in aid rates above €150,000. The greening element is not affected. Member states can raise levels of degressivity up to 100 per cent and reductions can be 'banded'. England and Scotland levy the minimum EU degressivity requirement. Scotland may introduce a cap of €600,000 from 2018 onwards. Wales has a banded policy:
  - 100% cap on payments above €300,000 (excluding greening);
  - 55% on payments between €250,000 and €300,000,
  - 30% on payments between €200,000 and €250,000 and
  - 15% on payments between €150,000 and €200,000.
- ***Pillar Transfer.*** This replaces *modulation*. A transfer of funds between the two CAP Pillars is allowed either way, to a maximum of 15% of funds. The rates can be different each year. No match-funding is required. Each of the devolved regions has taken this option at different rates: *England* – 12%, *Scotland* – 9.5%, *Wales* – 15%, *Northern Ireland* – 0%.
- ***Financial Discipline***. This is the mechanism by which direct payments are kept within the EU Budget. The threshold for financial discipline is set at €2,000 (€5,000 under SPS). Payments under this threshold are exempt.
- ***External Convergence.*** This is the term for all member countries receiving a fairer share of Pillar 1 funds.

Other Issues

- ***Sugar*** - Sugar quotas end on 30th September 2017.
- ***Conversion Rate*** – For non-Eurozone countries, BPS (calculated in euros) is converted into local currency using the average exchange rate throughout each September.

ESTIMATED BPS PAYMENT RATES

The rates below are estimated by The Andersons Centre for illustrative purposes. In Wales and Scotland every claimant has a different entitlement value based on their history which will converge in 2019 and it is therefore difficult to show budgeting figures. In these two countries, different initial entitlement values have been used to show how the 'winners and losers' as businesses move from the Historic method to a Regional Average Payment.

In the tables below the following exchange rates are used. 2014 – 2016 are actuals, 2017 are estimated. All the figures include the Greening Payment and are after Pillar Transfer and Financial Discipline.

Exchange Rate	2014	2015	2016	2017	2018	2019
€ = £	0.7773	0.7313	0.8523	0.85	0.85	0.85

England

Flat Rate Area Payments in England (forecast figures for 2017 onwards)

£/ha (acre)	2014	2015	2016	2017	2018	2019
Lowland	193 (78)	179 (72)	213 (86)	213 (86)	207 (84)	209(85)
SDA	155 (63)	178 (72)	211 (85)	212 (86)	206 (83)	207(84)
Moorland SDA	27(11)	47 (19)	56 (23)	56 (23)	54 (22)	55 (22)

Wales

The table below is for illustrative purposes. It uses 2014 gross entitlement values of €500, €250 and €60 per entitlement to project future BPS values.

Example Payments for Wales

	Gross Entitlement £/Ha (acre)					
2014	**2014**	**2015**	**2016**	**2017**	**2018**	**2019**
€500 (€202)	384 (155)	301 (122)	296 (120)	247 (100)	205 (83)	170 (69)
€250 (€101)	192 (78)	169 (68)	190 (77)	182 (74)	176 (71)	170 (69)
€60 (€24)	46 (19)	69 (28)	107 (43)	131 (53)	152 (62)	170 (69)

Based on 100ha farm including redistributive payments on the first 54ha, Assumes the same areas claimed going forward

Scotland

The first table below illustrates how payments are changing using an example gross entitlement value of €500, €100 and €30 per entitlement in 2014 for the three regions; Arable & Grassland (Region 1), Rough Grazing (Region 2) and Poor Rough Grazing (Region 3) respectively. Note: there is coupled support available of around €100 per yearling ewe in Region 3 (this has not been included in the figures below).

Example Payments for regions in Scotland

£/ha (acre)	2014	2015	2016	2017	2018	2019
Region 1	384 (155)	263 (106)	283 (115)	258 (104)	234 (95)	210 (85)
Region 2	76 (31)	49 (20)	51 (21)	44 (18)	38 (15)	32 (13)
Region 3	23 (9)	15 (6)	16 (6)	14 (6)	12 (5)	10 (4)

The example farms below illustrate how claimants' payments are changing over five years. They are for illustrative purposes only. *Note: They show the average rate per hectare. In practice where a farm's eligible land crosses payment regions, entitlements will have different rates depending on which region they were established in.*

Example A - is a 150ha intensive beef finisher or dairy farm. In 2014 the gross entitlement value was €400/entitlement. In 2015 all the land is in Region 1.

Example B – is a 150ha mixed beef and sheep farm with some arable land. In 2014 the gross entitlement value was €200/entitlement. In 2015 70ha is in Region 1; 50ha in region 2; with 30ha within region 3.

Example C – the final example is an extensive sheep farm, comprising 300ha which is within Region 3 in 2015. In 2014 the gross entitlement value was €50/entitlement.

Estimated Payments for example farms in Scotland

£/ha (acre)	2014	2015	2016	2017	2018	2019
Example A	307 (124)	227 (92)	251 (102)	237 (96)	223 (90)	210 (85)
Example B	154 (62)	116 (47)	129 (52)	123 (50)	117 (47)	111 (45)
Example C	38 (15)	22 (9)	22 (9)	18 (7)	14 (6)	10 (4)

Does not include any coupled beef and sheep payments. Assumes the same areas claimed going forward

4. MARKET SUPPORT

Market support measures are the other part of Pillar 1 funding, including intervention buying, export subsidies, quotas and tariff barriers. The main measures are tariffs which are unlikely to change much in the short term following the lack of WTO trade deal. Milk quotas in the EU ended on the 31st March 2015.

Sugar prices are supported within the EU. Following the 2006 reforms, 'institutional' sugar prices have been cut to reach a minimum EU beet price of €26.4 per tonne in 2009 to 2012. Although in Britain, actual prices paid are determined through the Inter-Professional Agreement between British Sugar and the NFU (refer to page 33).

Brexit Note: Tariffs that currently apply to UK imports are agreed by the WTO on behalf of the entire EU. They (invisibly) provide considerable support to UK farm-gate prices. What import tariffs the UK might implement upon Brexit is currently unknown but could have massive ramifications to UK agriculture in future years. This section of the Pocketbook will be developed in future Editions as more information becomes available.

5. SINGLE PAYMENT SCHEME

The BPS which replaced the Single Payment Scheme (SPS) used some of its principles so an overview is provided. Previous Editions of the Pocketbook are more comprehensive.

SINGLE PAYMENT SCHEME HISTORY

Major reforms of Pillar 1 of the CAP were implemented mostly in January 2005, with the introduction of the SPS. In November 2005 a reform of the Sugar Regime was agreed including price cuts and compensation to farmers starting with the 2006 sugar beet crop. In 2007 a reform of the Fruit and Vegetable regime was agreed. These subsequent reforms were incorporated into the SPS legislation. The latest changes were in 2008 when the 'Health Check' of the CAP was agreed. The SPS ended on 31st December 2014.

SINGLE PAYMENT SCHEME BASICS

The major, change of the SPS was ***decoupling***. This removed the link from farm support to production. In most member states (including Wales, Scotland and NI), the 'Single Payment' (SP) (also referred to as the 'Single Farm Payment') was made according to the support received by each claimant during the three years 2000-2002 (the '*reference* *period*'). This is known as the 'historic system' of SP allocation. England opted for a system which moved the payment to being calculated on a 'flat-rate' Regional Average Payment (RAP) per hectare with a transition period from 2005 to 2012, starting mainly historic and changing annually to become entirely a flat rate regional average. The three regional payments in England were; lowland (or non-SDA), non-moorland severely disadvantaged areas (SDAs) and moorland SDA.

In order to receive SPS payment, recipients had to farm 'eligible' land which was at their disposal on 15th May each year and be a 'farmer' – exercising an agricultural activity. They were also required to satisfy 'cross-compliance' rules, which are in two parts: 'Statutory Management Requirements' (SMRs; EU directives, largely already in force, on public and plant health, animal welfare and the environment) and keeping the land in 'Good Agricultural and Environmental Condition' (GAEC). They applied to the entire holding.

Recipients needed 'entitlements'. These were a new concept introduced for the SPS and can be considered as a 'right to receive aid'. Initial entitlements were awarded to the IACS claimant of agricultural land in 2005. They were transferable/tradable and could be sold with or without land, or leased only with an equivalent area of land. They were not attached to the land, they belonged to the business/ sole trader.

SPS PAYMENTS

Claims for payment were made annually by 15th May. Subsidy payments are calculated in euros then converted into sterling. The rate used was that on 30th September each year. The tables below shows the rates used (€1 = £)

	2005	**2006**	**2007**	**2008**	**2009**
€1= £	0.68195	0.6777	0.6968	0.7903	0.9093
	2010	**2011**	**2012**	**2013**	**2014**
€1= £	0.85995	0.86665	0.79805	0.83605	0.7773

Payments were subject to deductions. 'Modulation' saw a percentage of the Single Payment taken off and given to the Rural Development Fund (Pillar 2) see Section 5. In England it was 19%. 'Financial Discipline', a mechanism by which EU Farm Ministers could reduce payments to keep spending within stipulated budget thresholds was 2.45% and 1.3% in 2013 and 2014 respectively.

Every farm had a different payment per hectare each year until 2011 because their historic payments were unique. In Wales and Scotland these differences will persist until they change from the wholly historic system in 2015 under BPS (see Section 4) until 2019. Previous editions of the Pocketbook showed examples of how three different English farms' (arable, beef and sheep) payments changed from 2005 to 2012.

The following are actual rates of the area payments in 2014 in the three areas (or sub-regions) of England. 'Lowland' covers all non-SDA (Severely Disadvantaged Area) land, which is more than 84% of farmed land.

***2014** Flat Rate Area Payments in England*

Payments £/ha (acre)	Lowland	Non-Moorland SDA	Moorland SDA
before deductions	251.39 (102)	201.32 (81)	35.26 (14)
after deductions	192.87 (78)	154.45 (63)	27.05 (11)

SDA = Severely Disadvantaged Area *Converted at €1=£0.7773*
Deductions at 20.3% (modulation at 19% and FD at 1.3%)

6. RURAL DEVELOPMENT

Rural Development, or Pillar 2, supports environmental protection and improvement of the countryside, and encourages sustainable enterprises and thriving rural communities. The Rural Development regulation sets the legislative framework across the EU, providing a menu of schemes and aid from which member states can choose. There are Rural Development Programmes for each devolved region for the period 2014 to 2020. This round of EU Rural Development has 6 'priorities';

1. fostering knowledge transfer in agriculture and forestry
2. enhancing agricultural competitiveness and enhancing farm viability
3. promoting food chain organisation and risk management in agriculture
4. restoring, preserving and enhancing ecosystems dependent on agriculture
5. promoting resource efficiency and supporting a shift towards a low-carbon and climate-resilient agriculture
6. promoting social inclusion, poverty reduction and economic development in rural areas

The priorities will contribute to achieving the following objectives:

- The competitiveness of agriculture,
- The sustainable management of natural resources, and climate action,
- A balanced territorial development of rural areas

As many of the previous scheme contracts are for more than one year and will carry on for many years until the agreements are brought to an end, brief details of these schemes are also included in the sections below.

Brexit Note: Until the UK formally leaves the EU it will continue to receive support under the existing policies. All structural and investment projects, including agri-environmental schemes, signed before the UK leaves the EU will be fully funded, even when agreements continue beyond the UK's departure from the EU.

ENGLAND 2014 - 2020

Over its lifetime £3.5 billion will be invested in schemes to improve the environment and grow the rural economy. The schemes centre on;

- The environment (87% of funding) (£3.1 billion)
- Increasing productivity (4%)
- Rural economic growth including LEADER (9%)

***The Environment* – The Countryside Stewardship Scheme (CSS)**

The existing Environmental Stewardship Scheme (ESS), England Woodland Grant Scheme (EWGS) and capital grants from the Catchment Sensitive Farming (CSF) programme have been replaced by the Countryside Stewardship Scheme (CSS). The aim of the scheme is to support measures to 'restore, preserve and enhance the natural environment'. The scheme is open to farmers, foresters and land managersmostly through competitive application. It is run jointly by Natural England, Forestry Commission England and the Rural Payments Agency (RPA); it provides three tiers of funding:

- ***Higher-Tier*** - Multi-year agreements for environmentally significant sites, commons and woodlands where complex management requires one-to-one support from Natural England or the Forestry Commission to help build an application. Applicants select from 244 options and capital grants. Most agreements are by invitation.

- ***Mid-Tier*** - Multi-year agreements for environmental improvements in the wider countryside. Applicants choose from 120 management options and capital items. The minimum annual value must exceed £1,000. 'Priorities' for different areas have been identified. Agreements are scored against these and only those offering the best outcomes are given an agreement.
- ***Capital Grants*** - Funding up to £5,000 is available for 1 to 2 year grants for hedgerows and boundaries, improving water quality, developing implementation plans, feasibility studies, woodland management plans, woodland creation (establishment), woodland improvement and tree health.

Higher & Mid-Tier agreements normally run for five years (starting 1 January), although ten years may be offered if benefits will take longer to achieve. There is a menu of management options and capital items to choose from depending on the agreement. One agreement per holding is allowed, with no separate 'strands' for uplands or organics, although there are specific options for these types of land (see below).

- ***Organic*** - The scheme is non-competitive and provides 16 options exclusive to organic farmers and land managers including for conversion and maintenance. These options can be used alone through the Mid-Tier process or with other options within the Mid or Higher Tier as long as they are compatible with organic status. Conversion payments are paid for 2 years, except for permanent crops (3 years). For the duration of the agreement applicants must be registered with an Organic Control Body and the land must be in their first year of conversion at the start of the agreement.
- ***Uplands*** – There are 6 upland grants available; management of enclosed rough grazing, managing grazing for birds, management of moorland and supplements for moorland re-wetting, introducing or reintroducing shepherding and capital payments for Historic Building Restoration which are not upland specific.
- ***Facilitation Funds*** – Funding is available to deliver the CSS on a landscape scale. It is available to those organisations/people who have environmental land management skills and can help groups of land managers work together. The 'group' must manage at least 2,000 hectares (unless there is a smaller more obvious environmental boundary) and be spread across at least four neighbouring holdings.
- ***Scoring*** – Applications are scored against criteria. Applicants should use 'Statements of Priorities' and supporting maps for their area to identify the priority features and issues being targeted to help choose which options to include as part of an application. This means the application will score more highly. To further enhance their chances of an offer, applicants can choose options from the '***wild pollinator and farm wildlife package*** (WPFWP). These options are designed to benefit wild pollinators, farmland birds and other farm wildlife. Applications which select these options and meet the minimum area thresholds; 3% for Mid-Tier and 5% for Higher-Tier, will enhance their score. *All eligible applications are subject to the availability of budget.*
- ***Application window*** – There are various application windows, 2017 summarised here;

Mid Tier	10 March to 30 Sept 2017	
Higher Tier	10 March to 5 May	Expressions of Interest
	30 September	Full Applications
Boundaries and Hedgerows	1st February to 28th April 2017	
Woodland Management Plans and Tree Health		all year
Woodland Creation	3rd January to 1st March 2017 then 31st May 2017.	
Woodland Improvement	10th March to 5th May 2017 then 30th September 2017	

Similar application windows are expected in 2018 throughout.

***Increasing Productivity* – The Countryside Productivity Scheme**

About £140 million is available (2015-2019) through the Countryside Productivity Scheme to improve the competitiveness of farming and forestry businesses. Applicants bid for funds for projects which are innovative, use new technology and the latest research and which will improve skills & training in the business. Co-operation and collaboration with others in land-based sectors together with projects which benefit the environment in a number of ways i.e. tackle environmental problems whilst increasing productivity have been encouraged to bid for a share of the funds. Grants cover up to 40% of total eligible costs. The scheme was expected to open in rounds. The first in 2015, had a large number of applications and there was no round in 2016. Funds were available in the following areas in the first round, it is possible that these may change for future rounds *At the time of going to print, a further application round had been announced for 2017, but details were not available.*

- *Animal Productivity, Health and Welfare* – automated dairy cow lameness detection, rumination monitoring, on-farm analysis of foodstuffs, calving detectors, oestrus detectors, monitoring of pig production, static handling and weighing systems
- *Arable and Horticultural Productivity* – LED lighting, controlled atmosphere storage, remote crop sensors, crop robotics
- *Forestry Productivity* – woodland harvesting, extraction and small scale processing
- *Resource Management* – slurry application systems, air scrubbers & heat exchangers, livestock LED lighting, water management, poultry litter drying systems.

There are two types of grants; *Small Grants* –between £2,500 and £35,000 and *Large Grants* – funding between £35,000 and £1,000,000.

EIP-Agri grants (European Innovative Partnership for Agricultural Productivity & Sustainability) are a part of the Countryside Productivity Scheme. These are aimed at collaborative groups of farmers, foresters and researchers involved in agriculture or food, agricultural or agri-food businesses and non-governmental organisations. Funds of between £5,000 and £150,000 are available. This covers costs of running an innovative project for up to three years which seeks new ways of solving a recognised industry problem.

Rural Economic Growth

Funding for Rural Growth (worth £177 million) is available through Local Enterprise Partnerships (LEPs) or LEADER Local Action Groups (LAGs). LEPs are partnerships between public bodies and businesses whose role is to award grants to maximise local benefit. Each LEP its own strategy and local priorities. There are three types of grants:

- Business Development – to develop new or existing businesses
- Food Processing – for businesses that process agricultural & horticultural products
- Rural Tourism Infrastructure – to attract more visitors & prolong their stay

Applications are competitive, those projects which can show there will be business growth, job creation or money will be brought into the rural economy, will 'score' more highly. Grants are normally up to 40% of eligible costs, usually a minimum of £35,000 with a maximum grant of €200,000 (£170,000) but can differ. The programme is open for Expressions of Interest until 31st January 2018. Projects should be finished, paid for and grant claims submitted by 31st March 2019.

A LEADER scheme (worth £138 million) funds programmes run by local community partnerships called Local Action Groups (LAGs) and funds projects which improve the rural economy and create jobs.

ENGLAND 2007 - 2013

This section outlines the schemes in England under the RDP from 2007-2013. They are now closed to new applicants but many continue until their contract terms end so a brief description is included. Refer to previous editions of the Pocketbook for more detail.

Axis 2 Agri-Environmental Schemes

Administered by Natural England (NE) and the Forestry Commission and received approximately 80% of funding, the available schemes were:

- Environmental Stewardship Scheme (ESS)
- English Woodland Grant Scheme (EWGS)
- Energy Crops Scheme (ECS)

Environmental Stewardship Scheme (ESS); The Environmental Stewardship Scheme started in 2005 and last schemes were awareded in 2015. The scheme is closed to new applications. It comprised four elements:

- Entry Level Stewardship (ELS)
- Organic Entry Level Stewardship (OELS)
- Higher Level Stewardship (HLS)
- Uplands Entry Level Scheme (UELS)

ELS: designed to encourage many farmers nationally to adopt simple environmental management practices such as hedgerow management, stone wall maintenance, low input grassland, buffer strips and arable options. It was non-competitive. Points were awarded for management options adopted from a large range. Applicants had to achieve 30 points per hectare and received £30 per hectare per year. ELS agreements last for five years, the last started in 2015. In the LFAs the payment is £8 per hectare for parcels over 15ha.

OELS: was open to farmers with land registered as organic or in conversion and not receiving aid under the Organic Farming Scheme. OELS had similar options ELS. Participants received £30 per hectare per year for carrying out options on the organic land plus an additional £30 per hectare (organic land only) for farming the land organically. There was also an option to apply for organic conversion with a payment of £600 per hectare per year (for 3 years) for top fruit orchards and £175 per hectare per year (for 2 years) for improved land.

HLS: was targeted to achieving significant environmental benefits in high priority areas with the objectives being wildlife conservation, protecting historic environments, maintaining and enhancing landscape quality, encouraging public access and resource protection. It was a competitive application. Payment depends on management options adopted, and can include a capital items and per hectare payments. HLS agreements were normally for ten years with a break clause for either party after five.

UELS: Upland ELS was open to those who farmed within the SDAs. Farmers were able to have an ELS over all of their land and enter all their SDA land into the UELS. There were different points' targets depending on the classification of the land. Producers had to achieve the combined total. Similar to the ELS, applicants had to achieve the points target by selecting from a menu of 'options'. Once achieved the points equate to the level of payment. SDA Moorland parcels 15ha and above receive £23/ha; all other SDA land receives £62/ha.

The scheme was not available to farmers with other agri-environmental scheme agreements still running e.g. CSS and ESA schemes. In order that these farmers did not lose out after the HFA had finished, from 2011 there was an Uplands Transitional Payment

(UTP). The last UTP payment (received in March 2014) was £16.62/ha for Moorland and Common Land, Severely Disadvantaged Land (SDA) received £43.88/ha. The full rate was paid on the first 350ha, half rate on the next 350ha. No payment was made on land in excess of 700ha.

English Woodland Grant Scheme (EWGS): administered by Natural England and Forestry Commission, woodland grant options are within the new Countryside Stewardship Scheme.

Energy Crops Scheme (ECS); provided aid to plant Short Rotation Coppice and Miscanthus (elephant grass) on a minimum application size of 3 hectares.

Axes 1, 3 and 4 Schemes

The priorities socio-economic elements of the RDPE were improving competitiveness of farming, skills & knowledge transfer and development of the rural economy. This was centred on the following schemes:

- Farming and Forestry Improvement Scheme (FFIS)
- Rural Economy Grant (REG)
- Skills and Knowledge Transfer
- Rural Community Broadband Fund
- Paths for Communities
- Dairy Fund

In addition, Local Action Groups (LAGs) supported local projects, communities and businesses.

Farming and Forestry Improvement Scheme (FFIS); to make businesses more profitable and resilient whilst reducing the impact of farming on the environment. Grant rates of between 15% and 50% were available

Rural Economy Grant (REG); grants for large scale projects which would result in a significant change in performance for farming, forestry, agri-food businesses and micro businesses in rural areas of England. Funding up to 40% of eligible costs was available. The minimum grant was £25,000 up to about £1 million.

WALES 2014 - 2020

Throughout the current Welsh Rural Development Programme £953m is available to invest in a range of schemes to;

- Increase the productivity, diversity and efficiency of farming and forestry businesses. Improving competitiveness and resilience and helping them move from the 'historic' system of payments to the flat rate system and reducing their reliance on subsidies.
- Improve the environment by encouraging sustainable land management practices and the sustainable management of our natural resources and climate change
- Promote strong, sustainable rural economic growth and encourage community-led local development.

Funds are split between five key elements; Area-based measures (60% of funds), Investment measures (15%), Human and Social Capital measures (11%), LEADER and local development (10%), Technical Assistance (4%).

Area-based Measures

Most funding is available for the Area-based schemes and is through a continuation of the Glastir Programme together with some new measures which have been approved by the European Commission along with the wider Welsh Rural Development plan.

Glastir

Under the Rural Development Programme 2014-2020 Glastir is the main scheme through which funding for area based measures are channelled. Glastir has six elements;

- Glastir Entry (GE)
- Glastir Advanced (GA)
- Glastir Commons (GC)
- Glastir Woodlands (GW)
- Glastir Organic (GO)
- Glastir Small Grant Scheme

Note the Glastir Efficiency Grants (GEGs) are not available under the WRDP 2014-2020. Refer to the Gwlad e-newsletter for updates.

Glastir Entry; was not open in 2015 or 2016 for applications and is not expected to open in 2017. It is unclear whether a broad-based scheme such as Glastir Entry will be available again in Wales. It is a whole farm entry level management scheme. The first agreements commenced in 2012. Contracts are for five years and applicants must enter all eligible land they have control of for the full five years. Applicants have to obtain a points through selecting options for their farm which is either 34 (standard entry level threshold) or 17 (reduced entry level threshold) per hectare. Under Glastir 2014-2020 a number of options have been removed and others changed.

Payment for Glastir Entry is £34 per hectare for all land in the scheme or £17 per hectare for reaching the reduced threshold. Claim for payment is made annually on the SAF. To be eligible for the scheme, producers also need to comply with the Whole Farm Code; 13 standards of environmental practice. This attracts an additional payment of:

0 – 20 hectares	£15/ha
21 – 50 hectares	£8/ha
51 - 100 hectares	£2.75/ha

Glastir Advanced; addresses soil carbon management, water quality, water quantity management, biodiversity, the historic environment and improving access. It is a competitive scheme and applications are assessed against the objectives on target maps (Geographical Information System (GIS) maps) and are allocated a score based upon the ability to delivery towards the objectives. Farms are selected according to the score they achieve. Those that can deliver the most towards the objectives are then selected. At this level management is of a prescribed nature, payments consist of both capital and non-capital items. Glastir contracts are for 5 years and are whole farm commitments. Farmers are not now required to enter GE before they apply to the GA.

The Expression of Interest for Glastir Advanced 2018 opened on 28th February 2017 and closed on 31st March 2017. A similar application period is expected in 2018 for 1st January 2019 agreement start dates. The application window will be publicised in the Gwlad e-newsletter and on the Welsh Government website. Payments for Glastir Advanced are made annually, the value depends on the Management Options undertaken. Payment for capital works are made on completion and submission of a claim. Payment for complying with the Whole Farm Code (see above) is also made annually.

Glastir Commons is available for those who hold rights on Common Land and who have joined together to establish a Grazing Association. Application periods will be publicised in the Gwlad e-newsletter.

Glastir Woodlands provides funds for woodlands under the Glastir Woodland Creation Grant (WCG) and the Glastir Woodland Management (GWM) scheme. Under the WCG there are four funding streams; Establishment, Maintenance, Premium and Fencing grants. There are four categories of woodland, Establishment grants vary from £1,600/ha for the agroforestry category to £4,500/ha for trees planted in the mixed woodland-carbon category. Maintenance payments are available for 12 years at a rate of £60/ha/annum (5 years and £30/ha for agroforestry). A premium payment is also available for 12 years at a rate of £350/ha this is to compensate for the income foregone for the stock exclusion of agricultural land. It is not available for the agroforestry planting category. Fencing grants, of £3.48/m are available. The fourth Expression of Interest window for WCG opened on 20th March 2017 and closed on 1st May 2017.

Glastir Woodland Management (GWM) did not open for applications in 2016. At the time of writing it was unclear whether an Expression of Interest will be launched for the GWM scheme in 2017, previously payments were available for managing existing woodlands over 0.5ha. Payments ranged from £54 to £120/ha. A new Timber Business Investment Scheme has been launched (see later) for existing woodlands. A grant for small woodland planting is available through the Glastir Small Grant Scheme (see later). There is also a Glastir Woodland Restoration grant which makes funding available to replant areas of Larch that have been felled to help prevent the spread of phytophthora ramorum disease affecting trees. Funding is available for twice the area of larch which has been identified on the Statutory Plant Health Notice or felling licence. The 5th window for Expressions of interest opened on 5th June and closed on the 30th June 2017, further rounds are expected. Payment rates range from £1,900/ha to £2,770/ha.

Funding is also available via the ***Co-operative Forest Planning Scheme*** which offers support to new collaborations to develop project proposals which will encourage planning for the creation of broadleaved and conifer woodland. The window for Expressions of Interest opened on 14th November 2016 and closed on 30th April 2017.

Glastir Organic supports organic farming in Wales. It is a stand-alone scheme and farmers joining it remain eligible for other parts of Glastir. Conversion and maintenance contracts are for five years. Applicants must be an 'Active Farmer'. Support for ongoing training and skills development is available and applicants need to show they have a business plan in place. The maximum area supported per holding is 400ha. A maximum of 20ha of horticultural land may be entered into the contract. The Glastir Organic 2017 application window opened on 17th October 2016 and closed on 4th November 2016. At the time of writing there were no announcements when the next window will open.

Unlike the previous organic scheme there isn't any specific payment for arable crops, but other elements of Glastir have arable cropping options which organic farmers can make use of. The table below summarises the payment rates;

Glastir Organic Payment Rates

	Conversion		*Maintenance*	*Certification**
£/Ha	Years 1-2	Years 3-5	Years 1-5	
Horticultural	600	400	400	80
Enclosed Land	130	65	65	10
Rough Grazing	15	15	15	3

* Certification costs are capped at £500 per contract

Land with more than 40% land in horticultural crops in a temporary grassland rotation, as well as top fruit producers qualify for the highest payments (Horticultural). The Enclosed Land category includes all enclosed lowland. Rough Grazing includes enclosed upland, sole grazed commons, grazed woodland, as well as lowland bogs and heaths

Glastir Small Grant Scheme is a stand-alone scheme. It is competitive and offers grants of up to £7,500 for a set capital works which help tackle climate change, improve water management, restore traditional landscape features and increase Wales' native biodiversity. There are 3 themes under Glastir Small Grants; Carbon, Water, Landscape & Pollinators. Expressions of Interest opened in rounds for each of the themes, all have now closed with the last theme, Landscape and Pollinators closing in April 2017. It is unlikely there will be any further rounds. All projects must be completed and claimed for by 31st March 2018.

Investment Measures

Schemes under this element include:

The Farm Business Grant scheme is new in 2017, it provides support to farmers in Wales to improve both the economic and environmental performance of their agricultural holdings. It provides a 40% contribution towards capital investments in equipment and machinery that have been pre-identified as offering clear and quantifiable benefits to farm enterprises. Applicants can 'choose' from a specified list of capital items with standardised costs which are centred on five themes:

- Animal Health, Performance and Genetics
- Crop Management
- Resource Efficiency
- Energy Efficiency
- ICT

To be eligible, the business must be registered with Farming Connect and a partner must attend a 'Farming for the Future' event organised by Farming Connect. The scheme is competitive, applications are scored and ranked in order to the scoring criteria. The grant is from £3,000 to £12,000. The aim is to have three applications in the 2017-2018 financial year, each for two months. The first closed on 30th June. The second opened in August 2017 and the third will open in February 2018.

The Sustainable Production Grant replaced the Glastir Efficiency Grants which funded capital works to improve the resource efficiency of farms. Funds of up to 40% of eligible expenditure are available from £16,000 to £400,000 to improve farm profitability and environmental outcomes. Projects must address either; soil and crop management, handling and housing, animal or plant health welfare, crop storage issues or renewable energy production. The window for the second round of Expressions of Interest closed on 25th April 2016. At the time of writing the scheme was closed to applications and there were no details on future application dates.

The Food Business Investment Scheme (FBIS) is a discretionary scheme designed to help primary producers of agricultural products in Wales to add value to their outputs by providing support to those businesses that do first and/or second stage processing activities. It is also designed to improve the performance and competitiveness of their businesses; to respond to consumer demand; to encourage diversification and to identify, exploit and service new emerging and existing markets. FBIS covers capital investments in processing equipment along with and some associated costs. Priority is given to Micro, Small or Medium Enterprises (SME's). Applicants must demonstrate that a viable market has been identified for their product(s) and the project would not proceed without the grant. The grant rates range from 20% of the total investment up to 40% depending on size, location and whether both the input and output are agricultural products. The grant thresholds per project £2,400 to £5,000,000. The latest round of Expressions of Interest closed on 19th September 2017. The intention is for the scheme to open and close regularly.

The Timber Business Investment Scheme provides funding for capital investments which add value to forests and woodlands by supporting woodland management activities, timber harvesting and/or in-forest or small scale timber processing. The latest window for Expressions of Interest opened on 1st February and closed on 28th May 2017.

The Sustainable Management Scheme offers grants to collaborative groups looking to improve the resilience of businesses and communities to the impact of climate change or who are taking action to reduce greenhouse gas emissions or are improving the natural resources and the benefits they provide. Grants range from £10,000 to £700,000. The latest round of Expressions of Interest opened on 10th July and closed on 5th September 2017; further rounds are expected throughout the life of the Programme.

Other funding available may include support for entry into ***Quality schemes; Risk Management*** – subsidising insurance that will extend to losses incurred due to bad weather; ***Restoration of Forestry Potential*** – support for woodland and habitat restoration to mitigate natural disasters.

Human & Social Capital Measures

The main interventions available under this element include:

Knowledge Transfer & Innovation and Advisory Services – A ***Farming Connect*** programme commenced in October 2015. It is being delivered by Menter a Busnes and Lantra. It is a programme of knowledge transfer, innovation and advisory services targeting farming and forestry businesses. Many services are fully funded or subsidised up to 80%. Applicants must register for the programme. Those registered under the previous Farming Connect scheme must re-register. Support includes professional development and training, demonstration, coaching, workshops, specialist events. Lantra is responsible for delivering a new subsidised lifelong learning and development programme.

Co-operation and Supply Chain Development Scheme supports the development of new products or processes in agriculture, forestry and food. It aids short supply chains and local markets including those for biomass production. Also support for new and emerging Producer Groups is expected under this funding stream which will build on the Supply Chain Efficiencies Scheme and previous provisions for this kind of work under Farming Connect. The second window for Expressions of Interest opened on 19th March and closed on 9th May 2016.

LEADER & Local Development - LEADER Local Action Groups (LAGs) encourage innovation and achieve rural development. Under the Rural Community Development Fund (RCDF) the Welsh Government offers grants, primarily aimed at LEADER Local Action Groups (LAGs) and other community-Based organisations for investment funding across interventions designed to mitigate the impact of poverty in the countryside, improving conditions which can lead to future jobs and growth. The second Expression of Interest window closed on 30th June 2016. Further rounds are expected.

Other funding for diversification projects may be available through the ***Tourism Amenity Investment Support Scheme (TAIS)*** and the ***Micro Small Business Fund***, both providing grants for projects in the tourism sector.

Technical Assistance; Under this element funds are available for: ***Wales Rural Network*** – using existing schemes to help communicate the opportunities available under the WRDP, ***Glastir Support*** – Farmers can get technical advice

WALES 2007 - 2013

The following schemes operated in the last WRDP. Brief details have been included below:

Glastir continues in a similar format – see earlier

The ***Young Entrants Support Scheme*** (YESS), started in 2010, was available to young farmers (less than 40 years) who set up as head of a holding for the first time. It provided grant aid of 50% of eligible expenditure up to £15,000. It provided access to a Young Entrant's Business Enabler Service for advice on training, knowledge transfer and joint venture opportunities together with sign-posted access to funded mentoring services from established farmers and/or processors.

Farming Connect. This offered one-to-one support, guidance, advice and training. Up to five days subsidised support was available to produce a Whole Farm Plan. A subsidised Skills Development Programme was delivered by Lantra to provide access to practical and regulation linked courses. Help was provided to meet cross compliance measures. Support via Farming Connect remains available under the current WRDP through the Knowledge Transfer & Innovation and Advisory Services (see above).

SCOTLAND 2014 - 2020

The Scottish Rural Development Programme (SRDP) 2014-2020 is designed to help achieve sustainable economic growth in rural Scotland. The specific priorities are;

- Enhancing the rural economy
- Supporting agricultural businesses
- Protecting and improving the natural environment
- Addressing the impact of climate change
- Supporting rural communities

Up until 2020 there is £1.3bn available. The majority of funds will go towards supporting hill farming and agri-environment payments. Below is a summary of the schemes and the budgets available to fund them;

Less Favoured Area Support Scheme (LFASS) (£459m) - LFASS has been running in a similar format for many years. However, EU rules mean 2017 will be the last year that the current Less Favoured Area Support Scheme (LFASS) can operate. The EU is moving to a new 'Areas with Natural Constraints' (ANC) designation to replace the LFA. Schemes supporting farming in the ANC must be completely decoupled from production - so it is not possible to pay on the basis of stocking densities, enterprise mix etc. as the LFASS currently does. However, the EU Commission is offering an option to member states not to introduce a new scheme in 2018. It will possible to make 'parachute' payments for 2018. This allows member states to pay eligible producers in 2018, 80% of their 2017 payment. The Scottish Government will be taking up this option.

The 2017 LFASS is calculated as follows; eligible hectares are adjusted for non-ring fenced dairy land, variable minimum or maximum stocking density restrictions, grazing category and an enterprise mix multiplier. The adjusted hectares are then paid at the payment rates below depending on the grazing category and location of the land. There is a minimum payment of £385.

LFASS Payment Rates	*Grazing Category*	
£ per adjusted Hectare	A & B	C & D
Very Fragile	71.35	63.00
Fragile	62.10	54.51
Standard	52.16	34.12

Agri-environment Climate Scheme (£350m) – This scheme subsidises management and capital work for environmental purposes. It continue some of the support under the previous Rural Priorities scheme (see below). Support for organic conversion and maintenance is provided here. Applicants choose from options to support environmental management on arable, grassland, upland, peat, moorland & heath, wetland & bog, farmland habitats & features, small units, control of invasive non-native species, managing water quality & flood risk, public access, capital items including slurry storage and the management of scheduled monuments.

Most applications need a Farm Environment Assessment (FEA) which records key environmental features on farm and helps plan what to include in the application. Funding is available to complete the FEA. Support under the Agri-environment Climate Scheme is geographically targeted and it is necessary to check which of the 60 options are available in the applicant's area before applying. The scheme is expected to be open for applications from January to April each year. Claims are made annually on the SAF. Funds to help deliver landscape-scale environmental benefits may be available under the Environmental Co-operation Action Fund (see below). This scheme is delivered by RPID and Scottish Natural Heritage.

Forestry Grant Scheme (£252m) - The Forestry Grant Scheme (FGS) supports the creation of new woodlands, contributing towards the Scottish Government's target of 10,000 hectares of new woodlands per year and the sustainable management of existing woodlands. Support is available under eight categories;

- Woodland creation - to support the creation of new woodland that brings economic, environmental and social benefits. There are nine options. There is an initial planting payment (from £560/ha to £3,600/ha) and an annual maintenance payment for five years (from £96/ha to £624/ha). There is also a range of capital grants available for operations such as fencing and tree protection. There is no Farm Woodland Premium payment, but land remains eligible for BPS.
- Agroforestry - support for the creation of small scale woodlands (0.25-5ha per holding) on agricultural pasture or forage land which will allow for a mix of trees and sheep grazing. There is an initial planting grant; £1,860/ha at a stocking rate of 200 trees/ha or £3,600/ha for 400 trees/ha and an annual maintenance grant for 5 years; £48/£84/ha/year at a stocking rate of 200/400 trees/ha.
- Woodland Improvement Grant – several options provide capital grants for a range of activities to improve existing woodlands. These support forest management, activity to enhance the environment and the public's enjoyment of existing woodlands (Woodlands in and Around Towns (WIAT).
- Sustainable Management of Forests - there are nine options in this category. These support the management of existing woodlands with a high environmental value. Including control of grey squirrel & deer, predator control for Capercaillie and Black Grouse, public access, livestock exclusion, woodland grazing and low impact silvicultural systems.
- Tree Health - This provides support to prevent the spread of *Phytophthora ramorum (P. ramorum)* and restore affected woodlands.
- Harvesting and Processing - supports the development of the small-scale premium softwood and hardwood processing sector. Funding is available for equipment to increase harvesting in small, undermanaged woods.
- Forest Infrastructure – support for access into undermanaged or small woodlands.
- Forestry Co-operation – delivers landscape–scale projects involving a number of landowners – see Environmental Co-operation Action Fund below.

This scheme is being delivered by RPID and Forestry Commission Scotland, applications are online only.

Environmental Co-operation Action Fund (£10m) - This helps rural businesses work together to deliver larger (landscape- scale) environmental benefits through the Agri-environment Climate Scheme and Forestry Schemes which would not be achieved by businesses on their own. This scheme is delivered by RPID, Scottish Natural Heritage and Forestry Commission Scotland. At the time of writing, the scheme was being re-designed and was due to be re-opened but no dates were available.

New Entrants Support (£20m) - This provides start-up grants for new and young entrants through three schemes;

- Young Farmers Start-Up Grant Scheme - Young farmers or crofters starting an agricultural business for the first time or taking over an existing agricultural business. Applicants must be between 16 and 41 years at application with at least an NVQ level 2 or equivalent in agriculture or a minimum of five years agricultural experience. The business must demonstrate future standard outputs in the range of €10,000 to €600,000 (the level of output that could be expected on the average farm under 'normal' conditions). The grant is €70,000. There is an initial payment of €63,000 with the remaining being paid once business 'milestones' have been reached.
- New Entrants' Start-Up Grant – those who have started their business within 12 months prior to applying for the scheme. There is no upper age limit but must be at least 16. They must farm at least 3 hectares and demonstrate estimated standard outputs in the range of €600 to €9,999. The total grant is €15,000. There is an initial payment of €12,000 and the remaining payable on reaching business plan 'milestones'.
- New Entrants Capital Grant Scheme - for farmers and crofters who have been head of an agricultural business for up to five years before the application for support. Funding can be used for capital projects, such as the construction or improvement of agricultural buildings. The total amount of grant aid available in any two-year period is individuals; up to £25,000 and groups; up to £125,000.

  This support is delivered by RPID, Scottish Natural Heritage and Forestry Commission Scotland. Additional support and mentoring is delivered through the Advisory Service (see below).

Beef Efficiency Scheme (£32.5m) - This is a new five year scheme and is different from the Scottish Beef Suckler Support Scheme (see Top-up Schemes in Section 4 Basic Payment Scheme above). Its aim is to achieve economic and environmental improvements in the beef sector by raising genetic selection for traits such as growth rates, feed conversion, maternal behaviour, nutrition and disease resistance. Producers have to collect herd data. Participants receive an area payment for three years, expected to be worth £32 per calf. A further £12.5m will be available for targeted support for the beef sector through Knowledge Transfer and the Innovation Fund and the Advisory Service.

Crofting Agricultural Grant Scheme (£14m) - Crofting will continue to be supported under the SRDP. This provides grants to crofters to improve their crofts and help to sustain their business. Capital funding is available, including construction and renovation of agricultural buildings or for the establishment of Common Grazings Committees. The total grant available in any two year period is £25,000 for individual crofters and £125,000 for groups. The scheme is delivered by RPID, Scottish Natural Heritage and Forestry Commission Scotland. In addition the ***Croft House Grant Scheme*** provides grants to crofters to improve and maintain standards of crofter housing.

Small Farms Grant Scheme (£6m) - Provides support for small farms for capital projects, such as construction or improvement of agricultural buildings, including the cost of and transportation of materials, contractor costs and own labour. Holding must be between 3 and 30 hectares. The total grant available in any two year period is £25,000 for individual small farmers and up to £125,000 for groups of small farmers.

Farm Advisory Service (£20m) - It provides information and resources for increasing the profitability and sustainability of farms and crofts. Grants are available for Integrated Land Management Plans (ILMP) including specialist advice, mentoring new entrants and carbon audits. Events include workshops, farm meetings, conferences and training courses. Specifically for crofts and small farms there is a subscription service funded to provide access to advice and information. An advice line is available covering topics including cross compliance, the water framework directive, climate change etc. The scheme is delivered by SAC consulting and Ricardo Energy & Environment.

Knowledge Transfer and Innovation Fund (KTIF) (£10m) – supporting organisations to deliver vocational training, coaching, workshops, courses and farm visits designed to promote skills development and knowledge transfer. In addition funds cover the running costs of 'operational groups' which deliver improvements in competitiveness, resource efficiency, environmental and sustainability in the farming and forestry sector.

LEADER (£86m) – supporting individuals, communities and businesses to design and implement Local Development Strategies across Scotland together. Available through Local Action Groups (LAGs) who work with communities and businesses. In Scotland 21 LAGs implement Local Development Strategies. £20 million has been allocated for specific support for small business growth, including £10 million for farm and croft diversification, which is also available through LEADER.

Food Processing, Marketing and Co-operation (£70m) - In recognition of the fact that the food and drink industry is a key growth sector for Scotland. This scheme provides support for SMEs in the food and drink sector with start-up grants for new enterprises, and business development grants for existing businesses. This scheme is delivered through the Scottish Government's Food and Drink Division; usually three funding rounds per year.

Technical Assistance (£15m provisional) - Including the Scottish Rural Network for supporting and promoting rural development through the sharing of ideas and best practice. This includes SRDP implementation, evaluation and monitoring.

Broadband (£9m) - Support for communities to join together to deliver a broadband solution for their rural area. The scheme is delivered by Community Broadband Scotland.

Application Process

Under the current Rural Development Regulation there is a change to the application process. Apart from applications to the LFASS, there will be two levels of entry;

- Level 1 – applications for grants up to £75,000 with continuous local approval. For forestry the threshold will remain at £750,000
- Level 2 – applications for grants above £75,000 which will be considered nationally by an expert panel. Applications will also be limited to one per holding, per scheme, per year. This is to ensure that funding is spread more fairly in the future.

SCOTLAND 2007 - 2013

The schemes below were available under the previous Rural Development Programme, some agreements continue until the contract comes to an end even though the schemes are now closed to new applications.

Rural Development Contracts - Previously the SRDP was delivered through a single mechanism known as Rural Development Contracts (RDCs), this was divided into three tiers:

- Tier I: The Single Payment Scheme – through the cross-compliance requirements a basic level of environmental protection, food safety and animal welfare was provided.

- Tier II: Land Manager's Options - Farmers chose from a menu of options with applications being made at the same time as the Single Application Form (SAF).
- Tier III: Rural Priorities – This element was discretionary and competitive and it covered agri-environment, organic, farm business, forestry, young entrants and processing and marketing. Some of these agreements will still be running.

Less Favoured Area Support Scheme (LFASS) **-** this is still available – see earlier

Whole Farm Review **-** The other main support for farmers in Scotland was the Whole Farm Review, which granted aid for a business review, action plan and implementation, up to £2,400. This ran until the new Advisory Service was made available in 2016 – see earlier.

NORTHERN IRELAND 2014 - 2020

The Northern Ireland Rural Development Programme (NIRDP) has a budget of £623m which will be allocated across three specific areas:

- ***Competitiveness of Agriculture*** – The Farm Business Improvement Scheme is the main umbrella scheme. Under this is a portfolio of knowledge transfer through the Business Development Groups and targeted capital investment, central to this is the Business Investment Scheme (BIS) with up to £200m of funding available. There is an Agri-food Processing Investment Scheme (AfPIS), providing capital investment to improve the agri-food sector.
- ***Protecting the Rural Environment*** – Most funding is allocated to agri-environmental measures through the Environmental Farming Scheme (£173.5m). Five year agreements deliver a range of environmental measures. There are three levels, the 'Higher Level' is mainly for designated sites or priority habitats. A 'Wider Level' is for land outside these areas. A 'Group Level' facilitates collaboration between land owners to offer landscape agreements, such as for river catchment areas. The first tranche for EFS closed for applications on 31st March 2017. There will be funding for LFAs, whilst the Forest Service continues to provide grants to encourage the creation of new woodlands and the management of existing ones.
- ***Developing Rural Economies*** - Funds are available for a range of measures aimed at encouraging the economic development of rural areas through the LEADER Local Action Groups (LAGs) and the Rural Tourism Scheme.

ENVIRONMENTAL SCHEME PAYMENTS

There are many agri-environment schemes across the UK providing annual payments. The table below summarises the latest payments made for environmental schemes.

Environmental Scheme Payments, 2015 and 2016(provisional)

		£ Million	
		2015	2016
England:	Environmental Stewardship Scheme (c)	394	324
Wales:	Organic Farming Scheme	3	4
	Glastir	38	40
Scotland:	Less Favoured Area Support Scheme	65	66
	Land Managers Options (c)	5	2
	Rural Priorities (c)	28	14
N. Ireland	Environmentally Sensitive Areas	5	5
	Countryside Management Scheme	16	16
	Less Favoured Area Compensatory Allowances	16	16

Source: DEFRA, SGRPID, DARD, WAGDEPC. Agriculture in the UK 2016.
(c) Schemes that are now closed to new entrants.

IV. LABOUR

1. LABOUR COST

There are 8 National (UK) Bank Holidays in 2018; New Year's Day, Good Friday 30 March, Easter Monday 02 April, May Bank Holiday 7 May, Spring Bank Holiday 28 May, Summer Bank Holiday August 27, Christmas Day and Boxing Day.

MINIMUM WAGE

Agricultural workers are subject to the National Minimum Wage (NMW) as follows:

Minimum Wage	*From April 2017*
*25 Years and over **	*£7.50 per hour*
21 – 24 years	*£7.05 per hour*
18 – 20 years	*£5.60 per hour*
16 – 17 years	*£4.05 per hour*
*Apprentice ***	*£3.50 per hour*

** This will rise to £9.00/hour by 2020. This is the National Living Wage*

*** This is for apprentices under 19 or in their first year of apprenticeship, otherwise their relevant minimum wage should be used.*

The rates above apply from 1 April 2017, and are reviewed annually by the Low Wage Commission.

Many farmers pay a higher wage than legally necessary to attract greater calibre staff. More qualified workers such as machinery operators and livestock handlers command a premium. There are some occasions when the minimum wage is applicable in agriculture.

STATUTORY MINIMUM WAGE RATES - ENGLAND

The Agricultural Wages Board (England & Wales) ended in 2013 (Scotland, which has its own AWB is not affected). No changes can be made to existing agricultural workers employment contracts without mutual consent.

For workers Employed before 30th September 2013, Terms and Conditions under the Agricultural Wages Order (AWO) remain in place (unless there is a variation to the employee's terms and conditions of employment). For workers classified as Initial Grade under the 2012 AWO and employed before the 30th September 2013, the minimum wage increases in line with the National Living Wage.

For workers Employed after 30th September 2013, employers can decide on the rate of pay increases and other employment related benefits, with no standard increases dependent on skill level, responsibilities or qualifications.

STATUTORY MINIMUM WAGE RATES - SCOTLAND

The Scottish Agricultural Wages Board (SAWB) continues to operate. The following rates applied from the 1st April 2017;

	39 Hr Weekly Rate	Hourly Rate*	Overtime per Hour (2)
	£	£	£
All Workers (1).....................................	292.5	7.50	11.25
Level 2 apprentices **	171.60	4.40	6.60

1. *Hourly Rate.* This is a single rate irrespective of worker age.
2. *Overtime.* This is 1.5 times the normal rate starting after 48 hours have been worked in the week for those in their first 26 weeks of employment and after 39 hours for others.
3. *For* Appropriately qualified workers add £1.14 per hour
4. Those owning dogs as part of their work 5.60/dog/week (up to 4 dogs)
5. Accommodation provision (other than a house) £6.00/day off-set
6. Lvel 2 Modern Apprenticeships receive an hourly rate of £4.40

STATUTORY MINIMUM WAGE RATES - WALES

The abolition of the Agricultural Wages Board applied to England and Wales but the Welsh Government established its own Wages Board for Wales. The Agriculture Wages Order (Wales) 2017 sets out the rates from 1 April 2017;

Normal Hours (Standard Rates) Agriculture Order 2017

	39 Hr Weekly	Hourly Rate	Overtime Rate*	per Hour
		£	£	£
Grade 1.	Under 16 years	128.70	3.30*	4.95
	16-20	262.08	6.72	10.08
	21-24 years......................	274.95	7.05	10.57
Grade 2.	**25 and Over**	**292.50**	**7.50**	**11.25**
Grade 3.	Lead Worker	316.68	8.12	12.18
Grade 4.	Craft Grade......................	340.08	8.72	13.08
Grade 5.	Supervisory Grade...........	359.97	9.23	13.85
Grade 6.	Farm Management Grade	388.83	9.97	14.96
Apprentice:	Year 1 (all ages)	147.42	3.78	5.67
	Year 2 ~ 16-17 years	152.10	3.90	5.85
	Year 2 ~ 18-20 years	206.70	5.30	7.95
	Year 2 ~ 21 years and over	261.30	6.70	10.05

1. *Overtime rates are set at 1.5 times the basic hourly pay for all grades and categories of workers*
2. *On-call allowance is set as the sum of two hours of overtime pay.*
3. *Night work supplement is specified at £1.44 per hour.*
4. *Dog allowance is £7.63 per dog.*

WORKPLACE PENSION SCHEMES

By April 2018, all employers in the UK must offer a workplace pension scheme. Unless they actively opt-out, all workers must be automatically enrolled into a scheme if they are:

- Employed as a worker
- Aged between 22 and state pension age (varies according to age and gender) although workers between 16 and 74 have a right to *opt in*
- Earning at least £10,000 per year (although those earning £5,876 per year have a right to *opt in*).

The employer has an obligation to pay a minimum contribution into the pension as shown in the table, and the employee has an obligation to contribute to make up to at least the total minimum contribution (either employer or employee could pay more).

Date	*Employer contribution*	*Employee Contribution*	*Total Minimum Contribution*
To 6 April 2018	1%	1%	2%
6 April 2018 to 5 April 2019	2%	3%	5%
6 April 2019 onwards	3%	5%	8%

FARM MANAGERS SURVEY 2016

Farm managers are usually employed by private individuals and family trusts with most jobs in Central, Southern and Eastern regions of England but on a whole range of farm sizes. Most have formal agricultural qualifications in the form of either diplomas or, increasingly, degrees. Typical responsibilities on top of manual duties include day-to-day organisation, staff management, stock and machinery sales and purchases, and farm system decisions and can often include at least partial responsibility for investment decisions and financial control.

The average pre-tax cash earnings (average basic salary plus average bonus/profit share) for 2015 was £52,238. Factors such as age, experience, farm size, number of employees managed all influence pay levels. Predominantly farm managers are paid under fixed salary schemes, although often with bonuses or profit share arrangements alongside and some on a purely profit share basis. Holiday entitlements tend to be 21-30 days per year excluding public holidays.

On top of salaries, the majority of farm managers receive non-cash benefits, with the average pre-tax value in 2015 being £12,530. These are most often in the form of rent-free accommodation, mobile phone contracts and running costs of private car use but also include home lighting and heating costs and farm produce among others.

Reference: Farm Managers in 2016; Their Jobs and Their Pay. Crane R.T., and Cooksely R.D., Pub; Institute of Agricultural Management, 2016

TYPICAL ANNUAL LABOUR COST

Estimated for 2017/18 (from 1st April 2017), based on a minimum wage (Standard) Worker and ASHE Median Labour costs.

Minimum Wage Labour Costs (1)		**Hourly rate**	**Weekly**	**Annual**	**Cost per hour worked ***
			(39 hours)	(52 weeks)	(1755 hrs/yr)
		£	**£**	**£**	**£**
Standard worker Gross Basic Salary		7.50	292.50	15,262	8.70
National Insurance Contribution (NI)	13.8%	1.04	40.37	2,106	
Employers Liability Insurance (ELI)	1.0%	0.08	2.93	153	
Workplace Pension Employers Contribution	2.0%	0.15	5.85	305	
Minimum Cost to Employer		**8.76**	**341.64**	**17,826**	**10.16**
Overtime					**(450 hrs/yr)**
Typical additional hours/working week	10				
Number of weeks overtime worked	45				
Standard Overtime Rate		11.25	112.50	5,063	
NI & ELI		1.67	16.65	749	
Workplace Pension Employers Contribution		0.23	2.25	101	
Total Cost to employer for overtime hours		**13.14**	**131.40**	**5,913**	
Total Cost to employer for all hours		**9.65**	**473.04**	**23,739**	**10.77**
Employers Gross Earnings			405.00	20,325	9.22

Median Labour Costs (2)		**Hourly rate**	**Weekly**	**Annual**	**Cost per hour worked ***
			(40 hours)	(52 weeks)	(1800 hrs/yr)
		£	**£**	**£**	**£**
Median worker Gross Basic Salary *		8.84	353.74	18,457	10.52
National Insurance Contribution	13.8%	1.22	48.82	2,547	
Employers Liability Insurance	1.0%	0.09	3.54	185	
Workplace Pension Employers Contribution	2.0%	0.18	7.07	369	
Minimum Cost to Employer		**10.33**	**413.16**	**21,558**	**12.28**
Overtime					**(188 hrs/yr)**
Typical additional hours/working week *	4.0				
Number of weeks overtime worked	47				
Standard Overtime Rate		13.27	53.06	2,494	
NI & ELI		1.96	7.85	369	
Workplace Pension Employers Contribution		0.27	1.06	50	
Total Cost to employer for overtime hours		**15.49**	**61.97**	**2,913**	
Total Cost to employer for all hours			**475.14**	**24,471**	**12.59**
Employers Gross Earnings		10.54	406.80	20,951	9.50

1. **Standard Labour Costs** are based on the 'Standard Worker', as set by the UK Minimum Wage 2017 and Welsh Standard Agricultural Worker.
2. **Median Labour Costs** are based on the average farm worker earnings according to the Annual Survey of Hours and Earnings; In 2016, the median full time farm workers' gross salary was £392
3. *Per Hours worked: Average basic hours per* year = 1,755 hours, i.e. statutory holidays (23 days), public holidays (8 days) and illness (3 days), have been deducted from 52 weeks x 39 hours = 2028.

LABOUR HOURS AVAILABLE FOR FIELD WORK

This section calculates the theoretical maximum time a single worker could spend on field-work per month in 2018.

Hours available for field-work per worker per month in 2018

	Total Ordinary Hours (1)	Adjusted Ordinary Hours (2)	Per cent workable (3)	Available Hours (4,5,6)			Total Available Hours (7)		percent o/t at w-ends (8)
				Ordinary	Overtime				
Jan	176	162	50%	81	27	(66)	108	(147)	100%
Feb	160	148	50%	74	31	(60)	105	(134)	76%
Mar	168	156	60%	93	67	(63)	160	(156)	53%
Apr	160	148	65%	96	90	(60)	187	(156)	43%
May	168	156	70%	109	107	(84)	216	(193)	45%
Jun	168	156	75%	117	109	(84)	226	(201)	43%
Jul	176	163	75%	122	112	(88)	235	(210)	42%
Aug	176	163	75%	122	112	(88)	235	(210)	42%
Sep	160	148	70%	104	104	(80)	208	(184)	47%
Oct	184	171	65%	111	75	(69)	186	(180)	41%
Nov	176	162	50%	81	34	(66)	116	(147)	69%
Dec	152	140	50%	70	35	(57)	106	(127)	100%

1. *Ordinary Hours:* 8 hours per work day (less 8 bank hols). No deductions have been made for other holidays because they may be taken at various times of the year.
2. *After deducting* for illness (1.5% Nov. to Feb., 1% March to Oct.), and for contingencies and non-delayable maintenance (½ hour/day).
3. *Per cent Workable:* estimates severe weather, soil conditions e.g. waterlogging etc.
4. *Available Ordinary Hours:* Adjusted Ordinary Hours x Percentage Workable.
5. *Available Overtime Hours: Daylight hours above working day (8 hours)* to a maximum of 4 hours per day and 12 to 14 hours at weekends according to season. Same adjustments for illness and percentage workable.
6. Available Hours in brackets indicate hours available if headlights used, up to 4 hours/day (summer) and 3 hours/day (winter).
7. *Total Available Hours:* Time potentially to undertake fieldwork in daylight and (in brackets) with headlights.
8. *Overtime at Weekends.* Out of hours fieldwork that is undertaken in daylight.

Additional Notes

9. *Figures relate to medium land.* The percentage workability will be higher with light soils, less with heavy soils. On heavy soils, land may be almost 100% unworkable from late November to early March (or later, according to the season), particularly if un-drained. A rough estimate of variations in workability according to soil type (compared with the figures above) is as follows.

   Heavy land - March, October, November: 30% less; April: 20% less; September: 10% less; May to August: no difference. Light land — October to April: 15% more; May and September: 10% more; June to August: no difference.
10. *It must be remembered that indoor work*, e.g. livestock tending or potato riddling, can be continued over the full working week Also, some handwork in the field has to continue even in rain, e.g. sprout picking.
11. *Percentage workability* varies according to the particular operation, e.g. compare ploughing and harvesting.

2. SEASONAL LABOUR REQUIREMENTS

CROPS AND GRASS

On the following pages, data on labour requirements for various crops and types of livestock are given. Two levels are shown: average and premium. The average figures relate to the whole range of conditions and commercial farm sizes, i.e. small and medium-sized farms as well as large; the figures give all farms equal weight.

The premium rates do not denote the maximum rates possible, for instance by the use of high-powered tractors under ideal conditions, but relate to rates of work estimated to be obtainable over the whole season, averaging good and bad conditions, with the use of wide implements, relatively large tractors (150hp (111kW) to over 180hp (134kW)) and high capacity equipment in up to 8 hectare fields and over, where no time is wasted. Most farmers with more than 200 hectares (500 acres) of arable land ought to achieve at least the premium levels shown. Those with over 400 hectares (1,000 acres) will have still bigger machines and therefore faster work rates, and thus require 15 to 25% less labour per hectare than even the premium levels given.

The rates of work include:

- preparation,
- travelling to fields,
- minor breakdowns and
- other stoppages
- They relate broadly to medium and medium-heavy land

Some jobs, such as ploughing, may be done more quickly on light soils. Operations such as combine harvesting vary according to factors to do with the topography and other natural features of the farm as well as crop and yield.

The usual times of year when each operation takes place are shown; these relate to lowland conditions. They will vary between seasons, soil types, latitude and altitude. In particular, light land can be ploughed over a longer winter period and a high proportion of cultivations for spring crops may be completed in February in many seasons. All such factors must be allowed for in individual farm planning. Conditions in different seasons also affect, for instance, the number and type of cultivations required in seedbed preparation. Typical monthly breakdowns of requirements are given for various crops.

To illustrate the type of questions that need to be asked for full details of seasonal labour requirements on the individual farm, critical questions affecting timing are listed for cereals.

Note: These data are old and little new research has been completed to replace it with. However, productivity per labour unit has increased since then.

Winter Cereals

Operations	Labour-hours per hectare Average	Premium	Time of Year
Plough (1)................................	1.4	1.0	July to October (according to previous crop)
Cultivate (often power harrow).	1.0	0.7	September to October (according to previous crop) (½ Aug if ploughed in July)
Drill (often with power harrows followed by roll)	1.1	0.7	Mid-September to 3rd week October (according to previous crop and soil)
Apply Fertiliser.........................	0.3	0.2	
Spray	0.3	0.2	October-November
Top Dress (three times [2]).......	0.9	0.6	March and April
Spray (three or four [2])...........	1.0	0.5	March-June
Combine, Cart Grain, Barn Work	2.5	1.9	Mid-Aug to approx. 10th Sept
Later Barn Work (3)	0.7	0.4	September to June
Total.......................................	**9.2**	**6.2**	
Straw: Bale	1.3	0.8	Mid-August to end
Cart	3.5	2.6	September

Typical Monthly Breakdown

Month	Average	Premium	Notes
October....................................	2.4	1.7	Approx. 60% of Ploughing, Cults., Drill, Harrow
November	—	—	
December	—	—	
January	—	—	
February	—	—	
March	0.4	0.2	Part Top Dress
April	0.8	0.5	Part Top Dress, Spraying
May	0.3	0.2	Spraying
June	0.3	0.2	Spraying
July	—	—	
August	1.7 (+2.4 Straw)	1.3 (+1.7 Straw)	⅔ of harvesting (4)
September (harvest).................	0.9 (+2.4 Straw)	0.6 (+1.7 Straw)	⅓ of harvesting (4)
September (prepn. drill)...........	1.7	1.1	40% of Ploughing, Cults., Drill, Harrow

1. *Some cereal crops* are direct drilled or drilled after reduced, or minimal, cultivations, i.e. without traditional ploughing. Direct drilling reduces man-hours per hectare by about 2.5 (average) or 1.8 (premium), and minimal cultivations by about 1.2 (average) and 0.9 (premium).

2. *This is for winter wheat;* winter barley will often have one less top dressing and spraying and oats two less. Also see next page for harvest times for winter barley and oats.

3. *Later barn work* is excluded from monthly breakdown.

Spring Cereals

Operations	Labour-Hours per hectare Average	Premium	Time of Year
Plough (1)	1.4	1.0	July to October (according to previous crop and soil type)
Cultivate (often power harrow)	1.0	0.7	March (½ in second half February on light land)
Apply Fertiliser	0.3	0.2	
Drill (often with power harrow), plus roll	1.2	0.8	March (½ at end February on light land)
Top Dress (once, some possibly twice)	0.4	0.2	
Spray (two or three)	0.7	0.3	May
Combine, Cart Grain, Barn Work	2.4	1.8	Last ¾ of August (affected by variety and season)
Later Barn Work (2)	0.6	0.4	September to June
Total	**8.0**	**5.4**	
Straw: Bale (unmanned sledge)	1.3	0.8	Mid-August to end September
Cart	3.5	2.6	

Typical Monthly Breakdown

Month	Average	Premium	Notes
October	0.4	0.3	Ploughing. How much in
November	0.8	0.5	October depends on area
December	0.2	0.2	W. Wheat, Potatoes, etc.
January	—	—	
February	—	—	
March	2.4	1.6	All Cults. Drilling, Rolling, (nearly half in February on light land)
April	—	—	
May	1.1	0.6	Spray and Top dress
June	—	—	
July	—	—	
August (3)	2.4 (+2.6 Straw)	1.8 (+1.8 Straw)	Harvesting
September	— (+2.2 Straw)	— (+1.6 Straw)	

1. *Autumn drilling* preferable if possible to allow frost to crumble soils

2. *Later barn work* excluded.

3. *This is for spring barley*; spring wheat and oats partly September.

Crop Timings in a Normal Season:

Winter Wheat

Drilling mid-September to 3rd week October.
Harvesting mid-August to approx. 10th September.

Winter Barley

As for winter wheat, except that:

- Ploughing unlikely to start before cereal harvest, as usually follows a cereal crop.
- Harvesting some weeks earlier: mid-July to approx. 10th August.

Winter Oats

As for winter wheat, except that:

- Drilling usually first half of October.
- Harvesting earlier (late July or first half of August).

Spring Barley

Drilling end of February to very early April
Harvesting last half of August to early September

Spring Wheat

As for spring barley, except that:

- Drilling on average 1-2 weeks earlier (should finish in March) - lose more if later than barley.
- Harvesting, on average, 2 weeks later: last week August/first half of September (two-thirds in September).

Spring Oats

As for spring barley, except that:

- Drilling usually a little earlier.
- Harvesting is later than spring barley, earlier than spring wheat: end of August/beginning of September.

Critical Questions affecting Timing for Spring-sown Cereals

1. What was the previous crop?
2. Will the crop be ploughed traditionally, chisel ploughed, subsoiled, minimally cultivated, or direct drilled?
3. Months when winter ploughing is possible, on average (where relevant).
4. Is spring ploughing satisfactory (where relevant)?
5. Average period of cultivations and drilling.
6. Earliest dates for starting and finishing spring cultivations/drilling and latest dates for starting and finishing cultivations/drilling, ignoring extreme seasons (1 year in 10).
7. Effect on yield if drilling is delayed.
8. Is the crop rolled (a) within a few days of drilling or (b) later?
9. (a) Average period of harvesting.
   (b) Earliest dates for starting and finishing harvest, and latest dates for starting and finishing harvest, ignoring extreme seasons (one year in ten).

Critical Questions affecting Timing for Autumn-sown Cereals

1. What weed control is required, particularly of herbicide tolerant grasses?
2. What was the previous crop (affects time available and need for deep cultivations)?

3. Will the crop be ploughed traditionally, chisel ploughed, subsoiled, minimally cultivated, or direct drilled?
4. Earliest and latest drilling date, by choice.
5. Effect on yield if drilling is delayed.
6. In the spring: (a) whether crop is rolled, and when,
   (b) whether crop is harrowed, and when,
   (c) time of top dressings,
   (d) number of spray applications.
7. (a) Average period for harvesting.
   (b) Earliest dates for starting and finishing harvest, and latest dates for starting and finishing harvest, ignoring extreme seasons (1 year in 10).

Maincrop Potatoes

Operations	Labour-Hours per hectare Average	Premium	Time of Year
Plough	1.4	1.0	September to December
Cultivating, Ridging, De-stoning/ Clod Sep. (as required)	6.5	5.0	March, early April
Plant and Apply Fertiliser (1)	4.5	3.5	Last quarter of March, first
Apply Herbicide	0.3	0.2	three-quarters of April
Spray for Blight (av. 6 times)	1.2	0.9	July, first half August
Burn off Haulm	0.3	0.2	End September, early October
Harvest, Cart, Clamp (2)	15.0	10.0	End September, October
Work on Indoor Clamp	4.8	3.2	November
Riddle, Bag, Load	40.0	30.0	October to May
Total	**74.0**	**54.0**	

1. *Automatic planter.* Hand-fed planters: approx. 12hrs plus 8 (could be casual labour).
2. *Mechanical harvester,* excluding up to 25 hours for picking off on harvester - usually casual labour. None may be needed on clod and stone-free soils. Hand harvesting: additional approx. 80 hours of casual labour.

Typical Monthly Breakdown

Month	Average	Premium	Notes
October	12.2	8.2	80% of harvest, ½ burn off
November	5.9	4.0	Clamp work and ¾ plough
December	0.3	0.2	¼ plough
January	—	—	
February	—	—	
March	7.8	6.0	All fert', ½ cults', ¼ plant
April	3.5	2.7	½ cult's, ¾ plant
May	—	—	
June	—	—	
July	0.9	0.7	3 blight sprays
August	0.3	0.2	1 blight spray
September	3.1	2.0	20% harvest, ½ burn off

These figures exclude casual labour and riddling.

Early Potatoes

Operations	Labour-Hours per hectare Average	Premium	Time of Year
Plough	1.4	1.0	September to December
Cultivating, etc.	6.5	5.0	Late February, early March
Plant and Apply Fertiliser	4.5	3.5	Late February, early March
Apply Herbicide	0.3	0.2	1st half March (some in February on light land or in early season)
Further Spraying	0.3	0.2	
After-Cultivation/Spray	0.3	0.2	April, early May
Harvest, bag, load	30.0 (1)	25.0 (2)	2nd week June onwards. All June or till mid-July

1. Excluding 80 hours picking—usually casuals.
2. Excluding 60 hours picking—usually casuals.

Second Early Potatoes

Operations	Labour-Hours per hectare Average	Premium	Time of Year
Plough	1.4 (1)	1.0 (1)	September to December
Cultivating, etc	6.5 (1)	5.0 (1)	March
Plant and Apply Fertiliser	4.5 (1)	3.5 (1)	March
Apply Herbicide	0.3 (1)	0.2 (1)	Half 2nd half March, half 1st half April
Further Spraying	0.9 (1)	0.7 (1)	End April, May, early June
Harvest	15.0 (1)	10.0 (2)	Mid-July to end August

1. *Spinner or elevator-digger*, excluding picking and riddling—usually casual labour.
2. *Mechanical harvester*, excluding picking off on harvester/riddling - usually casual.

Sugar Beet

Operations	Labour-Hours per hectare Average	Premium	Time of Year
Plough	1.4	1.0	September to December
Seedbed Cults	3.2	2.2	Mainly March (some early April. Some late February in good seasons)
Load, Cart, Apply Fertiliser	0.7	0.4	
Drill (and Flat Roll)	1.8	1.1	Between mid-March and mid-April
Spray (herbicide: pre- and post-emergence)	0.6	0.3	Late March/April
Spray (x 2)	0.6	0.3	May/June
Spray (aphis)	0.3	0.2	July
Harvest (machine)	14.0	9.0	End September, October, November
Load	3.4	2.5	End September to early January
Total	**26.0**	**17.0**	

Typical Monthly Breakdown

Month	Average	Premium	Notes
October	7.2	4.6	45% harvest; + loading
November	8.2	5.3	45% harvest; ¾ ploughing; + loading
December	1.0	0.8	¼ ploughing; + loading
January	0.5	0.4	Loading
February	—	—	
March	3.8	2.3	Fert., most cults., some drilling
April	2.5	1.7	Some cults., most of drilling
May	0.3	0.2	Spray
June	0.3	0.15	Spray
July	0.2	0.15	Spray
August	—	—	
September	2.0	1.4	10% harvesting; + loading

Vining Peas

Operations	Labour-Hours per hectare Average	Premium	Time of Year
Plough	1.4	1.0	September to December
Cults, Fert. and Drill	2.3	1.6	Mid-Feb. to April
Post Drilling and Spraying	1.5	0.8	
Harvesting	19.0	14.0	July and early August
Total	**24.2**	**17.4**	

Drilling is staggered in small areas through the season, ranging from early varieties to late varieties.

Dried Peas

Month	Labour-Hours per hectare Average	Premium	Notes
October	1.2	0.8	
November	0.8	0.5	Stubble cult., Plough
December	—	—	
January	—	—	
February	0.2	0.1	Cult. x 2, harrow; drill & fert.
March	2.8	1.9	(80% March); light harrow
April	0.6	0.4	roll; and spray
May	2.5	1.2	
June	0.2	0.2	Scare pigeons; spray
July	1.8	1.1	Possible spray desiccant;
August	2.2	1.3	combine and cart, dry
September	0.5	0.3	Stubble cult.

Assumes direct combining.

Field Beans

Winter Beans

Operations	Labour-Hours per hectare Average	Premium	Time of Year
Broadcast Seed	0.6	0.4	
Apply Fertiliser	0.3	0.2	
Plough	1.4	1.0	September/October
Power Harrow	1.0	0.8	
Spray (pre-emergence)	0.3	0.15	
Spraying (two or three times)	0.8	0.35	Spring
Combine and cart and Barn-work	3.0	2.4	August

Spring Beans

Operations	Labour-Hours per hectare Average	Premium	Time of Year
Plough	1.4	1.0	September to December
Cultivate (often power harrow)	1.0	0.7	
Apply Fertiliser	0.3	0.2	
Drill, Roll	1.2	0.8	End Feb, early March
Spray (two or three times)	0.8	0.4	
Combine and cart and Barn-work	3.0	2.4	September

***Winter Oilseed Rape** (Desiccated)*

Month	Labour-Hours per hectare Average	Premium	Notes
October			
November	0.6	0.3	Spray herbicide and
December			insecticide if necessary
January	—	—	
February	—	—	
March			
April	0.8	0.4	Top dress twice
May	—	—	
June	—	—	Desiccate (1st half July);
July	2.4	1.7	combine (½ 2nd half July
August	2.0	1.4	½ 1st half Aug.); dry
August	1.6	0.9	Cults. (x 2), spray, drill, fert.;
September	1.6	0.9	harrow, roll, barn work (0.5)

Herbage Seed *(first production year)*

Undersown

Operations	Labour-Hours per hectare Average	Premium	Time of Year
Undersown	0.6	0.4	March, April
Roll	(0.6	0.4)	Straight after drilling
	0.4	0.3	September
	0.4	0.3	Late February, March
Harvest (by Combine): Mow	1.4	0.9	3 to 4 days before combining
Combine and Cart	4.5	3.5	Ital. Ryegrasses and Early *Perennials: late July.* *Intermed. Perennials: late July/early August.* *Late Perennials/White Clover: mid-August*
	6.0	4.5	Meadow Fescue: early July
	7.0	5.0	Cocksfoot: early July
	10.0	7.0	Timothy: mid-August
			Red Clover: late September

Direct Drilled in Autumn

Operations	Labour-Hours per hectare Average	Premium	Time of Year
Plough	1.4	1.0	
Seedbed Cults	2.2	1.6	Depends on previous crop—
Load, Cart, Apply Fertiliser	0.3	0.2	Usually July or August
Drill (with harrows behind)	0.8	0.6	As early as previous crop allows. This may be up to mid-Sept for ryegrass without detriment to the yield.
Roll (soon after drilling)	0.6	0.4	Meadow fescue and cocksfoot are best sown no later than July and it is risky to sow Timothy much later than this.

Grass

Production

Operations	Labour-Hours per hectare Average	Premium	Time of Year
Plough	1.4	1.0	Autumn drilling. If necessary.
Seedbed Cults	2.2	1.6	
Load, Cart, Apply Fertiliser	0.3	0.2	
Drill*	0.7	0.5	Mid-March to mid-April (1) or end July to mid-Sept.
Roll	0.6	0.4	Soon after drilling
Load, Cart, Apply Fertiliser* (three lots)	0.9	0.6	March to mid-August (2)
Top*	1.3	0.8	Mid-June to mid-July; if grazed only.

1. * These operations apply only where the seeds are undersown in a spring cereal crop soon after drilling. One extra harrowing and rolling is needed if undersown in an autumn-sown cereal crop.
2. *Spring drilling* may continue to mid-May to enable extra cleaning cultivations or the application of farmyard manure.
3. *P. and K.* may be applied in September - especially on undersown ley in year sown.

Conservation

Operations	Labour-Hours per hectare Average	Premium	Time of Year
Plough	1.4	1.0	Autumn drilling: If necessary.
Hay (5.5 tonnes per hectare)			
Mow	1.2	0.9	
Turn, etc	2.6	1.9	Two-thirds June, one-third
Bale	1.3	0.9	July
Cart....................................	6.0	4.5	
Total per hectare.........................	11.1	8.2	
Total per tonne...........................	2.0	1.5	
Silage (17 tonnes per hectare)			
Mow	1.2	0.9	
Turn, etc	0.7	0.5	Two-thirds May, one-third
Load....................................	2.3	1.7	June
Cart....................................	3.0	2.3	
Clamp	2.3	1.7	
Total per hectare.........................	9.5	7.1	
Total per tonne...........................	0.56	0.42	

Specialised Equipment Prices for Grass Conservation: see page 163.

Typical Monthly Breakdown

Production (figures averaged over the life of the ley)

	1-year ley undersown in spring		3-year ley undersown in autumn (1)		1-year ley drilled		3-year ley drilled	
	Ave.	Prem.	Ave.	Prem.	Ave.	Prem.	Ave.	Prem.
March	0.9	0.5	0.7	0.5	0.6	0.3	0.6	0.3
April	0.9	0.5	0.7	0.5	0.6	0.3	0.6	0.3
May	0.6	0.3	0.6	0.3	0.6	0.3	0.6	0.3
June	0.6	0.3	0.6	0.3	0.6	0.3	0.6	0.3
July	0.6	0.3	0.6	0.3	0.6	0.3	0.6	0.3
August	0.3	0.2	0.3	0.2	5.0	3.4	1.9	1.4
September...	0.6	0.3	0.3	0.2	3.2	2.2	1.4	1.0

1. *If ploughed after a cereal crop,* drilled early August to mid-September.

	1-year ley drilled in autumn (1)		3-year ley drilled in spring		Permanent Pasture	
	Ave.	Prem.	Ave.	Prem.	Ave.	Prem.
March	3.0	2.1	1.4	1.0	0.6	0.3
April	1.8	1.2	0.9	0.7	0.6	0.3
May	0.3	0.3	0.6	0.3	0.6	0.3
June	0.6	0.3	0.6	0.3	0.6	0.3
July	0.6	0.3	0.6	0.3	0.6	0.3
August	0.3	0.2	0.2	0.2	0.3	0.2
September	—	—	—	0.2	0.2	0.2
October	0.9	0.5	0.6	0.3	—	—
November	1.4	1.0	1.0	0.3	—	—
December	0.7	0.5	0.6	0.2	—	—

Conservation

	Hay				Silage			
	per hectare		per tonne		per hectare		per tonne	
	Av.	Prem.	Av.	Prem.	Av.	Prem.	Av.	Prem.
May	—	—	—	—	6.3	4.7	0.37	0.28
June	7.4	5.6	1.3	1.0	3.2	2.4	0.19	0.14
July	3.7	2.6	0.7	0.5	—	—	—	—

Kale

Production

Operations	Labour-Hours per hectare Average	Premium	Time of Year
Plough	1.4	1.0	September onwards
Seedbed Cults	2.2	1.6	March, April, early May
Fertiliser	0.3	0.2	April, early May
Drill	1.3	1.0	May
Roll	0.6	0.4	Straight after drilling
Spray (weed killer)	0.3	0.2	6 weeks after drilling

Catch Crop

Kale may be drilled up to the first week of July; the crop will be smaller but either an early bite or silage crop may have been taken from a ley earlier in the year, or the ground may have been fallowed and thoroughly cleaned during the spring and early summer. The smaller crop is also easier to graze using an electric fence.

The above operations will still apply although the times of the year will obviously be different, but there may be an additional three or so rotavations and two or three heavy cultivations if fallowed for the first half of the year or ploughed after an early bite. This means approximately an extra 10 (average) or 8 (premium) man-hours per hectare in April, May, June.

FIELD SCALE VEGETABLES

(Labour hours per hectare unless otherwise stated)

Cabbage Transplanting	Hand 150-160. Spring cabbage, Sept.-Oct.; summer, April; autumn, May-June Machine (3.5 gang). Spring cabbage 75, summer 85, autumn 100. Pulling and dipping plants. 20 per hectare transplanted.
Cabbage Harvesting	Early spring cabbage, 210, Feb.-April; hearted spring, 250, April-June; summer, 220, June-July; autumn, 220, Oct.-Dec.
Brussels Sprouts Transplanting	45 (machine) to 55 (hand), May-June.
Brussels Sprouts Picking	320-400: picked over 3-5 times, maximum approx. 3 hectares per picker per season. Early sprouts, Aug.-Dec.; late, Nov.-Mar.
Peas Hand Pulling	475-525 (150 per tonne). Early, June; maincrop, July-Aug.
Runner Beans (Picked)	Harvesting. 625 (175 per tonne), July-Sept.
Runner Beans (Stick)	Harvesting. 675, July-Sept.
Runner Beans (Stick)	Erecting Canes and String. 100-150, May-June.
Carrot Harvesting.	Elevator-digger: 260 (1 man + 12 casuals, 20 hours per hectare). Earlies, July-Aug.; maincrop, Sept.-Feb. Harvester: 30 (3 men, 10 hours per hectare). Riddle and Grade: (1° per tonne), Dec.-Feb.
Beetroot Harvest and Clamp.	25, Oct.-Dec. 12-15 man-hours per tonne to wash and pack.

Source: The Farm as a Business, Aids to Management, Section 6: Labour and Machinery. (N.B. This data is now dated, but it is still the latest known to the author.)

LABOUR FOR LIVESTOCK

This data is updated for 2018

Dairy Cows

Time Required per Cow Depending on Yield.

Yield of Cow	5,500	7,000	8,000	9,000
	hours per cow per month			
January	2.0	2.5	3.1	3.8
February	1.9	2.5	3.1	3.8
March	1.8	2.5	3.1	3.8
April	1.6	2.4	3.0	3.8
May	1.6	2.1	2.7	3.5
June	1.6	2.1	2.6	3.2
July	1.6	2.1	2.6	3.2
August	1.6	2.1	2.6	3.2
September	1.6	2.2	2.8	3.5
October	1.8	2.4	3.1	3.8
November	1.9	2.5	3.1	3.8
December	2.0	2.5	3.1	3.8
Total per Cow per Year	21	27.9	34.9	43.2
Average Seconds per Litre	*13.7*	*14.3*	*15.7*	*17.3*

No time is allocated here for dairy young stock. This schedule is based on a 100-cow herd. Low yielding cows tend to spend more time at grass and less housed. High milk yielders take more management time.
13.7 seconds per litre = 1 man per 725,000L
17.3 seconds per litre = 1 man per 575,000L
The most labour efficient milk producing operations in the UK achieve over 800,000 litres per employed man.

Hours staff Requirement per Cow per Year.

	Cow Annual Milk Yield (L)			
	5,500	7,000	8,000	9,000
Cows per Herd				
60	21.9	29.1	36.4	45.0
100	21.0	27.9	34.9	43.2
150	20.0	26.6	33.2	41.1
300	17.5	23.3	29.1	36.0
500	15.0	19.9	24.9	30.9

Labour Cost per Litre

	Cow Annual Milk Yield (L)			
ppl	5,500	7,000	8,000	9,000
Cows per Herd				
60	4.47	4.67	5.11	5.63
100	4.30	4.48	4.91	5.40
150	4.09	4.27	4.67	5.14
300	3.58	3.74	4.09	4.50
500	3.07	3.20	3.51	3.86

Earnings. The average earnings of 'dairy herdsmen' in 2017/18 is estimated to be £31,163 a year and working 2,770 hours (10 hours for 277 days). This includes relief milking etc. but no cover for young stock or fieldwork, such as hay and silage making.

Dairy Followers and Beef

No recent survey work has been published on labour requirements for beef animals and dairy followers. The following data is therefore only 'best estimates'. They are for average performance and average conditions, excluding fieldwork. Substantial variations occur, e.g. through differing management styles or economies of scale with differing herd sizes.

Calves (per head, early weaning)

	Labour hours per month	
Age Group	Average	Premium
0-3 months	2.3	1.6
3-6 months	0.9	0.6
(av. 0-6 months	1.6	1.1)
6-12 months, yarded	1.1	0.8
6-12 months, summer grazed	0.3	0.2
(av. 0-12 months, during winter (1)	1.3	0.9)
(av. 0-12 months, during summer (1)	0.9	0.6)

1. *Assuming 6 to 12-month olds housed in winter and grazed in summer, and calvings or calf purchases fairly evenly spaced throughout the year.*

Stores (per head)

	Average	Premium
Yearling, housed	1.0	0.7
2 year olds and over, housed	1.4	0.8
Out-wintered store	0.7	0.5
12 months and over, summer grazed	0.2	0.1

Dairy Followers

(Per 'replacement unit', i.e. calf + yearling + in-calf heifer.) (1)	Average	Premium
During winter	2.9	2.0
During summer	1.2	0.8

1. *Assuming calvings fairly evenly spaced throughout the year and heifers calving at 2 to 2.5 years old.*

Beef Finishing (per head)

	Average	Premium
Housed	1.8	1.2
Summer Grazed	0.2	0.1
Intensive Beef (0-12 months)	1.3	1.0

Suckler Herds (per cow)

	Average	Premium
Lowland Single suckling (av. whole year)	0.9	0.6
Lowland Multiple suckling (av. whole year)	2.9	2.1
Upland/Hill Single suckling (av. whole year)	1.1	0.7

Sheep *(per Ewe)*

	Labour hours per month	
	Average	Premium (4)
January	0.3	0.2
February	0.3	0.2
March	1.0 (1)	0.7
April	0.4	0.25
May	0.3	0.2
June	0.4 (2)	0.3
July	0.2	0.15
August	0.2	0.15
September	0.25	0.15
October	0.25	0.15
November	0.2	0.15
December	0.2	0.15
Total	4.0 (3)	2.75

1. Assuming mainly March lambing.
2. 0.3 if shearing is by contract.
3. A full-time shepherd, i.e. one who did no other work on the farm, would have a flock of 550 ewes for the average 4 hours per ewe per year to be achieved, assuming full-time assistance during lambing time. Some farms achieve 3 times this number of ewes per single worker.
4. In a national survey conducted in 1999 the average annual requirement for flocks exceeding 500 ewes was 2.9 hours per ewe.

Pigs

	Labour hours per month	
Age Group	Average	Premium
Breeding and Rearing, per sow	1.5	1.20
(Average 130 sows per worker, Premium 160)		
Feeding only, per 10 pigs	1.6	1.25
No. at a time, per worker:		
Average 1,200 per man, Premium 1,600		
No. per year, per worker:		
Average: 6,000 porkers, 4,800 cutters, 4,450 baconers		
Premium: 8,000 porkers, 6,400 cutters, 5,750 baconers		
Breeding, Rearing and Feeding, per sow (with progeny)		
Porkers, average 90 sows per worker, premium 110	2.4	2.0
Cutters, average 80-85 sows per worker, premium 100-105	2.6	2.1
Baconers, average 75-80 sows per worker, premium 95-100	2.8	2.2

Poultry *(large scale, automated)*

	Labour hours per month
Laying hens: battery cages (18,000 per full-time worker)	1.1 per 100
free range	4 per 100
Broilers: 32,500 at a time per full-time worker* (225,000 a year)	1.0 per 100

* additional help needed for catching and cleaning out (included in labour hours/ month)

3. STANDARD MAN DAYS

Standard Man Days (SMD) is a general estimate of the farm labour requirement per enterprise. A Standard Man Year is 2,200 hours. This is 45 weeks' work of 39 hours (after holidays, illnesses etc. have been deducted), plus an average of 10 hours overtime per week (45 x 49 = 2,205). These total hours are converted into 275 notional 8-hour Standard Man Days. This figure includes an assessment for overtime but can be increased by further overtime working.

Every farm enterprise requires a number of SMDs per unit of key input (per hectare, per cow etc.). The total SMD requirement for each enterprise is therefore calculated by multiplying by the size of the operation. The total labour needed on the holding is the sum of all the individual enterprises. An additional 15% has then traditionally been added to account for general maintenance, repairs and management. The total SMD requirement is then divided by 275 to find the number of full-time employees that will be required. This system can work when the labour requirement is constant during the year – e.g. some livestock enterprises. However, when labour use is seasonal, e.g. most field operations, it does not show the 'peaks and troughs' that are crucial in labour planning. It also fails to reflect that daylight hours, soil conditions, rainfall etc. will alter the amount of time available for fieldwork during the course of the year. SMD also does not recognise the efficiency of larger units, so SMD requirements fall per unit as the enterprise grows.

Crops (per hectare)	S.M.D.s
Winter Feed Wheat	1.15 / 1.75 (1)
Winter Milling Wheat	
Spring Wheat	
Winter Feed Barley	
Winter Malting Barley	
Spring Malting Barley	
Winter Oats	
Spring Oats	
Winter Oilseed Rape	1.10
Spring Oilseed Rape	1.00
Linseed	1.00
Winter Field Beans	0.90
Spring Field Beans	0.95
Dried Peas	1.60
Lupins	1.50
Vining Peas	3.00
Maincrop Potatoes	9.25 (2)
Early Potatoes	5.50 (2)
Sugar Beet	3.00
Herbage Seed (Ryegrass)	1.40
Hops	9.50 (2)
Kale (grazed)	1.40
Silage:~ one cut	1.60 (3)
two cuts	2.80 (3)
Grazing only	0.40 (3)
Hay for sale	1.80 (3)
Let Keep	0.40 (3)
Bare fallow / set-aside	0.20
Rough Grazing	0.20

Livestock *(per head) (4)*

Dairy Cows	4.00
Bulls	3.50
Beef Cows (single suckler including calf):	
lowland	1.35
upland/hill	1.68
Cereal Beef (0-12 months) (5)	1.90
18-month Beef (5)	1.60
Grass Silage Beef (5)	1.90
Finishing Suckler bred stores:	
Grass	1.10
Winter	1.10
Calves; to 6 months (5)	1.20
Ewes: lowland	0.50
upland	0.45
hill	0.40
Rams	0.50
Winter Finishing Store Lambs	0.30
Sows (including weaners to 30kg)	2.25
Boars	2.00
Other Bacon Pigs	0.25
Laying Birds: battery cages	0.017
free range	0.06
Pullets reared (5)	0.005
Broilers (5)	0.002

1. 1.15 if straw ploughed in; 1.75 if straw harvested. Highly mechanised larger farms will require no more than 0.75 S.M.D./ha of direct labour for cereals and other combinable crops (assuming straw ploughed in).
2. Excludes casual labour for harvesting.
3. Excludes any reseeding carried out – this is likely to be around 0.6 S.M.D./ha in the year reseeding is carried out.
4. Note that for grazing livestock, the S.M.D.s per head exclude field work, e.g. grass production and silage making, i.e. the labour for these has to be added to give total labour for these enterprises.
5. For these livestock, S.M.D. per annum should be based on numbers produced (sold) during the year. For all other livestock, average numbers on the farm at any one time during the year should be used (i.e. average of numbers at end of each month).

'Other Cattle' can refer to both beef animals and dairy followers (ref. detail on page 183).

This data is dated now and many commercial enterprises will have more efficient working practices, requiring fewer SMD per unit of output or input (hectare or head).

V. MACHINERY

1. AGRICULTURAL MACHINERY PRICES

This schedule is for 2018 purchase of new machinery, net of discounts and ex. VAT During the early and mid-2000's, machinery price inflation was significant because of dearer raw materials and currency fluctuations. Between 2010 and 2013, price changes were minimal, with some items actually falling in price. Between 2014 and 2015, general machinery costs increased by approximately 5%, although tractors specifically remained static in price. From 2015 to 2016, general machinery price inflation was static and for tractors was small at under 2%. Although official data does not exist for 2017 at the time of writing, the pound euro exchange rate (coupled with a small amount of input cost inflation) has resulted in new machinery prices increasing by approximately 10%. In addition, due to the weakening of sterling, demand for second hand machinery has been much higher for export markets which has also driven machinery prices upwards. No further price increase has been budgeted for 2018. Prices shown are a range as prices vary between makes and models. Machines with a star '*' denote those used in subsequent 'farmer' cost' calculations.

	Tractors	***£ Range***	
	(a) Two-Wheel Drive		
	80-90 hp	32,760	38,610
	90-100 hp	33,930	39,780
	(b) Four- Wheel Drive		
*	100-120 hp	46,800	58,500
*	125-140 hp	52,650	70,200
*	150-180 hp	76,050	91,260
	180-220 hp	87,750	117,000
	225-270 hp	107,640	146,250
	Extra for 50km/hr high road speed on 150hp-200hp tractor	3,500	6,500
	(c) Crawlers - rubber tracks		
*	230-300 hp	169,650	187,200
	340-400 hp	187,200	216,450
	450-550 hp	234,000	280,800

	Cultivating Equipment	***Price Range***			
	(a) Ploughs	*Variable width*			
		Mechanical		*Hydraulic*	
	Reversible:	*Adjustment*		*Adjustment*	
	3-furrow	11,700	14,625	—	
	4-furrow	14,040	16,965	16,965	19,890
	5-furrow	18,135	20,475	21,645	23,985
*	6-furrow	19,890	25,740	23,400	29,250
	7-furrow (mounted)	30,420	33,930	35,100	39,195
	8-furrow (mounted)	35,100	40,950	40,950	46,800
	(b) Furrow Presses				
	2.0-2.4 m double row			4,680	5,850
*	2.6-3.0 m double row			6,435	9,360

	(c) Front Presses (excluding linkage)		
	1.5 m single row	3,159	3,744
	3.0 m single row	4,388	7,020
*	4.0 m single row — hydraulic folding	7,605	9,945
	(d) Front Press Linkage		
	1.0 to 2.0 tonne	1,872	4,095
	(e) Other Cultivating Equipment		
*	Sub Soiler 2-3 leg	9,360	14,040
	Shakarator (3m)	11,115	15,210
	Low Disturbance Sub-soiler (5 leg 3.5m)	9,945	12,870
	Stubble Cultivator - discs and press (3m)	9,360	12,870
*	(heavy duty) (4m) hydraulic folding	16,380	22,230
	(6 m): hydraulic folding	19,890	31,590
	(8 m): hydraulic folding	25,000	40,000
	8-12m straw rakes (excl. roller)	12,500	25,000
*	Spring-tine Cultivator (3-4 m):	8,190	14,040
	(5-6 m): hydraulic folding	11,700	18,720
	Tine / Disc Cultivator Combinations (one-pass type)		
	(3-4 m) mounted	14,040	23,400
*	(5-6 m) trailed	29,250	49,140
*	Disc Harrows (3.6 - 4.4 m): trailed	15,210	24,570
	(4.4-6.0 m): trailed folding	29,250	40,950
	(8.0-12.0 m): trailed folding	40,000	60,000
*	Harrows (5-6 m): light-medium, hydraulic folding	9,360	16,380
*	Rotovator	10,530	16,380
	Power Harrow (with packer roller)		
	(3 m)	8,775	11,700
*	(4m)	14,040	18,720
	(4-6m): folding	25,740	35,100
*	Rolls: Triple gang, hydraulic folding (6 m)	7,020	12,870
	Five gang, hydraulic folding (12m)	19,890	25,740

		Price Range	
	Fertiliser Distributors, Seed Drills, Sprayers		
	(a) Fertiliser Distributors		
	Mounted Spinners		
	(700-1,200 litre): twin disc, hydraulic control	3,510	8,190
	(1,300-1,700 litre): twin disc, hydraulic control	5,850	9,945
*	(1,650-2,300 litre): twin disc, electronic control	9,360	14,040
	(3,200 litre): twin disc, electronic control	14,040	18,720
	Bag lifter (850-1,000kg)	2,340	2,925
	Variable rate and automated headland management	1,170	2,925

(b)	*Seed Drills - standalone mounted hydraulic or PTO fan driven*		
	4 m Tine coulters	18,720	21,060
*	4.8 m Tine coulters	21,060	23,400
	6 m Tine coulters	23,400	29,250
	12 m Tine coulters	52,650	76,050
	Extra for electric controls and variable rate	2,340	2,925
	4 m Disc coulters	28,080	30,420
	4.8 m Disc coulters	32,760	37,440
	6 m Disc coulters	39,780	46,800
	12 m Disc coulters	64,350	87,750
(c)	*Combined Cultivator Drills - trailed heavy duty machines*		
	3 m	29,250	40,950
	4 m	40,950	52,650
	6 m	46,800	70,200
	8 m	76,050	99,450
(d)	*Combined Power Harrow and Pneumatic Drill*		
*	3 m	18,720	26,910
	4 m rigid	25,740	32,760
	4 m folding	37,440	46,800
	6 m folding	52,650	64,350
(e)	*Direct Drill (4m Disc Coulter)*	52,650	58,500
	Direct Drill (6m Disc Coulter)	67,860	79,560
	Strip Till Drill (3m)	29,250	40,950
	Precision Maize Drill (12 row)	28,080	35,100
(f)	*Sprayers*		
	Mounted, 600-800 litre tank, 12 m boom	4,680	11,700
	Mounted, 1,000-1,800 l, 20-24 m hydraulic boom	23,400	40,950
	Trailed, 2,500-3,000l tank 18-24 m boom	32,760	49,140
	Trailed, 3,000-4,500l tank 24-36 m boom	37,440	67,860
	Self-propelled sprayers,		
*	2,500-4,000l tank, 24-36 m boom	105,300	157,950
	5,000-6,000l tank, 24 - 36m boom	163,800	222,300
	Extra for auto-shut-off and boom height control	6,435	10,530

Grass Conservation and Handling Equipment		***Price Range***	
(a)	*Silage Equipment*		
*	Forage Harvester: trailed, precision chop	35,100	52,650
	Self-propelled (3 m pick-up 400-600 hp)	210,600	304,200
	Maize attachment, 8 row	46,800	76,050
	Silage Trailer, 12 tonne, tandem axle	11,700	15,795
	Silage Trailer, 14 - 16 tonne, tandem axle	15,210	19,890
	Buckrake (push off)	4,095	8,190

(b)	*Haymaking Equipment*		
	Mowers 1.5-1.8 m, 1-2 drum	3,276	4,446
*	Disc Conditioner, mounted (2.4-3.2 m)	9,945	15,795
	trailed (3.2 - 3.8 m)	17,550	21,060
	Rake: single/double rotor, 3.2m-4.5m range	4,680	8,775
*	multiple rotors 8-10m range	17,550	35,100
	multiple rotors 12-15m range	37,440	45,630
	Tedder/swather		
*	5-7 m, 4-6 rotors	7,020	12,870
	8-11m multiple rotors	17,550	35,100
	Balers and Bale Handling: see 5(c) and (d) below		
(c)	*Silage Handling Equipment*		
	Silage shear bucket	2,340	3,510
	Silage grab	2,048	3,218
	Big Bale Silage Feeder, mounted	10,530	16,380
	Diet-feeder Wagon (6 tonne)	12,870	19,890
	Clamp Silage Mixer (10 tonne)	23,400	35,100

Grain and Straw Harvesting and Handling Equipment — ***Price Range***

(a)	*Combines*			
	Engine size hp	Cutterbar width metres (feet)		
	220-249	4.5-5.5 (14-18)	117,000	163,800
	250-299	5.4-6.6 (18-22)	140,400	198,900
	300-399	6.0-7.7 (20-25)	152,100	234,000
	400+	7.7-10.6 (25-35)	234,000	374,400
(b)	*Yield monitoring/mapping*		9,360	12,870
	Self-levelling options		14,040	21,060
(c)	*Balers*			
*	Conventional Balers		12,285	15,210
*	Round balers, twine tying and net wrap		26,910	38,610
*	Big Square Balers		81,900	117,000
(d)	*Bale Wrappers*			
	Big Bale Wrapper: trailed		10,530	18,720
	Big Square Bale Wrapper: trailed		23,400	32,760
	Combined Baler and Wrapper		40,950	64,350
	Bale Trailers, 30 ft - 35 ft long		4,095	5,850
	Accumulator, flat 8, mechanical		2,925	4,680
	Big bale accumulator		11,700	17,550
	Big Bale Shredder, silage or straw		7,020	10,530
	Big Square Bale Chasers		60,000	75,000

(e) Drying, Handling, Feed Processing Equipment

Grain driers and Grain storage:		
Rotary Cleaner, 10-20 tonnes/hour	16,380	22,230
Grain augers 150 mm, 6-8.5 m, with trolley	2,340	3,510
Grain conveyors, (25-50t/hour) (plus £145-185/m)	2,925	4,680
Hammer mill, 7.5-15 kW	4,680	5,850
Roller mill, 4-5.5 kW	3,803	4,680
Mixer, 750-1000 kg	5,265	5,850
Mill and mixer, 1,000-1,300kg, 3.7-5.5 kW	8,190	10,530

Potato, Sugar Beet and Vegetable Machinery	***Price Range***	
(a) Potato Machinery		
* De-stoner	52,650	70,200
* Bedformer, 1 bed	5,850	9,360
Bed tiller (1 bed)	10,530	14,040
* Planter: 2 row mounted	14,040	29,250
6 row	40,950	52,650
Haulm pulveriser (2 row):	7,605	10,530
* Harvesters: 2 row trailed manned/unmanned	140,400	169,650
2 row, self-propelled	175,500	257,400
4 row, self-propelled	374,400	468,000
Store loader (heavy duty)	29,250	35,100
Self-unloading hopper, 3-5 tonnes	12,870	16,380
Clod separator	12,870	16,380
Sizer, 5-30 tonnes/hour	12,870	17,550
Barrel washer, 8-10 tonnes/hour	29,250	40,950
Roller inspection table, 1.2 x 2.4 m	3,510	7,020
Weigher, automatic, 8-10 tonnes/hour	8,775	11,700
Box tipper with cross conveyor	17,550	29,250
Box filler, automatic	17,550	23,400
Bag stitcher (hand held)	585	1,755
Complete out of store grading line: 20 tonnes/hour	70,200	163,800
30 tonnes/hour	140,400	210,600

(b) Sugar Beet Machinery

*	Precision Drill:	6 row (pneumatic)	12,870	17,550
		12 row-18 row (pneumatic)	21,060	40,950
*	Hoe:	6 row-12 row (heavy duty)	9,945	16,380
	Harvesters:	Trailed, 4 row, tanker	105,300	117,000
		Trailed, 6 row, tanker	93,600	140,400
*	Self-propelled, 6 row, 18 tonne tank		374,400	468,000
	Cleaner-loader, with engine, 1-3 tonnes per minute		23,400	40,950
	6 Row Fodder beet harvester		76,050	117,000

(c) Vegetable Machinery

Onion windrower		12,870	15,210
Root crop digger: 1 webb		8,775	9,945
	2 webbs	10,530	12,870
Top lifting ve	single row, bunker	64,350	81,900
	twin row, bunker/elevator	111,150	146,250
	four row, elevator	152,100	181,350
	four row, self-propelled	351,000	421,200
Leek harvester (mounted)		29,250	46,800

Dairy Equipment	***Price Range***	
Water heater	936	2,106
Heat recovery unit	2,925	5,850
Plate Cooler	1,755	4,680
Variable speed vacuum pumps	10,530	12,870
Cow collars for heat-time monitoring (£ per cow)	82	105
Electronic auto-shedding systems	9,360	16,380
Auto-dipping and flushing system (£ per stall)	936	1,170

General		*Price Range*	
	Trailer, 12 tonne tipping grain/silage	12,870	15,210
*	Trailer, 14t tipping, tandem axle; grain/silage	14,040	18,720
	Grain Chaser Bin - 24t	55,000	65,000
*	F.Y.M. Spreader, (10 - 12 tonne)	12,870	18,720
	(12 - 14 tonne)	17,550	23,400
	Self-propelled Slurry / Digestate applicator with 24 boom	374,400	468,000
*	Loaders, front mounted	7,020	11,115
*	Materials Handler, telescopic boom (2.5-3.0 tonne)	52,650	70,200
	Skid steer loader (500-600 kg)	17,550	25,740
	Quad Bikes	4,095	7,605
	Vacuum Tankers (5,000-6,000 litre	5,850	8,190
*	Low Ground Pressure Tankers (9,000-11,000 litre)	14,040	18,720
	Slurry pump	4,680	5,850
	Slurry separator	32,760	40,950
	Cattle crush	1,170	3,510
	Cattle crush with weigher	2,340	4,680
	Cattle trailer (twin-axle)	4,095	5,850
	Yard scrapers	585	1,170
	Rotary brush (2-2.5 m)	2,340	2,925
*	Flat roll, ballastable (2.5-3 m)	1,463	2,340
*	Pasture topper (2.0-3.0 m)	1,404	2,925
	Hedge cutter:		
*	hydraulic angling; flail head	14,040	21,060
	7.6m reach, 1.3m flail head, double sided	32,760	40,950
	Ditcher: fully slewing	11,115	14,040
	Post hole digger	1,404	2,340
	Post hole driver	1,755	4,095
	Saw bench	1,755	2,925
	Log splitter	936	1,404
	Welder	293	1,755
	Angle Grinder	29	234
	Compressor	293	936
	Farm Security Camera (single basic camera)	117	234
	Farm Security Camera System (automatic and wireless)	1,287	1,638
	Tractor Guidance System (basic)	351	1,053
	Auto-Steer Guidance System	3,510	8,775

For complete milking parlour costs - see building costs on page 234.

2. CONTRACTORS' CHARGES, FARMERS' COSTS AND WORK RATES

Contractors' charges vary widely according to many factors: these are estimates for 2018. Farmer-contractors may charge less than dedicated contractors, since their overheads and fixed costs are sometimes *considered* partly covered by their own farming operations. However the service may not always be so complete, including specialist advice or access to new technology.

Farmers' own costs (including the value of the farmers' own manual labour) vary even more widely; those given (for 2018) are averages in every respect as costs vary according to soil types, size of farm, and so on; they are based on accounting cost procedures in that labour, tractor and machinery fuel, repairs and depreciation are included - no allowance has been added for general farm overheads, interest on capital, supervision/management or under-occupied labour during slack times. They assume four-wheel drive 150hp tractors for the majority of operations (these individual tractor costs are shown in the tractor costs schedule on page 202). 185hp tractors are assumed for work with a higher power requirement such as ploughing, cultivations, sub-soiling and big square baling. An additional fuel allowance for very heavy work has been added (i.e. higher than the average consumption assumed in the tractor costs schedule). The figures should not be used for partial budgeting. The machinery used in the calculations for farmers' costs is identified by a 'star' * adjacent to specific items of equipment in the machinery list in the previous section (an average has been used for the purchase price). In line with increasingly larger machinery on farm, many of the daily work rate assumptions have been reviewed in the farmers' cost calculations in recent years.

The contract charges and average farmers' costs are put side-by-side for tabular convenience, not to facilitate comparisons. Apart from the fact that contractors' charges must cover expenses omitted from the farmers' cost, the advisability or otherwise of hiring a contractor for a particular job depends on many factors (e.g. timeliness), varying widely according to farm circumstances; therefore, there are advantages and disadvantages not reflected in a cost comparison alone.

Assumptions: Contractors' costs are sensitive to factors including fuel costs, capital machinery prices, and local demand versus competition. Contractors' charges are based on red diesel at 50ppl. The farmers' cost calculations are based on fuel at 45ppl. However, many contractors are now making individual arrangements with customers regarding fuel (i.e. prices quoted before fuel – therefore using the farmer's fuel when on site). The contractor charges shown below include fuel. The rates of work include preparation, travelling to and from the fields and allow for minor breakdowns and other stoppages.

Machinery rings: Prices charged by farmers offering services through machinery rings are variable but are generally between farmers' costs and contractors' charges. There are exceptions, which mainly relate to relatively expensive items of machinery (e.g. root harvesters, de-stoners and combine harvesters), where the charges for services offered through machinery rings are close to and often less than farmers' costs. Machinery and Labour rings are great examples of Joint Ventures that can deliver cost savings for all the farming businesses involved. Structures and circumstances often vary between organisations / groups involved. Many farmers are also achieving similar benefits through machinery sharing arrangements often undertaken on a relatively informal basis.

Acknowledgement. The estimates for contractors' charges are partly supplied by the National Association of Agricultural Contractors (as collected through their survey).

* *Costs are per hectare unless stated. The figures represent a national average.*

Average Contractors Charges & Farmers Costs of Performing Mechanical Operations

Operation	Contract Charge £/ha *	Farmer's Average Cost £/ha *	Average Rate of Work (Ha per 8 hr day)
Cultivations			
Ploughing – light land	58.07	46.42	10.5
– heavy land	63.63	51.30	9.5
– with furrow press	6.92	9.39	8.5
Deep ploughing (over 30cm)	74.01	61.16	8.5
Rotovating - ploughed land	70.42	55.38	8.5
- grass		78.45	6
Sub-soiling/Flat lifting	59.30	46.53	10
Mole-ploughing – single leg	67.95	53.33	15
Stubble raking	23.47	33.25	15
Discing: shallow	48.18	29.76	16
Deep	53.13	36.98	13
Power harrowing – deep/on ploughing	59.30	47.45	9
Shallow/seedbed prep	51.89	35.59	12
Spring-tine harrowing	34.59	19.80	16
Pressing	37.07	23.19	16
One-pass tillage train (Solo/Discordon etc	67.26	47.18	16
Cultivation (Rexus Twin / Culti-press etc)	35.83	33.38	16
Rolling – flat (grassland)	26.09	15.15	15
– ring (seedbeds)	19.77	8.09	35
Drilling			
Rape drilling with flatlift/subsoiler	65.48	51.19	10
Cereal drilling – conventional	49.42	24.37	24
Combi-drilling	61.78	52.47	12
Cultivator drill (Vaderstad)	49.42	45.82	20
Direct drilling	58.07	55.37	16
Sugar beet drilling	51.97	52.10	10
Carrot/parsnip/onion precision drilling	78.26		
Grass seed (broadcast)	24.71	18.43	14
Grass seeding with harrow (e.g. Opico)	31.16	18.68	12
Cross drilling grass	74.13		
Chain harrowing	23.30	13.34	20
Maize precision drilling	44.48		
Maize Drilling Under Plastic	121.08		

Operation	Contract Charge £/ha *	Farmer's Average Cost £/ha *	Average Rate of Work (Ha per 8 hour day)
Fertilising & Spraying			
Fertiliser distribution	12.36	6.04	70
Extra for variable rate application	3.71		
Lime spreading (per tonne)	6.10/tonne		
Irrigating (excl. water costs) per inch	98.84		
Spraying (based on 200 l/ha & 24m boom	12.50	9.30	80
Spraying (120-150l/ha 36 boom)		7.51	140
Extra if less than 50 acres (20 ha)	4.32		
Liquid Fertiliser	14.83	11.16	68
ATV spraying	34.00/hr or 12.36/ha		
Slug-pelleting	8.90	2.86	56
Weed Wiping	25.95		
Avadex Spreading	19.77		
Combining			
Combining cereals	86.49	80.52	20.4
Extra for straw chopper on combine	6.30	*Farmer's cost assumes*	
Extra for seeding (Autocast)	9.02	*average of all machine size.*	
Extra for yield mapping	2.47	*and harvested areas*	
OSR harvesting – out of windrow	86.49		
– direct combining	86.49	80.52	20.4
Combining peas/beans	88.96	80.52	20.4
Combining grain maize	103.78		
Swathing OSR	44.48		
Grain carting to barn (per hour)	42.00/hr	32.05 /hr	
Grass & Forage			
Flail Topping margins per hour	44.88/hr		
Grass topping	32.12	19.50	15
Grass mowing	28.42	27.37	15
Tedding	16.31	13.10	25
Raking	17.30	18.23	25
Forage harvesting only – first cut	64.99	53.74	20
- other cuts	58.07	41.34	26
Forage harvesting, cart (3 trailers) and clamping (1st cut)	145.29		
Whole Crop forage harvesting, cart (3 trailers) and clamping	168.03		
Complete service – mow, rake, forage harvest, cart (3 trailers) and clamp	160.62		
Maize harvesting incl carting (3 trailers) and clamping	168.03		
Extra forage trailer (per hour)	40.50/hr	32.05	
Forage box	110.00/hr		

Operation	Contract Charge £/ha *	Farmer's Average Cost £/ha *	Average Rate of Work (Ha per 8 hour day)
Baling			
Baling (per bale) - 'small'	0.62/bale	0.27 / bale	8
- 80cm × 90cm	3.80/bale		
- 120cm × 70cm	4.60/bale	3.27 / bale	32
- 120cm × 90cm	5.60/bale		
- 120cm × 130cm	6.60/bale		
- Round 120cm	2.81/bale		
- Round 150cm	3.47/bale	2.08 / bale	17.6
Bale-wrapping – Round 120cm (6 layers)	5.40/bale		
- Round 120cm (with 4 layers)	4.89/bale		
- Round 120cm (without plastic)	2.30/bale		
- Square 120cm × 70cm (6 layers)	7.00/bale		
- Square 120cm × 70cm (4 layers)	5.45/bale		
- Square120cm × 70cm (without plastic)	2.42/bale		
Bale Chaser (per hour)	60.00/hr		
Root Crop Operations			
Potato harvesting – harvesting only	741.30	549.41	2.5
- Harvesting and carting	963.69	754.56	
De-stoning potato land	276.75	197.08	3.2
Potato ridging	85.25	50.72	9
Potato Planting	187.80	115.07	4
Sugar beet harvesting - harvesting only	237.22	254.22	10
- Harvesting and carting	276.75		
Irrigation (25 mm application / ha)	98.00		
Manure Handling - *see below for telehandler costs for loading*			
FYM spreading – tractor & rear discharge	49.50/hr	45.20	per hour
- tractor and side discharge spreader	44.50/hr		
Slurry spreading – tanker	50.00/hr	49.28	per hour
- umbilical	78.20/hr or 2.40/cube		
- extra pump	40.00/hr		
Slurry injection	54.83/hr		

Operation	Contract Charge £/ha *	Farmer's Average Cost £/ha *	Average Rate of Work (Ha per 8 hour day)
General / Rural Maintenance			
Hedge cutting - flail	39.70/hr	40.17	per hour
- saw-blade	48.20/hr	48.86	per hour
Hedge laying	15.50/metre		
Fence erection (with materials)			
– post and 4 Barb	5.00/metre		
– post, stock net & 2 Barb	6.10/metre		
– post and 3 rails	14.80/metre		
Quad bike (including man)		15.89	per hour
Tractor + Post Knocker + Man	37.50/hr		
Ditching using 360 deg digger	36.64/hr		
Tractor + trailer + man	39.50/hr	32.05	per hour
100 – 150 hp Tractor + man	35.50/hr		
150 – 220 hp Tractor + man	38.25/hr		
220 – 300 hp Tractor + man	48.47/hr		
300 hp + Tractor + man	65.00/hr		
Forklift/Telehandler + man	37.50/hr	33.43	per hour
Livestock Husbandry			
Sheep dipping	1.40/head		
Sheep jetting / showering	0.98/head		
Sheep – shearing ewes	1.54/head		
-- rams	3.17/head		
-- crutching	0.75/head		
Sheep ultrasound scanning	1.05/head		
Cattle ultrasound scanning	2.05/head		
Foot trimming – sheep	1.05/head		
- cattle	11.00/head		
- bulls	24.50/head		
Tractor + Man + Feeder Wagon		33.52	per hour
Livestock husbandry - Sheep & Cattle	14.00/hr		
Crimping (£/t)	9.82/tonne		
Mobile feed mixing and processing (£/t)	19.50/tonne		

CONTRACT FARMING AGREEMENTS

Generally these are formalised with a written agreement setting out the terms for the Farmer (who can be a landowner or tenant) and a Contractor. The Contractor can be a neighbouring farmer or traditional contractor. Contractor remuneration includes a guaranteed Basic Fee which is usually between £210 and £275/ha (£85-£110/acre) for combinable crops and should cover the majority of the fixed costs of the operation. It should not offer a margin for the contractor to incentivise him to farm the land to the best of his ability and therefore generate the maximum return to the farmer and contractor through the share of the divisible surplus. The Contractor provides all of the day-to-day labour and management to run the farming business, including provision of all cross-compliance and assurance scheme paperwork.

Following deduction of running costs (crop variable costs, drying, insurance, interest charges etc.) and the Farmers Basic Return, the surplus is split between the two parties. The split may typically be 70%-80% to the Contractor and 20%-30% to the Farmer. This incentivises good performance and management from the contractor. A second band of payment rate is sometimes introduced e.g. 50:50 split above a set level of surplus to enable the farmer to benefit from further rises in market prices. This is increasingly the case given the large volatility in cereal prices in recent years. The flow chart below demonstrates the flow of income and expenditure through a Contract Farming Agreement, applicable to all sectors of agriculture.

Income

Sales

Cull / Calf, Grain / Straw Sales

Basic Payment *

Environmental Scheme income **

↓

***Less,* Variable Costs**

Feed, Fertiliser, Seed, Sprays, Lime, Agronomy

Livestock Sundries, Vet and Med, Bedding, Livestock Purchases

↓

***Less,* Overheads**

Water, Electricity, Repairs, Office & Professional Fees, Interest

↓

Less,

Contractor's Basic Fee

Farmer's Basic Return

Depreciation

↓

Divisible Return

↙ ↘

xx% to Farmer — yy% to Contractor

* *can be included or excluded and the Farmer's first charge adjusted accordingly*

** *above caveat can also apply if the scheme covers a wider area than solely the land available to the contract farming agreement*

CONTRACT CHARGE FOR ALL OPERATIONS

For cereals and combinable break crops, 'stubble to stubble' charges (i.e. up to and including combine harvesting and carting the grain to store) are typically £333 to £420/ha (£135-170/acre). Variations depend on factors such as distance away, area contracted, field sizes, terrain type, soil quality, cultivation/crop establishment methods and which party provides the storage. At the lower end of the prices around £320 to £370 per hectare (£130-150/acre) it would be solely to cover field operations and carting grain to store, whereas higher prices stated above would be a complete management service to include hedge cutting, field infrastructure maintenance, crop walking and agronomy etc. Local competition affects prices, as with all contract charges. Some regions of the UK are very competitive for certain contract operations, for example hedge cutting or 'tractor and man' provision.

When comparing farmers' total power, machinery and labour costs with stubble to stubble contractors' charges, the former include cost items not included in the latter, e.g. the cost of farm vehicles, fixed plant such as grain stores, general farm maintenance and other down-time for full-time labour.

3. TRACTOR HOURS

Crops	Per Hectare Per Annum Average	Premium
Cereals	7.1	5.3
Plus, Straw	1.5	1.1
Potatoes	15.3	11.5
Sugar Beet	10.3	7.7
Vining Peas	7.5	5.6
Dried Peas	5.8	4.3
Field Beans	5.8	4.3
Oilseed Rape	7.1	5.3
Herbage Seeds:- 3 year crop	4.3	3.2
Hops (machine picked)	120.0	90.0
Kale (grazed)	3.6	2.7
Turnips/Swedes (Grazed/Lifted)	6/12	5/10
Fallow	0.6	0.5
Grass Ley Establishment	3.5	2.6
Making Hay	4.1	3.1
Making Silage:		
1st Cut	3.8	2.8
2nd Cut	3.0	2.3
Grazing:-		
Temporary Grass	1.7	1.3
Permanent Grass	0.9	0.7

Livestock	Average Per Head
Dairy Cows (Grazed / Intensive)	4/7
Other Cattle over 2 years	5
Other Cattle 1-2 years	4
Other cattle 0.5-1 year	2.25
Calves 0-0.5 year	2.25
Housed Bullocks	3
Sheep (per ewe)	1.25
Store Lambs	0.8
Sows	1.75
Other Pigs over 2 months	1
Laying Birds	0.04

1. *For livestock,* annual requirements are per head requirements above multiplied by average numbers during the year (i.e. average numbers at end of each month).

2. *As with labour,* the number of tractors required by a farm depends more on the seasonal requirements and number required at any one time than on total annual tractor hours. These can be calculated from the seasonal labour data provided earlier in this book. The soil type and size/power of tractors purchased are obviously other relevant factors. All figures are for 2018.

4. TRACTOR COSTS

	Four-Wheel Drive Tractors			
	120 h.p.		150 h.p.	
Initial Cost....................................	£58,500		£71,955	
	per year	per hour	per year	per hour
	£	£	£	£
Depreciation....................................	4,095	8.19	5,037	10.07
Insurance..	665	1.33	818	1.64
Repairs and Maintenance........................	878	1.76	1,079	2.16
Fuel and Oil......................................	2,528	5.06	3,283	6.57
Total	8,166	16.33	10,217	20.43

	185 h.p.		250 h.p.	
Initial Cost....................................	£96,525		£126,945	
	per year	per hour	per year	per hour
	£	£	£	£
Depreciation....................................	6,757	13.51	8,886	17.77
Insurance..	1098	2.20	1,444	2.89
Repairs and Maintenance........................	1,448	2.90	1,904	3.81
Fuel and Oil......................................	4,498	9.00	7,516	15.03
Total	13,800	27.60	19,751	39.50

Figures are estimates for 2018. Depreciation assumes all tractors are sold for 30% of their original value after 10 years, a slight change in assumption from previous years to reflect current markets. The depreciation schedule shown on page 207 demonstrates the average annual fall in value of machinery over its life (the middle columns are applicable to tractors). Annual repair costs are calculated at 1.5% of initial cost for all tractors. This assumes the majority of basic servicing work carried out by the farm's own labour. No interest on capital has been included. Fuel is charged at 45p/litre plus a 5% allowance for oil. Insurance costs vary depending on the policy type. The above assume the most common practise whereby tractor costs incur the majority of the insurance cost, with any implements of value up to circa £80,000-100,000 automatically covered by the tractor policy.

The hourly figures are based on 500 hours use per year. A greater annual use than this will mean higher annual costs but possibly lower hourly costs. On some larger farms and within many contracting businesses, many tractors do in excess of 1,000 hours per year, and even as high as 2,000 hours for some contractors. Earlier replacement at a given annual use will increase depreciation costs per hour but should reduce repair costs. The hourly figures are averages for all types of work: heavy operations such as ploughing obviously have a higher cost than light work. The variability of fuel usage is significant depending upon the type of work (light work vs. heavy cultivations) and can vary by up to 80%. The figures shown attempt to depict the average consumption from all types of work.

CONTRACT HIRE, PURCHASE OR HIRE PURCHASE OF MACHINERY

The farmer's cost for the various operations shown in the table above assume machinery and equipment is purchased outright. No interest charge is included in the calculations for the capital required to purchase the machinery. However, a farmer may purchase the machinery through a hire purchase (HP) agreement. Here, a deposit is paid up-front followed by a number of monthly or annual payments. The benefits of HP agreements are purely cash flow, allowing a business to spread the cost over say 3 years. For new equipment, the interest charge may be very low or even 0%, whereas using HP agreements to finance used machines will usually incur an interest rate currently of 3-7%. Once the HP agreement ends (i.e. all payments are complete), the farmer owns the item outright.

Another option is contract hire (CH) agreements. Here, a rental charge is paid for the equipment for a set time period. At the end of the period, the machine is returned to the company (although sometimes opportunities exist to negotiate a price to buy the machine). Contract hire agreements usually include a full service, maintenance and repair plan. The main advantage of these agreements is the ability to plan and budget costs, as the exact cost of operating that machine is known, with no un-expected repair bills or no need to budget what it will be worth upon resale. These are becoming popular with large arable and contracting businesses as it can be very cost-effective where machinery usage is high.

Another option which is increasingly popular is to use short-term hire agreements to hire key items of machinery as and when required. For example, many arable businesses contract hire combines and/or additional tractors at harvest time when extra machinery is needed. This allows them to access new technology without having large sums of capital tied up in machinery that sits idle for much of the year. The most cost-effective option depends on the specific circumstances of the farm business and will be determined by factors such as ability to access capital, annual usage and life expectancy.

Machinery Hire Costs

Typical Contract Hire charges (see above) for tractors are shown below (prices exclude insurance but include repairs/maintenance):

	Short-Term (8-10 weeks)	*52 weeks Contract*
110 hp tractor:	£450 - £500 / week	£180 - £220 / week
130 hp tractor:	£550 - £630 / week	£220 – £260 / week
165 hp tractor:	£750 - £850 / week	£280 - £330 / week
290 hp tractor (wheeled):	£1,100-£1,400 / week	£425 - £500 / week
130 hp telehandler	£525 - £575 / week	£280 - £330 / week
16 tonne Grain Trailer	£250 – £270 / week or £60-£70/day	
3,000g vacuum tanker	£350 - £400 / week or £100/day	
10t rear discharge spreader	£450 - £550 / week or £110-£130/day	
8ft road brush	£250 / week or £70/day (+ wear charges)	

HIRE OR OWN?

Whether it is best to hire or buy a machine depends on many factors, often specific to the farm's own circumstances. However, a common practise now, particularly on arable farms, is to hire one of the larger tractors only required for a short period of time, for example as used for autumn cultivations. This type of machine, and combine harvesters often sit idle for much of the year.

The tables below show the way a farmer can calculate whether it is most cost effective to hire or to buy for one specific example. Here, a large 250hp tractor is hired/used for 10 weeks of the year. It demonstrates the cost of the machine per hour on both a hired and owned basis excluding labour and fuel, (being the same whether the machine is owned or hired). It includes the cost of finance based on the average capital employed over the life of the asset at 5%; this is not shown in the tractor costs previously in the book. But, this is one of the main considerations between hiring and buying when the capital cost is so significant. The hire cost assumes a fixed charge for the 10 week period of £12,500 for a 60 hour week maximum (based on 50 being achieved), but assumes the overage charge on additional hours is £25/clock hour. Whether or not this is available at the same rate varies between suppliers of hired machines.

	£/hour on 500 hrs	
	Owned	*Hired*
Depreciation / Hire Charge	17.77	25.00
Finance	4.44	-
Repairs	3.81	-
Insurance	2.89	0.67
	28.91	**25.67**

The table below demonstrates the point at which, in this example for the above set of circumstances, it is more cost effective to buy the machine. This is above about 750 hours. However, this relies upon being able to achieve this level of output in the short space of time, which dependent on weather and cropping may not be realistic.

Total Cost Per Hour (£)

	Hours per Year						
	400	500	600	700	800	900	1000
Owned	34.08	28.91	29.17	26.18	23.94	22.20	20.80
Hired	32.08	25.67	25.56	25.48	25.42	25.37	25.33

Depreciation rates for low usage of high value machines matter, because depreciation by age rather than use makes the cost of ownership high. Where a business has high usage/demand for this machine in the spring and autumn, long-term hire costs would need to be considered. These are less per week but likely to cost more for the year and so usage is the key determinant.

UK AGRICULTURAL TRACTOR SALES PER YEAR

(Tractors over 50 HP)

Year	Average Tractor Size HP	Number of Units Sold	Per Cent change y/y
2007	134.0	15,540	+14.6%
2008	138.1	17,104	+10.1%
2009	143.4	15,013	-12.2%
2010	141.7	13,347	-11.1%
2011	144.3	14,094	+5.6%
2012	148.0	13,951	-1.0%
2013	150.7	12,498	-10.4%
2014	155.1	12,433	-0.5%
2015	157.0	10,842	-12.8%
2016	158.3	10,602	-2.2%
2017 (Jan-June)		6,142	

(data from the Agricultural Engineers Association).

TRACTOR POWER REQUIREMENTS

		hp/acre		hp/ha		kW/ha	
		av.	prem.	av.	prem.	av.	prem.
Combinable crops:	heavy land	1.20	0.85	3.00	2.10	2.24	1.57
	light land	0.90	0.65	2.20	1.60	1.64	1.20
Mixed cropping:	heavy land	1.35	0.95	3.35	2.35	2.50	1.75
	light land	1.00	0.70	2.50	1.75	1.86	1.30

Includes tractors, telehandlers, self-propelled sprayers and combines

5. ESTIMATING ANNUAL MACHINERY COSTS

Annual machinery costs consist of depreciation, repairs, fuel and oil, contract charges, and vehicle tax and insurance. These can be budgeted in three ways;

1) using information on past machinery costs on the farm (e.g. management accounts),

2) per hectare, by looking up an average figure according to the size and type of farm. Approximate levels are shown in the tables of whole farm fixed costs (page 221). This is obviously a guide only and masks huge variations between farms. It is essential to understand your own power and machinery costs given that they vary so significantly between businesses. However, averages may be a useful starting point.

3) Fully detailed calculations, costing and depreciating each machine in turn, including tractors, estimating repairs and fuel costs for each, and adding the charges for any contract work. The following tables give, for different types of machinery, estimated life, annual depreciation, and estimated repairs according to annual use (although this can vary considerably between soil types, weather conditions and the level of maintenance undertaken).

ESTIMATED USEFUL LIFE OF POWERED MACHINERY IN NORMAL USE

Estimated Useful Life (years)	Annual Use (hours)			
Equipment	50	100	200	300
Group 1:				
Ploughs, cultivators, harrows, rolls, ridgers, potato planting machinery, grain cleaners	15+	12+	12	10
Group 2:				
Disc harrows, seed drills, grain drying machines, feed mills/mixes	15+	12	10	8
Group 3:				
Combine harvesters, pick-up balers, rotary cultivators, hydraulic loaders	20+	20+	12+	10
Group 4:				
Mowers, forage harvesters, swath turners, rakes, tedders, hedge cutting machines, precision drills	15	12	10	8
Group 5:				
Fertiliser spreaders, combination drills, FYM spreaders, sprayers	15+	10+	8	7
Miscellaneous:				
Beet harvesters	12+	10	8	6
Potato harvesters	10+	10	8	5
Milking machinery	—	—	—	20+

	Annual Use (hours)					
	500	750	1,000	1,500	2,000	2,500
Tractors	18+	12	10	7	6	5
Electric motors	20+	12	10+	10	9	8

CAPITAL EMPLOYED IN MACHINERY

	£/acre		£/ha	
	average	premium	average	premium
Combinable Crops:	550	400	1,360	990
Mixed Cropping	780	550	1,925	1,360
Grazing Dairy:	200	140	420	270
Intensive Dairy:	475	330	1,175	815
Grazing Livestock:	180	130	445	320

This includes tractors, telehandlers, self-propelled sprayers and combines. It excludes fixed items such as parlours, livestock handling equipment and grain drying equipment. Large variations exist depending upon the use of contractors vs own equipment, as well as farm efficiency variations.

DEPRECIATION

There are two methods by which to calculate depreciation rates for agricultural machinery. The ***straight line*** method takes the difference between the estimated trade-in, second-hand or scrap value of a machine, and the purchase price of the machine. The loss in capital value over the period the machine is retained for is then divided by the age of the machine to arrive at the annual depreciation charge. This can then be used to arrive at the annual % depreciation rate to apply to that machine on a straight line basis over its useful life for budgeting purposes.

Example: If a machine costing £10,000 is retained for 8 years, at the end of which the trade-in value is £2,000, the depreciation has been £8,000. Over 8 years this equates to £1,000 per annum (i.e. 10% per year of the new price).

The ***diminishing balance*** method takes account of the fact that new machines lose a larger proportion of their capital value in the early years even with modest annual usage. Some estimated percentage rates of depreciation for different machine types under a diminishing balance basis are shown in the table below. *Clearly, in addition to the age of the machine, annual usage has an effect upon depreciation rates which is not necessarily accounted for below.*

AVERAGE ANNUAL FALL IN VALUE

Age of Machine	Complex. High depreciation rate		Traditional machines		Simple equipment: Low depreciation rate	
	Annual % Dep'n	Total % Dep'n	Annual % Dep'n	Total % Dep'n	Annual % Dep'n	Total % Dep'n
1	37.5	37.5	28	28	22	22
2	25	50	19	38	16	32
3	20*	60	15.3	46	13.7	41
4	16.5†	66	13.3*	53	12	48
5	14.2‡	71	11.8	59	10.8	54
6	12.5	75	10.7†	64	9.8	59
7	11.3	79	9.8	68.5	9.1*	64
8	10.3	82	9.0‡	72	8.4	67
9	9.3	84	8.2	74	7.7	69
10	8.5	85	7.5	75	7†	70

Complex: Machines such as potato harvesters, pea viners, etc.
Traditional Machines: with many moving parts, e.g. tractors, combines, balers, forage harvesters
Simple Equipment: with few moving parts, e.g. ploughs, trailers

* Typical frequency of renewal with heavy use.

† Typical frequency of renewal with average use.

‡Typical frequency of renewal with light use.

These figures have been calculated from a survey of machinery sale prices. Depreciation is calculated from the new price, asking price of the second hand machine, and its age. The asking price has been discounted by 5% to account for price negotiations. Prices for a variety of machinery and equipment types have been collated and categorised according to complexity.

Example: If a tractor (traditional machine) costing £80,000 is 5 years old, the value of the machine has depreciated on average by 11.8% per year, totalling a 59% fall in value. This means the tractor is now worth £32,800. The chart shows depreciation over the ten year period.

Depreciation of Machinery Categories over 10 years

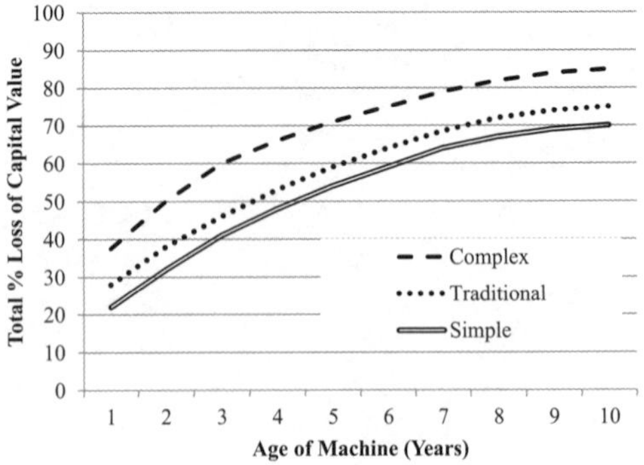

Total % Loss of Capital Value
100
90
80
70
60
50
40
30
20
10
0
1 2 3 4 5 6 7 8 9 10
Age of Machine (Years)
Complex
Traditional
Simple

ESTIMATED ANNUAL COST OF SPARES AND REPAIRS

These figures are based on a percentage of purchase price* at various levels of use

	Annual Use *(hours)*				Additional 100 hours
	500	750	1,000	1,500	use add
	%	%	%	%	%
Tractors	1-2	2-3	4	4-6	0.5

	Annual Use *(hours)*				Additional 100 hours
	50	100	150	200	use add
Harvesting Machinery:	%	%	%	%	%
Combine harvesters, self-propelled forage harvesters, self-propelled potato harvesters	1.5	2.5	3.5	4.5	2
Trailed forage harvesters, pick-up balers, potato & sugar beet harvesters	3	5	6	7	2
Other Implements and Machines:					
Ploughs, cultivators, harrows	4.5	8	11	14	6
Rotary cultivators, mowers, windrowers	4	7	9.5	12	5
Disc harrows, fertiliser spreaders, farmyard manure spreaders, combination drills, potato planters, sprayers, hedge-cutting machines.	3	5.5	7.5	9.5	4
Tedders, rakes	2.5	4.5	6.5	8.5	4
Seed drills, milking machines, hydraulic loaders	2	4	5.5	7	3
Grain driers, grain cleaners, rollers, hammer mills, feed mixers	1.5	2	2.5	3	0.5

* *When it is known that a high purchase price is due to high quality and durability or a low price corresponds to a high rate of wear and tear, adjustments to the figures should be made.*

SERVICE PLANS

Most tractor manufacturers now offer extended warranties or comprehensive service plans to cover the cost of all servicing, maintenance and repairs beyond the regular manufacturer warranty. This is usually for a pre-agreed period of time or maximum number of hours (usually this expiry date is determined by which comes first). Costs and offerings vary hugely between manufacturers and tractor models but the following gives an approximate guide. A 'standard' maintenance and repair plan for a 130hp tractor doing 500 hours per year for 5 years would cost an average of £1,350-£1,500/year. This is for a 'standard' maintenance and repair plan to include all servicing, most replacement parts, filters, maintenance fluids and routine labour.

There are 'premium' plans available to go a stage further and protect further parts of the machine. There are, however, always exclusions from these agreements such as tyres, glass and provisions for negligence. Given the rising cost of repairs (and machinery dealer labour costs), such plans can be beneficial for farming businesses, particularly contractors who can fix their repair costs. This therefore helps with budgeting and setting prices to charge customers. However, where annual usage is lower, they may not always be economical. Such agreements are a risk management strategy in protecting against large un-expected repair costs. This also gives peace of mind in the knowledge that the services were carried out by a qualified technician at the correct service intervals, rather than by farm staff who may lack knowledge and also can be undertaken on a rather ad-hoc basis, particularly during busy times of the year.

TYRES

The length of time a set of tractor tyres lasts before they need to be replaced will vary significantly depending upon a number of factors. These include soil type (stone content is the main determinant of tyre wear), the amount of yard work undertaken (feeding, loading grain etc), and the amount of road travelling undertaken. Many tractors will do in excess of 5,000 hours on a set of tyres assuming the machine does not do excessive road work. Front tyres on loader tractors are likely to require replacement earlier than rear tyres due to the weight of the loader (and items lifted) and the associated increase in wear that this creates when turning on yard areas. Clearly costs vary between tyre sizes but the largest variation can be seen between manufacturer makes due to perceived quality and therefore wear differences. The following table gives a guide for the prices of a range of different tractor tyres:-

Size	*Price Range*	*Size*	*Price Range*
320 R24	£160 - £440	540 R38	£620 - £1,240
340 R24	£220 - £440	600 R38	£800 - £1,470
420 R28	£340 - £590	650 R42	£950 - £2,290
480 R28	£370 - £880	710 R42	£1,360 - £3,000
520 R38	£560 - £1,490	800 R42	£1,800 - £3,450

As an example, new 520 R38 tyres for the rear and 480 R28 tyres for the front of a 150hp tractor would cost on average approximately £3,300 plus VAT, plus the cost of the fitting and old tyre disposal costs. This could be done on-farm where the correct equipment is held, otherwise most tyre fitters / tractor dealers would fit these. Typical labour charges for technicians vary between £30/hour and £65/hour. Larger and even flotation tyres are becoming increasingly popular for field-work, and in particular trailers, in an attempt to reduce soil compaction. These will cost significantly more to purchase.

BENCHMARK POWER AND LABOUR COSTS

One of the key areas where significant differences in costs between businesses is apparent is fixed costs. However, whilst many fixed costs such as property expenses, administration, rent and finance differ due to farm circumstances e.g. rented vs owner occupied; power/machinery and labour costs can be easily considered as a method of comparing financial performance and business efficiency. The table below gives some benchmark figures for different businesses in different sectors. For dairy, these costs are presented on a pence per litre basis on page 50.

Represents good financial performance	£ Per Hectare				
	Combinable Cropping		**Dairy (120 ha farms)**		
	Large	*Small-Medium*	*Spring Calving*	*All-Year-Round*	*Autumn Calving*
Power & Machinery	*800-2,000 ha*	*150-500 ha*	*5,250 l / cow*	*8,000 l / cow*	*7,000 l / cow*
Fuel	71	82	15	105	48
Light & Heat	20	22	54	68	55
Machinery Repairs	64	52	30	88	61
Contractors	20	27	275	316	309
Hire Costs	4	2	9	14	26
Depreciation	113	128	161	201	158
Total Power Costs	**292**	**314**	**544**	**792**	**657**
Labour					
Paid Labour	67	30	263	372	407
Family Labour	44	104	195	215	135
Total	**111**	**133**	**458**	**587**	**542**
Hectares / FTE	270	190	55	43	46

6. PRECISION AGRICULTURE

Precision farming is a method of farm management fundamentally centred on responding to very detailed variations in resource capability. The term has been adopted in recent years as a technology to map resource capacity such as land fertility or machinery passes so that each resource unit can be treated individually and precisely to maximise its productive capacity. It is estimated that about two thirds of UK arable land is farmed using some form of precision farming technology, dominated by the larger farms.

The cheapest and most cost effective piece of precision farming equipment is a tape measure. For example, measuring the 'operating' width of machinery compared with actual width of bouts to identify overlap is a critical starting point. Precision farming is of most benefit to farmers who are least precise in their resource allocation. This might be through considerable variation of in-field nutrient levels or soil types. Larger, more extensive operations that have less management and labour per hectare to examine and treat each small parcel of land (or other resource) individually, will be able to benefit more greatly through automated measurements of resource capacity such as soil fertility or pH in different areas. They can also benefit more by spreading the capital cost over more hectares. Whilst it has taken many years to develop, there are now a wide number of different technologies available. These are covered in the following sections.

Automated / Assisted Steering

This was the first precision farming technology to gather pace in UK agriculture. It ensures that machinery covers precisely the correct area of ground without overlaps or leaving any gaps. Systems vary from GPS controlled in-cab monitors which produce lines at pre-determined bout widths for the operator to follow on the screen (still requiring manual steering) to fully automated systems whereby the in-cab controls result in the tractor steering itself up and down the field at the selected bout widths. With the latter, the operator merely has to turn the tractor round on the headland and re-start it in its new bout before the GPS controls navigate it down the field again. Basic light bar systems cost £350-£900, whereas fully automated steering systems cost between £3,500 and £6,000. Costs can be reduced if tractors are purchased with in-built technology readily available, thus requiring the receiver to simply be moved from one tractor unit to the next. Most of these use freely available GPS signals which are generally accurate to between 10cm and 20cm depending on the system. The most sophisticated systems now allow farmers to operate Controlled Traffic Farming (CTF) systems whereby all vehicle types are kept solely on a precise layout of permanent traffic lanes year after year to reduce compaction and soil structure damage. This requires extensive machinery planning to ensure all working widths fit the desired traffic lanes. They also require more accurate GPS signals which are more expensive. For example, RTK (Real Time Kinematic) systems are generally accurate to 2cm, either having base stations on farm or utilising others via an annual subscription fee of circa £500-£750.

Variable Rate Fertiliser, Lime and Seed

The application of fertiliser at different variable rates across fields requires those fields to be mapped for nutrients to determine the nutrient balance at a very precise level of field area. This then allows applications to be tailored according to the requirement or yield potential of that precise piece of land. Service providers offer mapping of Phosphate, Potash, soil pH and other micro-nutrients using either grid methods or zoning linked to soil conductivity testing (i.e. soil type variations). These enable variable rate P, K and lime applications, as well as variable seed rates to better target inputs. The aim is to help produce an even crop across varying soil types within fields, whilst ensuring nutrients are only applied where required. Such a comprehensive service costs in the region of £8-£11/ha for all mapping services, often costing more in the early years until all zoning has been completed. The cost of individual soil tests for N, P, K and Mg is about £8 per sample. Machine compatibility with control boxes / existing tractor technology is important when considering precision farming techniques/services. When such variable rate nutrient application maps are overlaid with yield monitoring maps, nutrient applications can also be tailored to ensure those high yielding areas receive back the high level of nutrients removed through the high yielding crop.

For the variable application of nitrogen fertilisers, either granular or liquid, growers can choose between satellite based imagery systems for green leaf area index mapping or Active Light Source (ALS) tractor mounted sensors. The cost of preparing variable rate nitrogen plans using satellite based mapping services, which convert data into green leaf area/crop biomass maps, is approximately £1.50 per hectare. A number of images are taken during the growing season and applications adjusted accordingly in line with changes in crop development in different areas of the field. Tractor mounted sensors are becoming more popular due to the arguably more accurate real-time data gathered and processed whilst the machine is driving through the crop. By mapping crop biomass levels, nitrogen and sulphur fertilisers can be applied variably, as well as growth regulators and fungicides. Sensor manufacturers claim from long term trial results, savings of up to 20kgN/ha are possible with yield improvements of circa 3% in cereals. The cost of sensors and software are approximately £25,000 per unit, sufficient for a 1,000 ha arable unit.

The Future

The variable rate technology is now being applied to spray inputs, in particular fungicides and growth regulator products, utilising the green area index / crop biomass maps to better focus inputs for overall yield benefit and/or resource efficiency. Some growers are also now starting to map problematic weed areas within fields in order to target spray applications, as well as higher seed rates and differing cultivation strategies to better manage weed burdens within crops. The use of drones for visual imagery in order to produce such maps are also becoming more common.

Economic Benefits

Economic benefits result from better allocated inputs leading to savings of inputs, or higher yields. Inputs saved could include seed, fertilisers, sprays, machinery use, fuel and labour. Faster work-rates achieved can mean achieving more in periods of optimal weather conditions. Environmental benefits can also be achieved through correct input allocations and less wastage/leaching. Many growers report little cost savings actually achieved through variable rate seed and fertiliser applications, but do report yield improvements as a result of more even crops through the better targeting of the inputs within each field. Independent data on the economic benefits is difficult to obtain. A HGCA publication 71 (2009) suggests that costs and benefits of automated steering might be in the region of the table below, although this will vary considerably between farms and years.

Table of benefits for Assisted Steer Technology (HGCA Review 71)

Level	Arable area	Accuracy	Machines Adapted	cost £/ha	benefit £/ha	net £/ha
Assisted Manual Steer	300 Ha	+/- 40cm	2	1.25	2.50	1.25
Mid-Level DGPS*	500ha	+/- 10cm	2	12	14	2.00
RTK**	500ha high value crops	+/- 2cm	3	20	22	2.00

** DGPS = Differential Global Positioning System* *** RTK = Real Time Kinematic*

Knight S., Miller P. and Orson J. An up to date cost/benefit analysis of precision farming techniques to guide growers of cereals and oilseeds. HGCA Review 71. 2009

Acknowledgement: thanks to Ian Beecher-Jones 07967 637 985

7. OTHER MACHINERY COSTS

IRRIGATION COSTS

Estimated for 2018

Capital Costs

1. Pumps delivering from 30 to 200 cubic metres per hour from a surface water source, complete with monitoring equipment:-

Tractor PTO driven (pump only)	£1,100 - £4,500
Diesel engine driven pump unit	£22,000-£24,000 *(50-100 m^3/hr)*
	£22,000-£28,000 *(100-200 m^3/hr)*
Electric motor driven pump unit	£40,000 *(100 to 150 m^3/hr)*
Optional remote/wireless monitoring controls	£500 - £1,500
Variable speed drive option – fitted to electric motor	£800 - £5,000

Individual pumps for mounting on diesel engines range in price from £3,000 to £15,000 for capacities of between 50 and 250 cubic metres per hour. A sophisticated system, including pump house, pumps and control equipment to feed an irrigation system from a reservoir to cover a total area of approx. 400 ha (as and when required) would cost approximately £35,000 - £50,000 to construct and install.

2. Pipelines (averages £ per metre):-

Portable (excl. valve take offs):

50 mm: £2.00

75 mm: £4.50

100 mm: £7.00

125 mm: £9.20

150 mm: £11.00

Permanent underground PVC pipe 16 bar rating (excludes the cost of laying):

100 mm: £5.40

160 mm: £7.30

200 mm: £10.90

Hydrants:

100 mm x 100 mm: £120 (aluminium) £300 (underground)

150 mm x 125 mm: £150 (aluminium) £360 (underground)

3. Application Systems:-

(a) Hose reel systems (average cost per machine) complete with rain gun:

	Hose Length	Output	Acre inches/day	Cost
Small	180-250m	5-25m^3/hr	4.5-5.5	£5,000 to £11,000
Medium	300-400m	40-80m^3/hr	17-20	£13,000 to £22,000
Large	450-650m	70-120m^3/hr	28-33	£22,000 to £36,000

To add electric controls would cost an additional £3,500-£4,000.

(b) Irrigation booms (average cost per unit):

Small	18m boom (24m wetted width)	£5,000 - £6,000
Medium	30m boom (48m wetted width)	£6,300 - £7,000

Large	50m boom (72m wetted width)	£15,200 - £16,000
	64m boom (72m to 90m wetted width)	£16,500 - £17,000

(c) Pivot and linear systems:

Small Linear	200m width	£45,000 - £55,000
Large pivot	600m radius (100ha approx.)	£60,000 - £85,000

(d) Solid set sprinkler lines – semi-permanent systems (very specialist and not widely found):

63mm dia. pipework assemblies at 18m x 18m triangulated spacing	£1,500 - £1,800/ha
As above but with infra-red automated hand-held controls	£1,700 - £2,100/ha

(e) Specialist Drip Irrigation systems (excluding the header mains, control valves and filtration equipment) will cost approximately 4.50p per metre for 16mm tape for a one year life span with 20cm emitter spacing for 1.25L per linear meter (6mm wall thickness). For 20mm 10 year tape with 40cm emitter spacing, emitting 0.65L per emitter (47mm wall thickness), this will cost between 33p and 35p per metre.

4. Total:
If no source works are needed, as with water from a river, or pond, total capital costs are likely to vary between £1,200 and £2,300 per hectare requiring irrigation at regular intervals, depending on the site layout, levels of sophistication and automation of the system installed. The capital cost of constructing a reservoir to store irrigation water, usually filled during the winter, is typically in excess of £1.30/m^3 for clay-lined reservoirs (although considerable variations will exist depending on precise circumstances). Lining and fencing could double this cost. This cost could be off-set partly by the sale of sand / gravel depending upon the location. In addition, there may be a need for pump houses and other infrastructure depending upon the circumstances. New time limited abstraction licences are difficult to obtain, especially for summer abstraction. Hence there is an increasing trend towards constructing reservoirs that can be used to store water abstracted during the winter months.

Acknowledgement: thanks to Briggs Irrigation and Javelin Irrigation Systems

Water Sources

An abstraction licence is required if more than 20m^3 (4,400 gallons) of water per day are taken from surface or underground sources. Once an abstraction licence is obtained, the licence holder must comply with its conditions. *The rules and charges below are based upon the abstraction charges scheme for 2017/18.* A temporary abstraction licence is sufficient if more than 20m^3 of water per day is to be taken for less than 28 days, whereas a full abstraction licence is required if more than 20m^3 of water per day is to be taken for more than 28 days. In 2016, there were over 18,000 abstraction licences in place in England. If abstracting more than 10m^3 per day in Scotland, you must obtain authorisation from SEPA. If abstracting less than 10m^3 per day in Scotland, and comply with certain General Binding Rules (GBR), you do not require authorisation. Abstraction charges vary widely calculated by a formula combining the following factors together:

- Volume – annual licensed
- the Source Factor; whether the source is Environment Agency unsupported, supported or tidal
- The Season Factor; summer, winter or all year round
- The loss factor – high, medium, low or very low, depending upon what the water is authorised to be used for under the licence
- A minimum annual charge of £25

Annual Charge = Standard Charge + Compensation Charge
= V x A x B x C x SUC + V x B x C x D x EIUC

Where V = annual licensed volume (000 cubic metres)
A = Source factor
B = Season factor
C = Loss factor
D = Adjusted source factor
SUC = Standard Unit Charge (£/1,000 cubic metres)
EIUC = Environmental Improvement Unit Charge (£/1,000 cubic metres)

There were 22 regions 'supported' by the Environment Agency in 2017/18. Abstraction from these rivers is 3 times dearer than 'unsupported' sources. Abstraction from tidal sources costs 20% of 'unsupported' sources.

Winter abstraction charges (authorised for abstraction between 1st November and 31st March) cost 16% of all-year abstraction charges. Summer charges (1st April to 31st October) are 160% of the all-year charge.

An application charge of £135 (a higher application charge of £1,500 is due for those extracting water for use in electricity/power generation) and advertising administration charge of £100 is due, alongside an Annual Charge which is the sum of the Standard Charge and the Compensation Charge which are each calculated from a formula comprising the Standard Unit Charge (SUC) and the Environmental Improvement Unit Charge (EIUC) respectively. The Annual Charge is not payable for temporary licences. The charges for 2017/18 are as follows:-

Region (£/1000m³)	*Standard Unit Charges*	*Environmental Improvement Unit Charge (EIUC)*
Anglian	27.51	0.00
Midlands	14.95	0.00
Northumbria	16.66	0.00
Yorkshire	11.63	0.00
North West	12.57	3.86
Southern	19.23	0.00
South West (incl. Wessex)	19.71	12.91
Thames	13.84	2.30
Dee	14.40	0.00
Wye	14.40	0.00

Most abstractors must provide the Environment Agency with accurate records (known as 'returns') of how much water is taken in order to enable them to balance water resources between different users and check compliance with licence conditions. If a licence is in place and you have not extracted any water, a 'nil' return must be submitted. It is a cross-compliance breach to not submit an abstraction return form under GAEC 2.

Water Costs

A typical extraction cost for a non-tidal, non-supported farm in East Anglia for 25mm per hectare (250m^3 per hectare) applied through a rain gun (high loss factor) would be as follows:-

	£/ha	*Pence/m^3*	*£/acre inch*
Winter Abstraction only	1.65	0.66	0.68
All-Year Abstraction	10.31	4.12	4.24
Summer Abstraction only	16.49	6.60	6.78
Mains Water	400.00	160.00	164.00

This is clearly just the cost for the water. The capital invested plus the labour and any power requirement should also be accounted for which will vary according to individual circumstances.

Overall Operating Costs

Because of variations in individual farm circumstances in terms of source works and the irrigation system used, the overall cost of applying 25mm per hectare can range widely, from £85 to £155/ha. Very sophisticated systems distributing mains water over intensive specialist crops could be much more expensive.

Conversions and Calculations

The (approximate) imperial equivalents for metric values commonly used in irrigation are as follows:

- 1 cubic metre = 1,000 litres = 220 gallons (1 million gallons = 4,546 cubic metres).
- A pump capacity of 100 cubic metres per hour is equivalent to 22,000 gallons per hour (367 gallons per minute).
- 1,000 cubic metres is sufficient to apply 25 millimetres of water over 4 hectares, which is approximately equivalent to applying 1 inch over 10 acres. An acre inch is therefore 100 cubic meters (22,000 gallons), or a hectare centimetre is 100 cubic meters.
- The cost/volume conversion from a hectare of 25mm depth to an acre-inch is 0.411 or 2.433 from an acre-inch to a hectare 25mm.

GRAIN DRYING AND STORAGE

When reviewing different grain drying systems, consider it alongside existing or new grain storage options. This is because some drying systems necessitate certain storage facilities and vice versa. The tables below outline the cost of grain drying and storage for three options for a 500 hectare arable farm, assuming all grain is dried. Whilst in practical terms, not the entire harvest is necessarily dried, in most cases the vast majority of grain will be dried (or at least cooled) but just to various different extents depending on harvest moisture levels and crop condition.

Grain Drying and Storage Comparison	On Floor Drying & Storage	Continuous Flow Dryer & Concrete Floor Storage	Batch Dryer & Concrete Floor Storage
Capital Costs (per tonne):-			
Store Building	£70	£70	£70
Floor, Tunnels, Fans & Controllers (no stirrers)	£67		
Dryer (16t/hour) + Wet Intake Area		£29	
Dryer (25t/batch system) + Wet Intake Area			£17
Store / Dryer Longevity (years)	35	35 / 25	35 / 25
Interest/Opportunity Cost	4%	4%	4%
Cost per tonne per year			
	£/tonne	**£/tonne**	**£/tonne**
Depreciation	£3.91	£3.16	£2.68
Finance/Opportunity Cost	£2.74	£1.98	£1.74
Fuel & Electricity (per 5% moisture)	£2.50	£3.65	£3.70
Repairs & Insurance	£2.06	£1.92	£1.56
Total *(assuming total tonnage dried)*	**£11.21**	**£10.71**	**£9.68**

Handling costs in terms of elevators, conveyors, telehandlers and trailers to move grain into and out of drying systems are additional to the above figures and vary according to the layout of the infrastructure.

GRAIN DRYING

Choosing the most appropriate system depends on many factors. The capital cost of installing on-floor drying floors is significantly greater than a dryer and a concrete floor building to store grain post drying. On-floor drying requires minimal handling of grain post-harvest but time to monitor store moistures and temperatures over 3-6 months post-harvest is needed. On-floor drying is much slower so less suitable for those wishing to sell grain in September to November.

Continuous flow dryers require good building layout to limit the infrastructure required to convey grain from the dryer into different stores. Labour input for a modern automatic facility is minimal. Continuous flow dryers typically have low resale values being fixed and immobile. Mobile batch dryers are much cheaper but can require more handling of grain (forklift and trailers) unless they are automatic and sited suitably. The capital costs per tonne are therefore often much lower but running costs higher. These machines are popular on many farms, offering flexibility and a viable alternative where a suitable electrical connection is not available (the example above assumes an electrically powered batch dryer, but PTO powered machines are also popular). They also have a better second-hand value. They suit a farm with multiple grain storage sites and where storage does not allow grain to be cooled as each batch is cooled prior to un-loading, unlike continuous flow machines.

There could be a further cost requirement to cool the grain in store after being dried. This cost varies depending on the system used – pedestals or on-floor blowing are common. The costs of suitable fans vary between £1,500 and £4,000 depending on requirements. Ducting under the crop may also be required.

Introduction of the Renewable Heat Incentive has offered opportunities to use renewable fuels (woodchip, straw) to reduce drying costs. There is even a market for using drying systems to dry woodchip fuel to utilise grain drying facilities when not required for combinable crops.

There has been considerable investment in grain storage and drying facilities in recent years, which has been much needed, with many businesses having old and often inefficient facilities. Another alternative is Central Grain Stores. These organisations offer grain drying services for about £7.00 to £12.00 per tonne for 5% moisture drying for members and non-members respectively. Contractors' charges vary between £10.00 per tonne and £15.00 per tonne for drying grain by 5% moisture, although often prices quoted are much lower because less drying may be required on average.

Grain cleaning equipment gives flexibility if a crop sample is poor, bushel weights low, or admixture high to aid storage, drying and crop value. Superior crop quality, particularly niche crops, attracts premiums. A rotary cleaner with 25 tonne per hour cleaning output and 8-10 tonne per hour very fine cleaning output costs £17,000 - £20,000. Some drying systems enable cleaning systems to be added to their automated controls to enable a fully automated integrated system to be installed. Simpler cleaning systems cost significantly less to purchase but will not enable the same degree of cleaning capability.

GRAIN STORAGE

Clearly the capital costs detailed in the table above vary considerably depending on precise requirements and site circumstances. For example, an elaborate plant on a greenfield site, including weigh-bridge, intake pit, elevator, conveyors, ventilated storage bins, catwalk etc. in a new building could cost over £300/t. *See page 237.*

Contract Storage: typically £1.50 - £2.50/t per month with a handling charge of around £2.00 - £2.50 per tonne for loading into store and out of store. Large grain merchants offer storage including haulage for around £10/t for the four month period September to December (giving flexibility on marketing where no on-farm storage is available) with a further charge of £1.50/t per month for every additional month stored prior to sale post-Christmas. Handling charges will be in addition. Alternatively farmers can choose to buy into farmer owned co-operative grain store operations. Costs vary depending upon membership structures but are in the region of £100-£110/t for membership storage rights (normally partly in the form of a loan/investment), plus annual maintenance charges (including haulage) of typically £8-10/t, plus handling and drying charges of £2-£4/t depending on moisture levels. Additional drying charges normally apply for grain delivered with a moisture content in excess of 16%. The main benefits of membership in a co-operative store are the ability to use own buildings for other uses, as well as take away any on-going store management work, whilst retaining the benefit of flexible marketing. Often, co-operative stores will also allow non-members to store at a premium storage price of circa £12-14/t and premium handling and drying charges of £4-£12/t according to moisture levels. Retiring farmers can normally choose to sell their storage rights back to the co-operative or to other members, therefore releasing their invested capital.

LIVESTOCK HAULAGE COSTS

The cost of hauling livestock to market, to field, back to winter housing or other movements between grazing is a cost that is often over-looked. The table below demonstrates the farmers cost of hauling livestock per head per journey, for a number of different journey lengths.

Journey	*£ Per Head Per Journey*		
Length	Ewe	Finished Lamb	Finished Cattle
1 Mile	0.50	0.33	4.96
5 Miles	0.61	0.41	6.15
10 Miles	0.76	0.51	7.63
15 Miles	0.91	0.61	9.10
20 Miles	1.06	0.71	10.58
30 Miles	1.35	0.90	13.54

The costs calculated above include the cost of running a vehicle (pick-up/Landrover), based upon 12,000 miles annual mileage, attributing this cost on a per mile basis to the livestock transport cost (to reflect the fact that the vehicle is also used for many other purposes). The cost of running a livestock trailer (capital cost and repairs/maintenance) is based upon an average sized farm stock trailer with decks, capable of holding 30 ewes, 45 finished lambs, or 3 finished cattle, assuming it is kept for 10 years and used for 40 journeys per year.

In arriving at a cost per head, the calculations assume that the trailer is always fully occupied with one of the above livestock numbers. The costs per head by journey length assume one journey; therefore if the journey to market was 30 miles one-way and no return load was bought back (i.e. an empty trailer), the total cost of transporting those livestock to market would in fact be almost double that shown above (although recognising the fact that towing an empty trailer will use less fuel than when fully loaded). The labour costs calculated above exclude time for loading/un-loading but account for time spent driving between destinations averaging 30mph.

Specialist livestock hauliers charge either on a per day basis or a cost per head for specific journey lengths. As a result, charges vary widely depending upon the specific circumstances, such as distances and the size of groups etc. As a guide, to move breeding sheep from Yorkshire to the Midlands would cost approximately £3/ewe assuming the haulier is able to backload. Costs for hauling lambs to market over a distance of more than 40 miles would cost circa £2.00 - £2.50/lamb and £15-20/head for finished cattle. An articulated lorry and driver, fully equipped for livestock haulage, would typically cost £600-£750/day.

GRAIN HAULAGE COSTS

The AHDB's grain haulage survey has now ceased but indicative haulage costs per tonne of grain (and oilseed) in Great Britain for varying journey lengths are shown in table below. Given that the majority of combinable crops are sold on an ex-farm basis, haulage costs are less relevant to the farmer.

10 miles	*20 miles*	*40 miles*	*60 miles*	*100 miles*	*150 miles*
£4.60/t	£5.33/t	£6.80/t	£8.29/t	£11.25/t	£14.95/t

VI. OTHER FIXED COSTS DATA

1. WHOLE FARM FIXED COSTS

The following are a broad indication of the levels of fixed costs per hectare (acre) for various types and sizes of farm, estimated for 2018, including the value of unpaid family manual labour, including that of the farmer and spouse. The figures are based on the actual results from the Farm Business Survey (FBS) for the 2015-16 year (February to February), adjusted for subsequent changes in costs. The FBS is based on a sample of farms which does change over time, so there is not a consistent sample. This just emphasises that the costs given below should be used only as an indication and must be adjusted according to individual situations; see also further notes on the use of this data below.

The FBS is conducted by a consortium of Universities and Colleges across England on behalf of Defra. Although the survey is limited to England, the figures within this section are broadly applicable to most parts of the UK. Specific regional reports can be accessed via the FBS website (see www.farmbusinesssurvey.co.uk). Farm types are standardised across the country based on Defra's standard farm classifications. All of these costs, of course, vary widely according to many factors, especially the intensity of farming, e.g. the number of cows per 100 hectares on dairy farms, the hectares of intensive crops on general cropping farms and management ability.

The figures provided are averages. 'Premium' farms of the same level of intensity can have labour, machinery and general overhead costs at least 20% lower. However, the most profitable farms are often more intensive. They therefore have higher fixed costs per hectare associated with the great intensity - but with substantially higher total farm gross margins. Thus it is the net amount (Gross Margin – Fixed Costs) that matters.

The 'small' farm categories relate only to full-time holdings and do not include very intensive holdings occupying very small areas.

The term 'fixed costs' is used here as it is in gross margin analysis and planning; a full explanation of the differences between fixed and variable costs in this context is given on pages 3 and 4. Note that all casual labour and contract work has been included under fixed costs. In calculating enterprise gross margins on the individual farm, these costs are normally allocated as variable costs if they are specific to a particular enterprise and vary approximately in proportion to its size, i.e. are approximately constant per hectare of a particular crop or per head of livestock. Otherwise they are included as fixed costs. In both cases, however, they could be regarded as substitutes for regular labour and/or the farmer's own machinery - which are both items of fixed cost. It is therefore simpler if both are included, fully, as fixed costs. If one is comparing results from accounts set out on a gross margin basis, and some or all of the casual labour and contract work have been included as variable costs (especially on cropping farms, e.g. for potato harvesting using casual labour or a contractor's machine), the necessary adjustments need to be made in making the comparisons.

Notes on the Schedules

1. *Unpaid Labour:* Refers to the value of unpaid family manual labour, including that of the farmer and spouse.
2. *Machinery Depreciation:* This is based on current (i.e. replacement) cost. This gives a truer reflection of the real loss of value of machinery (as is apparent when replacement becomes necessary). It also allows easier comparison between different businesses. However, many farm accounts calculate depreciation on the 'historic' (i.e. original) cost of the machinery. This will tend to produce a lower figure. Depending on the age of the machine, and bearing in mind recent strong increases in machinery prices, the

historic method may underestimate depreciation by 10-20%. Note that both the Depreciation item and Repairs include vehicles.

3. *Leasing Charges:* The capital element, but not the interest, is included in depreciation; the proportion paid as interest varies according to the rate of interest paid and the length of the leasing period, but is typically 7%-10%.

4. *Machinery Running Costs:* This includes fuel, oil, repairs, servicing and vehicle tax and insurance. Separate figures for these elements are no longer available. As a general rule, fuel might make up a little over half of all such costs.

5. *General Overheads:* include general farm maintenance and repairs, office expenses, water, insurance, fees, subscriptions, etc.

6. *Rent & Interest:* Rent only relates to the actual rent paid by the average farm in that particular category. It is not an imputed rent for all land farmed by the business; thus, a fully owned-occupied farm will have no rental costs. Only actual interest paid by the average farm in that particular category is shown.

In making comparisons with fixed costs taken from farm accounts it is important to note that in the figures below unpaid manual labour is included; farm accounts will rarely include this. Also the figures below include average rent and interest; in farm accounts these will vary widely depending on the farm tenure and borrowing. Very low 'target' figures given in press articles often omit these items and can therefore be misleading; usually, too, they relate only to large, very well appointed farms. If an 'opportunity cost' for owner-occupied land (often fully paid for many years) is included, then the cost level rises further. Note too that the figures given below do not include management, whether paid or unpaid. The margin after deducting the fixed costs below from the total gross margin plus any other farm receipts represents the total return to management and own capital in the business.

Labour, machinery and buildings are the main items of 'fixed' costs subject to change with major alterations in farm policy. Each has a separate section in this book.

Mainly Dairying

£/ha (£/acre)	Under 75 ha		75 - 125 ha		Over 125 ha	
	(Under 185 acres)		(185 - 310 acres)		(Over 310 acres)	
Regular Labour (paid)	85	(34)	195	(79)	325	(132)
Regular Labour (unpaid)	680	(275)	355	(144)	185	(75)
Casual Labour	40	(16)	45	(18)	55	(22)
Total Labour	**805**	**(326)**	**595**	**(241)**	**565**	**(229)**
Machinery Depreciation	160	(65)	200	(81)	180	(73)
Machinery Running Costs	120	(49)	180	(73)	205	(83)
Contract	130	(53)	160	(65)	185	(75)
Total Power & Machinery...	**410**	**(166)**	**540**	**(219)**	**570**	**(231)**
Farm Maintenance	50	(20)	105	(42)	95	(38)
Water & Electricity	180	(73)	170	(69)	150	(61)
General Overhead Expenses ..	90	(36)	75	(30)	75	(30)
Total Overheads	**320**	**(130)**	**350**	**(142)**	**320**	**(130)**
Rent & Interest	155	(63)	205	(83)	255	(103)
Total Fixed Costs	**1690**	**(684)**	**1690**	**(684)**	**1710**	**(692)**

Mainly Cereals

£/ha (£/acre)	Under 200 ha (Under 490 acres)		200 - 400 ha (490 - 990 acres)		Over 400 ha (Over 990 acres)	
Regular Labour (paid)	50	(20)	75	(30)	100	(40)
Regular Labour (unpaid)	220	(89)	155	(63)	100	(40)
Casual Labour	10	(4)	15	(6)	10	(4)
Total Labour	**280**	**(113)**	**245**	**(99)**	**210**	**(85)**
Machinery Depreciation	120	(49)	140	(57)	125	(51)
Machinery Running Costs	100	(40)	110	(45)	105	(42)
Contract	95	(38)	80	(32)	80	(32)
Total Power & Machinery...	**315**	**(127)**	**330**	**(134)**	**310**	**(125)**
Farm Maintenance	35	(14)	35	(14)	30	(12)
Water & Electricity	60	(24)	65	(26)	60	(24)
General Overhead Expenses ..	100	(40)	75	(30)	90	(36)
Total Overheads	**195**	**(79)**	**175**	**(71)**	**180**	**(73)**
Rent & Interest	110	(45)	105	(42)	130	(53)
Total Fixed Costs	**900**	**(364)**	**855**	**(346)**	**830**	**(336)**

Large-Scale Cereal Farms (over 500 ha (1,250 acres)

Data from the Farm Business Survey indicates there are further economies of scale for cereals farms at even larger farm sizes. There are likely to be wide variations depending on the precise scale of these businesses (some of which are very large). The following figures may be used as a guide; Labour - £180 per ha (of which paid labour £110); Power & Machinery - £285 per ha; Other Overheads - £175 per ha; Rent & Interest - £135 per ha. This totals £775 per ha (£314 per acre).

Data for larger-scale General Cropping farms (see below) is not so conclusive. Costs on a 'per ha' basis do not necessarily seem to fall as farm size increases. This may be due to the larger proportion of (higher cost) root crops and vegetables seen on larger farm sizes.

General Cropping

£/ha (£/acre)	Under 150 ha (Under 370 acres)		150 - 225 ha (370 - 560 acres)		Over 225 ha (Over 560 acres)	
Regular Labour (paid)	45	(18)	75	(30)	180	(73)
Regular Labour (unpaid)	310	(125)	205	(83)	170	(69)
Casual Labour	20	(8)	25	(10)	55	(22)
Total Labour	**375**	**(152)**	**305**	**(123)**	**405**	**(164)**
Machinery Depreciation	120	(49)	140	(57)	175	(71)
Machinery Running Costs	120	(49)	140	(57)	160	(65)
Contract	130	(53)	120	(49)	80	(32)
Total Power & Machinery...	**370**	**(150)**	**400**	**(162)**	**415**	**(168)**
Farm Maintenance	30	(12)	25	(10)	40	(16)
Water & Electricity	85	(34)	75	(30)	95	(38)
General Overhead Expenses ..	70	(28)	90	(36)	70	(28)
Total Overheads	**185**	**(75)**	**190**	**(77)**	**205**	**(83)**
Rent & Interest	150	(61)	155	(63)	160	(65)
Total Fixed Costs	**1080**	**(437)**	**1050**	**(425)**	**1185**	**(480)**

With potatoes and/or sugar beet and/or field vegetables; grade 1 or 2 land.

Mainly Sheep/Cattle (lowland)

	Under 90 ha (Under 220 acres)		90 - 125 ha (220 - 310 acres)		Over 125 ha (Over 310 acres)	
Regular Labour (paid)	30	(12)	40	(16)	60	(24)
Regular Labour (unpaid)	460	(186)	400	(162)	260	(105)
Casual Labour	10	(4)	15	(6)	10	(4)
Total Labour	**500**	**(202)**	**455**	**(184)**	**330**	**(134)**
Machinery Depreciation	90	(36)	105	(42)	105	(42)
Machinery Running Costs	80	(32)	95	(38)	100	(40)
Contract	60	(24)	55	(22)	60	(24)
Total Power & Machinery...	**230**	**(93)**	**255**	**(103)**	**265**	**(107)**
Farm Maintenance	30	(12)	35	(14)	30	(12)
Water & Electricity	70	(28)	75	(30)	65	(26)
General Overhead Expenses ..	55	(22)	55	(22)	40	(16)
Total Overheads	**155**	**(63)**	**165**	**(67)**	**135**	**(55)**
Rent & Interest	85	(34)	100	(40)	105	(42)
Total Fixed Costs	**970**	**(393)**	**975**	**(395)**	**835**	**(338)**

Mainly Sheep/Cattle (upland)

	Under 130 ha (Under 320 acres)		130 - 200 ha (320 - 490 acres)		Over 200 ha (Over 490 acres)	
Regular Labour (paid)	15	(6)	20	(8)	25	(10)
Regular Labour (unpaid)	375	(152)	240	(97)	180	(73)
Casual Labour	15	(6)	10	(4)	15	(6)
Total Labour	**405**	**(164)**	**270**	**(109)**	**220**	**(89)**
Machinery Depreciation	65	(26)	60	(24)	60	(24)
Machinery Running Costs	60	(24)	55	(22)	60	(24)
Contract	25	(10)	20	(8)	30	(12)
Total Power & Machinery...	**150**	**(61)**	**135**	**(55)**	**150**	**(61)**
Farm Maintenance	15	(6)	15	(6)	15	(6)
Water & Electricity	50	(20)	35	(14)	35	(14)
General Overhead Expenses ..	25	(10)	25	(10)	20	(8)
Total Overheads	**90**	**(36)**	**75**	**(30)**	**70**	**(28)**
Rent & Interest	50	(20)	50	(20)	60	(24)
Total Fixed Costs	**695**	**(281)**	**530**	**(214)**	**500**	**(202)**

Other Farm Types

The other main DEFRA farm types are '***Mixed***', ***Pigs***, ***Poultry and Horticulture***. As the name suggests, the mixed category includes all farms where one enterprise is not sufficiently dominant for it to be allocated to one of the categories above. As it includes many different mixes of enterprises, the figures are unlikely to be useful for budgeting purposes.

Due to the intensity and variability of the Pig, Poultry and Horticultural farm types, the presentation of average 'per ha' figures would not be useful. Detailed historic FBS data for the different pig, poultry, and horticulture systems found in England are published online at the addresses given on page 6. For pigs, Askham Bryan: for poultry and horticulture, Reading, or go to www.farmbusinesssurvey.co.uk.

2. RENTS

One of the main factors affecting the rental level of agricultural land is the type of tenancy it is let on. There are three main types of agricultural agreements for letting land in England and Wales: Full or Agricultural Holdings Act (AHA) 1986, Farm Business Tenancies (FBTs, under the 1995 Act) and Seasonal Lets of less than 1 year. Since the introduction of the 1995 Act no new AHA tenancies can be created.

The Basic Payment Scheme provisions also need to be taken into account when comparing rents. The situation will vary from farm to farm and differ between the different regions of the countries of the UK. The tenant is the only person who can claim the Basic Payment (BP). In seasonal lets (grazing agreements) the Licensor should be the claimant. In an AHA tenancy agreement the rental is struck independently of the Basic Payment in that the tenant will have been awarded the Single Payment entitlements in 2005 which will have been converted to Basic Payment entitlements on 1st January 2015 and at the end of the tenancy the ownership remains with the tenant or his/her successors. With FBTs the assumption is that the tenant is claiming a 'full' BP, and if land becomes available without BP entitlements then rental levels will be lower than those shown below.

Rents for land have been increasing over recent years. The tables below show rents up to 2015 and are therefore a little dated and do not pick up current trends. They also include lettings which may not be at full value for one reason or another i.e. lets to other family members and do not correspond to some of the headline rates often seen. The fall in almost all agricultural sectors has had some impact on rents over the past year, particularly dairy and to some extent cereals, with evidence of rents stabilising or even reducing. But with output prices now rising, this is not expected to continue. Tender rents, especially in the cropping sector, often remain above levels that can be economically justified.

Unless otherwise stated the figures in this section relate to farms let with a combination of crops, grass and rough grazing in England; they include housing and buildings, as available.

Agricultural Holdings Act Tenancies:

The average rent for lowland, excluding woodland and rough grazing for farms under full Agricultural Tenancies is likely to be approximately £200 per ha, *£80 per acre*, in 2017/18. The levels on large mixed arable farms (i.e. including potatoes, sugar beet and/or vegetables) on very good soil, or well-equipped dairy farms, will tend to average £200 to £250 per hectare *(£80 to £101 per acre)*. Rents on moderate, below average, quality farms, particularly with full repairing and insuring leases are likely to average £125 to £150 per hectare *(£50 to £60 per acre)*.

Farm Business Tenancies:

On average FBT rents will remain higher than those above for AHA tenancies, although this is not always the case especially for lowland cattle and sheep land. When reviewing AHA rents the scarcity value is ignored, but FBT rents (unless they have an agreed alternative rent review formula) reflect an open market and therefore the gap is wider. For cereals land of reasonable quality, offers used to follow the price of a tonne of wheat (!) per acre, but in recent years there has been very little on offer for under £495 per hectare (*£200 per acre*). However this may prove to have been a high point. The fall in commodity prices led to prices stabilising and although prospects have improved and there is more confidence, Tenants seem a little more cautious and in the main Landlords appear to realise that Tenants need to get over a difficult couple of years. Nevertheless, rents for maize land and other alternatives destined for Anaerobic Digesters are putting a base in the market. Local markets for potato land can command high values and even cause agents to try and increase 3-5 year agreements on the back of this but it must be remembered there has to be a rotation. A sensible rent for new agreements throughout 2017/2018 for arable land would be £300 to £370 per hectare (£120 to £150 per acre) although many are expected to be ahead of this.

Farm Business Survey 2015-16:

The following figures are the latest National Statistics produced by Defra showing the estimates of farm rents in England from the 2015/16 Farm Business Survey (FBS). Results from the 2015/16 Survey are referred to as the 2015 results. It should be borne in mind that rough grazing may be included in the figures given in the table below and the figures relate to the 2015/16 (Feb-Feb) year mainly covering 2015. Some farms are likely to be let at below competitive rates, for various reasons.

Average Rent by Type of Agreement:	£/ha	*(acre)*
Full Agricultural Tenancies	180	*(73)*
Farm Business Tenancies for 1 year and over......................	209	*(85)*
Seasonal Lets of less than one year.....................................	162	*(66)*

Full Agricultural Tenancies in England:

Average Rent by Farm Type: (£ per ha [acre])	2011	2012	2013	2014	2015
Cereals	172 (70)	182 (74)	190 (77)	192 (78)	194 (79)
General Cropping	192 (78)	203 (82)	201 (81)	200 (81)	204 (83)
Dairy	186 (75)	193 (78)	195 (79)	201 (81)	194 (79)
Cattle & Sheep (LFA)	66 (27)	59 (24)	64 (26)	73 (26)	79 (32)
Cattle and Sheep (Lowland)	148 (60)	152 (62)	160 65)	152 (62)	160 (65)
All	159 (64)	163 (66)	170 (69)	176 (71)	180 (73)

Farm Business Tenancies – One year and over:

Average Rent by Farm Type: (£ per ha [acre])	2011	2012	2013	2014	2015
Cereals	192 (78)	211 (85)	223 (90)	231 (93)	234 (95)
General Cropping	307(124)	264(107)	290(117)	309(125)	274 (111)
Dairy	184 (74)	195 (79)	206 (83)	218 (88)	230 (93)
Cattle & Sheep (LFA)	78 (32)	77 (31)	76 (31)	79 (32)	78 (32)
Cattle and Sheep (Lowland)	121 (49)	121 (49)	124 (50)	134 (54)	142 (57)
All	179 (72)	176 (71)	196 (79)	207 (84)	209 (85)

Source of Data

DEFRA (Farming Statistics): Farm Rents 2015/16 – England. In the past DEFRA rental statistics were collected via the Tenanted Land Survey (TLS) and these were reported on in previous editions of the Farm Management Pocketbook. Following a review in early 2009 DEFRA decided that the Farm Business Survey (FBS) data should be the main source and the Tenanted Land Survey (TLS) should be discontinued. The FBS is an annual survey conducted by trained Interviewers. The FBS collects data at business level and collects data for up to 15 agreements per business, with a sample of around 1,900 farm businesses. The 2016-17 Survey is due to be published in March 2018.

RICS Rural Land Market Survey:

Previous editions of the Pocketbook have included average rental levels. These are now available on the Pocketbook website at www.thepocketbook.co.uk

3. LAND PRICES

SALE VALUE OF FARMLAND, ENGLAND AND WALES

Current Agricultural Land Prices (CALP)/RICS/RAU

A CALP/RICS Farmland Price Index (England and Wales) began in 1995. It covers sales of vacant possession land in England and Wales. It is calculated by dividing total value of sales by total area sold. Figures for the most recent half-yearly periods are subject to revision as further information becomes available. More recently the survey has been undertaken by the RICS and the RAU (Royal Agricultural University).

As can be seen from the table below, the volume of land traded in any year, and included in the Index, is low – probably only between 0.1%-0.2% of the total agricultural area of England and Wales. The relative scarcity of land for sale has contributed to the increases in prices seen since the early 2000's. Such a 'thin' market can also make prices sensitive to a small number of large transactions. For this reason, in recent years, the RICS has moved away from the transaction-based figures, to using opinion-based data as its headline land price figures. Both are presented in the table below. The *'transaction'* based measure uses actual sales and includes a residential component (where that component is estimated to be worth less than 50% of the total value of the land). Milk quota was excluded. The *'opinion'* based measure, is an estimate of bare land only, no residential component is included and therefore it tends to be less than the transaction-based figure.

CALP/RICS Farmland Price Index 2007-2016

		No. of Sales	Area sold '000		Weighted Average Price £			
					Transaction Based		Opinion Based	
			Ha	acres	Ha	acres	Ha	Acres
2007	H1	141	7.0	17.3	11,156	4,515	8,849	3,581
	H2	230	10.8	26.7	14,144	5,724	10,438	4,224
2008	H1	233	8.9	21.9	15,829	6,406	12,965	5,247
	H2	278	11.7	28.9	16,348	6,616	12,335	4,992
2009	H1	181	6.3	15.6	15,204	6,153	12,172	4,926
	H2	256	11.4	28.2	16,133	6,529	12,716	5,146
2010	H1	162	6.6	16.3	15,948	6,454	13,529	5,475
	H2	262	12.0	29.6	17,458	7,065	14,445	5,846
2011	H1	154	4.2	10.6	18,631	7,540	15,110	6,115
	H2	298	12.3	30.4	20,650	8,357	16,096	6,514
2012	H1	166	4.69	11.6	20,586	8,331	16,378	6,628
	H2	254	8.5	21.0	20,650	8,357	16,761	6,783
2013	H1	188	5.02	12.4	21,656	8,764	18,387	7,441
	H2	311	11.9	29.4	24,278	9,825	19,160	7,754
2014	H1	213	6.15	15.2	24,137	9,768	19,934	8,067
	H2	233	11.2	27.7	24,979	10,109	20,319	8,223
2015	H1	149	4.90	12.1	22,921	9,276	20,828	8,429
	H2	388	12.0	29.6	27,302	11,049	20,524	8,306
2016	H1*	196	6.60	16.3	27,062	10,952	19,706	7,975
	H2*	242	11.6	28.7	25,286	10,233	19,921	8,062
2017	Estimate				25,204	10,200	19,891	8,050

* = *Provisional*

Farmland prices have weathered the economic downturn of recent times far better than other asset classes. 'Lifestyle' purchasers were replaced by investors and farmers keeping the demand and the price of land high as the economy faltered. Since 2009, very low rates of borrowing money and negligible returns for cash investments have fuelled farmland values. This has been coupled with tight supply of land and improved farm commodity prices. But the fall in commodity prices over the last couple of years and an increase in supply has slowed the pace at which prices have been rising over the last few years.

In the first half of 2015, the transaction based index (see above) recorded a fall in the average weighted price, however with 'lifestyle' buyers returning to the market, prices increased again in the second half of the year. In 2016, transaction based prices have eased back again with the opinion based measure stable over the year. The uncertainty surrounding Brexit is cited as one of the main reasons for prices easing. Availability has also declined and as prices have eased at a time when supply has also fallen, has led many commentators to forecast decreases in values over 2017. The decline is expected to be greater for commercial farmland, rather than blocks with a residential component.

The fundamentals driving farmland values such as low supply, tax advantages of owning land and the competition from a variety of land uses remain. In the short term (at least) the weak pound will help commodity prices and subsidy payments. Land prices could drop back (along with other asset classes) when base rates rise, leading to higher costs of borrowing money and fixed interest investments start to generate a return. As always there is a wide variation in prices; location and soil quality remain the key drivers for commercial land. Farmland prices for the period 1995 to 2006 are in previous editions of the Pocketbook.

Other Land Price Series

In past editions of the Pocketbook, Inland Revenue and Valuation Office (VO) land price returns have been published, covering 30 years up to 1996/97 and 1993-2004 respectively. These series contained detailed splits between vacant possession and tenanted land, farms (including houses and buildings) and bare land, and also by size, land class and region. This information is still available from past editions of the Pocketbook. Data in the VO series does not continue beyond 2004, although limited information is available on the website, www.voa.gov.uk. Previous editions also include the Oxford Institute/Savills (1) Series, 1937-2000. Much of the data included in this section is available from the RICS website – www.rics.org

SALE VALUE OF FORESTS AND WOODLANDS

Forests

The figures in this section relate to planted land sold (over 20 hectares) so that values include the value of the property (land) and the timber. They focus on properties that are predominantly conifer.

During 2016, £79.19m of forestry properties were traded throughout GB. This is a drop of 47% compared to (the record year of) 2015. Although it must be noted, 2015 was dominated by the £50m sale of the UPM portfolio and 2016 is on a par with 2014 sales at £82.9m. Properties in Scotland continue to dominate the market, with around 67% of total sales, although England recorded an unusually high percentage of sales at 29%, with Wales registering a lower than normal amount. Forestry continues to be attractive to investors especially due to the tax benefits available to owning woodland. Income tax is not payable on timber sales. There is potentially 100% relief on Inheritance Tax (IHT) and any gains attributable to standing or felled timber are exempt from Capital Gains Tax (CGT).

Forestry continues to deliver excellent returns. Over the last decade, the average return from UK forestry has been 18.8% (Source: IPD) and interest going forward is expected to be driven by demand for timber and incentives to use wood as an energy source. As economies start to recover and movement in the development and construction sectors increase, demand for timber both as a material and for fuel should grow further.

Woodlands also often present opportunities for wind turbines and hydro-electric schemes and biomass projects.

After a long period of buoyancy in the timber market, prices fell in 2015, mainly due to the strong Pound. The first half of 2016 saw an upturn in the market, driven mainly by the sawn fencing market but also by the weakening of the Pound. The vote to leave the EU has seen Sterling weaken further, providing a boost, making domestic timber relatively cheaper than imports. The sawmilling sector and in particular the construction sector, are exposed to the economy and exchange rates. Biomass and the board sector are less so, leading to an imbalance in both demand and payability between logs and roundwood. The vote to leave the EU has added uncertainty to the timber markets.

The figures below are for the UK and are predominantly upland with at least 50% coniferous content. Values vary with many factors; only size of block and age are recorded here, but yield class is also important.

Value of Forestland: £ per stocked ha:

By Size Range (approx.)	2015	2016
	£/ha *(£/acre)*	£/ha *(£/acre)*
20 to 50 hectares	8,400 *(3,400)*	8,000 *(3,238)*
51 to 100 hectares	7,500 *(3,035)*	8,200 *(3,318)*
101 to 200 hectares	9,100 *(3,683)*	6,150 *(2,489)*
Above 200 hectares	7,500 *(3,035)*	7,400 *(2,995)*

By Age Band	2015	2016
	£/ha *(£/acre)*	£/ha *(£/acre)*
Young (1 to 10 years)	6,050 *(2,448)*	3,600 *(1,457)*
Mid-rotation (11 to 20 years)	7,050 *(2,853)*	6,000 *(2,428)*
Semi-mature (21 to 30 years)	10,200 *(4,128)*	9,100 *(3,683)*
Mature (31 to 40 years)	8,625 *(3,490)*	4,900 *(1,983)*
Mature (over 40 years)	6,400 *(2,590)*	4,800 *(1,942)*

Woodlands

The value for small woodland decreased in 2010 as demand from lifestyle buyers for less commercial, more amenity and sporting woodland was hit by the economic climate. As the economic climate picks up this is reversing. Values remain at their highest adjacent to centres of population and for properties of high amenity value. Sales in the South of England are in the £8-12,000/ha range, whereas £2-5,000/ha is more typical for other locations or where amenity values are lower.

Source: UK Forest Market Report (2016)

4. PUBLIC LIABILITY INSURANCE

Public liability insurance is not a legal obligation. However, it is necessary if the general public is interacting with your business in any way, whether deliveries, visitors, etc. With a rising emphasis on encouraging the public to understand farming including visiting farms, this should be a necessity for all farms.

These figures are per year, per farm. Prices of some providers are the same for each band, as they calculate their quotes differently. Often public liability comes with product and environmental liability. These figures are solely for farming, and not other activities that might take place on a farm such a contract farming, other diversifications such as a shoot, livery or a farm shop.

	Mixed Farm (130 ha)	Dairy (130 ha)	Arable (250 ha)
£5m	£360	£360	£320
£10m	£450	£450	£430

5. BUILDINGS

BUILDING COSTS

Building costs are notoriously variable. Many factors influence a contractor's price, including distance from his yard, size of contract, site access, site conditions, complexity of work, familiarity with the type of work and his current work load. There will also be differences in efficiency and standard of work between contractors and, as is often the case with farm buildings, the absence of detailed specification by the client may mean different contractors will not have quoted for identical buildings. The number of extras that are found to be required after a contract has been agreed will also vary.

The costs given below are an approximate guide. They refer to new buildings, erected by contractor on a clear level site and exclude VAT and grants that may be available. More detailed information is available in the following publications. The books and journals giving general building cost information generally assume knowledge of how to take off quantities for building work.

Specialised Information on Farm Buildings

- Farm Building Cost Guide. Published by SAC Building Design Services, Aberdeen.
- Standard Costs. Published by the Scottish Government. Used when claiming government grants on a standard-cost basis. It is now dated (2001)
- The Farm Buildings Handbook. Published by the Rural and Industrial Design and Building Association, Stowmarket.

General Building Cost Information

Books are produced by a number of publishers with annual or more frequent new editions and updates. Examples are Laxton's Building Price Book, Spon's Architects' and Builders' Price Book, and Wessex Comprehensive Building Price Book. Regularly updated cost information is also given in several professional and trade journals.

Constituent Parts

Frame, Roof and Foundations		*per m² floor area*
1. Open-sided timber framed pole barn with round pole uprights on concrete bases, sawn timber rafters and purlins, high-tensile galvanised steel cladding to roof and gable ends above eaves, hardcore floor, eaves height 4.8 m, 9 m span, no side cladding, rainwater drainage to soakaways.		£80
2. Open-sided steel portal-framed building with fibre-cement or plastic coated steel cladding to roof and gables above eaves, hardcore floor, eaves height 4.8 m, no side cladding, rainwater drainage to soakaways.		
9 m span		£135
13.2 m span		£125
18 m span		£115
3. Cost breakdown of 2 above;		
Materials:	portal frame and purlins	26%
	foundations	3%
	roofing	16%
	rainwater and drainage	3%
	hardcore and blinding	2%
	Total Materials	50%
Erection:	portal frame and purlins	19%
	foundations	2%
	roofing	19%
	rainwater and drainage	5%
	hardcore and blinding	5%
	Total Erection	50%

Roof cladding		*per m²*
1. Natural grey fibre-cement, 146 mm corrugations fixed with drive screws		
Materials	£15.00	
Fixing	£12.50	
Total		£27.50
2. Extra for coloured sheet		£2.50
3. Deduct for translucent sheets		£0.55
4. Deduct for PVC-coated steel		£3.00
5. Deduct for high-tensile corrugated galvanised steel sheeting		£4.00
		per m run
6. PVC 150 mm half-round gutter on fascia brackets, including stop-ends and outlets		£27.50
7. PVC 100 mm rainwater pipe with fixings, swan-neck and shoe		£45.00
8. Fibre-cement close-fitting ridge		£40.00
9. Fibre-cement ventilating ridge		£45.00

Walls and Cladding		*per m²*
1. Concrete blockwork, fair faced and pointed both sides		
150 mm thick		£50.00
215 mm thick		£70.00
215 mm thick hollow blocks		£70.00
215 mm thick hollow blocks, filled and reinforced		£90.00
2. Extra for rendering or roughcast to blockwork on one side		£25.00
3. Vertical spaced boarding 21x 145 mm with 19 mm gaps including horizontal rails, all pressure treated		£28.00
4. Fibre-cement vertical cladding, including rails		£43.00
5. Corrugated high-tensile steel side cladding, including rails		£37.50
6. Wall element: 215 mm thick blockwork, including strip foundation (base 750 mm below ground level), 2.5 m height above ground level	£180 per m run	

Floors		*per m²*
1. Concrete floor 100 mm thick, Gen 3 mix, on 150 mm hardcore, including excavation:		£36.50
Breakdown:		
(a) excavate, level and compact	£3.50	
(b) hardcore	£5.00	
(c) blinding	£2.40	
(d) damp-proof membrane	£2.10	
(e) premixed concrete spread and compacted	£19.00	
(f) float finish	£4.50	
2. Extra to above for		
(a) 150 mm instead of 100 mm	£6.00	
(b) laying concrete to falls	£2.00	
(c) broom or textured finish	£2.00	
(d) Carborundum dust non-slip finish	£3.50	
(e) insulating concrete	£12.50	
3. Reinforced concrete slatted floors for cattle		
(a) cattle loading		£77.50
(b) tractor loading		£90.00
4. Reinforced concrete slats for pigs		£60.00
5. Insulating floor, including excavation and base		
(a) 27 mm expanded polystyrene, 38 mm screed		£52.50
(b) insulating concrete with lightweight aggregate		£45.00
(c) as (b) with 20 mm screed		£52.50
6. Form channel in concrete	£5.00 per m run	
7. Excavate for cast 1 m3 in-situ concrete bases for stanchions	£140.00 each	

Services and Fittings		*per m²*
1. Drainage: 100 mm PVC pipe laid in trench, including 750 mm deep excavation and backfil	£29.00 per m run	

	Breakdown:	
	(a) excavate and backfill	£18.00
	(b) 100 mm PVC pipe laid	£10.00
	Extras:	
	(c) add to (a) for 1 m deep	£4.00
	(d) add to (b) for 150 mm pipe	£7.00
2.	Excavate soakaway and fill with stones	£120 each
3.	Trap and grid top, 100 mm PVC	£29.00 each
4.	Yard gully with heavy duty road grating 400 x 300 mm	£200 each
5.	Inspection chamber 900 mm deep, 450 x 600 mm opening and medium duty cast iron cover	£400 each
6.	Above-ground vitreous enamel slurry tank on concrete base, 1000 m^3	£55,000 each
7.	Reception pit, 20 m^3	£6,000 each
8.	Slurry channel beneath (not including) slats, 1.8 m deep, 3m wide	£500 per m run
9.	Lighting: 1.5 m 60W single fluorescent unit, including wiring and switch	£135 each
	Extras:	
	(a) PVC conduit	£6.50
	(b) screwed steel conduit	£12.00
10.	Power: 13A switched outlet	£24.00 each
11.	Diagonal feed fence, fixed, including posts (painted)	£135 per m run
12.	Tombstone feed fence, fixed, including posts (painted)	£145 per m run
13.	Feed bunker	£80 per m run
14.	Hay rack, wall fixing	£85 per m run
15.	Cubicle division, galvanised, fixed in place	£110 each
16.	Fencing: three-rail timber with posts, all pressure treated	£30.00 per m run
17.	Gate, 3 m wide, galvanised steel, including posts set in concrete	
	(a) medium duty	£250 each
	(b) heavy duty	£325 each
	Deduct for painted instead of galvanised finish	£30

Complete Buildings

Fully Covered and Enclosed Barn

Portal frame, 18 m span, 6 m bays, 6 m to eaves, 3 m high blockwork walls with sheet cladding above, 6 m sliding doors at either end, 150mm thick concrete floor	£210 per m^2 floor area

Cows and Cattle Housing

1.	Covered strawed yard, enclosed with ventilated cladding, concrete floor, pens only, with 4.0 m^2 per head floor area	£750 per head
2.	Extra to 1 for 4.0 m wide double-sided feeding passage, barrier and troughs	£300 per head
3.	Kennel building	£450 per head

4.	Portal framed building with cubicles	£1,500 per head
5.	Extra to 4 for feed stance, feeding passage, barriers and troughs	£625 per head
6.	Extra to 4 for slatting of cubicle passages	£640 per head
7.	Covered collecting yard, 1.1 m² per cow	£225 per head
8.	Milking parlour building, example: 5.5 x 11.5 m for 8/16 parlour	£20,000
9.	Parlour equipment, herringbone parlours:	
	(a) low level, 1 stall per point	£3,850 per point
	(b) pipeline	£3,150 per point
	(c) extra for meter and auto cluster removal	£2,150 per point
	(d) auto feed dispenser	£900 per point
10.	Dairy building	£335 per m² floor area
11.	Bulk tank and washer	£8.50 per litre
12.	Loose box, 16 m² floor area laid to falls, rendered walls	£350 per m² floor area
13.	Bull pen and open run	£13,500
14.	Cattle crush and 20 m race	£6,500
15.	Slatted floor cattle building for 120 growing cattle (1.7 m² pen space per head) with drive-through feed passage/troughs	£1,500 per head

Silage		*per tonne stored*
1.	Timber panel clamp on concrete base with effluent tank	£80
2.	Precast concrete panel clamp with effluent tank	£110
3.	Glass-lined forage tower and unloader	£250

Slurry Storage		*per m³ stored*
1.	Lined lagoon with safety fence	£45.00
2.	Glass-lined steel slurry silo	
	small (400 m³)	£60.00
	medium (1,200 m³)	£55.00
	large (3,600 m³)	£50.00
3.	GRP below-ground effluent tank, encased in concrete	
	small (12 m³)	£500
	large (36 m³)	£450

Sheep Housing		
1.	Penning, troughs, feed barriers and drinkers installed in suitable existing building	£38 per ewe
2.	Purpose-built sheep shed with 1.35 m² pen space per ewe concentrate troughs, feed passage and barrier for forage feeding	£225 per ewe
	Extras:	
	(a) softwood slatted floor panels, materials only	£10.00 per m²
	(b) slatted panels as (a), made up, plus supports	£31.50 per m²

Pig Housing		*per sow and litter*
1.	Farrowing and rearing	
	(a) Prefabricated farrowing pens with crates, side creep areas, part-slatted floors, including foundations, electrical and plumbing work	£3,500
	(b) Steel-framed farrowing house with insulated blockwork walls, part-slatted pens with side creeps in rooms of eight with off main passage	£3,950
	(c) Flat-deck rearing house 3-6 weeks with fully perforated floors to pens, 0.25 m^2 per pig pen area	£150 per weaner
	(d) Prefabricated veranda house including foundations, electrical and plumbing work, 0.3m^2 per pig internal lying area	£120 per weaner
2.	Finishing	*per baconer*
	(a) Prefabricated fattening house with part-slatted floors, trough feeding	£265
	(b) Prefabricated fattening house with part-slatted floors, floor fed	£255
	(c) Steel framed building with insulated blockwork walls, part-slatted floors, trough fed	£110
	(d) Automatic feeding systems for items (a), (b) and (c) above:	
	dry-feed system with ad-lib hoppers	£675
	dry on-floor feeding	£16.00
	wet feeding	£23
3.	Dry sows and boars	*per sow*
	(a) Yards with floor feeding	£375
	(b) Sow cubicle system	£600
	(c) Yards with electronic feeders	£1,050
	(d) Yards with individual feeders	£1,250
	(e) Two-yard system with flat-rate feeding	£1,350
	(f) Boar pens as part of sow house	£2,750 each
4.	Complete pig unit	
	Building costs calculated on basis of three-week weaning, 23 pigs per sow per year to bacon, excl. external slurry or dung storage, feed storage and handling/weighing facilities:	
	(a) Breeding and rearing only	£2,100 per sow
	(b) Breeding with progeny to bacon	£3,750 per sow

Poultry Housing and Equipment		*per bird*
1.	Intensive enriched cages with automatic feeding and egg collection; (new traditional cages were banned from 1st January 2003;only enriched cages complete with nest box, perches and scratching area are now allowed)	£24.00-£28.00
2.	Perchery/barn	£22.00-£27.00

3.	Free Range: new sites stocked at 9 birds per m^2,	£27.50-£35.00
	existing sites stocked at 11.7 birds per m^2	£22.50-£29.00
	smaller mobile units will cost	£32.00 plus
4.	Broiler Breeders, deep litter, 0.167 m^2 per bird	£29.00
5.	Pullets (cage and floor reared)	£16.50
6.	Broilers, deep litter, 0.05 m^2 per bird	£9.50-£10.50
7.	Turkeys, 20,000 pole barn fattening unit (cost varies with size of unit and degree of automation)	£21.00-£28.00

Grain Storage and Drying		*per tonne stored*
1.	Intake pit, conveyor, elevator, overhead conveyor and catwalk, storage bins within existing building	£240
	extra for low volume ventilation of bins	£95
2.	As 1 in new building	£340
3.	Portable grain walling for on-floor storage in existing building	£55
4.	On floor grain storage in purpose-built building	£125
	Extras:	
	(a) low volume ventilation	£9.00-£10.00
	(b) on-floor drying with above-ground main duct and laterals	£135
	(c) add to (b) for below-ground laterals	£17.00
5.	Sealed towers for moist grain, including loading and unloading equipment	£165-£210

Potato Storage		*per tonne stored*
1.	Pallet-box store with recirculation fans	£240
	Pallet boxes, 1 tonne	£85
2.	Bulk store, building only	£225
	Ventilation system: fans, main duct, below-floor lateral ducts	£55

Roads and Fences	*per m length*
3.2 m wide hardcore road with drainage ditches using locally excavated material	£35.00
using imported hardcore (£6.15/m^3)	£50.00
extra for bitumen macadam surfacing, two coats	£57.00
Traditional 7-wire stock fence	£8.50
High tensile 7-wire stock fence	£6.50

Construction Equipment Hire	*hourly rate, with driver*
Excavator	£30.00-£40.00
Tipping lorry	£40.00-£55.00
10-tonne crane	£50.00-£70.00
	weekly rate
Concrete mixer, 100 litre (5/3)	£50
Compressor and heavy breaker	£140

STORAGE REQUIREMENTS

Bulk (cubic metres (feet) per tonne):

		m^3/tonne	ft^3/tonne
Beans		1.2	(43)
Wheat, peas		1.3	(46)
Barley, rye, oilseed rape, linseed, fodder beet		1.4	(50)
Oats		1.9	(68)
Potatoes		1.6	(57)
Dry bulb onions		2.0	(71)
Concentrates:	meal	2.0	(71)
	cubes	1.6	(57)
Grass silage:	18% DM	1.3	(46)
	30% DM	1.6	(57)
Maize silage		1.3	(46)
Silage: large round bales		2.5	(88)
Wheat straw	small bales	13.0	(464)
Barley straw	small bales	11.5	(411)
Hay	small bales	6.0	(214)
Wheat straw	large round bales	20.0	(714)
Barley straw	large round bales	18.0	(643)
Hay	large round bales	8.0	(286)
Brewers' grains		0.9	(32)

(With straw and hay the storage requirement clearly depends on the packing density; the above are simply typical averages).

Boxes (floor area in square metres (feet) per tonne):

Potatoes:	0.5 tonne boxes, 5 boxes high	0.52	(5.6)
	1.0 tonne boxes, 4 boxes high	0.52	(5.6)
	1.0 tonne boxes, 5 boxes high	0.45	(4.8)

Bags (floor area in square metres (feet) per tonne):

Feedstuffs:	2 bags high	1.6	(17)
Fertiliser:	6 bags high	1.1	(12)
	10 bags high	0.7	(8)

VII. TAXATION

Note: *no responsibility can be taken for any errors or omissions in the information presented in this section or for any action taken on the basis of the information provided. Professional advice should always be sought before taking any decision that may affect your tax position.*

1. INCOME TAX

RATES OF INCOME TAX

	Tax Rate %	Income Band 2017-18	Income Band 2018-19	*Dividend Tax Rate % 16-17 and 17-18**
Basic rate	20	£0 - £33,500	tba	*7.5*
Higher rate~	40	£33,501 - £150,000	tba	*32.5*
Additional rate	45	over £150,000	tba	*38.1*

*~ in Scotland the Higher Rate band begins at £31,500 * subject to confirmation*

A Dividend Tax Allowance exempts the first £5,000 of dividend income from tax and then the rates shown in the table will apply to the excess. For 2018-19 the threshold will fall to £2,000.

For 2017-18 and 2018-19 Savings Income (primarily bank and building society interest) is exempt from tax up to a limit of £5,000. If taxable Savings Income exceeds this figure then the standard marginal tax rates set out in the table above apply.

ALLOWANCES AND RELIEFS

Personal Allowance

This is £11,500 for 2017-18. The basic personal allowance for income tax is gradually reduced to nil for individuals with adjusted net incomes in excess of £100,000. The reduction is £1 for every £2 over the limit. The 2018-19 basic personal allowance is not yet set although there is a Government aspiration to raise it to £12,500 by 2020/21.

The previous (higher) age related allowances have now been aligned with the basic personal allowance.

Married Couples Allowance

This was abolished from the tax year ended 6th April 2001 except for couples where at least one spouse was born before 6th April 1935. From 2005-06 the allowance has been available to couples in a civil partnership where at least one partner was born before 6th April 1935. The relief is given as a reduction in income tax restricted to the lower of 10% of the allowance (£844.50 for 2017-18) or the total tax liability.

Personal Pension Schemes

Tax relief is obtainable for contributions to a pension. There are limits on how much of the contribution is eligible for relief – both yearly and lifetime. The annual allowance is £40,000 for 2017-18. The lifetime allowance is £1m for 2017-18, and will rise by inflation for 2018-19.

From 2016-17 onwards the £40,000 annual limit is progressively reduced for those earning above £150,000 per year.

2. NATIONAL INSURANCE

The tables below set out the National Insurance contributions for the 2017-18 year;

Class 1 (not contracted out)

Employee's weekly earnings	Employee
£157 or less	Nil
£157.01 to £866	12%
Over £866	2%

Employer contributions are 13.8% on weekly earnings over £157

Class 2

Self-employed flat rate .... £2.85 a week

Class 3

Non-employed (voluntary) flat rate .... £14.25 a week

Class 4

Self-employed. On profits or gains
between £8,164 and £45,000 .... 9%
over £45,000.. 2%

3. PRIVATE COMPANY TAXATION

RATES OF CORPORATION TAX

The rates set out in the table below apply to profits made in any financial year (FY) from 1st April to 31st March. FY17 therefore covers 1st April 2017 to 31st March 2018. Profits are chargeable at the following rates;

	FY17	FY18	FY19
All profits	19	19	*19*

The previous Small Companies rate and marginal relief rate were abolished for FY15.

The rate is proposed to drop to 17% for the FY 2020

COMPANY TAXATION – OTHER ISSUES

Capital Gains

Capital gains of companies are charged at the appropriate rate of Corporation Tax. The indexation allowance is still available to reduce capital gains made by Companies.

Distributions

Dividends are not deductible in arriving at the amount of Corporation Tax profit. However, the recipient of distributions will be exempt from paying Income Tax on the first £5,000 of dividend income received (dropping to £2,000 for 2018-19). Above that, basic rate taxpayers will pay a rate of 7.5% on dividend income. Higher rate taxpayers are liable to pay tax at 32.5% on that part of their dividend income falling above the higher rate limit. Taxpayers with income in excess of £150,000 will be liable to tax on dividends at 38.1%.

Losses

Carry back of losses not set against other income is restricted to one year. Losses can be carried forward and offset against profits of the same trade.

4. AGRICULTURAL BUSINESSES: OTHER ITEMS

ASSESSING SELF-EMPLOYED PROFITS

Self-employed people are assessed for tax in any tax year on the basis of the profits recorded in the annual accounts which end in that tax year, i.e. on a 'current year basis'.

LIVESTOCK

Dairy cows or breeding livestock may be treated on the herd basis or on a trading stock basis;

Herd Basis

Under the herd basis valuation changes are not included in the trading account, nor are additions to the herd, but sales from the herd and replacements are. On the sale of all or a substantial proportion (normally taken as 20% or more) of the herd, no tax is paid on any profit over the original cost price, nor is there any relief for loss.

Trading Stock Basis

Purchases, sales and valuation changes are all included in the trading account. Under this method stock should be valued at the lower of cost (or cost of production) and net realisable value. Where animals are home-produced and it is not possible to ascertain actual costs from farm records the 'deemed' cost may be used. This is 60% of market value for cattle and 75% for sheep and pigs.

STOCK VALUATION: CROPS

Crops should generally be valued at the cost of production (or net realisable value, if lower). Costs which are directly attributable to buying, producing and growing the crops should be included. The deemed cost method allows 75% of market value to be used although this method should only be used where it is not possible to ascertain actual costs.

ALLOWANCES FOR CAPITAL EXPENDITURE

Machinery and Plant

1. The same rules apply whether the machinery and plant is new or second hand. An annual writing down allowance of 18% p.a. is available on a reducing balance basis on capital expenditure incurred on the provision of plant and machinery. Qualifying expenditure is added to the asset 'pool' and the writing down allowances are given on the residue of expenditure in that pool.
2. The Annual Investment Allowance ('AIA') gives 100% relief for a set amount of qualifying expenditure per accounting period. The allowance fell to £200,000 after the 31st December 2015 and will stay at that level for the lifetime of the current Parliament. The limit is proportionally increased or decreased where the chargeable period is longer or shorter than a year. A group of companies can only receive a single allowance. Expenditure on cars does not qualify, although expenditure on long life assets, or on 'integral features' can be claimed.
3. An 8% rate applies to expenditure incurred on certain listed 'integral features' in a building and on long life assets. Expenditure brought forward will obtain the 8% rate.
4. 100% first year allowances can be claimed for expenditure incurred by any business on designated energy-saving plant and machinery and environmentally beneficial technologies and products. The lists of items which qualify can be found on the Government's Energy Technology Product lists, which is at www.eca.gov.uk.

Cars

For expenditure on motor cars purchased in or after April 2009, the regime is based on CO_2 emissions. For cars purchased after April 2015 those with CO_2 emissions exceeding 130gm/km are allocated to the 8% special rate pool. All other cars go into the general 18% rate pool apart from new cars with emissions of 75gm/km or less which get a special 100% first year allowance. For unincorporated businesses, cars have their own separate pools where there is an element of private use.

Machinery Leasing

Tax allowances for rental payments on financial leases are spread to reflect the commercial depreciation of the asset. This may mean that full tax relief for rental payments may not be gained in the years in which the payments are made.

Buildings

Farm buildings, fencing, drainage and other improvements (including up to one-third of farmhouses) used to qualify for a writing-down allowance of 4% annually, given equally over 25 years. These allowances have now been completely phased out.

LOSSES

Losses can normally be set against other income in the year they are incurred and in the prior year. If other income is insufficient in the year when the loss occurs and in the prior year, unrelieved losses can be carried forward and set off against future profits from the same trade. Special rules apply to prevent abuse of loss relief provisions by 'hobby' farmers who are not running their farms on a commercial basis with a view to producing a profit: normally losses are disallowed against other income after 5 consecutive years of loss. Trading losses may be set against capital gains in the same year as the loss.

PROFIT AVERAGING

This relief is to enable farmers, other than companies, to average their taxable profits. Following a change from April 2016 there is an option to do this for either two or five consecutive years.

Under the two-year option profits can be averaged if profits of one year are 75% or less of the profits of the other year. Total profits for the two years are equally divided between the two years.

Under the five-year option either the average of the first four years' relevant profits must be less than 75% of the last year's relevant profits or vice versa or the relevant profits of one or more of the five tax years to which the claim relates must be nil (or there is a loss).

5. CAPITAL GAINS TAX

APPLICATION AND RATES

Applies to capital gains made by an individual. Capital gains accruing to companies are chargeable to Corporation Tax. A capital gain is the difference between the acquisition value and the sale price. The first £11,300 of capital gains (for the 2017-18 year) realised by an individual in a tax year are covered by their annual exemption.

Disposals of non-business assets attract capital gains tax of 10% for Basic Rate taxpayers or 20% for Higher and Additional rate taxpayers. Rates of 18% and 28% respectively apply on gains from residential property which is not the main home.

The lower rates of CGT apply where total taxable gains and income, after taking into account all allowable deductions including losses, personal allowances and the CGT annual exemption, are less than the upper limit of the income tax basic rate band. The higher rate will apply to gains or any parts of gains above this limit.

Exempt assets include a principal private residence (e.g. farm house, if non-exclusive business occupation applies) if occupied as such, normal life assurance policies, animals and tangible movable properly (i.e. chattels) disposed of for £6,000 or less.

Capital Gains Tax is chargeable only on the disposal (including gifts) of assets. Capital Gains Tax is not payable on death. Payment of Capital Gains Tax is due on 31st January following the tax year of disposal.

RELIEFS

Losses

Should a transaction produce a loss, this may be set against any long term chargeable gains arising in the same year or, if these are insufficient, those accruing in subsequent years. Losses brought forward will be used only to the extent necessary to reduce untaxed gains for the year to £11,300.

Where a trading loss can be set against other income in the same or prior year for income tax purposes, any unused loss can be set against capital gains for those years.

Improvements

Spending that has increased the value of the asset can be offset against any gain. In the case of agricultural property, allowance would be made for any capital expenditure undertaken to improve the property.

Indexation and Taper Relief

Indexation and Taper relief for individuals has now been abolished for any disposals taking place on or after 6th April 2008. Indexation allowance is still available for capital gains arising in companies.

Entrepreneurs Relief

Entrepreneur's relief applies to certain disposals of business assets by an individual. The relief, which must be claimed, gives an effective rate of Capital Gains Tax of 10% for eligible gains of up to £10m for disposals after 6th April 2011 (lower limits applied before this date). The limit is a lifetime limit per individual. The assets which qualify for entrepreneurs' relief are in line with those which qualified for business asset taper relief. This covers:

- a trading business carried on by an individual alone or in partnership;
- assets of such a trade following cessation;

- shares or securities in a trading company where the individual owns 5% or more and is an officer or employee

The conditions for the relief must have been satisfied throughout a qualifying period of a year before the disposal.

Editorial Note: *The rules for Entrepreneurs' relief are complex, particularly in cases of disposals of part of the business. The rules are similar to the previous Retirement Relief and are particularly tricky in cases of disposals of farmland and related assets and trade. It is recommended that professional advice is sought where it is anticipated claiming this relief, particularly as given the increase in the lifetime allowance combined with the increase in tax rate for non-business assets, the tax savings can be greatly increased.*

Rollover

Payment of tax may be deferred on gains accruing from the sale of business assets (including land and buildings occupied and used for trade purposes, fixed plant and machinery and from the sale of shares in a family business) if part or all of the proceeds are spent on acquiring new qualifying assets. The tax is deferred by deducting the gain from the acquisition price of the new asset. It can only be claimed if the new asset is acquired within 12 months before and 3 years after the disposal of the old assets. Disposal and acquisition dates for Capital Gains purposes are generally contract, not completion, dates.

Holdover

Payments of tax may be deferred where disposal is by gift. This relief only applies to gifts of business assets, land which qualifies for agricultural property relief at either the 100% or 50% rate under Inheritance Tax (see next section) and gifts which lead to an immediate charge to Inheritance Tax (e.g. gifts into a discretionary trust). The amount of the chargeable gain which would normally have accrued to the donor will be held over; the value at which the donee is deemed to acquire the asset will be its market value reduced by the amount of the donor's chargeable gain held over. Where deferral is not available, payment of tax by interest bearing annual instalments over 10 years will be allowed for gifts of land, controlling share holdings and minority share holdings in unquoted companies.

6. STAMP TAXES

Stamp Duty is charged at 0.5 per cent of consideration paid (purchase by cash, other stocks or shares) on the transfer of shares and securities.

Stamp Duty Land Tax is charged on the transfer of an interest in land; both sales and leases. Following reforms, the tax is now levied on the value that falls into each bracket at the prevailing rate for both residential and non-residential property. The rates applicable are:

Residential property	Rate	Non-residential and mixed use	Rate
Value up to £125,000..........	nil	Value up to £150,000.............	nil
£125,001 to £250,000..........	2%	£150,001 to £250,000.............	2%
£250,001 to £925,000..........	5%	£250,001 or more	5%
£925,001 to £1,500,000.......	10%		
£1,500,001 or more.............	12%		

Purchases of residential property other than by individuals with a value of over £500,000 are subject to a 15% rate.

Stamp Duty Land Tax is payable on leases calculated according to the net present value of the rent payable over the term of the lease.

7. INHERITANCE TAX

APPLICATION AND RATES

This tax is charged on lifetime gifts and transfers on death. The rate for 2017-18 is 40%, on amounts chargeable to Inheritance Tax above the nil rate band of £325,000.

The nil rate band is potentially increased for surviving spouses or civil partners who died on or after 9th October 2007. From this date the nil rate band may be increased by the unused proportion of the deceased spouse or civil partner's nil rate band.

From the 2017-18 year a Main residence nil rate band has been introduced. This will commence at £100,000 and rise to £175,000 by 2020-21. It will be in addition to the usual nil rate band but only be applicable to the main house of the deceased if transferred to a direct descendent. Any unused portion can be transferred between spouses.

Outright gifts to individuals are exempt from tax at the time of the gift. If the donor lives for a further seven years then the transfer is fully exempt. Gifts into accumulation and maintenance trusts and interest in possession trusts no longer receive special treatment - all other gifts will be taxed at half the above rates at the time of the transfer.

Tax is charged on the value of an individual's estate at death plus the value of all gifts made within seven years of death. Allowance is made for any tax paid on lifetime gifts included in the value of the estate on death. Relief is given for outright gifts made more than three years before death according to the following scale:

Years between gift and death	0-3	3-4	4-5	5-6	6-7
Percentage of the full tax charge	100%	80%	60%	40%	20%

Exemptions include: transfers between husband and wife; the first £3,000 of gift made by a donor in the income tax year and separately up to £250 per year to any number of persons; gifts made out of income which form part of normal expenditure; marriage gifts within limits of £5,000 for a parent, £2,500 for a lineal ancestor and £1,000 for other donors.

RELIEFS

Agricultural Property Relief

Relief may be available for agricultural land. Subject to a general rule that the agricultural land must have been occupied by the transferor (or by his controlled company) for two years, or owned by the transferor for 7 years and occupied for agricultural purposes by someone else before any relief is granted. The relief is at two different rates. If the basis of valuation is vacant possession (or there is the right to obtain it within 12 months), the taxable value of the land is reduced by 100%. If the basis of valuation is tenanted value, the taxable value of the land is reduced by 50% of that tenanted value. Ownership and occupation periods normally include prior periods of ownership or occupation by husbands and wives. From 1st September 1995, 100% relief applies to new lettings of agricultural land as Farm Business Tenancies. Agricultural Relief includes agricultural land in the European Economic Area (EEA).

Editorial Note: *There has been much publicised activity and tax cases concerning APR claims, particularly attempts by the HMRC to reduce or deny the relief on claims for farmhouses. Care must be taken to protect the relief particularly where the attached land is either let out on a Farm Business Tenancy or under a contract farming arrangement.*

Business Property Relief

Relief is also available in respect to 'business property' transferred during lifetime or on death. The relief extends to the business assets of a proprietor and the interest of a partner or controlling shareholder in the business capital of a company. The value of such property, providing certain tests are satisfied (e.g. it has been owned by the transferor for two years preceding transfer), is reduced by 100%. Where a partner or controlling shareholder owns assets (e.g. land) that the business uses, the value will be reduced by 50%. Shareholdings in unquoted companies receive a 100% reduction in market value.

Lifetime gifts of property eligible for Agricultural and Business Property Relief have to be retained (or replaced by similar property) until the death of the donor (or earlier death of the donee) if those reliefs are to be available when the tax (or additional tax) becomes payable subsequent to the donor's death

In the case of the transfer of property eligible for APR and BPR, the tax can be paid by annual instalments over ten years free of interest.

8. VALUE ADDED TAX

Agricultural businesses with a turnover of taxable goods and services in excess of £85,000 per annum must register for VAT. Businesses with a turnover below this figure can voluntarily register. Those with sales of less than £83,000 may apply for de-registration. The standard VAT rate has been 20% since January 2011. Most agricultural products are zero rated for VAT purposes. VAT has to be paid on certain inputs. Registered businesses are eligible to reclaim the tax paid where the goods or services purchased have been used in the production of zero-rated supplies.

A flat rate scheme is available to farmers as an alternative to registering for VAT. Farmers under the flat rate scheme do not have to submit tax returns or account for VAT and consequently cannot reclaim tax. They can, however, charge (and keep) a flat rate addition of 4% when they sell to VAT registered customers' goods and services which qualify. This addition is not VAT but acts as compensation for losing input tax on purchases. The registered person paying the flat rate amount to the farmer can recover it as if it were VAT, subject to the normal rules for reclaiming. The local VAT office may refuse to issue a certificate to participate in the flat rate scheme if this would mean the farmer would recover substantially (£3,000) more than through the normal system.

A flat rate scheme operates for small businesses generally and is an alternative that farmers can use if they have taxable supplies of no more than £150,000. This scheme operates in a different way to the flat rate scheme for farmers in that a business charges the normal rate of VAT on sales. However, the VAT which the business has to remit to Customs and Excise is calculated by multiplying the value of gross sales by a rate specified for each particular trade sector. The rate for agriculture is 6.5% except for businesses supplying agricultural services, when the rate is 11%.

***Editorial Note**: Farmers and landowners must always consider the VAT implications when considering any new or additional farming activities on the land or within the buildings, particularly where supplies are made to the public who cannot recover any VAT which may be charged on the service or goods provided from the farm.*

VIII. FARM BUSINESS MANAGEMENT

1. DEFINITIONS OF FARM MANAGEMENT TERMS

VALUATIONS AND CAPITAL

Valuations

Valuation is essentially a process of estimation. Various methods are possible, according to the purpose intended. The basis should be consistent throughout the period or any series of figures.

1. *Saleable crops in store.* At estimated market value less costs still to be incurred, e.g. for storage and marketing. Both may be estimated either at the expected date of sale or at the date of valuation.
2. *Growing crops.* Preferably at variable costs to the date of valuation, although estimated total cost can alternatively be used.
3. *Saleable crops ready for harvesting* but still in the ground. Preferably as valued in point 1 above, less estimated harvesting costs, although they can alternatively be treated as described in point 2 above.
4. *Fodder stocks (home-grown).* Normally at variable costs when calculating gross margins although this can be misleading for management purposes. Estimated market value (based on hay-equivalent value according to quality for example) includes the opportunity cost of the fodder in the livestock margin. Fodder crops still in the ground, e.g. kale, treated as point 2 above.
5. *Stocks of purchased materials (including fodder).* Priced at cost (net of discounts).
6. *Machinery and equipment.* Original cost (net of grants and discounts), less accumulated depreciation to date of valuation – this gives a valuation on the 'historic' cost basis. Alternatively at estimated market value.
7. *Livestock.* At current market value, less cost of marketing. Fluctuations in market value expected to be temporary should be ignored.

Capital

Tenant's Capital. The estimated total value of capital on the farm, other than land and fixed equipment. There is no easy way of determining this sum precisely and estimates are made in several ways depending on the information available and the purpose for which the estimate is required. One method is to take the average of the opening and closing valuations (at either market value or cost) of livestock, crops, machinery and stores (feed, seed, fertilisers). See also pages 250 (following section).

Landlord's Capital. Value of the land and fixed equipment (including buildings).

OUTPUT TERMS

Revenue (or Income). Receipts adjusted for debtors at the beginning and end of the accounting period. Items such as CAP support, revenue grants, contract receipts and wayleaves are included.

Returns. Revenue including valuation changes (add closing, deduct opening, valuation) so if valuation goes up, this adds to the returns.

Gross Output. Returns plus the value of produce consumed in the farmhouse or supplied to workers for which no payment is made, less purchases of livestock, livestock products and other produce bought for resale.

Enterprise Output. The total value of an enterprise, whether sold or retained on the farm. It therefore equals Gross Output of the enterprise plus the market value of any of the products kept on the farm (transfers out). The Basic Payment should not be apportioned to individual enterprises. Products transferred from another enterprise to be used in the production of the enterprise whose output is being calculated are deducted at market value (transfers in). Instead of the accounting year the "harvest year" can be used for crops which means valuations may not be relevant.

(Enterprise) Output from Forage. Primarily the sum of the enterprise outputs of grazing livestock, but includes keep let and occasional sales, e.g. of surplus hay, together with an adjustment for changes in the valuation of stocks of home-grown fodder. However, fortuitous changes in stocks caused by yield variations due to the weather, the severity or length of the winter, or minor changes in livestock numbers or forage area can be either ignored (if small in relation to total annual usage) or included in miscellaneous output.

Adjusted Forage (Enterprise) Output. Output from Forage less rented keep and purchases of bulk fodder.

Standard Output. The average enterprise output per hectare of a crop or per head of livestock calculated from average yield data and either national or local average price.

INPUT TERMS

Expenditure. Payments adjusted for creditors at the beginning and end of the accounting period. Capital expenditure is not included.

Costs. Expenditure adjusted for valuation changes (add opening, deduct closing, valuation), with the following adjustments: Add; depreciation on capital expenditure including machinery, any loss made on machinery sales (add to depreciation) and the value of payments in kind to workers if not already included in their earnings. Deduct; purchases of livestock, livestock products and other produce bought for resale, any profit made on machinery (deduct from depreciation), allowance for private use of farm vehicles (deduct from machinery costs), the value of purchased stores used in the farmhouse (e.g. electricity) or sold off the farm (deduct from the relevant item).

Inputs. Costs with the following adjustments, made in order to put all farms on a similar basis for comparative purposes. Add: the value of unpaid family labour, including the manual labour of the farmer and spouse, and, in the case of owner-occupiers, an estimated rental value (based on average rents of similar farms in the area), less any cottage rents received. Deduct: any mortgage payments and other expenses of owner-occupation, interest payments and the cost of paid management. A proportion of the rental value of the farmhouse may also be deducted.

Fixed Costs. See pages from 221 whole Farm Fixed Costs.

Variable Costs. See page 1.

MARGIN TERMS

Management and Investment Income. Gross Output less Inputs. It represents the reward to management and the return on tenant's capital invested in the farm, whether borrowed or not. It is mainly used for comparative purposes, all farms having been put on a similar financial basis by the adjustments made to costs in calculating Inputs.

Net Farm Income. Management and Investment Income, less paid management, plus the value of the manual labour of the farmer and spouse. It represents the return to all tenant's type capital and the reward to the farmer for his or her manual labour and farmer's management.

Profit (or Loss). Gross Output less Costs. This represents the surplus or deficit before imputing any notional charges such as rental value or unpaid labour. In the accounts of owner-occupiers it includes any profit accruing from the ownership of land.

Farm Business Income. This term is increasingly being used in FBS costings, and is similar to 'Profit' above. It represents the return to all unpaid labour and to all their own capital in the farm business including land and farm buildings.

Gross Margin. See page 1.

Net Margin. A term sometimes used to denote Gross Margin less direct labour and machinery costs charged to an individual enterprise. This is not, however, nationally accepted terminology. Increasingly Net Margin in the enterprise context is being used to denote the profit of an enterprise by taking its gross output less its 'complete enterprise costs', but see page 2.

AREA TERMS

Total Hectares. All hectares comprising the farm.

Hectares. Total hectares less areas of woods, waste land, roads, yards, buildings, etc.

Adjusted Hectares. Hectares reduced by the conversion of rough grazing into the equivalent hectares of average quality grassland. This is the figure often used for lowland farms when calculating "per hectare" results.

Forage Hectares. Total hectares of forage crops grown, less any hectares exclusively used by pigs or poultry and the area equivalent of any home-grown fodder fed to livestock reared in cereal systems. Also, the area of rough grazing is converted to its grassland equivalent (see Adjusted Hectares). Forage crops are all crops including grass, rough grazing, maize and whole crops grown specifically for grazing livestock, but excluding catch crops and crops harvested as grain and pulses.

Adjusted Forage Hectares. Forage hectares adjusted as follows; add the area equivalent of keep rented, deduct the area equivalent of keep let; deduct the area equivalent of occasional sales of fodder, e.g. surplus hay, and seed cuts (note: hay and seed grown regularly for sale should be regarded as cash crops, not forage crops); add or deduct the area equivalent of planned changes in the valuation of stocks of home-grown fodder (fortuitous changes in stocks resulting from weather conditions may be ignored); convert rough grazing into their grassland equivalent if not already done. The following adjustments also may be made: add the area equivalent of catch crops and of grazing from cash crops of hay or seed: add the area equivalent of purchased fodder.

In calculations such as Gross Margins per Forage Hectare, Adjusted Forage Hectares are usually used. If the area equivalent of purchased fodder has been added, the cost of purchased fodder must not be charged as a variable cost: this is probably the best calculation for comparative purposes. Alternatively, when considering all the grazing enterprises taken together, purchased fodder can be deducted as a variable cost and no addition made for its area equivalent.

2. CAPITAL REQUIREMENT AND RETURN

TENANT'S CAPITAL

1. *Machinery.* Costs of new machinery are given from page 187. Written-down values in 2018 are likely to average £345-£1,400 per hectare (£140-£560/acre) of actively farmed land (excluding fallow and rough grazing) depending on farm types. Average values for different farm types for 2015/16 are detailed on the next page.
2. *Breeding Livestock.* The 2018 average of breeding livestock value per hectare can be anything up to £1,800 (£730/acre) for an intensive (outdoor) dairy/livestock farm. Intensive (housed) pig and poultry units will be substantially more but a meaningless figure having minimal land. Approximate average market values of various categories of breeding livestock (of mixed ages in the case of adult stock) are as follows (actual value will vary according to average age and weight, quality, breed and market conditions):

Average market values of various breeding livestock

	Breeding Herd		
	Newly calved	Average	Cull
Holstein/Friesian Dairy Cows	£1,200	£800	£400
Channel Island Dairy Cows	£1,000	£590	£180
Suckler Beef Cows	£1,500*	£1,000	£500
Pure-bred Beef Cows	£1,875*	£1,250	£625

* *Calf at Foot < 3 months*

	Replacements		
	Holstein Friesians	Ayrshires and C.I. Breeds	Beef Cattle
In Calf Heifers	£1,080	£900	£1,300
1-2 years	£800	£700	£890
6-12 months	£600	£500	£590
Under 6 months	£340	£280	£360
Dairy Calf	£150	£150	£225

	Other Livestock		
	Newly Lambed	Average	Cull
Ewes	£150	£110	£70
Rams	£495	£290	£85
Sows and In-Pig Gilts	£220	£156	£92
Boars	£1,000	£540	£85

3. *Working Capital.* This is defined as the current assets of a business less its current liabilities. It is the liquid capital needed to finance the cash flow through the production cycle, the length of which varies considerably between different crop and livestock enterprises and different combinations of these enterprises. It can include the cost of purchased fattening stock, feed, seed, fertilisers, regular labour, machinery running costs, general overhead costs, rent and living expenses. This capital will vary between farm business types. Specialist root crop and vegetable farm businesses will have significantly higher working capital requirements than livestock and combinable cropping businesses. The only accurate way to estimate working capital requirement is to complete a full cash flow estimate for the production cycle of the business.

Average Tenants Capital per Hectare

Average Tenant's Capital for different English farm types for 2015-16:

Farm Type Group	Average No. Hectares	Breeding Livestock	Crops and Stores	Machinery and Equipment	Total Tenant's Capital	
		£/ha	**£/ha**	**£/ha**	**£/ha**	***£/acre***
Mainly Dairying:						
Small	60	1,095	125	853	2,881	*1,167*
Medium	82	1,141	242	1,327	3,687	*1,493*
Large	113	1,339	276	1,190	3,679	*1,490*
V. Large	216	1,271	325	1,135	3,679	*1,490*
Average	149	1,271	299	1,157	3,653	*1,479*
Mainly Cereals:						
Small	189	14	566	835	1,842	*746*
Medium	265	47	628	902	2,294	*929*
Large	398	52	554	799	1,940	*786*
V. Large	711	57	572	815	2,140	*867*
Average	300	41	578	836	2,041	*827*
General Cropping:						
Small	133	24	455	764	1,878	*761*
Medium	203	41	441	875	1,790	*725*
Large	240	80	763	1,103	2,530	*1,025*
V. Large	941	55	451	794	1,943	*787*
Average	343	51	485	838	1,988	*805*
Mainly Sheep/Cattle (Lowland):						
Small	90	388	110	573	1,871	*758*
Medium	99	632	121	730	2,289	*927*
Large	159	533	140	623	2,099	*850*
V. Large	375	449	108	393	1,638	*662*
Average	126	478	118	571	1,942	*787*
Mainly Sheep/Cattle (Upland Less Favoured Area):						
Small	101	464	61	419	1,401	*567*
Medium	166	422	45	344	1,212	*491*
Large	227	483	49	329	1,358	*550*
V. Large	416	629	87	372	1,542	*625*
Average	164	495	60	371	1,380	*559*

Source Farm Business Data

- Trading livestock, crops in store and other liquid assets are not included separately as they are not assets of production and vary according to marketing styles and time of year. They are included in the Total Tenant's Capital.
- Farm size is measured by labour units normally required on farms of these sizes: Small = 1-2 full time equivalent workers (FTE), Medium = 2-3 FTE, Large = 3-5 FTE and Very large = over 5 FTE. 'Very Small' (less than 1 FTE) has been omitted here. The average is for all farms of 1 FTE or more, considered 'full time farms'.
- The above (rounded) data is from Farm Business Survey results for England compiled annually by University/Colleges (as listed on page 4). The value of Basic Payment entitlements is excluded as are other assets not named above, such as debtors. The variation in capital per farm size is a reflection of the range of farming systems and the small sample numbers in some categories.

RETURN ON CAPITAL

Return on Tenant's Capital

Return on tenant's capital is calculated by taking the management and investment income (MII) of a business as a percentage of the tenant's capital (see definitions in section 1 of this chapter). Because MII is before deduction of any interest, this return is 'gross', i.e. before allowing for cost of finance. However, it should be borne in mind that MII includes no charge for management but that a rental value for owner-occupied land and the value of the unpaid labour of the farmer and wife have been deducted.

Return on Landlord's Capital

The return on landlord's capital is calculated by taking the rental income, less any ownership expenses (mortgage, insurance, repairs etc.), expressed as a percentage of the land value. With farmland in 2017 averaging possibly £25,000 per hectare (£10,110 per acre) (see page 228) with vacant possession (assuming no special amenity or house value), an average lowland existing rent of, say, £350 per hectare (£140 per acre) (see page 226), and assuming ownership expenses at £87 per hectare (£35 per acre), the (net) return of £263 per hectare (£106 per acre) averages 1%. This takes no account of land capital valuation change.

Return on Capital to Individual Enterprises

On a mixed farm it is difficult to ascertain the return on enterprise capital, except perhaps for a full-time pig or poultry enterprise. It would also be of limited use. It would require the arbitrary allocation both of costs and capital inputs that are common to several, or all, of the enterprises on the farm.

What is relevant and important is the extra (net) return from an enterprise either to be introduced or expanded, as calculated by a partial budget, related to the extra (net) capital needed. The 'net' in brackets relates to the additional returns to gross margins less any additional (or plus any reduction in) 'fixed' costs, bearing in mind that another enterprise may have to be deleted or reduced in size; and, regarding capital, to the fact that deletion or reduction of another enterprise may release capital.

In most cases of 'marginal' substitution, it is differences in the value of breeding livestock and differences in variable costs that are particularly relevant, but the timing of both inputs and sales are also obviously very important.

'Marginal' Capital Requirements

These are for small changes in crop areas or livestock numbers and can be estimated as follows:

- Crops: variable costs until payment of sale.
- Dairy Cows and Egg Production: value of the cow* or hens, plus food until payment of product.
- Other Breeding Livestock: average value of stock*, plus variable costs to sale (payment) of the progeny (e.g. lambs) – or their transfer to another enterprise (e.g. weaners to the pig fattening enterprise).
- Rearing Breeding Livestock (e.g. heifers, shearlings, gilts, pullets): cost of the calf, lamb, weaner or chick, plus variable costs until they produce their first progeny/milk/eggs.
- Fattening Livestock and Production of Stores: cost of stock, plus variable costs till sale.

* Value of breeding stock, including dairy cows: either the average value over their entire breeding or milk producing life (see table on page 250) or their value when they first

produce progeny can be taken. The latter will give the lower return on (marginal) capital and is thus the severer test.

Home-reared stock: where stock to be used for milk or egg production, breeding or fattening are home-reared, there are two possibilities:

(a) either they can be valued at variable costs of production when they are transferred from the rearing to the 'productive' enterprise; in this case the return on (marginal) capital will be estimated over the combined rearing and 'productive' enterprise.

(b) or they can be valued at market value at point of transfer. This is the procedure if one wishes to work out a return on (marginal) capital for the rearing and the 'productive' enterprises separately.

Return on 'Marginal' Capital

This is sometimes expressed as the gross margin less fuel and repair costs of the enterprise expanded as a percentage of the 'marginal', or extra capital. However, two points have to be remembered:

(a) If another enterprise has had to be reduced in size to enable the enterprise under consideration to be expanded, the capital released and the gross margin forfeited by reducing the size of the first enterprise must be brought into the calculation in estimating the net result of the change.

(b) All the above statements on 'marginal' capital refer to small changes. If the change is large enough to cause changes in labour, machinery, rent or building requirements, the capital changes brought about may be considerably greater.

Return on Investments in Medium-Term and Long-Term Capital

This calculates the Rate of Return and the Discounted Yield.

Example: If a £5,000 investment results in an annual net return of £500 (after deducting depreciation, but ignoring interest payments) and with no capital salvage value:

$$\textit{Rate of Return on Initial Capital} = \frac{500}{5{,}000} \times 100 = 10\%$$

$$\textit{Rate of Return on Average Capital} = \frac{500}{2{,}500} \times 100 = 20\%$$

Care has to be taken when using the return on '*average*' capital as the capital has still been spent, it is just that half has been written off. It is more accurate to calculate the '*Discounted Yield*', which is the discount rate that brings the present value of the net cash flows (which means ignoring depreciation) to the value of the investment. The tables from page 259 may be used.

'Short-Cut' Estimates of the Discounted Yield on Depreciating Assets

The Discounted Yield falls between the simple Rates of Return on Initial and Average Capital. In fact, for investments lasting 5 to 15 years, when the Rate of Return on Initial Capital is 10 per cent and on Average Capital 20 per cent, the Discounted Yield will be almost exactly halfway between, i.e. about 15 per cent. However, this is only so providing the anticipated annual net cash earnings are fairly constant — or fluctuate unpredictably around a fairly constant level.

There are three circumstances when the Discounted Yield will get closer to the Rate of Return on Initial Capital (i.e. the lower per cent return) and further from the Rate of Return on Average Capital:

(a) The longer the life of the investment.

(b) The higher the Rate of Return.

(c) The higher the net cash flow is in the later years of the investment compared with the earlier years.

When the opposite circumstances occur, the Discounted Yield will be closer to the Rate of Return on Average Capital (i.e. the higher per cent return).

There are varying degrees of estimation and uncertainty in calculating future net annual earnings of investments. The following short-cuts might reasonably be used where the annual net cash earnings are expected to be fairly constant - or fluctuate unpredictably (e.g. through weather effects on yields) around a fairly constant level. (W.O. period = write-off period; R.R.I.C. = rate of return on initial capital).

1. Where

(i) the W.O. period is 5 years or less,

(ii) the W.O. period is 6 - 10 years and the R.R.I.C. is 15 per cent or less,

(iii) the W.O. period is 11 - 20 years and the R.R.I.C. is 10 per cent or less,

calculate the Return on Capital as being approximately midway between the Rates of Return on Initial and Average Capital, i.e. by calculating the Rate of Return on 2/3 of the original investment.

For example, following the earlier example above:

$$\frac{500}{3,333} \quad x\ 100 = 15\%.$$

2. Where

(i) the W.O. period is 6 to 10 years and the R.R.I.C. exceeds 15 per cent,

(ii) the W.O. period is 11 to 20 years and the R.R.I.C. is between 10 per cent and 25 per cent,

(iii) the W.O. period exceeds 20 years and the R.R.I.C. is 10 per cent or less,

calculate the Return on Capital on 80 per cent of the original investment.

For example, again following the earlier example:

$$\frac{500}{4,000} \quad x\ 100 = 12.5°\%.$$

3. Where

(i) the W.O. period is 11 to 20 years and the R.R.I.C. exceeds 25 per cent,

(ii) the W.O. period exceeds 20 years and the R.R.I.C. exceeds 10 per cent. Take the Return on Capital to be the R.R.I.C.

In borderline cases, use method 1 rather than 2, or 2 rather than 3 if there is a tendency for the cash flow to be higher in the earlier years, e.g. because of tax allowances on machinery. Take 2 rather than 1, and 3 rather than 2, if the likelihood is that the cash flow will be lower in earlier years and increase in later years.

However, where the annual cash flow is expected to vary (apart from unpredictable fluctuations) it is safer to make the full D.C.F. calculation. This is particularly so where the variation is both up and down and where further periodic investments are to be made during the life of the project.

3. INTEREST RATES

Rate of interest on Bank Loans

Overdraft borrowing rates are typically 2.5% to 3.5% above Base Rate. Main range is 1.5% above to 4.0% above. Extremes are likely to be 0.8% above and 7% above. Particularly low margins over base have become rare, especially for new lending agreements. Annual arrangement fees based on the total facility can add substantially to the cost of borrowing. Base rate is at an all-time low of 0.25%, a ¼ point fall from 0.5% where it had been since 2009, itself an all-time low. However it is always prudent for budgeting purposes to allow an additional 0.5% as changes can be fast if they are made. A 0.5% rise in base rate is now proportionally a very large increase in borrowing rates. Whilst the Governor of the Bank of England says a rate rise is not imminent, sentiment is starting to rise.

Fixed Rate Mortgages

The table gives typical mortgage rates on domestic dwellings. Note that this is taken from the current mortgage marketplace. Each offering is different with varying retention clauses, booking fees or early redemption costs. The lowest interest rate is not necessarily the best mortgage.

Typical Fixed Rates on Residential Mortgages

Fixed Rate	90% LTV*	75%	65% LTV*
2-year	2.0%	1.1%	1.0%
5-year	2.8%	1.9%	1.7%
10-year	n/a	3.7%	3.0%

* *LTV = Loan to Value (the percent the financier loans against the capital value)*

Annual Percentage Rate (APR)

This is the effective rate of interest calculated on an annual basis and should be used when seeking to make a true comparison between interest charges on money borrowed from different sources. The APR allows for the fact that when interest is applied to accounts at half yearly, quarterly or monthly intervals an element of compounding will arise.

For example, £100 borrowed for one year at a quoted annual nominal interest rate of 6% (e.g. 5.75% over base rate of 0.25%) with interest charged quarterly, will lead to an accumulated interest charge of £6.136 (i.e., giving an APR of just under 6.14%). The higher the annual nominal interest rate and the more frequently the interest charges are applied to the account, the more pronounced the compounding element becomes. For example, an annual nominal interest rate of 10% produces an APR of 10.25% with half yearly charging, 10.38% with quarterly charging and 10.47% with monthly charging.

In the case of some loans and hire purchase agreements, interest charges may be quoted as a flat rate on the original amount borrowed. The APR will be considerably greater than the flat rate if the loan is repaid by equal periodic instalments, comprising part capital and part interest, so that the borrowing is completely repaid by the end of the agreed term.

The Real Rate of Interest.

When preparing profit and loss budgets to estimate how worthwhile an investment in a fixed asset (machinery, buildings, land) is, it is usual to price inputs and outputs at present-day values even when most costs and returns are expected to rise due to inflation over the life of the investment. Where this real terms approach is adopted a more realistic estimate of the effect on profitability can be gained by basing charges for capital on the real rate of interest rather than the APR.

The real rate of interest is the APR adjusted for the annual rate at which prices relevant to the investment are expected to increase. A crude estimate of the real rate of interest can be obtained by simply subtracting the expected rate of price increase from the APR; for example, if the APR were 8% and the expected rate of inflation 3%, the real rate of interest would be 8 – 3 = 5%.

4. FINANCIAL RATIOS

Common Ratios

The following ratios are standard guidelines using '*normalised*' output prices, i.e. those in an average year. These are used as guidelines for advisors, students, agricultural commentators and farmers alike:

% of Gross Output	*Arable*	*Dairy*	*Mixed*	*Upland*	*Intensive stock*
Variable Costs	32	39	37	47	65
Labour+	12	15	21	17	12
Machinery	18	17	19	14	5
Sundry Fixed Costs	9	9	10	12	4
Rent & Interest	12	13	9	8	4
Profit *	17	17	4	2	10
Basic Payment Support	14	5	14	19	2

+ *including drawings*
* *to cover, tax, capital repayments, reinvestments*

These are only rough guidelines and need to be considered with great care. Values vary with type and size of farm. Unpaid manual labour of the farmer and family has been included and a rental value has been allowed for owner-occupied land. Higher rent and finance can be justified on more profitable farm systems. In years when output is lower, all these percentages, other than profit, will rise.

The Basic Payment as a percentage of output is also included to compare against profit. Being greater than total farm profit in some cases, it identifies the dependence of several farm businesses to direct subsidy.

Farm Survey Ratios

The following are rounded averages based on farm surveys in recent years on a large sample of all types of farm, assuming a Management and Investment Income (see page 248) of 10% of Total Output is made. It is to be noted that Total Output includes the market value of any production retained for use/consumption on the farm (e.g. cereals for feed or seed). Unpaid labour (value of manual labour by the farmer and spouse) is included. Rent includes the rental value of owner-occupied land and interest charges are not included in the costs. Casual labour and all contract work are included in fixed costs. Costs are a lower proportion and the margin a higher proportion in profitable years (and on more profitable farms), and *vice-versa* in low profit years.

Average Financial Ratios calculated from Farm Business Survey (England)

	% Total Output		% Total Gross Margin		% Total Fixed Costs	
	2014	2015	2014	2015	2014	2015
Gross Margin (*inc. SPS*)	62%	63%				
Variable Costs:						
(excl. casual labour and contract)	38%	37%	60%	59%	62%	58%
Fixed Costs:						
Labour: Paid (inc. unpaid)	19%	20%	30%	32%	31%	31%
Power & Machinery (inc. contract)	20%	20%	31%	32%	32%	31%
Rent/Rental Value	15%	16%	24%	26%	24%	25%
General Overheads	7%	8%	12%	13%	12%	13%
Total Fixed Costs	61%	64%	97%	102%	100%	100%
Margin	**2%**	**-2%**	**3%**	**-2%**	**3%**	**-2%**

Lending Criteria

Another set of standards widely used by lending and leasing institutions looks at Total Finance Charges (rent, interest, leasing charges, etc.), as a percentage of Gross Output and Gross Margin;

Finance as a % of Gross Output	Finance as a % of Gross Margin	Lending Criteria
0-10%	0-15%	Normally very safe
11-15%	16-22.5%	Common range, should be safe
15%	24%	Average Farm in 2014/15*
16-20%	23-29%	Care required
20% plus	30% plus	Potentially dangerous

* *Interpretation from Farm Business Survey data*

As lenders will be well aware, these ratios must be regarded with caution and in conjunction with the farm's level of net worth (% equity) and its trend in recent years, recent trends in its profitability and the potential borrower's record of expenditure both on and off the farm, together with his or her character and potential. Also, some enterprises and types of farming are more risky than others.

DISCOUNTING TABLE A

Discount Factors for Calculating the Present Value of Future (irregular) Cash Flows

Year	Percentage																	
	2%	3%	4%	5%	6%	7%	8%	9%	10%	11%	12%	13%	14%	15%	16%	18%	20%	25%
1	0.980	0.971	0.962	0.952	0.943	0.935	0.926	0.917	0.909	0.901	0.893	0.885	0.877	0.870	0.862	0.847	0.833	0.80
2	0.961	0.943	0.925	0.907	0.890	0.873	0.857	0.842	0.826	0.812	0.797	0.783	0.769	0.756	0.743	0.718	0.694	0.64
3	0.942	0.915	0.889	0.864	0.840	0.816	0.794	0.772	0.751	0.731	0.712	0.693	0.675	0.658	0.641	0.609	0.579	0.51
4	0.924	0.888	0.855	0.823	0.792	0.763	0.735	0.708	0.683	0.659	0.636	0.613	0.592	0.572	0.552	0.516	0.482	0.41
5	0.906	0.863	0.822	0.784	0.747	0.713	0.681	0.650	0.621	0.593	0.567	0.543	0.519	0.497	0.476	0.437	0.402	0.33
6	0.888	0.837	0.790	0.746	0.705	0.666	0.630	0.596	0.564	0.535	0.507	0.480	0.456	0.432	0.410	0.370	0.335	0.26
7	0.871	0.813	0.760	0.711	0.665	0.623	0.583	0.547	0.513	0.482	0.452	0.425	0.400	0.376	0.354	0.314	0.279	0.21
8	0.853	0.789	0.731	0.677	0.627	0.582	0.540	0.502	0.467	0.434	0.404	0.376	0.351	0.327	0.305	0.266	0.233	0.17
9	0.837	0.766	0.703	0.645	0.592	0.544	0.500	0.460	0.424	0.391	0.361	0.333	0.308	0.284	0.263	0.225	0.194	0.13
10	0.820	0.744	0.676	0.614	0.558	0.508	0.463	0.422	0.386	0.352	0.322	0.295	0.270	0.247	0.227	0.191	0.162	0.11
11	0.804	0.722	0.650	0.585	0.527	0.475	0.429	0.388	0.350	0.317	0.287	0.261	0.237	0.215	0.195	0.162	0.135	0.09
12	0.788	0.701	0.625	0.557	0.497	0.444	0.397	0.356	0.319	0.286	0.257	0.231	0.208	0.187	0.168	0.137	0.112	0.07
13	0.773	0.681	0.601	0.530	0.469	0.415	0.368	0.326	0.290	0.258	0.229	0.204	0.182	0.163	0.145	0.116	0.093	0.06
14	0.758	0.661	0.577	0.505	0.442	0.388	0.340	0.299	0.263	0.232	0.205	0.181	0.160	0.141	0.125	0.098	0.078	0.04
15	0.743	0.642	0.555	0.481	0.417	0.362	0.315	0.275	0.239	0.209	0.183	0.160	0.140	0.123	0.108	0.084	0.065	0.04
20	0.673	0.554	0.456	0.377	0.312	0.258	0.215	0.178	0.149	0.124	0.104	0.087	0.073	0.061	0.051	0.037	0.026	0.01
25	0.610	0.478	0.375	0.295	0.233	0.184	0.146	0.116	0.092	0.074	0.059	0.047	0.038	0.030	0.024	0.016	0.010	.004
30	0.552	0.412	0.308	0.231	0.174	0.131	0.099	0.075	0.057	0.044	0.033	0.026	0.020	0.015	0.012	0.007	0.004	.001

Example: The Present Value of £2,000 received 10 years from now, at 8 per cent discount rate of interest = 2,000 x 0.463 = £926.

Conversely, £926 invested now, at 8 per cent compound interest, will be worth £2,000 in 10 years' time.

ANNUITY / DISCOUNTING TABLE B

Discount Factors for Calculating the Present Value of Future Annuity (i.e. Constant Annual Cash Flow) Receivable in Year 1 to n inclusive.

Year	Percentage																	
	2%	3%	4%	5%	6%	7%	8%	9%	10%	11%	12%	13%	14%	15%	16%	18%	20%	25%
1	0.980	0.971	0.962	0.952	0.943	0.935	0.926	0.917	0.909	0.901	0.893	0.885	0.877	0.870	0.862	0.847	0.833	0.80
2	1.942	1.913	1.886	1.859	1.833	1.808	1.783	1.759	1.736	1.713	1.690	1.668	1.647	1.626	1.605	1.566	1.528	1.44
3	2.884	2.829	2.775	2.723	2.673	2.624	2.577	2.531	2.487	2 444	2.402	2.361	2.322	2.283	2.246	2.174	2.106	1.95
4	3.808	3.717	3.630	3.546	3.465	3.387	3.312	3.240	3.170	3.102	3.037	2.974	2.914	2.855	2.798	2.690	2.589	2.36
5	4.713	4.580	4.452	4.329	4.212	4.100	3.993	3.890	3.791	3.696	3.605	3.517	3.433	3.352	3.274	3.127	2.991	2.69
6	5.601	5.417	5.242	5.076	4.917	4.767	4.623	4.486	4.355	4.231	4.111	3.998	3.889	3.784	3.685	3.498	3.326	2.95
7	6.472	6.230	6.002	5.786	5.582	5.389	5.206	5.033	4.868	4.712	4.564	4.423	4.288	4.160	4.039	3.812	3.605	3.16
8	7.325	7.020	6.733	6.463	6.210	5.971	5.747	5.535	5.335	5.146	4.968	4.799	4.639	4.487	4.344	4.078	3.837	3.33
9	8.162	7.786	7.435	7.108	6.802	6.515	6.247	5.995	5.759	5.537	5.328	5.132	4.946	4.772	4.607	4.303	4.031	3.46
10	8.983	8.530	8.111	7.722	7.360	7.024	6.710	6.418	6.145	5.889	5.650	5.426	5.216	5.019	4.833	4.494	4.192	3.57
11	9.787	9.253	8.760	8.306	7.887	7.499	7.139	6.805	6.495	6.207	5.938	5.687	5.453	5.234	5.029	4.656	4.327	3.66
12	10.58	9.954	9.385	8.863	8.384	7.943	7.536	7.161	6.814	6.492	6.194	5.918	5.660	5.421	5.197	4.793	4.439	3.73
13	11.35	10.635	9.986	9.394	8.853	8.358	7.904	7.487	7.103	6.750	6.424	6.122	5.842	5.583	5.342	4.910	4.533	3.78
14	12.11	11.296	10.563	9.899	9.295	8.745	8.244	7.786	7.367	6.982	6.628	6.302	6.002	5.724	5.468	5.008	4.611	3.82
15	12.85	11.938	11.118	10.380	9.712	9.108	8.559	8.061	7.606	7.191	6.811	6.462	6.142	5.847	5.575	5.092	4.675	3.86
20	16.35	14.877	13.590	12.462	11.470	10.594	9.818	9.129	8.514	7.963	7.469	7.025	6.623	6.259	5.929	5.353	4.870	3.95
25	19.52	17.413	15.662	14.094	12.783	11.654	10.675	9.823	9.077	8.422	7.843	7.330	6.873	6.464	6.097	5.467	4.948	3.99
30	22.40	19.600	17.292	15.372	13.765	12.409	11.258	10.274	9.427	8.694	8.055	7.496	7.003	6.566	6.177	5.517	4.979	4.00

Example: The Present Value of £500 a year for the next 10 years, at 12 per cent discount rate of interest = 500 x 5.650 = £2,825. This is the same answer that would be obtained by multiplying 500 by each discount factor (at 12 per cent) in Table A for each year from 1 to 10, and adding together the ten resulting figures.

To obtain the Discounted Yield of a constant annual net cash flow, divide this into the original investment and look up the resulting figure in the table above, against the number of years. Example: an investment of £1,000 is estimated to produce £80 a year additional profit over 10 years (before charging interest). Add £100 depreciation a year = £180 annual net cash flow. 1000 / 180 = 5.56. This equals just over 12 per cent (the 10 years /12 per cent figure being 5.650).

COMPOUNDING TABLE A

The Future Money Value of £1 after n Years with no additional payments made

Year	Rate of Interest %																
	2%	3%	4%	5%	6%	7%	8%	9%	10%	11%	12%	13%	14%	15%	16%	18%	20%	25%
1	1.02	1.03	1.04	1.05	1.06	1.07	1.08	1.09	1.10	1.11	1.12	1.13	1.14	1.15	1.16	1.18	1.20	1.25
2	1.04	1.06	1.08	1.10	1.12	1.14	1.17	1.19	1.21	1.23	1.25	1.28	1.30	1.32	1.35	1.39	1.44	1.56
3	1.06	1.09	1.12	1.16	1.19	1.23	1.26	1.30	1.33	1.37	1.40	1.44	1.48	1.52	1.56	1.64	1.73	1.95
4	1.08	1.13	1.17	1.22	1.26	1.31	1.36	1.41	1.46	1.52	1.57	1.63	1.69	1.75	1.81	1.94	2.07	2.44
5	1.10	1.16	1.22	1.28	1.34	1.40	1.47	1.54	1.61	1.69	1.76	1.84	1.93	2.01	2.10	2.29	2.49	3.05
6	1.13	1.19	1.27	1.34	1.42	1.50	1.59	1.68	1.77	1.87	1.97	2.08	2.19	2.31	2.44	2.70	2.99	3.81
7	1.15	1.23	1.32	1.41	1.50	1.61	1.71	1.83	1.95	2.08	2.21	2.35	2.50	2.66	2.83	3.19	3.58	4.77
8	1.17	1.27	1.37	1.48	1.59	1.72	1.85	1.99	2.14	2.30	2.48	2.66	2.85	3.06	3.28	3.76	4.30	5.96
9	1.20	1.30	1.42	1.55	1.69	1.84	2.00	2.17	2.36	2.56	2.77	3.00	3.25	3.52	3.80	4.44	5.16	7.45
10	1.22	1.34	1.48	1.63	1.79	1.97	2.16	2.37	2.59	2.84	3.11	3.39	3.71	4.05	4.41	5.23	6.19	9.31
11	1.24	1.38	1.54	1.71	1.90	2.10	2.33	2.58	2.85	3.15	3.48	3.84	4.23	4.65	5.12	6.18	7.43	11.64
12	1.27	1.43	1.60	1.80	2.01	2.25	2.52	2.81	3.14	3.50	3.90	4.33	4.82	5.35	5.94	7.29	8.92	14.55
13	1.29	1.47	1.67	1.89	2.13	2.41	2.72	3.07	3.45	3.88	4.36	4.90	5.49	6.15	6.89	8.60	10.70	18.19
14	1.32	1.51	1.73	1.98	2.26	2.58	2.94	3.34	3.80	4.31	4.89	5.53	6.26	7.08	7.99	10.15	12.84	22.74
15	1.35	1.56	1.80	2.08	2.40	2.76	3.17	3.64	4.18	4.78	5.47	6.25	7.14	8.14	9.27	11.97	15.41	28.42
20	1.49	1.81	2.19	2.65	3.21	3.87	4.66	5.60	6.73	8.06	9.65	11.52	13.74	16.37	19.46	27.39	38.34	86.8
25	1.64	2.09	2.67	3.39	4.29	5.43	6.85	8.62	10.83	13.59	17.00	21.23	26.46	32.92	40.9	62.7	95.4	265
30	1.81	2.43	3.24	4.32	5.74	7.61	10.06	13.27	17.45	22.89	29.96	39.12	50.95	66.2	85.9	143	237	807

COMPOUNDING TABLE B

The Future Money Value of £1 after n Years*

Year	Rate of Interest %																	
	2%	3%	4%	5%	6%	7%	8%	9%	10%	11%	12%	13%	14%	15%	16%	18%	20%	25%
1	1.02	1.03	1.04	1.05	1.06	1.07	1.08	1.09	1.10	1.11	1.12	1.13	1.14	1.15	1.16	1.18	1.20	1.25
2	2.06	2.09	2.12	2.15	2.18	2.21	2.25	2.28	2.31	2.34	2.37	2.41	2.44	2.47	2.51	2.57	2.64	2.81
3	3.12	3.18	3.25	3.31	3.37	3.44	3.51	3.57	3.64	3.71	3.78	3.85	3.92	3.99	4.07	4.22	4.37	4.77
4	4.20	4.31	4.42	4.53	4.64	4.75	4.87	4.98	5.11	5.23	5.35	5.48	5.61	5.74	5.88	6.15	6.44	7.21
5	5.31	5.47	5.63	5.80	5.98	6.15	6.34	6.52	6.72	6.91	7.12	7.32	7.54	7.75	7.98	8.44	8.93	10.3
6	6.43	6.66	6.90	7.14	7.39	7.65	7.92	8.20	8.49	8.78	9.09	9.40	9.73	10.07	10.41	11.1	11.92	14.1
7	7.58	7.89	8.21	8.55	8.90	9.26	9.64	10.03	10.44	10.86	11.30	11.76	12.23	12.73	13.24	14.3	15.50	18.8
8	8.75	9.16	9.58	10.03	10.49	10.98	11.49	12.02	12.58	13.16	13.78	14.42	15.09	15.79	16.52	18.1	19.80	24.8
9	9.95	10.46	11.01	11.58	12.18	12.82	13.49	14.19	14.94	15.72	16.55	17.42	18.34	19.30	20.32	22.5	24.96	32.3
10	11.17	11.81	12.49	13.21	13.97	14.78	15.65	16.56	17.53	18.56	19.65	20.81	22.04	23.35	24.73	27.8	31.15	41.6
11	12.41	13.19	14.03	14.92	15.87	16.89	17.98	19.14	20.38	21.71	23.13	24.65	26.27	28.00	29.85	33.9	38.58	53.2
12	13.68	14.62	15.63	16.71	17.88	19.14	20.50	21.95	23.52	25.21	27.03	28.98	31.09	33.35	35.79	41.2	47.50	67.8
13	14.97	16.09	17.29	18.60	20.02	21.55	23.21	25.02	26.97	29.09	31.39	33.88	36.58	39.50	42.67	49.9	58.20	86.0
14	16.29	17.60	19.02	20.58	22.28	24.13	26.15	28.36	30.77	33.41	36.28	39.42	42.84	46.58	50.66	60.0	71.04	109
15	17.64	19.16	20.82	22.66	24.67	26.89	29.32	32.00	34.95	38.19	41.75	45.67	49.98	54.72	59.93	71.9	86.44	137
20	24.78	27.68	30.97	34.72	38.99	43.87	49.42	55.76	63.00	71.27	80.70	91.47	103.8	117.8	133.8	173	224.0	429
25	32.67	37.55	43.31	50.11	58.16	67.68	78.95	92.32	108.2	127.0	149.3	175.8	207.3	244.7	289.1	404	566.4	1318
30	41.38	49.00	58.33	69.76	83.80	101.1	122.3	148.6	180.9	220.9	270.3	331.3	406.7	500.0	615.2	933	1418	4034

* Equal payments made at the beginning of each year.

AMORTISATION TABLE

Annual Charge to write off £1,000

Write-off	Rate of Interest															
Period	2	3	4	5	6	7	8	9	10	11	12	13	14	15	16	18	20
5 years	212	218	225	231	237	244	250	257	264	271	277	284	291	298	305	320	334
6	179	185	191	197	203	210	216	223	230	236	243	250	257	264	271	286	301
7	155	161	167	173	179	186	192	199	205	212	219	226	233	240	248	262	277
8	137	142	149	155	161	167	174	181	187	194	201	208	216	223	230	245	261
9	123	128	134	141	147	153	160	167	174	181	188	195	202	210	217	232	248
10	111	117	123	130	136	142	149	156	163	170	177	184	192	199	207	223	239
11	102	108	114	120	127	133	140	147	154	161	168	176	183	191	199	215	231
12	95	100	107	113	119	125	133	140	147	154	161	169	177	184	192	209	225
13	88	94	100	106	113	120	127	134	141	148	156	163	171	179	187	204	221
14	83	89	95	101	108	114	121	128	136	143	151	159	167	175	183	200	217
15	78	84	90	96	103	110	117	124	131	139	147	155	163	171	179	196	214
16	74	80	86	92	99	106	113	120	128	136	143	151	160	168	176	194	211
17	70	76	82	89	95	102	110	117	125	132	140	149	157	165	174	191	209
18	67	73	79	86	92	99	107	114	122	130	138	146	155	163	172	190	208
20	61	67	74	80	87	94	102	110	117	126	134	142	151	160	169	187	205
25	51	57	64	71	78	86	94	102	110	119	127	136	145	155	164	183	202
30	45	51	58	65	73	81	89	97	106	115	124	133	143	152	162	181	201
40	37	43	51	58	66	75	84	93	102	112	122	131	141	151	160	180	200

Example: £30,000 is borrowed to erect a building. The annual charge to service interest and capital repayment on the £30,000, repayable over 10 years at 12%, is 30 x £177 = £5,310. Where the write-off period of the building is equal to the repayment period of the loan (10 years), then the average annual depreciation plus interest will equal £5,310.

The proportion of the total annual charge representing the average amount of capital repaid per annum can be readily determined by dividing the sum borrowed by the number of years of the loan: (in the above example this is £30,000 ÷ 10 = £3,000/year). The remainder is clearly the average amount of interest paid per annum: (in the above example, £5,310 — £3,000 = £2,310/year). The year to year variations between the two items (i.e. capital repaid and interest) are shown in the Mortgage Repayment Data tables (2 pages further on) , which demonstrate the way the capital repayment part increases and the interest part decreases over time.

SINKING FUND TABLE

The sum required to be set aside at the end of each year to make £1,000

No. of	Rate of Interest															
Years	2	3	4	5	6	7	8	9	10	11	12	13	14	15	16	18	20
5	192	188	185	181	177	174	170	167	164	161	157	154	151	148	145	140	134
6	159	155	151	147	143	140	136	133	130	126	123	120	117	114	111	106	101
7	135	131	127	123	119	116	112	109	105	102	99	96	93	90	88	82	77
8	117	112	109	105	101	97	94	91	87	84	81	78	76	73	70	65	61
9	103	98	94	91	87	83	80	77	74	71	68	65	62	60	57	52	48
10	91	87	83	80	76	72	69	66	63	60	57	54	52	49	47	43	39
11	82	78	74	70	67	63	60	57	54	51	48	46	43	41	39	35	31
12	75	70	67	63	59	56	53	50	47	44	41	39	37	34	32	29	25
13	68	64	60	56	53	50	47	44	41	38	36	33	31	29	27	24	21
14	63	59	55	51	48	44	41	38	36	33	31	29	27	25	23	20	17
15	58	54	50	46	43	40	37	34	31	29	27	25	23	21	19	16	14
16	54	50	46	42	39	36	33	30	28	26	23	21	20	18	16	14	11
17	50	46	42	39	35	32	30	27	25	22	20	19	17	15	14	11	9
18	47	43	39	36	32	29	27	24	22	20	18	16	15	13	12	10	8
19	44	40	36	33	30	27	24	22	20	18	16	14	13	11	10	8	6
20	41	37	34	30	27	24	22	20	17	16	14	12	11	10	9	7	5
25	31	27	24	21	18	16	14	12	10	9	7	6	5	5	4	3	2
30	25	21	18	15	13	11	9	7	6	5	4	3	3	2	2	1	1
40	17	13	11	8	6	5	4	3	2	2	1	1	1	1	—	—	—

MORTGAGE REPAYMENT DATA

Items per £1000 invested; where I = Interest, P = Principal repaid, L = Loan outstanding

Loan of	3%			4%			5%			6%			8%			10%		
5 years	I	P	L	I	P	L	I	P	L	I	P	L	I	P	L	I	P	L
1	30	188	812	40	185	815	50	181	819	60	177	823	80	170	830	100	164	836
2	24	194	618	33	192	623	41	190	629	49	188	635	66	184	645	84	180	656
3	19	200	418	25	200	424	31	200	424	38	199	435	52	199	447	66	198	458
4	13	206	212	17	208	216	21	210	220	26	211	224	36	215	232	46	218	240
5	6	212	0	9	216	0	11	220	0	13	224	0	19	232	0	24	240	0
10 years																		
1	30	87	913	40	83	917	50	80	920	60	76	924	80	69	931	100	63	939
2	27	90	823	37	87	830	46	83	837	55	80	844	75	75	856	94	69	868
3	25	93	730	33	90	740	42	88	749	51	85	758	69	81	776	87	76	792
4	22	95	635	30	94	646	37	92	657	46	90	668	62	87	689	79	84	709
5	19	98	537	26	97	549	33	97	561	40	96	572	55	94	595	71	92	617
6	16	101	436	22	101	448	28	101	459	34	102	471	48	101	494	62	101	516
7	13	104	332	18	105	342	23	107	353	28	108	363	39	110	384	52	111	405
8	10	107	224	14	110	233	18	112	241	22	114	249	31	118	266	40	122	282
9	7	111	114	9	114	119	12	117	123	15	121	128	21	128	138	28	134	148
10	3	114	0	5	119	0	6	123	0	8	128	0	11	138	0	15	148	0

MORTGAGE REPAYMENT DATA (CONTINUED)

Loan of 20 years	3%			4%			5%			6%			8%			10%		
	I	P	L	I	P	L	I	P	L	I	P	L	I	P	L	I	P	L
1	30	37	963	40	34	966	50	30	970	60	27	973	80	22	978	100	17	983
5	25	42	802	34	39	818	43	37	833	53	34	847	72	30	872	92	26	893
10	19	49	573	26	48	597	33	47	620	41	46	642	58	44	683	76	41	722
15	11	56	308	15	58	328	20	60	347	26	61	367	38	64	407	51	66	445
20	2	65	0	3	71	0	4	76	0	5	82	0	8	94	0	11	107	0
25 years																		
1	30	27	973	40	24	976	50	21	979	60	18	982	80	14	986	100	10	990
5	27	31	854	36	28	870	45	25	884	55	23	897	75	19	920	95	15	938
10	22	36	686	30	34	712	38	33	736	47	31	760	66	27	802	86	24	838
15	16	41	490	22	42	519	29	41	548	37	41	576	54	40	629	72	39	677
20	9	48	263	13	51	285	18	53	307	23	55	330	35	59	374	48	62	418
25	2	56	0	2	62	0	3	68	0	4	74	0	7	87	0	10	100	0

MORTGAGE REPAYMENT DATA (CONTINUED)

Loan of	4%			5%			6%			8%			10%			12%		
30 years	I	P	L	I	P	L	I	P	L	I	P	L	I	P	L	I	P	L
1	40	18	982	50	15	985	60	13	987	80	9	991	100	6	994	120	4	996
5	37	21	903	47	18	917	57	16	929	77	12	948	97	9	963	118	7	974
10	32	25	786	42	23	811	51	21	833	71	18	872	92	14	903	113	11	927
15	27	31	643	35	30	675	44	29	706	63	26	760	83	23	807	104	20	846
20	20	38	469	27	38	502	34	38	535	51	38	596	69	37	652	88	36	701
25	12	46	257	17	49	282	21	51	306	33	56	355	46	60	402	61	63	448
30	2	56	0	3	62	0	4	69	0	7	82	0	10	96	0	13	111	0
40 years																		
1	40	11	989	50	8	992	60	6	994	80	4	996	100	2	998	120	1	999
5	38	12	943	48	10	954	58	8	964	79	5	977	99	3	986	119	2	992
10	36	15	874	45	13	896	56	11	915	76	8	944	97	5	964	118	4	977
15	32	18	789	42	16	821	52	15	850	73	11	895	94	9	928	115	6	951
20	28	22	687	37	21	726	47	20	762	67	17	823	88	14	871	110	11	906
25	24	27	562	32	27	605	40	26	645	59	24	718	80	22	778	102	20	826
30	18	33	410	24	34	450	31	35	489	48	36	563	66	36	628	86	35	685
35	11	40	225	15	43	252	20	47	280	31	53	335	45	58	388	60	61	437
40	2	49	0	3	56	0	4	63	0	6	78	0	9	93	0	13	108	0

Note—All figures rounded to nearest £.

6. FARM RECORDS

The following records should be kept for management purposes:

BASIC WHOLE FARM FINANCIAL POSITION

1. Cash Analysis Book, fully detailed.
2. Petty Cash Book.
3. Annual Valuation, including physical quantities of
   - i. Harvested crops in store
   - ii. Livestock (breeding and fattening) at (near) market value, less any variable costs yet to be borne.
   - iii. Fertilisers, seeds, sprays, casual labour or contract work applied to growing crops should be recorded, but "cultivations" and manure residues can be ignored for management purposes.
   - iv. Fertiliser, seed, sprays and other sundry direct items in store,
4. Debtors and creditors at the end of the financial year.

OTHER FINANCIAL AND PHYSICAL RECORDS

5. Output (quantities and value) of each crop and livestock enterprise for the "harvest year" (or production cycle). It may be possible to get information of sales from a fully detailed cash analysis book (although, for crops, the financial year figures will then have to be allocated between crops from the current harvest and those from the harvest in the previous financial year in order to check on the accuracy of the opening valuation of crops in store; this is particularly a problem with Michaelmas ending accounts). The following records of internal transfers and consumption will also be required:
   - (a) Numbers and market value of livestock transferred from one livestock category to another, e.g. dairy calves to dairy followers or beef enterprise, or dairy heifers to dairy enterprise.
   - (b) Quantity and market value of cereals fed on farm and used for seed.
   - (c) Quantity and market value of milk and other produce consumed by the farmer or his employees, used on the farm (e.g. milk fed to calves), or sold direct.
6. A monthly record of livestock numbers; preferably reconciled with the previous month according to births, purchases, deaths, sales and transfers.
7. Costs and quantities of concentrate feed to each category of livestock, including home-grown cereals fed on the farm.
8. Allocation of costs of seed, fertiliser, sprays, casual labour and contract work specific to an enterprise. This is in order to calculate gross margins, where required.
9. Breeding record for cows, including bulling dates, date(s) served, type of bull used, pregnancy testing, estimated calving date, actual calving date, and date when dried off.

10. For each crop, total output and yield per hectare, in both quantity and value. Include each field where the crop has been grown and its approximate yield, where this can be satisfactorily obtained.

11. For each field, keep one page to cover a period of say, ten years. Record on this, each year, crop grown, variety sown, fertiliser used, sprays used, date sown, date(s) harvested, approximate yield (if obtainable), and any other special notes that you feel may have significance for the future.

12. A rotation record. On a single page, if possible, list each field down the side and say, ten years along the top. Colour each field-year space according to the crop grown, e.g. barley yellow, potatoes red, etc.

13. It is important to note that other farm records are required for legislative and cross compliance purposes including:

    i. Livestock movements, identification, flock and herd records etc.

    ii. Nitrate Vulnerable Zone (NVZ) records and calculations including livestock loadings, manure storage, fertiliser plans and usage etc.

    iii. Pesticide application and storage records, risk assessments

    iv. Farm waste storage and disposal records and necessary exemptions / permits / transfer certificates

    v. Integrated Pollution and Prevention Controls (IPPC) records (for pig and poultry units)

    vi. Soil Protection reviews and risk assessments

    vii. Financial (HMRC) records including VAT, PAYE, NI etc.

IX. MISCELLANEOUS DATA

1. CONSERVATION COSTS

Note: Costs vary widely, depending on geographical location and the type and size of the job. Markets for such services can be highly localised, sparse in some areas, competitive in others. Also, refer to contracting charges on page 194.

Hedges

Hedge Cutting. Flailing £39.70/hour to £48.20/hour for sawblade cutting (contract charges). Average of 3-5 miles per day depending on trim quality and obstacles.

Hedge Laying (Making hedges stock proof and rejuvenated by selective cutting and positioning). Manual hedge laying approximately 20 to 40m/day depending on hedge thickness (single or double), amount of timber to clear, access to hedge, style of hedge and varieties in hedge. Cost £15.50/metre for dense hedge and less for younger hedges

Hedge Planting. Single row = 3-4 plants per metre, double row 6 plants per metre

- Plants average 54p - £1.36 each (mixed species); spiral guards 40p; canes 16p.
- Labour: Planting up to £2.90-£3.90/metre, professional contractor up to 100-150 metres/day. Preferably October/March.
- Overall from £3.40/metre; unfenced, single width, self-planted;
to £30.00/metre; double width & double rabbit fenced, contract planted.

Hedge Coppicing. By hand: 2 men and a chain saw, £6.35-£7.35 per metre plus burning debris. Contractor: tractor mounted saw, driver and 2 men, 12.5 metres per hour, £44.00/hour.

Devon Hedges. Maintenance, flailing annually and occasional mechanical recasting banks when eroded. Flailing costs as above and recasting with Backhoe excavator £27.00/hr.

Fencing

Fencing (labour and materials): stock proof post and 4-barb £5.00/metre, rabbit proof (dug in) £6.10/metre (per side). Post and 3 rails £14.80/metre

Dry Stone Walls

Dry Stone Walling. Highly variable cost depending on stone type, stone grading availability, structure, vehicular access and local competition (people pay more for private walls in gardens than fields). As a guide: Cost of graded stone from £200/tonne, varying enormously on local stone, type and availability. Some are priced in Square-Face-Yards (about 4SFY per tonne). Cost of wall building is from as low as £45 (highlands) to £250 (Cotswolds) per square metre (normally quoted per square metre but grants awarded per linear metre). Most are around £90-110/m^2. Partial grants might be available in some areas e.g. within National Parks.

Trees

Amenity tree planting; (half acre block or less)

- Transplants average £1.12; shelter plus stake and tie £1.38; stake 58p; whip 85p. Rabbit spiral guard 38p; netlon guard 56p; cane 17p.
- Trees per man day: farmer 200, contractor 400; (large-scale, 33 man days/ha). Optimal time November to April.

Shelter Belts; Per 100 metre length

- 100 large species (oak, lime, etc.) £57; 66 medium species (cherry, birch, etc.) £49; 100 shrubs, £40;
- 166 tree stakes, shelters and ties, £300;
  (site preparation, weed control, labour and fencing extra)

Woodland Establishment.

- Conifers £235/1,000 (2m spacing), broadleaves £460/1000 (3m spacing).
- To supply and plant transplants; conifer £3.40/tree, oak or beech £4.20-£4.70 each, (2-3ft tall) in tubes dependent on shelter size and species.
- Rabbit fencing £6.08/metre (dug in), deer fencing £8.70/metre, deer and rabbit fencing £10.70/metre
- Contract planting labour: Conifers at 2m £1,660/ha; broadleaves at 3m £1,140/ha; forest transplants £320/1,070/ha.

Forestry, General.

- 2-man tree surgery team £570/day
- Contract labour: chain sawing £25/hr,
- Brush cutting £15.60/hr,
- Extracting timber/pulp £5.60-£12.50/tonne,
- Chemical spot weeding 11p-15p/tree, or £3306/hectare
- Rhododendron control range from £750-£2,700/hectare dependant on stem diameter (largest over 7cm) and accessibility.

Pollarding and Tree Surgery.

- Pollard: £105/mature tree; Pollarding: 2 or 3 trees/day. Pollard every 20-40 years.
- Tree surgery from £190/tree. Dependant on size and number. Best in winter.

Ponds and Ditches

Pond Construction. Butyl lining (0.75mm) £6.20/m^2; other linings up to £4.40/m^2. Contract labour: 150 Komatsu £33/hr.; bulldozer D6 LGP £51/hr, 13t 360° excavator £45/hr (excluding haulage), labour £13.00/hr. Flail-mowers from £19.80/hr (machine only). Autumn (dry ground conditions).

Pond Maintenance. Hymac £46/hr.; Backhoe £25.00/hr. 100 m^2/day (contractor). Timing: probably winter; time depends on ground condition and species whose life cycles may be disturbed. Every 15 to 50 years.

Ditch Maintenance. Backhoe excavator £25.00/hr; 13t 360° excavator £45/hr (excluding haulage), labour £13.00/hr. preferably in winter. Every 3 to 7 years on rotation.

Grassland

Permanent Grass Margins at Field Edges. To provide wildlife benefits and help control pernicious weeds, reducing herbicides at the field edge. (A sterile strip provides virtually no wildlife benefit and the initial establishment costs may be offset by savings in maintenance costs in future years.)

Seed costs per 100 metres of seeds as follows.

- 2m grass margins, £3.00-£3.10; (4-6 year ley £150.50/ha)
- 6m grass margins, £9.00-£9.30;
- beetle banks, £7.50 (6m wide) (£5.00/kg, 25kg/ha).

Establishment of Wildlife Grassland Meadow. £200-300/ha for ground preparation, depending on cultivations, weed burden and total area, more for heavy land or exceptional weed burden. Seed costs very variable, but as a guide:

- Native Perennial wild flowers and grasses, £16/kg, 20kg/ha = £320/ha
- Pollen and Nectar mix for bumble bees and butterflies £5.80/kg, 20kg/ha = £116/ha
- Bird Seed sward £4.40/kg, 12kg/ha = £53/ha for single year crop, £4.00/kg, 50kg/ha = £200 for longer sward.
- Single species native grass seeds vary from £3.55/kg (e.g. Creeping Red Fescue) to £60/kg (Sweet Vernal).
- Single species native perennial wild flower seeds vary from £29/kg (Corn Cockle) to £695/kg (Cowslip)
- Buffer strip grass margin mix for cross compliance and agri-environmental features, £4.00/kg drilled at 25kg/ha = £100/ha. Costs of ground preparation and drilling are usually higher than the seed.

Acknowledgement: Thanks to Cotswold Seeds and the Forestry Commission

2. GRASS, FORAGE AND ENVIRONMENTAL SEEDS

SEED PRICES AND SEED RATES

(for 2018)

Crop	Price £/kg	Seed Rate kg/ha		Cost £/ha
Grass Leys				
1 year Westerwolds	£2.50	35		87.5
2 year leys	£2.56	35		89.6
3-4 year leys	£3.80	35		133
4-6 year leys	£4.30	35		150.5
Long-term ley	£4.24	30		127.2
Permanent Grass	£4.86	32.5		157.95
Drought Resistant	£6.35	32.5		106.38
Mixed and Clover Leys				
White Clover ley	£5.00	30		150
Red Clover ley	£4.15	30		124.5
Timothy/M. Fescue ley	£4.60	32.5		149.5
Fodder Crops				
Fodder Kale	£9.80-13.50	5		49-68
Swedes	£42.80	0.7	precision drill	28.96
		4.0	seed drill	172
Stubble Turnips	£3.80	3.75 kg	drilled,	14
		5.0 kg	broadcast	19
Maincrop Turnips	£11.40	3.75 kg	drilled,	43
		5.0 kg	broadcast	57
Rape	£3.10	10		31
Rape/Kale hybrid	£8.00	7.50		60
Mustard	£1.80	15		30
Rape and Turnip mix	£3.62	0.5 kg	rape	
		1.50kg	turnips	7.24
Kale, Swede & Turnips	£14.50	0.6 kg	kale,	
		0.2 kg	swede	
		0.7 kg	turnips	21.75
Cover Mixes, Environmental and Equine				
Game Cover mixture	£3.96	25		99
Game Maize	£4.18	27.5		114.95
Forage Maize: Silage				175
Vetch	£1.48	67		99.16
Quinoa & Kale mix	£9.90	7.5		74.25
Field Corner mixture	£11.45	25		286.25
Horse grazing	£5.60	35		196
Gallop mixture	£3.98	125		497.5

Crop	Price £/kg	Seed Rate kg/ha	Cost £/ha
Individual Varieties			
Westerwold Ryegrass	£2.50	35	87.5
Italian Ryegrass	£2.56	35	89.6
Perennial Ryegrass	£4.30	25 to 40	107.5 - 172
Hybrid Ryegrass	£3.70	35	129.5
Cocksfoot	£5.20	20 to 25	104 - 130
Red Clover Ley	£8.90	15	133.5
White Clover Ley	£9.30	7	65.1
Timothy	£5.00		
Meadow Fescue	£4.70		
Sweet Vernal	£60.00		
Reed Canary Grass	£18.00	7.5	135
Lucerne	£7.40 (inoculated)	20	148
Sainfoin	£2.65	87	230.55
Millet	£2.40	25	60
Sunflower	£4.40	25	110
Sorghum	£3.70	20	74
Countryside Stewardship			
Beetle Bank	£4.98	25	124.5
Buffer Strip	£5.32	25	133
Autumn Sown Bumblebird Mixture	£8.14	30	244
Autumn Sown 2-year Legume Fallow	£6.37	33	210
Flower Rich Margin	£12.68	25	317

COVER AND CATCH CROPS

A 'catch' crop is grown between two 'cash' crops to catch nutrients which might otherwise be lost from weather erosion. A cover crop is grown over winter to protect and enrich soil. Catch and cover crops can be used to help meet Ecological Focus Area (EFA) obligations as part of the Basic Payment scheme's Greening requirements in England and Scotland.

	Establishment Deadline	*Minimum Retention Date*
Catch Crops	31 August of scheme year	1 October of scheme year
Cover Crops	31 October of scheme year	15 January of following year

For Greening, cover and catch crops must consist of both a cereal and a non-cereal species separately from rye, barley, oats, vetch, lucerne, mustard, phacelia and oilseed radish. Undersown grass is also eligible. For more detail on EFAs, refer to page 142. Cover and Catch Crops clearly have a cost of establishment and destruction (although some graze it) and can act as a green bridge, resulting in a build-up of pests. But they also have several benefits:

- Correcting soil C:N ratio (see below)
- Fixing soil nitrogen
- Increasing soil organic matter which helps to retain soil nutrients and moisture facilitating crop establishment and higher yields for following crops
- Improving soil structure, which reduces cultivation requirements
- Providing a canopy to reduce soil erosion and slow nutrient loss
- slowing leaching of nutrients (eutrophication) and volatilisation of nitrogen compounds

A C:N ratio compares the ratio of carbon to nitrogen in organic matter. The ideal C:N for soil is 24:1. The ratio for wheat straw and microorganisms is 80:1 and 8:1 respectively. Thus, land farmed for cereals crops often has a C:N above optimum, and leafy crops help to reduce it. Fertiliser does the same but at a cost.

Crop	Seed Cost £/kg	Seed Rate kg/ha	Cost £/ha
Black Oats*	1.60	25	40
Forage Rye*	0.95	40	38
White Mustard*	1.84	12	22
Lucerne*	6.40	25	160
Phacelia*	3.50	10	35
Vetch*	1.48	25	37
Clover	5.00	10-15	50 - 75
Radish	2.45	12	29
Oilseed Radish*	8.40	12-15	100 - 126

**EFA Cover and Catch Crop Compliant*

3. FIELD DRAINAGE

Field drainage has been over-looked in recent years. Most agricultural land has been drained at some point, although some will have been over 100 years ago (clay pipes). Much was re-drained in the 1960's and 1970's when generous grants assisted with the capital cost. Despite the age of some of these systems, many still function, although require regular maintenance. This may include clearing out-falls, ditches, or field drains (jetting).

The costs of installing drains per metre shown below include the cost of operating a trenching machine, supplying and laying perforated plastic pipe to an average depth of 800mm by trencher with 40/20mm cleaned washed porous fill (drainage stone) laid over the pipe to within 375mm of the surface:

60 mm diameter	£4.50 - £5.00/metre
80 mm diameter	£5.50 - £6.00/metre
100 mm diameter	£7.50 - £7.75/metre
160 mm diameter	£9.50 - £11.50/metre

In some soil types (very rare), soil can be used as backfill. This could save £2.50-£3.50 per metre in cost depending upon the depth of the trench required to get the falls correct and the type of drainage stone selected. However, porous backfill improves the effectiveness of drains by keeping the openings in the pipe clear and enabling fast penetration of water into the drain. The choice to use permeable backfill should depend on soil type not cost. The above rates apply to comprehensive schemes of 4 hectares or more. Smaller areas and patching up work can cost up to 50% more due to the cost of transporting and tracking trenching equipment across fields for small areas of work. Patching up / repairing old drainage systems is common practise as a cheaper alternative to new comprehensive systems. 100mm diameter drainage pipe costs approximately £1 per metre.

Digging new open ditches (1.8m top width, 1.25m depth) costs £2.20-£3.00 per metre compared with improving existing ditches at £1.20 to £1.80 per metre depending on the amount of material that needs to be removed. However, most contractors charge on an hourly basis for this work with a 360 digger at approximately £37/hour.

Mole draining costs in the region of £65-£100 per hectare (see contractor charges). Mole draining is effectively a secondary drainage method which is used where a drainage system already exists. The mole plough creates a cavity for the water to travel through. This practise is best suited to heavy land / clay based soils, where mole cavities will remain in place for some time.

Total Costs per hectare for complete schemes vary on the distance between laterals, soil type, area to be drained, region of the country and the time of year when the work is to be undertaken. The cost of a scheme with 20m spacing between laterals and using permeable backfill will typically be in the range of £2,200 to £3,200 per hectare (£900-£1,300 per acre). Comprehensive schemes using little / no permeable backfill cost about £1,300 - £1,800 per hectare. Backfilling with soil, rather than with permeable material (washed gravel), may reduce the cost by almost half but is only possible on certain soil types. Certain soil types which are particularly suitable for mole drainage may permit spacing between laterals to be increased to 40m or even 60-80m in some instances. Where this is possible costs will be reduced proportionately.

Acknowledgement: thanks to Rob Burtonshaw 01926 651540

4. FERTILISER

FERTILISER PRICES

Compounds	Analysis			Price Per Tonne
	N	**P_2O_5**	**K_2O**	**£**
	0	26	26	272
	0	24	24	252
	0	18	36	267
	0	20	30	253
	0	30	15	250
	0	30	20	271
	5	24	24	280
	8	24	24	296
	10	26	26	327
	11	15	20	243
	13	13	20	242
	15	15	20	265
	16	16	16	260
	22	4	14	214
	20	10	10	222
	25	5	5	199
	26	0	15	217

Straights	Price per tonne £
Ammonium Nitrate: UK (34.5% N)	190
Ammonium Nitrate: Imported (34.5% N)	182
NS grade: UK (27% N, 30% SO_3)	178
Sulphate of Ammonia (21% N, 60% SO_3)	175
Urea (46% N.): granular/ prills	253
Liquid Nitrogen (26% N, 5% SO_3)	148
Triple Superphosphate (TSP) (46% P_2O_5)	270
DAP (18/46/0)	351
Muriate of Potash (MOP) (60% K_2O)	250

Average price (p) per kg:			
	N :	55.1	(UK AN)
	P_2O_5 :	58.7	(TSP)
	K_2O :	41.7	(MOP)

The prices above are for fertiliser delivered in 600kg bags; delivery in bulk averages £7.00/tonne less; collection of bags by farmers £8/tonne less. They are based on forward prices in October 2017 and spring 2018; they vary according to area and bargaining power. They assume delivery in 25-27 tonne loads; add approximately £4.30/tonne for 10 tonne loads, £8.70 for 6-9 tonne loads, £20 for 4-5 tonne loads.

FERTILISER VALUE OF SLURRY & MANURE

Nutrient Values of Common Farm Yard Manure Types

		(kg N/t)	*(kg P_2O_5/t)*		*(kg K_2O/t)*	
	Dry Matter %	Total N*	Total P	*Available P*	Total K	*Available K*
Cattle FYM	25	6.0	3.2	*1.9*	9.4	*8.5*
Pig FYM	25	7.0	6.0	*3.6*	8.0	*7.2*
Sheep FYM	25	7.0	3.2	*1.9*	8.0	*7.2*
Duck FYM	25	6.5	5.5	*3.3*	7.5	*6.8*
Horse FYM	25	5.0	5.0	*3.0*	6.0	*5.4*
Goat FYM	40	9.5	4.5	*2.7*	12.0	*10.8*

FYM = Farmyard Manure

* Crop-available nitrogen depends on application timing, and time taken to incorporate, but RB209-2017 quotes 10% of total N in most conditions, 10-50% for poultry.

** Refer to RB209 for different dry matter FYMs.

Note: these nutrient contents are for guidance only and will vary between different livestock systems and storage methods. Analysis should be performed to understand the specific values of manure.

Source: RB209-2017

Manure Output per Head during the Housing Period

	Undiluted Excreta t or m³	Total Kg *N*	Total Kg *P_2O_5*	Total Kg *K_2O*
1 dairy cow ~ *6,000 to 9,000 litres milk yield*	11.6	60	26	46
1 beef cow ~ *>500 kg*	8.2	41	15.5	33
1 finishing pig ~ *per place ~ 86% occupancy*	1.6	10.6	5.6	5.6
1,000 broiler hens ~ *per hen place ~ 85% occupancy*	19	330	220	340

Note: These figures should not be used for calculating NVZ compliance as they only allow for the time spent in the buildings and therefore exclude manure deposited in fields during grazing. Refer to the DEFRA NVZ guidance booklets for NVZ calculation methodology and annual manure output tables.

LIME

Prices average around £23.50 delivered and spread per tonne with an application rate of 6 tonnes per hectare per application, typically every 4 years, or 1.25 tonnes per hectare of arable land per year.

Lime price varies according to type of dressing, grade of mineral (such as particle size and consistency), location and ease of spreading and could be as low as £2.50 per tonne ex-quarry to £26 ex-quarry. A short haul would cost about £5.50 and spreading approximately £4.75 per tonne, adding about £10 to the ex-quarry cost.

BIOSOLIDS (SEWAGE SLUDGE)

Biosolids act as good soil conditioner and fertiliser to farmers, whilst providing the most environmentally favourable method for water companies to dispose of the sludge. Biosolids vary in nutritional composition depending on processing and location, but RB209 (2017) describes its content as follows:

Biosolid Key Composition

	Digested Cake	Thermally Dried Pellets	Lime Stabilised
Dry Matter	25%	95%	25%
Total Nitrogen *kg/t*	*11*	*40*	*8.5*
Total Phosphate (kg P_2O_5/t)	*11*	*55*	*7*
Total Potash (kg K_2O /t)	*0.6*	*2*	*0.8*
Available N *kg/t (10-20%)*	1.6	6	1.2
Available P_2O_5 *kg/t*	5.5	28	3.5
Available K_2O *kg/t*	0.5	1.8	0.4
Available SO_3 *kg/t*	8.2	23	7.4
Guideline Price £/t applied*	£5.00	£35	£5.00

Nutrient data taken from Fertiliser Manual RB209 (2017)
** Prices can be much lower depending on region and Water Company.*

Application rates vary according to terrain, soil analysis and plant need, but an application of 25 tonnes dry solids per hectare is the typical maximum rate. Thermally dried and lime stabilised cakes are far less common than digested cake. A Biosolids Assurance Scheme coming into use in coming months is expected to make the product considerably more acceptable for use on land used to grow grains for high-value processing which has not been the case in many firms to now.

COMPOST

The new RB209 (2017) has a detailed section on the nutrient value of compost. It summarises typical nutrient values of green compost (non-food) as follows:

	Green Compost
Dry Matter	60%
Total Nitrogen *kg/t*	*7.5*
Total Phosphate (kg P_2O_5/t)	*3.0*
Total Potash (kg K_2O /t)	*6.8*
Available N *kg/t (10-20%)*	0.0
Available P_2O_5 *kg/t*	1.5
Available K_2O *kg/t*	5.4
Guideline value £/t applied	£3.15

It sensibly points out that nutrient provided by compost (or other organic matter) probably won't precisely match the nutrient requirement of the following crop so all added nutrient might not have the same economic value. Equally, some other fertiliser might still be required. RB209 also comments on typical figures for food compost and digestate from anaerobic digestion, entire and separated.

5. AGROCHEMICALS

AGROCHEMICAL COSTS

Names of the active ingredients are given below, with their principal use. These materials should be applied in accordance with the manufacturers' recommendations. Application rates vary and there are differences between the prices of various proprietary brands. The list is not intended to be exhaustive and there is no implied criticism of materials omitted.

The variation in costs per hectare is because of varying application rates rather than price variation between suppliers. It is priced on the purchase of chemical alone, i.e., not the agronomy service.

Crop	Function		Material	Cost £/ha per application
Cereals	Herbicides	General	Mecoprop-P	6.30 - 14.49
			Tri-allate	40.20
			Flufenacet & Pendimethalin	24.66 - 49.32
			Metsulfuron-methyl	16.73
			Mesosulfuron & Iodosulfuron	35.65
			Diflufenican	3.56 - 5.94
			Flufenacet & diflufenican	17.10 - 34.20
			Flupyrsulfuron-methyl & thifensulfuron-me	23.94
		Cleavers	Fluroxypyr	4.58 - 6.10
			Amidosulfuron	18.25
			Florasulam & Fluroxypyr	14.32 - 21.48
		Wild Oats	Pinoxaden & Cloquintocet-mexyl	22.25 - 57.85
		Wild Oats & Blackgrass	Clodinafop-propargyl	8.80 - 13.75
			Fenoxaprop-P-ethyl	1.32 - 2.06
			Flurasulam & Pyroxsulam	17.55 - 23.40
	Growth Regulator		Chlormequat	1.90 - 3.80
			2-chloroethylphosphonic acid	5.75 - 11.49
			2-chloroethylphosphonic acid + Mepiquat Chloride	10.74 - 21.48
			Trinexapac-ethyl	5.20 - 10.40
	Fungicides		Azoxystrobin	30.30
			Fenpropimorph	15.68 - 20.90
			Epoxiconazole	9.75 - 13.00
			Tebuconazole 250gm	6.15 - 8.20
			Prothioconazole	18.08 - 36.16
			Chlorothalonil	5.10 - 7.65
			Epoxiconazole & Boscalid	25.50
			Pyraclostrobin	6.90 - 13.80
			Prothioconazole & bixafen	33.50 - 41.88

Crop	Function	Material	Cost £/ha per application
		Epoxiconazole & Fluxapyroxad	31.53 - 39.41
		Epixiconazole & Metcanzole	34.00
		Epoxiconazole & Isopyrazam	25.50 - 34.00
		Chlorothalonil & Propiconazole	12.00 - 24.00
		Bixafen, Fluopyram & Prothioconazole	45.60 - 57.00
		Benzovindiflupyr & Prothioconazole	28.50 - 38.00
	Seed Dressing		
		Prothioconazole & Clothianidin	13.75 - 22.00
		Silthiofam	24.38 - 39.00
	Aphicide	Pirimicarb	10.92
		Lambda-Cyhalothrin	3.40
	Slug Killer	Metaldehyde 3%	
		Mini slug pellet	11.55 - 16.17
		Durum pellet	6.90 - 8.05
		Ferric-Phosphate	15.85 - 22.19
Oilseed Rape	Herbicides	Propyzamide	23.73
		Metazachlor	17.10 - 28.50
		Clomazone	16.56
		Aminopyralid & Propyzamide	36.04 - 42.40
	Insecticide	Deltamethrin	4.70
		Pirimicarb	10.92 - 16.38
		Cyhalothrin	1.20
		Alphacypermethrin	3.31 - 6.58
		Lambda-Cyhalothrin	5.03
	Fungicide	Iprodione & Thiophanate-methyl	24.44 - 36.66
		Tebuconazole	4.10 - 8.20
		Metconazole	20.00
		Boscalid	17.69 - 35.37
	Dessicant	Glyphosate	5.85
Potatoes	Herbicides:	Metribuzin	13.19 - 26.37
		Prosulfucarb	19.50 - 32.50
		Diquat	6.00 - 12.00
		Clomazone	17.63
	Blight Control	Cymoxanil & Mancozeb	10.40
		Fluazinam	8.70
		Mancozeb & Metalaxyl	38.00
	Insectaicides		
	Nematodes	Fosthiazate	240 - 480
	Haulm Dessicant	Diquat	25.48

Crop	Function		Material	Cost £/ha per application
			Cyazofamid	18.50
Sugar Beet				
	Herbicides:	Pre-emergence	Chloridazon:	12.25 - 50.0
			Band Spray (1/3 rate)	7.08 - 16.65
		Post-emergence	Phenmedipham:	6.69 - 11.15
			Metamitron	2.36 - 5.54
			Triflusulfuron-methyl	23.04
	Insecticide		Pirimicarb	10.92
Beans	Herbicide		Bentazone	67.91
			Pendimethalin	13.50 - 16.20
			Clomazone	16.56
	Fungicide		Chlorothalonil	15.30
			Tebuconazole	8.20
			Azoxystrobin	30.30
Peas and Beans				
	Herbicide		Pendimethalin & Imazamox	47.56
	Insecticide		Pirimicarb	10.92
			Lambda-Cyhalothrin	5.03
Maize	Herbicide		Nicosulfuron	13.50 - 20.25
			Bromoxynil	22.68
			Mesotrione	28.00
Brassicas	Herbicides		Metazachlor	18.71
			Pyridate	69.62
Broadleaved Grass weeds and volunteer Crops				
	Cereals		Fluazifop-P-butyl	21.60 - 32.40
			Clethodim	21
			Propaquizafop	12.78 - 27.39
			Cycloxydim	26.69 - 44.49
Grassland	Herbicides		MCPA	10.50 - 17.50
General	Weed and Grass Killer			
	Couch Grass Control		Glyphosate	5.85 - 9.00
			Clopyralid & Fluroxypyr + MCPA	39.24 - 78.48

The above prices are based on retail prices paid by farmers (August 2016) and reflect the discounts available where there are competing products from several manufacturers. The range in prices per hectare reflects the varying application rates.

Average rates for agronomy only are £12.75/ha for cereals or maize only and rising to £21-£32/ha for potatoes and other vegetable and perishable crops.

Acknowledgement: Thanks to Bartholomew's

AGROCHEMICAL RATES

This table summarises the agrochemical spend for the main crops in Chapter 2, with a breakdown of what each figure is comprised of. Clearly the variation can be considerable between soil-types, regions, farms and even fields, but this offers a starting point from which individual costings can be derived.

	Herb-icides	Fung-icides	Insect-icides	PGR	Other	Total Ag-chemical
Feed Winter Wheat	98	116	7	17	5	244
Milling Winter Wheat	98	121	7	17	9	252
Second F. Wheat	108	121	7	17	5	259
Spring Wheat	62	53	7	17	5	144
Winter Feed Barley	77	79	7	17	5	186
Winter Malting Barley	77	79	7	17	5	186
Spring Malting Barley	62	53	7	17	5	144
Winter Oats	57	44	7	17	5	131
Spring Oats	36	34	7	9	5	91
Winter Oilseed Rape	108	76	7	17	14	223
Spring Oilseed Rape	52	55	7	17	14	145
Winter Beans	62	47	7	0	10	126
Spring Beans	62	42	11	0	10	124
Blue Peas	77	53	11	0	10	150
Marrowfats	67	92	11	0	16	186
Maincrop Potatoes	31	189	48	0	480	748
Early Potatoes	16	98	25	0	249	388
Sugar Beet	165	47	11	0	16	239

6. SEED

DRILLING RATES

	Thousand Grain Weight (g/1000 grains)												
Seeds Planted per m²	**35**	**38**	**41**	**44**	**47**	**50**	**53**	**56**	**59**	**62**	**65**	**68**	**71**
150	53	57	62	66	71	75	80	84	89	93	98	102	107
175	61	67	72	77	82	88	93	98	103	109	114	119	124
200	70	76	82	88	94	100	106	112	118	124	130	136	142
225	79	86	92	99	106	113	119	126	133	140	146	153	160
250	88	95	103	110	118	125	133	140	148	155	163	170	178
275	96	105	113	121	129	138	146	154	162	171	179	187	195
300	105	114	123	132	141	150	159	168	177	186	195	204	213
325	114	124	133	143	153	163	172	182	192	202	211	221	231
350	123	133	144	154	165	175	186	196	207	217	228	238	249
375	131	143	154	165	176	188	199	210	221	233	244	255	266
400	140	152	164	176	188	200	212	224	236	248	260	272	284
425	149	162	174	187	200	213	225	238	251	264	276	289	302
450	158	171	185	198	212	225	239	252	266	279	293	306	320

Measured in Kg/Ha

SEED ROYALTY RATES

Seed Royalty rates for autumn 2017 and spring 2018

	£/ha	£/tonne
Wheat	8.44	47.17
Winter Barley	7.76	45.10
Spring Barley	9.47	50.08
Oats	5.85	37.96
Peas	9.94	41.42
Beans	13.16	57.47
Oilseed Rape	10.14	2,281
Linseed	4.78	97.53
Triticale	8.73	46.66

Seed purchased from a merchant includes a royalty for the seed breeder. Farmers who home save seed are legally obliged to pay the royalty irrespective of the purpose of the sowing (e.g. includes cover crops). If seed is cleaned and dressed, the royalty is taken at this point (per tonne), if not, the farmer is responsible for paying (per hectare). Some older varieties no longer have royalty charges. It is illegal to sell or buy seed (such as between farmers) unless licensed. View eligible varieties at BSPB website

HOME SAVED SEED COSTS

	Value of Old Crop £/t	*Cleaning & Dressing £/t*	*Testing £/t*	*Royalty £/t*	*Total Cost £/t*
Feed Wheat	140	78	1.20	47	**266**
Milling Wheat	146	78	1.20	47	**272**
Spring Wheat	146	84	1.00	47	**278**
Winter Feed Barley	126	84	2.40	45	**258**
Winter Malting Barley	140	84	2.40	45	**271**
Spring Malting Barley	148	84	2.40	50	**284**
Winter Oats	130	87	4.70	38	**260**
Spring Oats	130	87	4.40	38	**259**
Winter Rape	310	4,450	74.8	2281	**7,116**
Spring Rape	310	4,450	137	2281	**7,178**
Winter Beans	170	57	2.50	57	**287**
Spring Beans	175	57	2.50	57	**292**
Blue Peas	200	52	3.10	41	**297**
Marrowfats	225	62	4.10	83	**374**

The old crop seed is from 2017 harvest. Cleaning and dressing figures are based on costs for a mobile cleaner on a 350 hectare farm, and likely amounts of seeds required for each crop (the lower the tonnage, the higher the cost). Single purpose or basic seed treatments included. Testing costs assume a single test (one variety) per species (Germination only; £36/test). Royalty rates as above.

7. FEED

FEED PRICES

Prices are delivered May-October 2018 set in July 2017; there is a range of differences in the ingredients and delivery destinations. For hauls over 10 miles in 25 tonne loads. Additional farm delivered cost for bags ranges from £22 to £30 per tonne.

			£/tonne
Cattle	Dairy:	High Energy Parlour (21% CP)	215
		Dairy Concentrate 41%	250
		Medium Energy Blend (18% CP)	195
	Beef	Pellets (16% CP)	210
		Concentrate (34% CP)	240
	Calf	Milk Substitute (bags)	1,800
		High Fat Replacer (bags)	1,600
		Calf Weaner Pellets.	275
		Calf Rearer Nuts (16% CP)	212
Sheep	High Energy Lamb Pellets (17% CP)		240
	Medium Energy Sheep Feed (16% CP)		210
	Lamb Finisher Nuts		205
	H.E.Ewe Feed 19%		220
Horses	Horse and Pony Pencils/Cubes (bags)		325
Pigs	Sow Nuts (17% CP)		230
	Early Grower Pellets (22% CP)		270
	Grower/Finisher Pellets (19% protein)		240
	Sow Concentrate (43% CP)		300
	Grower Concentrate (45% CP)		305
Poultry	Chick Crumbs		270
	Layers Pellets 18%		240
	Broiler Grower Feed		300
	Turkey Grower Feed		270
Straight Feeds	Fishmeal (66/70% CP)		1,100
	Soya Bean Meal (Hipro; 50% CP)		290
	Rapeseed Meal (34-36% CP)		190
	Palm Kernel Meal/Cake (17% CP)		115
	Sunflower Seed (30/33% CP)		150
	Soya Hull Pellets		135
	Wheatfeed Meal (14-18% CP)		115
	Wheatfeed Pellets (14-18% CP)		120
	Maize Gluten (19-20% CP)		155
	Molasses (Cane) (5% CP)		200
	Sugar Beet Pulp (Molassed Nuts/Pellets)		155

Feed Prices (Continued)	*£/tonne*
Distillers Wheat Pellets	175
Distillers Maize Pellets	170
Maize (Whole)	175
Wheat (May / June)	156
Barley (May / June)	137
Beans (May / June)	184

FEEDSTUFF NUTRITIVE VALUES

Typical Energy and Protein Contents of Some Common Feeds and cost per unit

Type of Feeds	£/T	Dry Matter g/kg	ME MJ/kg DM	CP g/kg DM	p/kg DM	p/MJ ME	p/g CP
Forages:							
Barley Straw	65	860	7	10	7.56	1.08	0.76
Grass Silage (typical clamp)	22	250	10.8	150	8.85	0.82	0.06
Hay (typical meadow)	55	850	8.8	100	6.51	0.74	0.07
Maize Silage	19	300	11	90	6.35	0.58	0.07
Pasture (rotational grazed)	4	180	11.5	160	2.49	0.22	0.02
Whole-crop Wheat (fermented)	37	350	10.5	95	10.48	1.00	0.11
Cereals:							
Barley (home grown *)	120	860	13.2	120	13.95	1.06	0.12
Oats (home grown *)	120	860	12.5	120	13.95	1.12	0.12
Wheat (home grown *)	130	860	13.6	130	15.12	1.11	0.12
Maize	150	880	13.8	90	17.05	1.24	0.19
Roots:							
Fodder Beet	6	180	12	60	3.48	0.29	0.06
Potatoes	30	200	13.3	100	15.00	1.13	0.15
Wet By-Products:							
Brewers Grains	35	260	11.5	250	13.46	1.17	0.05
Straights:							
Cane Molasses	200	750	12.7	40	26.67	2.10	0.67
Distillers Maize Grains	170	900	14	310	18.89	1.35	0.06
Distillers Wheat Grains	175	900	13.5	340	19.44	1.44	0.06
Dried Molassed Sugar Beet Pulp	155	900	12.5	100	17.22	1.38	0.17
Field Beans	160	880	13.3	290	18.18	1.37	0.06
Maize Gluten Feed	180	880	12.8	210	20.45	1.60	0.10
Palm Kernel Meal	135	900	11.4	200	15.00	1.32	0.08
Wheat-feed	95	880	11.3	190	10.80	0.96	0.06

* Home grown feed should be costed to the livestock enterprise at the value the grain could otherwise be sold at, i.e. the opportunity cost of the crop.

8. AGRISTATS

These basic agricultural statistics relate to the UK farming and food sectors. The main source of data is the Defra Publication 'Agriculture in the UK 2016'. All figures are for the UK and relate to the 2016 year unless otherwise stated.

INDUSTRY STRUCTURE

Agriculture's Economic Contribution	UK	England	Wales	Scotland	N.I.
Gross Output (£m)	23,149	17,116	1,447	2,829	1,758
Total Income from Farming* (£m)	3,610	2,460	157	749	244
Agriculture's Share of the Economy**	0.51%	0.47%	0.69%	0.86%	1.02%
Agriculture's Share of Employment	1.35%	1.02%	3.63%	2.31%	5.50%

* *Total Income from Farming (TIFF) is essentially the profit of the farming sector. These are provisional figures.*

** *Based on agriculture's share of gross value-added – 2015 data.*

The wider agri-food sector (including farming, food manufacturing, wholesaling, retailing and catering) contributed £110bn or 6.6% to national gross value-added in 2015, and employed 3.9 million people, 13.2% of the total UK workforce. Total consumer' expenditure on food, drink and catering was £203bn.

Agricultural Workforce	2012	2014	2015	2016
Regular Full-time	*73,000*	72,000	73,000	-
Regular Part-time*	*44,000*	43,000	43,000	-
Seasonal, Casual and Gang	67,000	66,000	67,000	-
Salaried Managers	11,000	11,000	-	-
Total Employees	183,000	181,000	183,000	176,000
Farmers, Partners Directors and Spouses				
Full-time	141,000	140,000	142,000	139,000
Part-time*	158,000	155,000	152,000	151,000
Farmers, Partners Directors & Spouses	298,000	294,000	294,000	290,000
Total Labour Force	481,000	476,000	476,000	466,000

* *Part-time is less than 39 hours in England and Wales, less than 38 hours in Scotland and less than 30 hours in Northern Ireland.*

***UK Farmed Areas** '000 Hectares*

	2000	**2010**	**2014**	***2015***	***2016***	***2017 Est*****
Wheat	2,086	1,939	1,936	1,832	1,823	1,795
Barley	1,128	922	1,080	1,101	1,122	1,150
Oats	109	124	137	131	141	140
Mixed Corn, Triticale, Rye	25	29	26	35	45	36
Total Cereals (excl. maize)	**3,348**	**3,014**	**3,179**	**3,099**	**3,132**	**3,121**
Oilseed Rape	332	642	675	652	579	553
Linseed	72	44	15	15	27	30
Peas (harvested dry)	84	42	32	44	51	52
Field Beans	124	166	107	170	177	170
Potatoes	166	138	141	129	139	145
Sugar Beet	173	118	116	90	86	103
Veges & Salad grown in open	117	119	116	123	112	112
Top & Soft Fruit	38	34	33	36	35	34
Other Horticulture	16	14	15	16	14	16
Maize	104	164	183	187	194	200
Other Arable Crops	75	102	109	116	120	112
Bare Fallow	533	174	160	214	262	230
Total Tillage	**5,182**	**4,771**	**4,881**	**4,891**	**4,928**	**4,878**
Temporary Grass (<5 years)	1,226	1,232	1,396	1,167	1,144	1,130
Total Arable	**6,408**	**6,003**	**6,277**	**6,058**	**6,072**	**6,008**
Permanent Grass (>5 years)	5,364	5,925	5,824	6,078	6,118	6,053
Total Grass*	6,590	7,157	7,220	7,245	7,262	7,183
Total Tillage & Grass*	**11,772**	**11,928**	**12,101**	**12,136**	**12,190**	**12,061**
Sole Right Rough Grazing	4,445	4,055	3,930	3,801	3,961	3,880
Common Rough Grazing	1,228	1,228	1,199	1,199	1,199	1,194
Total Rough Grazing	**5,673**	**5,283**	**5,129**	**5,000**	**5,160**	**5,074**
Land for Outdoor Pigs	0	10	8	9	10	10
Utilisable Agric.l Area (UAA)	**17,445**	**17,221**	**17,238**	**17,145**	**17,360**	**17,145**
Woodland	499	773	897	961	978	988
Other Land on agric.l holdings	279	274	318	320	323	325
Total Agricultural Area	**18,223**	**18,268**	**18,453**	**18,426**	**18,661**	**18,458**

* *Excluding Rough Grazing*

** *2017 Estimate provided by The Andersons Centre*

The Utilisable Agricultural Area (UAA) comprises around 71% of the total UK land area. Of the remaining 29%, 4% is woodland and other land on agricultural holdings. The 25% of 'non-agricultural' land broadly splits equally between forest land, urban areas and 'other' land uses. The latter category includes villages, small towns, transport infrastructure, non-urban wasteland, and inland water. The total UK land area is approximately 24.3 million hectares.

Livestock Numbers

'000 Head		2005	2010	2015	2016	2017
Total Cattle and Calves		**10,770**	**10,170**	**9,919**	**10,033**	**10,133**
of which:	Dairy Cows	1,998	1,830	1,895	1,897	1,890
	Beef Cows	1,751	1,668	1,576	1,596	1,576
Total Sheep and Lambs		**35,416**	**31,084**	**33,337**	**33,942**	**33,244**
of which:	Female Breeding	16,935	14,740	16,024	16,304	16,504
Total Pigs		**4,862**	**4,460**	**4,739**	**4,865**	**4,950**
of which:	Female Breeding	470	427	408	415	425
Poultry		**173,909**	**163,867**	**167,579**	**172,607**	**174,399**
of which:	Table Fowl	111,475	105,309	107,056	110,639	111,639
	Laying Flock	49,034	47,107	49,509	50,798	51,560
	Other Poultry	13,400	11,451	11,014	11,170	11,200
Farmed Deer		33	31	*32*	*32*	*32*
Goats		96	93	100	*100*	*100*

Historic data from Defra June Survey, 2017 forecasts by The Andersons Centre

Size Distribution of 'commercial' Holdings - 2016

By Area on Holding	Holdings - '000	Area - '000 Ha	% of Holdings	% of Area
Under 20 hectares	101	726	46.3	4.1
20 to 50 hectares	43	1,428	19.7	8.1
50 to 100 hectares	32	2,316	14.7	13.2
100 hectares and over	41	12,994	18.8	74.4
Total	218	17,463	100	100

Average Size of Enterprises

Hectares	2005	2011	*Number*	2005	2011
Cereals (excl. maize)	49.4	59.0	Dairy Cows	68	80
Oilseed Rape	34.4	46.6	Beef Cows	27	28
Potatoes	11.6	15.2	Breeding Sheep	217	218
Sugar Beet	20.3	23.6	Breeding Pigs	80	72
			Broilers	37,953	42,692

Data not updated since 2011.

Age of Farm Holders	2000	2005	2007	2010	2013
Under 35 years	5	3	3	3	3
35-44 years	18	14	12	11	10
45-54 years	26	23	23	25	25
55-64 years	26	29	29	29	28
65 years and over	25	31	33	3332	34
Median age	56	58	59	59	59

DEFRA data. Does not measure amount of farming controlled by each age group, or who the active decision maker is.

FINANCE

Total Income From Farming (TIFF)

	Real terms, 2016 prices		Current Values	
	Total Income from Farming	TIFF per Entrepreneur *	Total Income from Farming	TIFF per Entrepreneur *
	£ Million	£	£ Million	£
1990	3 401	13 252	1 827	7 100
1991	3 418	13 430	1 958	7 700
1992	4 498	17 759	2 662	10 500
1993	6 208	24 698	3 768	15 000
1994	6 771	27 278	4 161	16 800
1995	7 788	31 904	4 904	20 100
1996	6 849	28 387	4 487	18 600
1997	3 949	16 511	2 647	11 100
1998	2 676	11 379	1 821	7 700
1999	2 756	12 078	1 897	8 300
2000	1 948	8 857	1 372	6 200
2001	1 992	9 281	1 418	6 600
2002	2 607	12 394	1 902	9 000
2003	3 328	16 169	2 494	12 100
2004	2 988	14 768	2 304	11 400
2005	2 762	13 793	2 193	11 000
2006	2 670	13 435	2 183	11 000
2007	2 861	14 503	2 403	12 200
2008	4 446	22 779	3 844	19 700
2009	4 550	23 646	4 016	20 900
2010	4 226	22 023	3 826	19 900
2011	5 434	27 959	5 043	25 900
2012	4 895	25 175	4 620	23 800
2013	5 585	28 991	5 367	27 900
2014	5 297	27 479	5 285	27 400
2015	3 903	20 206	3 769	19 500
2016	3 610	18 816	3 610	18 816

** TIFF per full-time entrepreneur equivalent. DEFRA Data*

TIFF is Total Income From Farming. It is the business profits plus remuneration to farmers, partners and directors and others with an entrepreneurial interest in the business. It is calculated on a calendar year basis and is the main aggregate measure of UK farming's income (profitability). There are no imputed charges (such as a rental value for owned land or value of the farmer's own labour).

Average English Farm Business Income (FBI) (Real Terms 2016/17 Prices)

Farm Type	*2013/14*	*2014/15*	*2015/16*	*2016/17 (prov.)*
Cereals	51,400	46,000	36,000	*38,000*
General Cropping	70,100	53,000	63,600	*77,500*
Dairy	91,100	85,500	44,600	*22,500*
Grazing L'stock (Lowland)	15,600	18,900	12,200	*19,000*
Grazing Livestock (LFA)	15,000	14,900	19,300	*24,500*
Specialist Pigs	67,600	50,400	22,000	*57,000*
Specialist Poultry	163,000	129,500	108,200	*74,000*
Mixed	30,700	22,000	18,700	*29,000*

FBI is the main farm-level measure of farming income (profitability). It is similar to TIFF but is based on a March to February year and calculated per farm rather than aggregated for TIFF.

TIFF Accounts - Inputs and Outputs *(2016)*

Inputs	**£m**	***Outputs***	**£m**	*%*
Animal Feed	4,527	Wheat	1,627	*7.0%*
Seeds	731	Barley	717	*3.1%*
Fertilisers	1,144	Oats and other cereals	90	*0.4%*
Pesticides	978	Oilseed rape	555	*2.4%*
Hired labour	2,541	Potatoes	747	*3.2%*
Depreciation: equipment	1,824	Sugar beet	150	*0.6%*
Depreciation: buildings	1012	Fresh vegetables	1,329	*5.7%*
Depreciation: livestock	1,222	Fruit	668	*2.9%*
Maintenance: materials	951	Plants and flowers	1,202	*5.2%*
Maintenance: buildings	655	Other crops	990	*4.3%*
Fuels	768	Cattle	3,409	*14.7%*
Electricity & heating fuel	367	Sheep	1,457	*6.3%*
Agricultural services	1,089	Pigs	1,103	*4.8%*
Veterinary expenses	457	Poultry	2,511	*10.8%*
Net rent	572	Milk	3,296	*14.2%*
Interest and finance fees	537	Eggs	603	*2.6%*
Other goods and services	3,175	Other livestock	350	*1.5%*
		Other agricultural	1,089	*4.7%*
		Non-ag income	1,257	*5.4%*
Total Inputs	***22,550***	***Total Gross Output***	***23,150***	*100.0%*
Total Income From Farming	3,610	Single P.t/Subsidy	3,010	
Balance	***26,160***	***Total Output***	***26,160***	
		Total crops	4,876	*21.1%*
		Total horticulture.	3,199	*13.8%*
		Total livestock	8,480	*36.6%*
		Livestock products	3,899	*16.8%*
		Other	2,696	*11.6%*

***Balance Sheet of UK Agriculture** (2015 – latest data)*			£m	£m
Assets:	Fixed:	Land	228,085	
		Buildings, plant and machinery	34,052	
		Breeding livestock	5,918	
	Total Fixed Assets:			*268,055*
	Current	Trading livestock	4,259	
		Crops and stores	4,027	
		Debtors and cash deposits	5,726	
	Total Current Assets:			*14,012*
		Total Assets:		***282,067***
Liabilities:	Long term:	Bank and Building Society loans	9,219	
	Med-term:	AMC and SASC	2,011	
		Other (inc. family loans)	510	
		Total Long and Medium Term Liabilities		*11,740*
	Short-term	Bank overdrafts	2,289	
		Trade credit	1,651	
		Hire purchase and leasing	1,482	
		Other	44	
		Total Short-term Liabilities:		*5,466*
		Total Liabilities:		***17,206***
Net Worth:				**264,861**
% Equity (Net worth as a % of Total Assets):				93.90%
Total Income from Farming (TIFF) 2015 as % of				
	a) Net Worth:			1.36%
	b) Total Assets:			1.28%
	c) Tenants Capital:			9.03%

Note: no charge has been made for farmers' own labour or management

PRODUCTIVITY

UK Crop Yields

(tonnes per hectare)	(harvest year) 2010	2011	2012	2013	*2014*	*2015*	*2016*	*Average 10-16*
Wheat	7.7	7.7	6.7	7.4	8.6	9.0	7.9	*7.9*
Barley (all)	5.7	5.7	5.5	5.8	6.4	6.7	5.9	*6.0*
Winter Barley	6.4	6.1	6.4	6.4	7.2	7.7	6.4	*6.7*
Spring Barley	5.2	5.4	5.0	5.7	5.9	6.0	5.6	*5.6*
Oats	5.5	5.6	5.1	5.4	6.0	6.1	5.8	*5.7*
Oilseed Rape	3.5	3.9	3.4	3.0	3.6	3.9	3.1	*3.5*
Linseed	1.6	2.0	1.5	1.8	2.7	1.9	1.8	*1.9*
Field Beans	3.5	3.4	3.3	3.2	4.2	4.4	3.7	*3.7*
Dried Peas	3.5	4.1	2.4	3.7	4.0	4.1	3.7	*3.7*
Potatoes (all)	43.8	47.3	37.0	45.4	47.3	48.6	44.8	*45.1*
Sugar Beet*	55.1	75.4	60.7	72.1	80.1	68.8	66.1	*70.5*

* *Adjusted to 16% sugar*

UK Livestock Output

(kg unless stated)	2011	2012	2013	*2014*	2015	2016	*Average 11-16*
Milk Yield (litres/cow)*	7,563	7,477	7,542	7,897	7,894	7,636	7,668
Beef Carcase Wgt**	345	347	342	*349*	*355*	*351*	*348*
Lamb Carcase Wgt Δ....	19.0	19.1	19.0	*19.0*	*20*	*19*	*19*
Pig Carcase Wgt •	78.0	78.0	79.0	*81.0*	*81.0*	*82*	*80*

* *litres per annum* ** *steers, heifers & young bulls*

Δ *clean sheep and lambs* • *clean pigs*

FOOD

Self Sufficiency* (%)	2003	2015		2003	2015
*All Food ***..................	*64*	*60*	*Indigenous-type Food*	*77*	*76*
Crops:..........................			*Livestock:*		
Wheat	124	102	Beef and Veal.........	70	80
Barley	120	124	Mutton and Lamb...	86	93
Total Cereals................	113	100	Pig-meat................	49	62
Oilseed Rape	108	109	Poultry-meat..........	91	87
Potatoes	82	77	Milk	102	102
Sugar	76	56	Hen Eggs...............	87	85
Fresh Vegetables	63	55			
Fresh Fruit	8	14			

* *ratio of UK production to UK human consumption* ** *2003 and 2016*

Food Spending*	2008	2010	2011	2012	2013	2014
Food and Drink at Home	23.00	24.50	24.92	25.98	26.62	26.27
Eating-Out Expenditure	8.16	8.54	8.79	8.95	9.29	9.41
All food and Drink	31.17	33.04	33.71	34.93	35.92	35.68

* *expenditure on Food and Non-alcoholic Drinks (£ per person per week) DEFRA*

Producers Share*	1990	2000	2010	2012	2013	2014	2015
Basket of Goods....	***43***	***35***	***37***	***39***	***38***	***40***	***40***
Wheat (bread)........	16	10	8	11	11	9	9
Potatoes	31	27	20	22	22	17	14
Carrots	31	38	41	47	44	34	35
Apples	51	40	42	44	37	34	34
Milk......................	35	28	32	35	31	39	38
Beef......................	57	44	48	54	58	50	50
Lamb	57	43	56	53	53	52	52
Pork	55	47	39	40	36	40	40
Chicken.................	44	37	38	39	40	39	40
Eggs......................	36	29	27	31	34	32	32

* *farmer's share of retail price (per cent) DEFRA.*

9. RATE OF INFLATION; PRICE AND COST INDICES

INFLATION DATA

Calendar Year	RPI*: % yearly change	RPI: Index 1987=100	CPI** % yearly change	CPI Index 2015=100	*Agricultural Prices Index, 2010 = 100* *Outputs*	*Inputs*
1988	4.9	107	-	50	69.4	53.0
1989	7.8	115	5.2	52	74.0	55.8
1990	9.5	126	7.0	56	75.3	58.4
1991	5.9	134	7.5	60	74.1	60.5
1992	3.7	139	4.3	63	74.1	62.1
1993	1.6	141	2.5	64	78.2	64.7
1994	2.4	144	2.0	65	78.8	64.8
1995	3.5	149	2.6	67	85.9	66.3
1996	2.4	153	2.5	69	83.7	69.9
1997	3.1	158	1.8	70	73.1	68.1
1998	3.4	163	1.6	71	68.4	65.3
1999	1.5	165	1.3	72	65.6	65.1
2000	3	170	0.8	73	63.6	66.3
2001	1.8	173	1.2	74	68.8	68.2
2002	1.7	176	1.3	75	65.7	67.8
2003	2.9	181	1.4	76	70.1	69.0
2004	3	187	1.3	77	71.6	72.9
2005	2.8	192	2.1	78	69.6	75.3
2006	3.2	198	2.3	80	72.3	78.1
2007	4.3	207	2.3	82	82.2	84.8
2008	4	215	3.6	85	98.9	103.2
2009	-0.5	214	2.2	87	95.0	95.9
2010	4.6	224	3.3	89	100.0	100.0
2011	5.2	235	4.5	93	113.5	112.3
2012	3.2	243	2.8	96	118.8	114.2
2013	3.0	250	2.6	99	125.8	117.0
2014	2.4	256	1.5	100	114.6	112.1
2015	1.0	258	0.0	100	105.0	106.8
2016	1.8	263	0.7	101	104.5	104.5
2017 (so far)	*3.2*		*2.4*		*114.1*	*110.0*

* *Retail Price Index*

** *Consumer Prices Index*

Inflation of food-based Component of CPI

Per Cent	2000	2005	2010	2013	2014	2015	2016	Jun-17
CPI (Overall Index)	2.1	3.3	4.5	2.6	1.5	0.0	1.6	2.6
All goods	0.3	3.1	4.6	2.0	0.6	-2.1	0.7	2.6
All Services	4.1	3.6	4.3	3.2	2.5	2.9	2.5	2.7
Food & non-alcoholic drinks	15.0	3.4	5.5	1.9	-0.2	-2.9	-1.1	2.3
Food	1.7	3.0	5.0	2.1	-0.3	-3.2	-1.0	2.6
Bread & Cereals	1.3	2.1	6.4	3.3	-0.6	-2.4	-0.3	3.1
Meat	0.7	0.9	5.4	2.5	0.6	-4.1	-2.3	1.4
Fish	1.6	6.6	9.2	5.2	2.6	-5.0	1.1	12.6
Milk, Cheese & Eggs	2.7	0.2	2.6	1.8	0.5	-5.4	-2.4	2.8
Oils & Fats	-2.2	6.7	11.8	0.9	-0.6	-6.2	4.8	5.2
Fruit	1.2	7.9	3.7	-0.1	0.3	-0.8	2.1	3.2
Vegetables inc. Potatoes	3.0	2.9	3.4	2.3	-4.7	-4.7	-1.6	2.2
Sugar, Jam & Sweets	2.8	5.6	7.5	0.1	1.8	-0.1	-2.4	1.1
Food Products	-0.5	0.7	3.2	2.9	0.6	0.0	-0.7	-0.9

Weighting of food-based Component of CPI

parts per 1000	2000	2005	2010	2013	2014	2015	2016	2017
CPI (Overall Index)	1000	1000	1000	1000	1000	1000	1000	1000
All goods	591	536	549	534	540	532	517	525
All Services	409	464	451	466	460	468	483	475
Food & non-alcoholic drinks	121	106	108	106	112	110	103	103
Food	109	93	96	93	99	97	91	91
Bread & Cereals	19	15	16	16	17	16	15	15
Meat	27	23	22	21	22	22	21	20
Fish	5	4	4	4	4	4	4	4
Milk, Cheese & Eggs	14	13	14	13	14	14	12	12
Oils & Fats	2	2	2	2	2	2	2	2
Fruit	9	8	9	9	10	10	9	9
Vegetables inc. Potatoes	18	14	15	14	15	14	13	13
Sugar, Jam & Sweets	12	12	11	11	12	12	12	13
Food Products	3	2	3	3	3	3	3	3

AGRICULTURAL PRICE AND COST INDICES

Producer Prices	**2010**	**2012**	**2013**	**2014**	**2015**	**2016**
Feed Wheat	100	144	153	121	101	101
Feed Barley	100	160	159	120	106	103
All Cereals	100	150	153	121	103	101
Oilseed Rape	100	139	127	100	95	105
Potatoes (all)	100	122	156	104	106	136
Sugar Beet	100	104	106	109	110	92
Desert Apples	100	118	117	104	105	103
All Fresh Vegetables	100	109	110	103	106	115
All Fresh Fruit	100	104	105	98	101	107
All Crop Products	*100*	*124*	*129*	*108*	*103*	*107*
Milk	100	114	128	128	99	91
Cattle	100	129	138	123	126	122
Sheep	100	105	102	106	99	105
Wool	100	75	101	103	83	83
Pigs	100	106	117	112	92	90
Poultry	100	105	109	106	105	105
Eggs	100	124	131	122	119	101
All Animal Products	*100*	*115*	*123*	*119*	*107*	*103*
All Products	*100*	*119*	*125*	*114*	*105*	*104*
Input Prices						
Seeds	100	105	114	101	96	98
Fertilisers	100	125	113	107	101	83
Agro-chemicals	100	102	98	103	103	102
Energy and Lubricants	100	122	123	119	101	97
Animal Feeding Stuffs	100	128	139	121	108	105
Plant Maint' & Repair	100	106	108	110	111	112
Machinery & Equip'	100	94	97	116	121	121
Building Maintenance	100	110	110	111	109	108
General Expenses	100	107	110	110	109	111
All Inputs	*100*	*114*	*117*	*112*	*107*	*105*

Source: DEFRA Agricultural Price Index

10. METRIC CONVERSION FACTORS

Metric to Imperial		*Imperial to Metric*	
Area			
1 hectare ($10,000m^2$)	2.471 acres	1 acre	0.405 ha
		1 square mile	259 ha
1 square km	0.386 sq. mile	1 square mile	2.590 sq. km
1 square m	1.196 sq. yard	1 square yard	0.836 sq. m
1 square m	10.764 sq. feet	1 square foot	0.093 sq. m
Length			
1 mm	0.039 inch	1 inch.	25.4 mm
1 cm	0.394 inch	1 inch	2.54 cm
1 m	3.281 feet	1 foot	0.305 m
1 m	1.094 yard	1 yard	0.914 m
1 km	0.6214 mile	1 mile	1.609 km
Volume			
1 millilitre	0.0352 fluid oz	1 fluid oz	28.413 ml
1 litre	35.2 fluid oz	1 fluid oz	0.028 litre
1 litre	1.76 pints	1 pint	0.568 litre
1 litre	0.22 gallon	1 gallon	4.546 litres
1 cubic m	35.31 cu feet	1 cubic foot	0.028 cu m
1 cubic m	1.307 cu yard	1 cubic yard	0.765 cu m
1 cubic m	220 gallons	1 gallon	0.005 cu m
1 ha of 10mm water	22,000gallons	1 acre-inch	$102.75 m^3$
Weight			
1 gram	0.0353 oz	1 oz	28.35 gm
1 kg	35.274 oz		
1 kg	2.205 lb	1 lb	0.454 kg
50 kg	0.984 cwt		
1 tonne (1,000 kg)	19.68 cwt	1 cwt.	50.80 kg
1 tonne	0.984 ton	1 ton	1.016 tonne
Milk			
1 litre	1.03 kg		
1kg	0.971 litre		
1 litre	1.709 pints	1 pint	0.585 kg
I tonne	213.63 gallon	1 gallon	4.681 kg

Yields and Rates of Use

1 tonne/ha.	0.398 ton/acre	1 ton/acre	2.511 tonnes/ha
1 tonne/ha.	7.95 cwt/acre	1 cwt/acre	0.125 tonne/ha
1 gram/ha	0.014 oz/acre	1 oz/acre	70.053 g/ha
1 kg/ha	0.892 lb/acre	1 lb/acre	1.121 kg/ha
1 kg/ha	0.008 cwt/acre	1 cwt/acre	125.5 kg/ha
1 kg/ha (fert.)	0.797 unit/acre	1 unit/acre	1.255 kg/ha
1 litre/ha	0.712 pint/acre	1 pint/acre	1.404 litre/ha
1 litre/ha	0.089 gal/acre	1 gal/acre	11.24 litres/ha

Power, Pressure, Temperature

1 kW	1.341 hp	1 hp	0.746 kW
1 MW	1,000kW		
1 kilojoule	0.948 Btu	1 Btu	1.055 kilojoule
1 therm	10,000 Btu	1 Btu	0.0001 therm
1 lb f ft	1.356 Nm	1 Nm	0.738 lb f ft
1 bar	14.705 lb/sq.in.	1 lb/sq.in	0.068 bar
°C to °F	x1.8, + 32	°F to °C	-32, ÷ 1.8

INDEX

HOW HAS THE POCKETBOOK HELPED YOU?

Here at The John Nix Pocketbook office, we are always very interested and humbled by the feedback we receive of how the book has helped our readers achieve their farming aims and ambitions.

If you have a particular way in which The John Nix Pocketbook has helped you, we would love to hear from you. No matter how big or how small. Please contact us via enquiries@thepocketbook.co.uk and tell us your story on how John Nix has improved your rural business or farm management.